YES, I AM YOUR BROTHER

Understanding the Indigenous African American Muslim

NURI MADINA

authorHOUSE®

AuthorHouse™
1663 Liberty Drive
Bloomington, IN 47403
www.authorhouse.com
Phone: 1 (800) 839-8640

Painting illustrated on cover is by Nuri Madina
and entitled "Joseph's Beautiful Coat"

Published by AuthorHouse 08/04/2016
and
New Earth Publishing, Chicago, Illinois 60615

2016 Edition
Edited by: Camille LaRay

ISBN: 978-1-5246-1346-4 (sc)
ISBN: 978-1-5246-1348-8 (hc)
ISBN: 978-1-5246-1345-7 (e)

Library of Congress Control Number: 2016909457

Print information available on the last page.

This book is printed on acid-free paper.

Contents

Introduction

I have read many success books and have wanted to write one for some time, but I was stymied by how to approach such a book in light of the many unique circumstances that African Americans face. That is not to say that universal principles would not apply since that which is in any man is in every man. It is influences that we come under that manifest these potentialities. Scripture I discovered is the ultimate source of universal success stories. I also found Prophet Muhammad, the Prayers and the Peace Be Upon Him (PBUH)[1] to be a model for success in all aspects of life. We also need real-life examples of success and Imam W. Deen Mohammed, May G-d be pleased with him (RAA) was a person, I found living that exemplary life in our time.

Prophet Muhammad (PBUH) lived in Arabia, 1,400 years ago and after a lifetime of virtuous behavior, he received Revelation from Allah (G-d),[2] that is now recorded and preserved in the Holy Qur'an. His message, that is accepted and lived by Muslims to this day, is that "There is no G-d but Allah, and Muhammad is His Messenger."

Honorable Elijah Muhammad was born in Sandersville, Georgia on October 7, 1897, and for years until his passing in 1975 he built and led the Nation of Islam. It was this movement that produced strong, disciplined men, and African American leaders, such as Malcolm X, Muhammad Ali, Louis Farrakhan and the son of Elijah Muhammad, Imam W. Deen Mohammed (RAA). That movement also inspired me and brought me into its teaching and disciplines. Its promises were fulfilled at Elijah's passing when Wallace D. Mohammed (RAA) became its leader and my leader and teacher.

Imam Mohammed (RAA) was known by many names and titles though he rejected most of the titles. Born Wallace D. Mohammed (RAA), he was also known as the clear voice for humanity, the spokesman for human salvation, and the sense-maker. Though he can clearly be seen and identified in each of these archetypes, the scriptural descriptions of him - Mujeddid, Mahdi, Meshia - still fuel controversy. He accepted the role of Mujeddid[3] which simply means one who appears every one hundred years to revive the religion, or bring it back to its original form. That is what he did for the religion of Al-Islam. But he was always comfortable with just *brother* or simply Wallace. Imam Mohammed (RAA) was called the "Former Nation of Islam leader," in an article printed by the Associated Press upon his passing September 9, 2008. This is technically correct but it ignores the 30 years of accomplishments he's had since that position. His best name - "America's Imam" - may have been coined by Ahmed M. Rehab, executive director of the Chicago chapter of the Council on American-Islamic Relations, in his September 10, 2008, blog. It does not address the total dimension of his life but it reflects the humility he sought throughout life and the high station that humility and pure heart brought as a reward. When he became leader of the Nation of Islam in 1975, he shunned the trappings of wealth and power. He lived briefly in his father's lavish Hyde Park home in Chicago but quickly noted that the house was too big and created too much distance between him and his family.

In 1992, Senator Paul Simon of Illinois was instrumental in Imam Mohammed (RAA) being invited as the first Muslim to deliver the prayer and invocation on the floor of the U.S. Senate. Senator Alan Dixon was present and said of Imam Mohammed (RAA): "I am proud to have one of my constituents from the State of Illinois to be the first Muslim to pray in the United States Senate." U.S. Senator Orrin Hatch of Utah, who helped arrange the event, said, "This is a great day for the U.S. Senate and the United States to have Imam Mohammed here today in the U.S. Senate; there is not a better man in America or better religious leader who is trying to do what is right for his people."

In 1986, I ran for State Representative in the 24 District of Chicago and I asked Imam Mohammed (RAA) for advice. He told me to practice patience and study the story of the Prophet Yusuf (Joseph) (PBUH), in the Qur'an. In studying it I found that, except for the Prophet Muhammad (PHUH), few prophets had the whole spectrum of their lives explained in the depth that Joseph's (PBUH) story was told in both the Bible and the Qur'an.[4]

On a basic level it is simply the story of a young boy, who because of the jealousy of his brothers, is sold into slavery, but because of his faith and righteousness rises into power in a foreign land. But we should also see the story in a social context, as a story of any enslaved people and in the interactions of any individual psyche. In both contexts, no people fit the profile of the rejected, enslaved, restricted, and confined as clearly as African Americans. Our enslavement involved our European, Christian, and Muslim brothers (historians now acknowledged that a significant number of these slaves were Muslim) and now we find ourselves in this industrial giant America (a modern Egypt). The subsequent discrimination and Jim Crow laws represented continued confinement and restricted opportunity, so for most of our time in this country, we have been servants in the house of the master.

Almighty G-d, Allah says in the Qur'an: 28:5 *"And We wished to be gracious to those who were being depressed in the land, to make them leaders (in Faith) and make them heirs."* It is because of this oppression and darkness of ignorance that we have been favored with the bright light of truth from G-d that can light the whole world.

The language of popular culture and protest has long described life here in America as "the belly of the beast," Egypt and modern "Babylon," while a succession of leaders issued a clarion call for us to free ourselves. Marcus Garvey was known as the black Moses, appealing to a great number of blacks in America. Malcolm X also called Elijah Muhammad our black Moses and called the United States and the white man in America the pharaoh. W. D. Fard, who fashioned the theology and the strategy known as the Nation of Islam, and gave it to Elijah Muhammad, though not African American himself, identified blacks as the lost tribe of Shabazz (Sheba). Fard borrowed philosophies and strategies from many of the African American patriots before him, and humbly acknowledged: "I can stand on the top of the earth and proclaim that the most beautiful nation is here in the wilderness of North America." Building upon Fard's plan, Elijah Muhammad popularized Islamic terminology and inspired a whole nation of black people with exhortations of self- help and racial superiority.

Imam Mohammed (RAA) advanced the languages of Islam and common humanity while creating an environment that ultimately lead to the election of the first African American president, Barack Hussein Obama. Among all of these leaders, there was recognition of a stronger and more intractable bondage, indeed a self- imposed confinement, beyond the chains of chattel slavery. Cultural icon Bob Marley echoed this theme in the language of his music and lifestyle. In *Redemption Song,* he sang: "Emancipate yourselves from mental slavery; none but ourselves can free our mind." Other great leaders appealed to the circumstances of blacks in America. Denmark Vesey and Nat Turner helped to advance militancy, and because of our unrewarded contributions, David Walker wrote: "America is more our country than it is the whites."

In Scripture, it is said that Moses (PBUH) went to the mountaintop. Allah says in the Qur'an "Did not we give you two eyes, one tongue, and two lips, but have you made any haste to travel the highway that is steep?" The steep highway is the one up to the mountaintop. Imam Mohammed (RAA) said, "Once you get up to the top, you feel like a conqueror. You look down and it feels like the valley and all around belongs to you. You feel like everything out there is yours because you have made it up." Dr. Martin Luther King Jr. echoed similar statements when he proclaimed, "I've been to the mountain top." He meant that he had a vision of the end of Jim-Crowism, segregation, and racism in America. He proclaimed his dream to the world and brought world attention to the cruelty of the slave masters, though he acknowledged, as did Moses (PBUH), that he might not be able to lead us into the "promise land". But here we are now and in the words of Marcus Garvey: *"Up you mighty nation, you can accomplish what you will."*

"God's time [Emancipation] is always near. He set the North Star in the heavens; He gave me the strength in my limbs;He meant I should be free." Harriet Tubman to Ednah Dow Cheney, New York City, circa 1859.

1. In the Holy Qur'an, 33:56, Allah Most High say: *"Allah and His angels send blessings on the Prophet: O ye that believe! Send ye blessings on him, and salute him with all respect."* It is also reported in Hadith, or sayings of the Prophet Muhammad, by Abu Hurayrah, that The Messenger of Allah said: "Whoever sends one salah *(prayer)* upon me, Allah will send ten upon him." Therefore, when the name of any Prophet is mentioned, we follow his name with the words, "The Prayers and the Peace be upon him," which we have abbreviated here, PBUH or "The Prayers and the Peace be upon them," (PBUT).
   Similarly, when companions, disciples, scribes and family of Prophet Muhammad are mentioned (Arabic: رضي الله عنه *raḍiya 'llāhu 'an-hu*, *[abbreviated here RAA], or* ***'an-ha*** *for females*), an Arabic phrase meaning, "May God Be Pleased with Him" is recited. This is also used to confer prayer upon scholars, teachers, or parents. We have followed Imam Mohammed's name with this expression of respect in this book. If you find that we have omitted these salutations in the mentioning of any of these figures, we ask that **you** be mindful and wish the prayers and the Peace of G-d upon them or that G-d be pleased with them.
2. Muslim Journal: On the spelling of the word God as G'd, what was the intent, expectations or focus for using that particular spelling, omitting the letter "o"?
   Imam Mohammed: During interactions with Jews and Christians, I had been seeing very often the spelling G-d for God with the "o" left out. I recall from my early years in the Nation of Islam, under the Hon. Elijah Muhammad, I recall him criticizing the spelling of G-o-d, that in reverse reads dog. I noticed that a lot of the publications, a lot of the papers that I read from the Jewish people never had the "o" in there, so you can't read dog into it. It is absent there, and you wonder why is it absent? I didn't have to think about it. It's absent because they are offended by the reverse spelling, as the Hon. Elijah

Muhammad was. I began to think that we should also reject the spelling "God." That is why I began to write in my own writings or in my own transcription of my speeches, to insist that it be written without the "o". I put an apostrophe, but really maybe an hyphen would be even better. Interview with Imam W. Deen Mohammed at Indianapolis Airport, by Imam Michael "Mikal" Saahir

3. Hadith: "Allah shall raise for the ummah centennial reformers who will renew (or) revive for it religion."-Recorded by Abu Dawud
4. Chapter headings are translations from the 12th Surah (Chapter) of the Holy Quran, Yusuf, and narrate the story of Joseph (PBUH). Each Chapter is mirrored in some respect in the story of the African American. Yusuf (PBUH) is the Arabic name for Joseph (PBUH) and both are used interchangeably here.

NOTE: Except where noted differently, Qur'anic verses (ayats) and references in this work are from the Abdullah Yusuf Ali translation of the Holy Qur'an.

Dedication

This book is dedicated to my children, my sons and my grandchildren, (who appear on the following page), to whom my unlimited love goes out. They are a great part of my blessings from Allah (G-d) and they also remind me all the time of all the other beautiful children of the world and of the world's future. I have come to realize that you can accomplish much in this life but from a perspective of eternal time and benefit to the whole, even that can be miniscule. We have to look at life in a larger perspective than our time-limited here and now.

Allah Most High says: *Verily We shall give life to the dead, and We record that which they send before and that which they leave behind, and of all things have We taken account in a clear Book (of evidence). Al-Qur'an36:12*

Modern science, health advances, and social progress, have all served to expand the human life span. But still, living beyond 80 years is a blessed feat. Allah said of our Prophet (PBUH) that he had lived a lifetime among his people there in Arabia even before the Revelation of Qur'an to him and that was near his 40th year. And Prophet Joseph (PBUH) was said to have received "power and knowledge" when he reached his age of full strength and that is considered in tradition to be age 40. We know that this age landmark is more symbolic of a maturity in all dimensions than it is of literal years so whether we have reached 40 or 80, we have to nevertheless be mindful of the adage that "life is short."

Prophet Muhammad(PBUH), however, gave us the key to extending our short run of the life of this world:

"When a human being dies, all of his deeds are terminated except for three types: an ongoing sadaqah (charity), a knowledge (of Islam) from which others benefit, and a righteous child who makes du'a for him." Muslim and others

We can extend the work of our lives from our short 80 plus years to 80 or more, through our children, and that 160 can extend to centuries and even thousands of years through useful knowledge. The stars have been out there for millions of years because they are serving their purpose of providing guidance to mankind.

Every second of life is a gift and not one second of it is guaranteed. So what can you do beside do good and try to leave good?

Right to left, son, Ismail, grandson, Nuri III, son, Zakee with granddaughter Kenzie Lou in arm, the author with grandchildren, Maleah, Malik and Elijah, and sons, Nuri II and Abd-eljaami.

12:1 Alif, Lam, Rar. These are the symbols (or Verses) of the perspicuous Book.

Chapter 1

What Do You Say?

It was toward the end of my mother's life before I began to fully understand what she had been trying to teach me since the beginning of my life. As early as I can remember, I knew that the adults in my life expected much of me. I am a convert to Al-Islam from Christianity for nearly 50 years and I remember the values of decency my parents instilled in me and found no conflict between those values and Al-Islam.

My mother was a mental health specialist and we joked often that she was giving me free therapy. I would share insights from the teachings of Imam Mohammed (RAA) and my mother never challenged any of them. However, she often remarked, when I would announce something Imam Mohammed (RAA) had said, "What do you say?"[1] I now understand her to also be asking me "what do you see?" I know she meant no disrespect to my leader but her comment still gave me a sense of unease. It was Allah's Words in the Qur'an that clicked in my mind and helped me understand what she was saying. "There are signs in the earth and there are signs in you."[2] The word *ayat,* which is used for signs, is the same word used by Allah to describe the verses in his holy book. She was telling me that to truly know and understand what I was being taught, I needed to internalize the concepts. Internalization is the process of establishing your own beliefs, attitudes, and values. This is a step beyond depending on a leader to direct you. What you are taught is good, but until it becomes a part of the voice of guidance inside your own soul, you're always dependent upon the leader.

What do we really know except what we connect to in the material universe around us or in our own life's experience? This material creation is, in fact, more of a model and a metaphor of what's going on in our own psyche. Our mother is our first teacher as children just as Mother Earth or Mother Nature is our first introduction to the physical world. My mother was pointing to the need to be responsive just as G-d intended all of us to be; expressing and creating something in our own life and society from this knowledge. She was also addressing the need for independent thinking and personal responsibility.

We should see the characters and conversations in the story of Joseph (PBUH), indeed all Scripture, in a community context and also as elements of our own individual psyches. If there are signs within the story, we should find their meaning in our life.

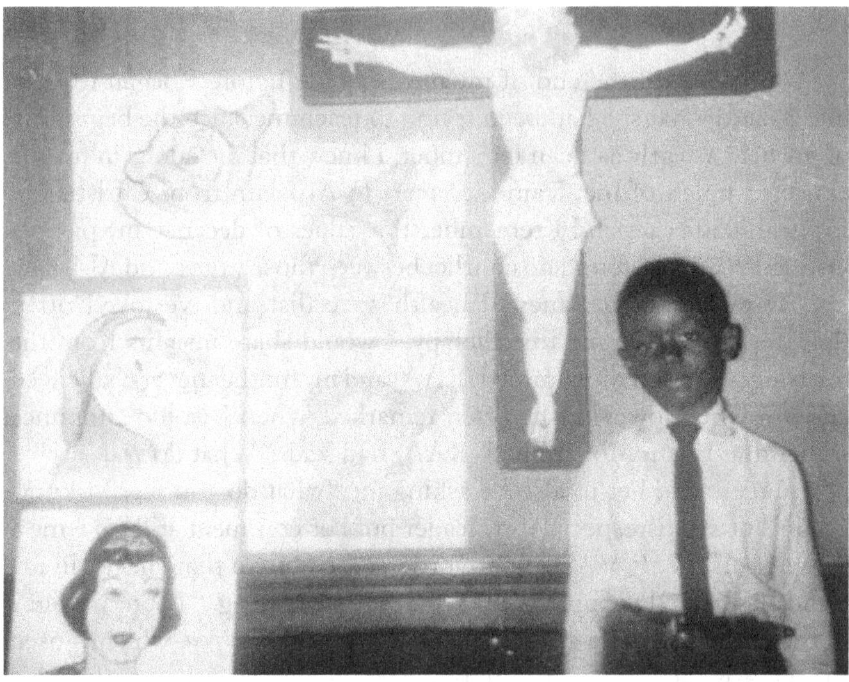

A young Edward Alexander, later to become Nuri Madina, a second-grader at Holy Angels grammar school on Chicago's Southside, the mid-1950s, with early artwork, including Snow White, dwarfs and a depiction of Jesus (PBUH) on the cross in the background. Christianity and the concept of a man-god permeated the atmosphere of America and it was impossible to live in this environment and not be influenced by it. We breathed the air. My teachers there looked over my development, as Pharaoh said: "Did we not cherish thee as a child among us, and didst thou not stay in our midst many years of thy life?" *Holy Qur'an 26:18.* During this same time the Muslims in the Nation of Islam, under the leadership of Honorable Elijah Muhammad were believing in their own man-god-- an "allah" that came in the person of Master Fard Muhammad. Photo courtesy of Nuri Madina

12:2 We have sent it down as an Arabic Qur'an, in order that ye may learn wisdom.

Chapter 2

Clear Message in a Pure Vessel

When we begin to see things through the mind's eye, we will see that the material world is a language-a language beyond the narrow definition of communication between human beings but communication directly from G-d to man's soul and intellect. We do not worship anything other than the Creator of the heavens and earth in all His Glory and Purity, and we acknowledge that His Proper Name is Allah. It is translated as G-d. Arabic speaking Christians refer to G-d as Allah and we use the terms interchangeably here. As with everything, we have to always be aware of corrupt language and thus, we say there is no is G-d but Allah and we avoid any negative interpretation in reference to G-d.

The Evolution of Language

Allah's first word of Revelation to Muhammad (PBUH) was *Iqra* or *read*! *Iqra bismi Rabbika lathi Khalaq,* read in the name of your lord who created. *Iqra* is commonly translated *read*, but it also means, *proclaim*, *rehearse*, *transmit*, *deliver*, or *recite a message*. From this same word we get *Qur'an* - the book that is meant to be *read, proclaimed, rehearsed or delivered.* The term *Quraanan Arabiyyan* can be interpreted as *an Arabic Qur'an*, but it can also be understood as a proclamation or a recital that states itself clearly and precisely.

Why Arabic? Ahmadiyyah founder, Hazrat Murza Ghulam Ahmed, wrote in his book, "Arabic-the Mother of all Languages" that Arabic is the first revealed language and thus the mother and original source for all the languages of the world. Evidence to support this claim is to be found, according to the author, "in the highly organized system of *Mufradaat* possessed by Arabic. These Mufradaat are the so-called 'root words'—the 'simples', or elementary symbols of speech - which are the divinely communicated basis for all human articulation, and which are so varied and of such as comprehensive character as to serve the needs of not only ordinary speech, but also the demands of all knowledge, religion, philosophy, culture and science."[1]

In the Arabic language, the word "arab" or arabah (from i'rab), is probably derived from a Semitic root related to nomadism. It means clean, clear and precise. These people held their tongue in such high regard that they called themselves Arabs meaning "those who speak clearly." This was in contrast to "ajam," others who they described as speaking indistinctly or mute. The Arabs did not create great art. Their artistic nature found expression through one medium only: speech. Their supreme art was oral poetry. [2,3,4,5]

Among the Arabs, two tribes were especially distinguished in this art-the Quraish and the Hawazin. We know that Prophet Muhammad (PBUH) never exhibited the least bit of arrogance but it was reported that once, for the sake of giving thanks to Allah, he said: "Verily, I am the *most perfect* Arab amongst you. My descent is from the Quraish and my speech is the tongue of the Banu Sa'd." (a branch of Hawazin). A Dictionary of Islam, Thomas Hughes, p. 368. Other commentators translate the first statement as 'I am the *most eloquent* among you.'

In the Qur'an, the word *Arab* is never used for the country of Arabia, but rather to identify the residence of Ismail, the son of Abraham (PBUH) as an "uncultivated land."[6] In the Old Testament, the word *midbar* is used for Ismail's (PBUH) home, meaning a desert or a barren land, which closely corresponds to the Qur'anic description. Centuries before the actual revelation of the Quran, the Arabs had evolved a language capable of expressing and containing the wisdom of the Qur'an. The Revelation of the Qur'an to Prophet Muhammad (PBUH) actually introduced a new language, a new Arabic to the people of that wilderness. That people had not received Revelation before.[7] This lack of revelation corresponds to the barrenness and lack of cultivation in the land. By contrast, for centuries, Bani Israel (Children of Israel) had received a succession of prophets and developed their civilization to the heights of the ancient world (including the glorious reigns of David and

Solomon). The spirit of the Qur'an is the spirit of knowledge and truth that was promised in the Bible to the people of the book.[8]

When the Qur'an was revealed, Prophet Muhammad (PBUH) had, as Allah tells us "...lived a lifetime already among his people." That lifetime had been one inclined to uprightness or ***hanifa***, just like Prophet Ibrahim (PBUH). Even before receiving Revelation, he was known as As-Saddiq, The Truthful One, and Al-Amin, the Trustworthy One. Thus, the Qur'an was not something foreign to his nature, or something different from the natural life he had been living. Whatever Allah asks of us is already implicit in our nature. We say that every child is born Muslim; until the environment changes him. Prophet Muhammad (PBUH) never let the environment change him.

Prophet Muhammad (PBUH) said that in the future people would see Christ Jesus (PBUH) and himself together. Jesus, the Christ (PBUH), was questioned by those who wanted to make him divine, to raise him to a level of Lord or patron among them and he replied: "I in you and you in me." He was saying that the same original nature, the same innocent human life — the soul, the mind, the thinking, the behavior—the Muslim (submissive to the Will of G-d) nature that G-d put in me, is in each of you. When the Christian says, "Christ within me," he is saying the same thing that we are saying, when we say "every human being is born Muslim." This innocent human nature is intended by G-d to be the cornerstone of society just as the black stone is the cornerstone of the Kaaba in the sacred shrine in Mecca,[9] to which every other stone of the building is aligned. When we make Hajj to the sacred site, in reverence, we kiss the black stone.

Painting by Nuri Madina of Imam W. Deen Mohammed (RAA) and Pope John Paul II at the Vatican, October 28, 1999. Both Imam Mohammed (RAA) and Pope John Paul II are symbols of the respective faith communities of Christians and Muslims and in that powerful symbolism, I believe that the Prophet's words can be seen: That in the Last Day, you would see Him, Muhammad (PBUH) and Christ Jesus (PBUH) together. In just brief minutes of comments to the audience assembled at the Vatican in Rome Imam Mohammed (RAA) summarized his whole Mission and described the time that we are living in. He noted that both he and the Pope shared values and belief in a virtuous life and that we have to look for opportunities for religions to meet. He said: "I have devoted my life to building bridges" and "inclusion is in my heart." He described this era that we live in as a time of the "revival of the true life that G-d put into the human souls when He created the first person." He stressed that our Unity is built on the diversity that G-d Himself created: "G-d is One, His Creation is One Whole. There is One Universal Law for all matter; for all material things and everything is related."

Photo courtesy of https://www.google.com/search?q=Imam+MOhammed%2B Vatican&biw =1080&bih=563&source=lnms&tbm=isch&sa= X&ved= 0ahUKEwj W2o37__zLAhWJ6SYKH b7yCy0Q_AUICSgE#imgrc= GJDLsDOY0x4ypM%3A

The Qur'an then builds on that original nature and that potential that was already in man and if we remain pure we are blessed with the double portion of His Mercy, through the increase in understanding of G-d's message. The Book is also known as the criterion. It is the standard by which we distinguish the *pure from the impure*, *the natural from the unnatural*, and that which produces life from that which brings death--*the just from the unjust.*

Therefore, despite the superiority of the language, we should not conclude that this was the primary reason for Allah revealing the Qur'an in Arabic. The primary reason was that the prophet Muhammad (PBUH) was an Arab. He was the best choice for Prophet and he spoke Arabic. He stressed in his Last Sermon, that there was no superiority of an Arab over a non-Arab or a non-Arab over an Arab. For those non-Arabic speakers, learning Qur'anic Arabic doesn't mean giving up our own cultural identity, or favoring those born speaking "common Arabic." Al-Islam comes to enhance our own culture, not rob us of it. Allah says "We sent not a messenger except (to teach) in the language of his (own) people, in order to make (things) clear to them."[9] Prophet Muhammad (PBUH), who expressed purity in his own life was therefore the ideal vessel for the delivery of a pure and clear message. We have been blessed to see Muhammed the Prophet (PBUH) as the embodiment of Qur'an rather than seeing him solely in his flesh body[10] and to avoid the mistake that Christians made of seeing Jesus (PBUH) in 'person' as opposed to 'personality.'

12:3 We do relate unto thee the most beautiful of stories, in that We reveal to thee this (portion of the) Qur'an: before this, thou too was among those who knew it not.

Chapter 3

G-d's Plan for Human Life is Beautiful

The highest life for us as human beings is living the Word of G-d's pure Revelation. When it comes into our life, it opens up a more beautiful and more productive life for us than we had before.

When and Why Revealed?

"The subject matter of the Surah Yusuf indicates that it was revealed during the last stage of the Holy Prophet's residence at Makkah, when the Quraish were considering the question of either killing, exiling or imprisoning him. Some of the unbelievers, probably at the instigation of the Jews, put this question to test him: "Why did the Israelites go to Egypt?" The Jews knew that their story was not known to the Arabs for there was no mention of it whatever in their traditions and the Holy Prophet had never even referred to it before. They expected that he would either be unable to answer it or evade it. He may afterwards try to get the answer from some Jew, and thus he would be totally exposed. But, contrary to their expectations, the tables were turned on them, for Allah revealed the whole story of Prophet Joseph then and there, and the Holy Prophet recited it on the spot." *Sayyid Abul Ala Maududi - Tafhim al-Qur'an - The Meaning of the Qur'an*

Transmission and Arrangement of the Quran

The Prophet, called ***ummiyee***, or common man, unlettered man, received the revelation of the Qur'anic Surahs over a period of 23 years, whenever God chose to bestow new revelation on him. Passages and Surahs were revealed in connection with certain events and addressed particular situations when they actually took place. At times, several Surahs, particularly the longer ones, were revealed to him concurrently.

It is said that the Qur'an was revealed on the prophet's heart. Similarly, the believers heard the recitals and most of them, ***Hafis***, loved the revelation and committed it to their memory--by heart. Even the common man knew the book and just as today, would correct an error when it was being recited. It will always be in the heart of believers, and Allah says "He has appointed angels over the Book to protect it."

The arrangement of the Surahs in Qur'an did not follow the chronological order of revelation. Rather the Prophet (PBUH) was instructed by the Angel Gabriel where to place every new passage and he indicated its position mainly by reading the Surahs in a specific order, particularly in prayer. When Caliph Abu Bakr instructed Zaid ibn Thabit to collect the original writings of the Qur'anic revelations, Zaid produced a whole copy of the Qur'an. It was arranged in the order we have today. This was done in the first two years after the Prophet's death since Abu Bakr ruled for less than two years.

Later at Caliph Uthman's time, copies were produced and sent to various centers of the Muslim state to be the reference copy in each center. These also, produced by Zaid ibn Thabit, were based on the first collection. There was no disagreement among the Prophet's companions with regard to the ordering of the Surahs, which indicates that the arrangement was made by the Prophet (PBUH) himself.

Clear teachings, clearly expressed form the basis of the Qur'an and that is what we are obligated to stand upon as authority. But it is also allegory presented in symbolic or picture language. The Prophet said, "for every verse there is an explicit and an implicit meaning." Explicit means that it is very clear and anyone who wants to can see it. Implicit means that there is some wisdom there, another language even, for the special people who have insight and good hearts. Allah blesses others with the understanding of that symbolic language, if they are fit and as He wills.[1]

Allah says those who prefer the allegorical over the clear basic teachings are those who have in their heart a perversion-a defect, corruption, poison, rot or illness. Basically, they have bad intention. The plain common sense logic is, therefore, more important than the picture language.

Tafsir

Imam Mohammed's (RAA) teachings and interpretations are referred to as his Tafsir. In technical terms, the word tafsir is used to describe the explanation, interpretation, and commentary on the Qur'an and this includes the extraction of its legal rulings and grasping its underlying reasons. The word is derived from the root *'fassara'* which means to explain or to expound. Mufassir (pl. mufassirun) is the term used for the person doing the Tafsir, i.e. the 'exegete' or 'commentator'. Tafsir (exegesis) of the Qur'an is the most important science for Muslims because the right application of Islam is based on proper understanding of the guidance from Allah. Without tafsir, there would be no right understanding of various passages of the Qur'an.

The word ta'wil also means explanation and interpretation of the Qur'an. It is derived from the root word *'awwala.'* Some scholars consider Tafsir to refer to the 'outer' (zahir) meanings of the Qur'an, while Ta'wil is considered to refer to the explanation of the inner and concealed meanings of the Qur'an, as far as a knowledgeable person can have access to them. Others are of the opinion that there is no difference between tafsir and ta'wil.

Prophet Muhammad (PBUH) said I leave you two things, the Qur'an, and my Sunnah. The Qur'an itself is a hadith. The best tafsir is the explanation of the Qur'an by the Qur'an itself. The next best is the explanation of the Qur'an by Prophet Muhammad (PBUH). If nothing can be found in the Qur'an or in the Sunnah of the Prophet, one turns to the reports from the *sahaba* or companions.

Interpretation

Mutashabihat is defined as things that are susceptible to various interpretations and is generally considered to have three elements:

- Something known to Allah only
- Something with more than one dimension
- Something requiring further explanation

The Dictionary of Islam, Noor Foundation-International, Inc. identifies the word's root as *Shabaha*, meaning to liken, resemble or render a thing dubious to anyone, and renders the word, *"susceptible to various interpretations."* I have found Qur'an Commentator, Abdullah Yusuf Ali's commentary to be most illustrative of this meaning. In commenting on Surah 3 Ayat 7, he states in Note 346.

"This passage gives us an important clue to the interpretation of the Holy Qur'an. Broadly speaking it may be divided into two portions, not given separately, but intermingled: viz. (1) the nucleus or foundation of the book, literally "Mother of the Book". (2) the part which is not entirely clear. It is very fascinating to take up the latter, and exercise our ingenuity about its meaning, but it refers to such profound matters that are beyond human language and though people of wisdom may get some light from it, no one should be dogmatic, as the final meaning is known to Allah alone. The commentators usually understand the verses "of established meaning *(mukham)* to refer to the categorical orders of the *shari'at* (or the law), which are plain to everyone's understanding. But perhaps the meaning is wider: the "Mother of the Book" must include the very foundation on which all law rests, the essence of Allah's message, as distinguished from the various illustrative parables, allegories, and ordinances." Thus, a meaning may be similar but can be given different "color" based on the context.

G-d gave revelation to prophet after prophet, but generation after generation missed the mark, misunderstood, changed the word, and generally went astray. Today we are seeing Muslims throughout the world discover the dignity of their own human souls and demand that their leaders order society in a fair, decent, and civilized manner. For centuries leaders in the West and in the Muslim world insisted on giving the people an infantile understanding of Scripture and the important things in life. Imam Mohammed's (RAA) tafsir has been accurately described as "meat" of knowledge as he noted: "the Qur'an reveals to us the most important construction is not the material construction, it is the linguistic or language construction." I think the greatest benefit of Imam Mohammed's (RAA) tafsir and commentaries is that they have made us independent thinkers and unwilling to ever again accept anything less than the highest and best understanding of man's purpose.

12:4 Behold! Joseph said to his father: "O my father! I did see eleven stars and the sun and the moon: I saw them prostrate themselves to me!"

Chapter 4

I Have a Dream

There are many accepted meanings of the life and history of the Prophet Joseph (PBUH). He is a model of patience, a truthful, honest and charitable person. He is a dreamer, and interpreter of dreams--a psychic who understands the mysteries of the mind. What his personality enables him to do over time is to transform concepts from the invisible realm of idea and concept (dreams) into the visible realm of (material) reality. Thus, he represents a level of consciousness through which we are brought increase on all levels.[1]

We all dream of a better life, and Joseph (PBUH) showed how we reach an ultimate destiny by overcoming obstacles, limitations, restriction and confinement throughout our life. James Allen writes in "As A Man Thinketh", *"The dreamers are the saviors of the world. As the visible world is sustained by the invisible, so men, through all their trials and sins and sordid vocations, are nourished by the beautiful visions of their solitary dreamers…" p23* [2,3]

Dreamers always seem to be looking beyond the material reality in front of them, into outer space, to the cosmic realm and seeing things not everyone can see "Jabir b. Abdallah: A group of men from the Jews came to the Prophet Muhammad (PBUH) and one of them said to him: "Muhammad tell me about the stars, the sun, and the moon which Joseph (PBUH), that were bowing down to him, what were their names?" The Prophet was quiet and did not make any answer, then Gabriel revealed the names to him. The Prophet said: "Will you believe if I tell you their names?" The Jews said: "Yes." So he said: "They are Harthan, Tariq, Dhiyal, Dhu Al-Kitfan, Qabis, Wathab, 'Amudan, Fulayq, Masbah, Daruh, Dhu Al-Far', Diyya, and Nur. The Jew said: "By, God, those are their names." *Prophets in the Quran: an Introduction to the Quran and Muslim exegesis, Brannon Wheeler.*

We as a community share a common origin, with common experiences and common aspirations and dreams. It was said referring to the assassination of Dr. Martin Luther King Jr. "They said we will shoot the dreamer and see what happens to his dream..." They did not understand that his dream was not just for himself. It was the dream of our ancestors and the dream for the whole community.

Sun, Moon, and Stars

The word *"kaukab"*, used for stars, means both "star" and "constellation." Similarly, "the word "Kochab" in Hebrew means both "star" and "constellation." The significance, therefore, of reference to the "eleven stars" is clear. Just as Joseph's (PBUH) eleven brethren were eleven out of the twelve sons of Jacob (PBUH), so also are there twelve constellations or signs of the Zodiac.

As society evolved men found they could increase their means of subsistence by concentrating greater energies on agriculture. For it to be successful, they had to observe the heavenly order and acquire the knowledge that it offered. The production of the earth had a regular and constant relation to the heavenly bodies. It became necessary to know the exact duration and succession of the seasons and the months of the year. An error here and the entire food supply for the coming winter might be jeopardized. Recall how older farmers, even in modern time, follow the Almanac, like a Bible, for cultivating.

The sun came to be seen as the first and supreme force of the entire creation of cause and effect. The masses in Egypt, like those in many cultures, conscious of the essential benefits of the sun to their life, fell into the habit of confusing the benefits with the benefactor the unseen giver of the blessings. They fell into the mistaken habit of accepting Osiris, the symbol of the sun, as a person, and in time they formulated a personality and a history to describe his various attributes and works while he supposedly lived in the flesh among them. The church followed this same model in reference to the Prophet Jesus

(PBUH). The real sign of the sun is that of Khalifa in human life, the potential of powerful light in us that G-d intends to light the world.

Next in importance was the moon, which, by her phases and periods, regulated time. Following her were the stars and planets, which, by their appearance and disappearances on the horizon and nocturnal hemisphere, marked the minutest divisions. All these formed an entire system of astronomy upon which a "calendar" was based. In ancient Egyptian religion, the Sun, as well as the Moon, are called eyes and together they represent the two eyes of the human being that give us vision and perception.

Prophet Abraham (PBUH) likewise recognized the beauty and artistry of these heavenly bodies. But like the real scientific thinker, he looked for the cause of those effects and for the planner and creator of those effects.[4] Abraham (PBUH) was patient enough to wait until he reached the conclusion of his search. He came to see the shortcomings and infirmities of the created things: sun, moon, stars, natural forces and influences, and to see that whatever power they had was inferior to He who had created them.[5] Like his forefather, Abraham, (PBUH) Joseph (PBUH) saw the proper relationship that G-d wants us to have to these great phenomena of the universe.[6]

Human and Community Development

Imam Mohammed (RAA) described the Prophet Yusuf (PBUH) as representing the third level of evolution in human and community development and cited the references in Qur'an in which this evolution is described: "G-d made the human being from clay, then from sperm or semen, then from a clot, then from a fetus lump. Then He brought bones into the lump. And He clothed the bones with flesh and then another creation" Holy Qur'an, 23:17 says that there are seven tracts above you and a like number in you.[7,8] We must go through seven steps and then the seventh is conscience or spirit. 'Con' means "with"; "science suggests knowledge or facts."

All life evolves in stages. Each level builds on the ones below, and this is the great message of the Qur'an ayat, 23:17. We must master one stage in order to move up to the next. We are taught this in the process of elementary school as we pass through each grade before we graduate. When I attended the 5th grade at Holy Angels School in Chicago, the 6th-grade class was small so both grades shared the same classroom and teacher. I was allowed to study in both classes. At the end of the year, I was passed from the 5th. grade to the 7th grade. Although I appreciated advancing I still sometimes wonder if I might have missed something in the 6th. grade.

There is much Scriptural support that these stages represent levels of knowledge and social development. *"It is He Who created everything on the earth for you and then directed His attention up to heaven and arranged it into seven regular heavens. He has knowledge of all things."* (The Qur'an, 2:29)

Allah closes this ayat with the words: "He has knowledge of all things" which implies that the creation and arrangements of these heavens (leadership) also represent the organization and evolution of knowledge. "Seventh heaven" is commonly used to describe a state of great joy and satisfaction. When we know a thing we are satisfied, so it is knowledge that brings about illumination.[9] Thus heaven is the full illumination of the mind. When the leadership is properly illuminated, which implies not only rational establishment but also an ethical base, that new heaven will bring about a new earth. The new earth is the masses of the people benefiting from the knowledge and the material resources of G-d's earth.

In the context of the individual evolution, Imam Mohammed (RAA) also described these levels in terms of intellectual developments and identified the Prophets, the concepts personified, that represent each level. Each of the seven Prophets is a potentiality in us. Allah also describes the Prophet's Ascension through these levels,[10] and the event is reported in detail in Hadith.[11]

Seven Heavens-The Night Journey

It was narrated by Abbas bin Malik:"… *that Allah's Apostle described to them his Night Journey saying, "While I was lying in Al-Hatim or Al-Hijr, suddenly someone came to me and cut my body open from here to here." I asked Al-Jarud who was by my side, "What does he mean?" He said, "It means from his throat to his pubic area," or said, "From the top of the chest." The Prophet further said, "He then took out my heart. Then a gold tray of Belief was brought to me and my heart was washed and was filled (with Belief) and then returned to its original place. Then a white animal which was smaller than a mule and bigger than a donkey was brought to me." (On this Al-Jarud asked, "Was it the Buraq, O Abu Hamza?" I (i.e. Anas) replied in the affirmative). The Prophet said, "The animal's step (was so wide that it) reached the farthest point within the reach of the animal's sight. I was carried on it, and Gabriel set out with me till we reached the nearest heaven.*

When he asked for the gate to be opened, it was asked, 'Who is it?' Gabriel answered, 'Gabriel.' It was asked, 'Who is accompanying you?' Gabriel replied, 'Muhammad.' It was asked, 'Has Muhammad been called?' Gabriel replied in the affirmative. Then it was said, 'He is welcomed. What an excellent visit his is!' The gate was opened, and when I went over the first heaven, I saw Adam there. Gabriel said (to me). 'This is your father, Adam; pay him your greetings.' So I greeted him and he returned the greeting to me and said, 'You are welcomed, O pious son and pious Prophet.'

Prophet Muhammad thus ascended through each successive heaven meeting Prophets on each one. Yahya (John and his cousin Isa (Jesus) on the second heaven; Yusuf (Joseph) on the third; Idris on the fourth; Harun (Aaron) on the fifth; Musa (Moses) on the sixth. Jibril (Gabriel) introduced Muhammad to the Prophets on each level and told him to greet them. The Prophet greeted each one and each one said, "You are welcomed, O pious brother and pious Prophet."

The Prophet said when he left Moses, Moses wept. "Someone asked him, 'What makes you weep?' Moses said, 'I weep because after me there has been sent (as Prophet) a young man whose followers will enter Paradise in greater numbers than my followers.' Gabriel continued ascending with the Prophet and "then Gabriel ascended with me to the **seventh** heaven and asked for its gate to be opened. It was asked, 'Who is it?' Gabriel replied, 'Gabriel.' It was asked,' Who is accompanying you?' Gabriel replied, 'Muhammad.' It was asked, 'Has he been called?' Gabriel replied in the affirmative. Then it was said, 'He is welcomed. What an excellent visit his is!' So when I went (over the seventh heaven), there I saw Abraham. Gabriel said (to me), 'This is your father; pay your greetings to him.' So I greeted him and he returned the greetings to me and said, 'You are welcomed, O pious son and pious Prophet.'

Then I was made to ascend to Sidrat-ul-Muntaha (i.e. the Lote Tree of the utmost boundary) Behold! Its fruits were like the jars of Hajr (i.e. a place near Medina) and its leaves were as big as the ears of elephants. Gabriel said, 'This is the Lote Tree of the utmost boundary. Behold! **There ran four rivers, two were hidden and two were visible.** I asked, 'What are these two kinds of rivers, O Gabriel?' He replied,' As for the hidden rivers, they are two rivers in Paradise and the visible rivers are the Nile and the Euphrates.' Then Al-Bait-ul-Ma'mur (i.e.

the Sacred House) was shown to me and a container full of wine and another full of milk and a third full of honey were brought to me. I took the milk. Gabriel remarked, 'This is the Islamic religion which you and your followers are following.'

After greeting Abraham (PBUH), the Prophet led them all in Prayer. The resources of these major prophets are in every human being. Although this potential is inherent, it is limited and it is through revelation that the potential is liberated and the evolution is completed on the social plane. The Prophet (PBUH) led the Prophets (PBUT) in prayer and his establishment of society at Madina is a sign of that completion.

The Bible also speaks of the Creation of the world in periods of seven days.[12] To better understand the nature of these developments, and get the greatest benefit from this perspective, we have to look beyond the Prophets (PBUT) as individual human persons. We have to see them as *mental dispositions, orientations in the intellect, and levels of social development.*[13]

Abraham (PBUH)

Prophet Abraham (PBUH) representing the seventh level is a personification of the correct thinking of the free thinker. This orientation of the intellect made it possible for the human curiosity to engage the material world and come to understand that everything G-d created embodies science and knowledge. We discover that everything in the material world is subject to laws that govern them. This faculty is analytical thinking and it evolves *into exact sciences and higher education.*

This faculty also demonstrates a respect for the unseen. Our mind searches for answers beyond the material constraints. We know Abraham studied the heavenly order until he discovered its limitations and this told him that there must be something beyond these things that did not have limitations and infirmities. Because he remained faithful to finding that, the straining of his brain ignited a higher power of intuition and cognition that propelled his vision beyond the gravity of matter-the seen—to the realm of the unseen. And even there he found the same system of laws governing it all.

There we conclude that the universe is one consistent whole, that there is a universal law governing it and that the permanent order is greater than the passing interruptions and disruptions that are coming and going. That is what began the real process of higher learning and education, so Abraham is the Father of our intellect and socially, the father of higher education.

Adam (PBUH)

Adam (PBUH) represents our common origin from one human soul. His thinking was different than Abraham's (PBUH) in that it personifies the natural intelligence in the common individual person that evolves with human nature. Allah says: He taught Adam (PBUH), the nature of all things.[14] His light and that of the other levels of development were not the light of Revelation. It was the light of human nature, their bodies agreeing with the nature G-d created, became light.

Adam (PBUH) was made from clay[15] Clay can be molded into shape, so we know that G-d shaped that first man exactly the way He wanted him-in the most excellent mold.[16,17] Clay will hold its shape, just the way its master or a sculptor has molded it, and when it *hardens* it will not change its shape unless you break it.

When it has hardened into shape, it *resonates*. You can tap it and it will produce a *sound* depending on its own nature—its composition, its thickness, and its shape. So G-d says He created man from sounding clay meaning that we all have the capacity for expression.

Education

It is no accident that the science of education has incorporated these same levels of development. In 1956, Benjamin Bloom headed a group of educational psychologists who identified three domains or categories of educational activities, or separate types of learning, called Bloom's Taxonomy of learning domains. Taxonomy is the practice and science of classification. They include:

Cognitive: mental skills (*Knowledge*)
Affective: growth in feelings or emotional areas (*Attitude*)
Psychomotor: manual or physical skills (*Skills*)

Within the cognitive domain, they developed a classification of levels of intellectual behavior important in learning. Bloom found that over 95 % of the test questions students encounter require them to think only at the lowest possible level-the recall of information. Bloom identified six levels within the cognitive domain, from the simple recall or recognition of facts, as the lowest level, through increasingly more complex and abstract mental levels, to the highest order which is classified as evaluation.[18]

Each level must be mastered before the next one can take place.[19] The levels expand the higher we go up into evolution, so on the higher levels, we have more capacity, more functionality. In the educational context those levels and their functions are as follows:

1. ***Knowledge***: arrange, define, duplicate, label, list, memorize, name, order, recognize, relate, recall, repeat, reproduce state.
2. ***Comprehension***: classify, describe, discuss, explain, express, identify, indicate, locate, recognize, report, restate, review, select, translate,
3. ***Application***: apply, choose, demonstrate, dramatize, employ, illustrate, interpret, operate, practice, schedule, sketch, solve, use, write.
4. ***Analysis***: analyze, appraise, calculate, categorize, compare, contrast, criticize, differentiate, discriminate, distinguish, examine, experiment, question, test.
5. ***Synthesis***: arrange, assemble, collect, compose, construct, create, design, develop, formulate, manage, organize, plan, prepare, propose, set up, write.
6. ***Evaluation***: appraise, argue, assess, attach, choose, compare, defend, estimate, judge, predict, rate, core, select, support, value, evaluate.

Allah confirms in Qur'an that He revealed these important stages of development to His Messenger over 1,400 years ago and the enduring power of these concepts is still evident today.

Success is to be measured not so much by the position that one has reached in life, as by the obstacles which he has had to overcome while trying to succeed.

– Booker T. Washington

The Fruit of Islam (FOI), the men "who belong to Islam in North America" from one of its many Temples in America's large and small cities and towns, assembled in front of the residence of Honorable Elijah Muhammad in Chicago, to be reviewed and to salute him in the early 1970s. The event was part of the wedding celebration of Muhammad's granddaughter, Ayesha Muhammad, and included a parade down Cottage Grove Avenue, with FOI from across the country, floats representing the Muslim businesses along Cottage Grove and 79th. Street and the Muslim schools called Universities of Islam. The military drill and discipline that was taught to the FOI was modeled in part on Booker T. Washington's teachings in the late 1800's and incorporated by W. D. Fard into the training of the Nation of Islam. Photo by John Fleming courtesy of Nuri Madina

12:5 Said (the father): "My (dear) little son! relate not thy vision to thy brothers, lest they concoct a plot against thee: for Satan is to man an avowed enemy!

Chapter 5

Keep That to Yourself

"Earn help for fulfilling your needs by being discrete, for every owner of a blessing is envied." Recorded by At-Tabari

Envy

The word *Ikhwatikun* means *'to thy brothers'* and brother is defined as a "Person of the same descent, land, creed or faith with other or others." Dictionary of the Holy Qur'an, Abdul Mannan Omar. But, jealousy and envy can make us do terrible things, even to our own brother.[1] They destroy the person from within. Mental health professionals say they can manifest in many ways from rash violence to chronic depression.

This is the same disposition that brought about Satan's rejection of G-d's plan for the human being in the earth.[2] He saw his role being diminished. He saw man's creation from mud as inferior to his creation from fire. He saw rational knowledge as the only thing that should rule over humanity, not conscience or human sensitivity.

Discouragement

Satan has attributes just like Allah has attributes, and among them are the Discourager and the Punisher. He denies us the noble position and the abundance that our Lord Creator intends for us. He does this through subtle suggestion; through whispering into the heart of man. In the Bible, it says that the serpent in the garden was the most subtle of all creatures.[3] Subtle means shrewd, crafty or devious. If we look at how the serpent moves, its body moves from side to side on a seemingly crooked path, but it still continues moving forward toward you.

Allah says that Satan approaches us from a vantage point we can't see.[4] He doesn't confront us face to face. He's observing us and approaching us through our own human nature, our subconscious. He threatens us with poverty.[5] We are all motivated by need and when we feel inadequate or insecure that is a sense of lack or poverty.

We should not advertise our plans and our dreams to everyone we come into contact with. Dr. Catherine Ponder suggests that one important reason is that it opens us up to the negative forces and people that are certain to come at us when we try to do something positive. If we are not strong in our conviction, we may become weakened by their efforts. Continually talking about your goal can also give you a false sense of accomplishment, making you less likely to actually go after it.

There are many people that get their satisfaction just from being seen as accomplishing something instead of actually accomplishing it. We tell people how great our plan is and we can begin to "Believe in our own press release." That jolt of satisfaction and pride is enough for many of us. We feel so satisfied, in fact, that we lose the motivation to really accomplish the task. Why should we go through the sweat and effort of accomplishment, when we're already being pumped up by those who just blow up our ego balloons so we can float away?

A lot of times other's opinions will block us. Dreams are powerful and if we hold onto the dream long enough and continue working toward it, we will eventually succeed. Allah says "Man attains only what he strives for" and "the object of his striving will soon come into view."[6] But we are always surrounded by people with materialist views, i.e., they only believe in what they can see, what is manifest. If the means and resources are not readily visible, then their mind can't visualize the result. This is not to say that we should surround ourselves with yes-men. It also helps to surround ourselves with people who have some connection to our dream. We need objective viewpoints; we need to be circumspect and we need people who will play the proverbial "devil's advocate." (Ever wonder why they call them that?) We also have to be sensitive to advice that may carry ulterior motives. But at the end of the day, we have to make our own decision. We have to believe in ourselves, in Allah, and in what we are doing. If it is good, then we know G-d is with it.[7] And the believers say, just as did the two spies of Moses (PBUH), if G-d is with us, we are assured of victory.[8]

When we fantasize about our goals we have to think about not only the rewards of our effort but also about the price we're going to pay to achieve them. We will have to devote time to accomplishing them and that time will come at the expense of something else. Sometimes we will have to sacrifice friends, sometimes there are expenses such as the costs of college or special training. This makes our vision more realistic and also enables us to develop a realistic plan for getting there.

12:6 "Thus will thy Lord choose thee and teach thee the interpretation of stories (and events) and perfect His favour to thee and to the posterity of Jacob - even as He perfected it to thy fathers Abraham and Isaac aforetime! for Allah is full of knowledge and wisdom."

Chapter 6

G-d Chooses Whom He Pleases

The rulers in the society believe no one can gain knowledge or have intelligent vision without them giving it to them. They have their own opinion as to who should be worthy and who should receive G-d's blessing, but G-d chooses whom he pleases.[1] That vision of eleven stars and the sun and the moon making sajdah to Joseph (PBUH), is the process by which we are blessed with knowledge on the highest levels. The twelve brothers, of which Joseph is one, represent the streams of knowledge and wisdom that flow from creation and human experience and feeds the intelligence. The sun represents divine knowledge. The moon represents revealed knowledge that must be interpreted. When all of this has submitted to Joseph he has reached the destiny that G-d intended.

Heaven can be viewed as the full illumination of the mind. Allah's description of the Hereafter is gardens with rivers flowing beneath. In the time of Moses (PBUH), Pharaoh - the ruler of Egypt - boasted, "look at these palaces with streams flowing beneath."[2] Metaphorically, *Nahar*, from *Nahara*-streams flowing, represents prosperity and power.[3] Even today we use the expressions *income stream* and *cash flow*. Palaces, like our houses and most buildings, are built on foundations rooted in the Earth. The taller the structure, the deeper the foundation must be rooted. His boast was of the great scientific and material establishment, rooted in material creation and the streams of knowledge that fed it. One definition of science is *systematic knowledge of the physical or material world* and logic is the system or principles of reasoning applicable to any branch of knowledge or study. Pharaoh therefore understandably had difficulty understanding Moses' (PBUH) message of an unseen Supreme G-d Who had created everything.[4]

The ancient Egyptian people excelled in many ways. For thousands of years, they were a great material power that also possessed advanced knowledge of the human mind and psyche. Psychology came from ancient Egypt to the western world through the Greeks and others. But all of this paled in comparison to G-d's intended blessing for Joseph (PBUH). What was it that Joseph should expect from G-d's perfected favor? It is the same thing that his fathers Jacob (PBUH), Isaac(PBUH), and Abraham(PBUH) received. Joseph (PBUH) was put in the pit/well. Jacob's (PBUH) father Isaac (PBUH) re-dug wells that had originally been dug by his father, Abraham (PBUH).[5] Jacob (PBUH) met Joseph's (PBUH) mother Rachel at the well.[6] Wells are dug into the material earth in order to bring water, the nourishment of material and spiritual life up to the surface.

Similarly, Joseph's (PBUH) father Jacob (PBUH) had experience with dreams. He saw in his dream a ladder extending to heaven and angels ascending and descending the ladder. I saw in my own life, the need to descend into my own subconscious and bring incorrect thinking, concepts, attitudes, beliefs, and habits from those dark, hidden recesses into the light of the heavens, into my consciousness, in order to analyze and deal with them. I needed then to descend with those cleansed elements back down the ladder into my everyday life on earth. In a broader context, Imam Mohammed (RAA) identified the need for real social reform as climbing a moral ladder.

Knowledge and wisdom is always the favor of G-d, but all human knowledge belongs to G-d and over every possessor of knowledge is He, the One complete in knowledge.[7] The twelve streams of knowledge is world leadership ruled by scientific disciplines and G-d's gift of revelation is above them all.[8] The worlds of business, politics, education, social sciences, religion all eventually reach the limits of their rational potential and when they do, it takes a "Word" from G-d to enlighten their endeavors and enable them to take another step up in human progress.

12:7 Verily in Joseph and his brethren are signs (or symbols) for seekers (after Truth).

Chapter 7

Twelve-the Leadership and the World

Four

What is the origin of the twelve streams of knowledge? Allah created Adam (PBUH) from one *nafs* - one soul or spirit. That spirit needs to have material expression to be visible to us and manifest in a material world. G-d placed Adam PBUH) in the Garden (the perfect spiritual consciousness and the uncorrupted environment). In scripture it says, four rivers went out of the Garden and supplied life to the known world.[1] They represent universal streams of knowledge and the four main areas of human influence: business, education, politics, and religion.[2] Prophet Muhammad (PBUH) re-ordered the social model of those major powers or influences that left the Garden in the beginning and he established himself in the four dimensions of character: leader, husband, military man, and peacemaker.

That Four[3] then branches out and evolves into many other influences. When four is multiplied by 10, it represents 40 or the completion in universal dimension. Imam Mohammed (RAA) identified America's promise to her slaves of "40 acres and a mule" as our "ability to pursue our G-d given potential, which is our divine inheritance."[4] In his own penchant for satire, Imam Mohammed (RAA) dubbed W. D. Fard as WD40, after the well-known lubricant. No doubt he was referring to Fard's success in unlocking the "rusty minds" of African Americans and his prayer that we would one day attain that universal dimension.

In January 1941, Franklin Roosevelt outlined his "Four Freedoms" declaration before a joint session of congress where he identified four basic rights he believed all humankind should enjoy: freedom of speech, freedom of unfettered worship, freedom from want, and freedom from fear.[5] Imam Mohammed (RAA) received the Four Freedoms Medals, from the Roosevelt Institute as one of many luminaries, whose life's work embodies FDR's Four Freedoms and who carry forward the legacy and values of Franklin and Eleanor Roosevelt. Previous recipients include Secretary and Presidential Candidate, Hillary Clinton, Bill Moyers, Muhammad Yunus, Aung San Suu Kyi, President Bill Clinton, President Jimmy Carter, Nelson Mandela, Bishop Desmond Tutu, Jonas Salk, the Dali Lama, Thurgood Marshall, and Elie Wiesel.

Twelve

The ancient people developed the psychology of their worship from the canopy of the heavens. A complete day is 24 hours - 12 hours of day and 12 hours of night - and together they represent the whole world, the world of the spiritual and rational. This twelve is the original pattern of time that the material universe is set upon.[6] The twelve zodiac signs indicated the proper time for sowing, mowing, and harvesting and all other activities of that period of time. In scripture, when Jacob (PBUH) blessed his twelve sons, he identified each of them by their nature and by their representation in of one of the constellations: Judah was the lion; Aquarius, the water bearer; Dan, the Serpent; and Issachar, the crab. The phrase "Issachar is a strong ass, is explained by the fact that there are two stars in the zodiac sign Cancer called "the two asses."[7] "Joseph is a fruitful bough, whose branches have gone over the wall," represents him in November, in the constellation Sagittarius, when the vine has grown to its fullness. "His bow abode in strength," is explained by a reference to the constellation in which he is drawing his bow. The Mysteries of Osiris, Ancient Egyptian Initiation by Dr. R. Swinburne Clymer (1951), p108

When Jesus (PBUH)called his twelve disciples together, it meant he brought the scientific leadership of that time under his rule and his message was for us to have that leadership within ourselves. We have to harness twelve disciplines, metaphysically and spiritually and gain mastery over heavenly or spiritual science. Jesus (PBUH)then called them together and said, "Now come away from the water; let us go on land and become fishermen of men. In other words, go to agriculture, go to industry, go to the factory and save the man." (Imam Mohammed [RAA], May 2008)

Moses (PBUH) sent twelve spies into Jericho to bring back a report on how to take the city. Ten spies came back reporting that there were giants there and that they could not be successful. Two of them, whom the Qur'an described as "G-d fearing" and tradition has identified as Joshua (PBUH) and Caleb, came back and reported that if it was G-d's Will, they could have it all. Those two represent the rational and scientific thinkers among us that know we can accomplish anything which G-d wills.[8] Later, Jacob (PBUH) will advise his sons how to enter Egypt by each of them using a different gate or port of entry. Those ten are the same ones among us today and all of them have the same middle name - doubt, fear, and 'we can't'.

In the Bible narrative of Joseph (PBUH), there were two brothers, Reuben and Judah, who rejected the idea of killing Joseph (PBUH).[9] They understood that slaying Joseph (PBUH) represented more than just the slaying of an individual.[10] Joseph (PBUH) had not succumbed to sin and would never lose G-d in his heart. That would be the real death. It has been the same with our community. There have always been those conscious ones among us who have held on to righteous principles. They have held on to the belief that G-d is a G-d of Mercy and Justice who will never abandon his true servants and believers. These are the ones that have kept the movement and our communities alive.

All of us will one day face physical deterioration and death. We will face all kinds of decline: economic, social, and physical. G-d says at the judgment he will bring us back down to our fingertips. Ask someone who is cripple or who has poor vision if they have dreamed of themselves in the afterlife or in heaven and they will mostly likely tell you that they see themselves as whole and healthy. That would be a hollow reward, to come back to a supposedly higher life with the same infirmities and ills that we have now. We need a better perspective of death, one that inspires hope instead of fear.

Devoid of the spiritual boundaries of the garden, those rivers, these material influences take on a life of their own. They divided further, and by the time of Moses (PBUH), they had evolved into twelve. You will find that in the history of modern society much human progress in the four important human endeavors has been made by Jews, the followers of Moses (PBUH).[11] But that spiritual consciousness that began in their heart hardened over an extended period of rebelliousness and, whereas in Genesis the rivers flowed from a Garden, by this time they were springing from a rock.[12] Moses (PBUH) struck the rock in response to the people's request for water; the water sprung forth and each head/influence knew its place. In the Gardens that Allah promises, there are rivers flowing beneath.[13]

When Moses (PBUH) went to Pharaoh with G-d's message to let His people go, Pharaoh was arrogant and didn't respond until plagues came upon him. Then he would relent, but every time G-d would remove the plague, his heart would harden and he would change his mind. The guidance of Allah, when we accept it, will penetrate any external conditions and soften the heart and bring it back to its original condition.[14]

Seekers

The word used for "seekers", *sailina,* from Sa 'ala is defined in the Dictionary of the Holy Qur'an (Abdul Mannan Omar) as a *Seeker [after Truth], Questioner, Solicitor or Begger, who ask (for help)*, and is used one other time in Qur'an at 41:10 where it is translated "those who seek (sustenance)."[15] Allah says there are signs in the earth and in us, and here we are told of the signs in Joseph (PBUH) and his brothers. We respond to these signs first as believers. We then gain certainty in our belief and arrive at reason and wisdom.[16] All of the prophets were thinkers and truth seekers and since this type is always trying to make sense of himself and the world around him, he will eventually free himself from the burdens of ignorance and myth.

Abraham (PBUH) asked to know things for a certainty in addition to his faith. The thinker comes to know G-d, the inscrutable, by questioning the mysteries of himself, of which he is capable of gaining some understanding. That study of the human existence will engage the mind of the scientist, the thinker, and the student, as long as the world endures; so we are all students in that sense. We are constantly learning from the Mother Book, Nature. For example, the Islamic calendar is a lunar calendar where months begin when the first crescent of a new moon is sighted. Since the Islamic lunar calendar year is 11 to 12 days shorter than the solar year, the months migrate throughout the seasons. Allah says in the Qur'an that he made the moon as signs for counting the time. Imam Salim Mu'min recently made the point, in reference to the debate over the scientific calculation of the moon sighting for the beginning of Ramadan and the Eid Al-Fitr, as opposed to the actual sighting of the moon, that if you depend solely on calculations and discard the effort to sight the moon, your calculations will have removed the new crescent as a sign. "When you remove a sign, you remove the great body of knowledge that the sign represents. The new crescent is a sign." This reminds us that Allah has given us a most trustworthy hand to hold in the *Fitr* (Original Pattern) of His Creation and that of our own souls. This is what Imam Mohammed (RAA) called "creation supported social logic" and what will serve us regardless to what *Alamin* or worlds or systems of knowledge evolve.

12:8 They said: "Truly Joseph and his brother are loved more by our father than we: But we are a goodly body! really our father is obviously wandering (in his mind)!

Chapter 8

I'm Better Than He

The brothers are so unrepentant in their arrogance that they see their father as wandering in the mind. Reflect back on G-d's creation of Adam (PBUH) and Iblis' assertion that G-d, in making man, was making a mistake, saying, "I am better than he.[1] "*That innocent creature you're making is no match for us of such great knowledge. He is no match for this complex society that has evolved. He's only going to make mischief and create bloodshed. He's going to make a lot of boo-boos arriving at the state you want him at.*" It's like a person looking down on an infant because he defecates in his diaper, not recognizing that he could be a great man in the making and not realizing that we all started off in diapers. Little did Iblis know, he was making the biggest mistake of all by not recognizing, in his arrogance, that Allah is all Knowing and has the power to subsume all little schemes into His big one. This attitude that "I am better than he," was fueled by jealousy and arrogance and is the root of today's racism, apartheid, and genocide.

The four rivers have become heads or influences within themselves. Even as they branch out into twelve influences and institutions of human society, they each still want life interpreted through their perspective only. Business wants to define everything in terms of finance, market forces, and bottom lines. Some companies will sell products they know will cause death to a small percentage of people, but they've calculated how much it costs to defend and settle the resulting lawsuits and, as long as the profits outweigh those costs, they'll consider those casualties a cost of doing business. And we are all familiar now with the military's concept of "collateral damage" that justifies whatever it wants to do in the name of power and dominance.

I am amazed at the pharmaceutical advertising on television today for ailments that could easily have been avoided through a healthy diet. Throughout the script that is claiming the benefits of the drug, another script is running which reminds us that this drug may cause blindness, loss of appetite, sudden drop in blood pressure, paralysis, stroke, hypertension, loss of consciousness, and sudden death.

Crusades

The Crusades occurred hundreds of years ago, but the same attitude and jealousy that led to these Christian "Holy Wars" is very much alive today. W. D. Fard taught in his lessons that history is most qualified to reward all research. Four hundred years after the Crusades, William Gladstone (1809-98), the British Prime Minister, stated in the House of Commons, "as long as the Qur'an remains in the world, there would be no peace in the world"—almost word for word of our bigots and Qur'an burners of today. The language of Imam Mohammed (RAA), the concepts, "Remake the World," [2] and "Words Make People" had a profound effect on Muslims and the world. It was a language of inclusion, a language that put the interests of community above those of the individual. It was a language that made us look beyond the races, the nationalities, and the differences we have and look first to our common human origin. He promoted interfaith dialogue to discuss our common goals and common interests.

When I ran for office in 1986, I incorporated this language into my political platform, but 30 years ago it was not language that resonated with the voting public.

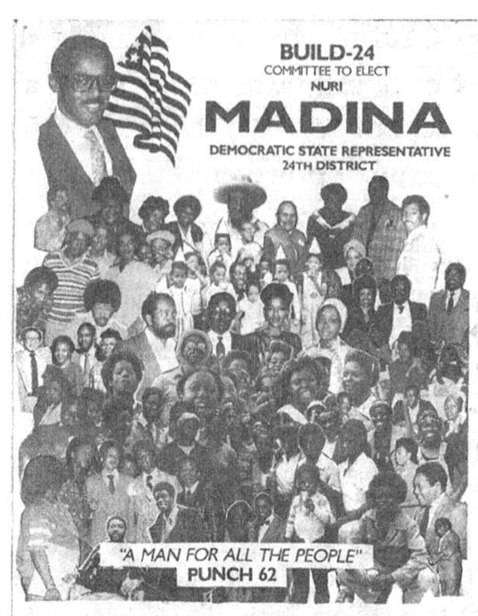

HIGHLIGHTS

Political Philosophy:

Everybody has to be included, and the individual concern should be addressed only after the community life has been put into focus.

Moral and ethical concerns must be promoted. We are morally obligated to oppose any movement, influence or element that restricts or limits the good healthy life of the community.

America and its political system is the ideal environment for African American people to survive and prosper. It is a protection for all racial, religious and cultural minorities, and we should utilize the system to advance our communities as others have done.

We embrace the Constitution of the United States and its Preamble, and particularly its emphasis on the sacredness of life, the individual rights, the emphasis on preserving the Union, the obligation of the government and the limitations placed on government.

BUILD-24 Platform:

URBAN DEVELOPMENT—

- Unity among residents, merchants, and institutions.
- A fair distribution of all state resources.
- Tenant Management in CHA

SOCIAL SERVICE NETWORK—

- More concern and efficiency in all public agencies and with public servants.
- Programs for the hungry, the homeless, the lonely, the depressed and the unemployed.
- Particular concern for families and single parent households

SELF-HELP JOBS—

- Revive community shopping to generate economic development
- Create jobs through rehabilitation of abandoned buildings & new construction in vacant areas.

NEIGHBORHOOD RESPONSIBILITY

- Organize a network of all individuals and institutions
- Assist and support the work of the Block Clubs and Community Organizations.

BACKGROUND-COMMUNITY SERVICE

18 years experience in developing and assisting African American culture, with emphasis in discipline and grassroots organizing. Background in publishing community newspapers, and organizing youth groups, business organizations, and community residents. A member of the Muslim community since 1968. Professional expertise: BA in Public Information, Columbia College, and 87 of 88 hours completed at John Marshall Law School.

HEADQUARTERS
4355 S. Calumet, Chicago, IL 60653 312/373-2022

Cover and page 2 of my campaign literature. Imam Mohammed's (RAA) language laid the groundwork for the "post-racial" leadership that a majority of Americans are embracing today. Courtesy of Nuri Madina

The attacks on September 11, 2001 (9/11) could have overshadowed the progress that this new language made. Muslims had begun to be seen as a part of the fabric of American society. We should remember Imam Mohammed (RAA) raising the American flag in the Temple on Stony Island in Chicago and instituting New World Patriotism Day celebrations on the Fourth of July. I have no doubt that had he not built such an "Ark," a vessel of protection that sailed over the stormy seas of a changing society, and the relentless rain of concerns and cultural decay, Muslims would have been interned just like the Japanese were during World War II. Many pioneer Muslims remember white Americans referring to us a "Black Japs" after the Pearl Harbor attacks. After 9/11, extremists responded by fanning the flames of hatred, mistrust, and resentment against our Muslim population. You will always have people that do not want progress; they want dissension and conflict. They want human beings fighting each other. They cast the wars in Iraq and Afghanistan as Crusades against Muslims. And now the world's scourge of ISIS is being used to cast shade over the image of Peace and Oneness that Islam presents.

Actions speak louder than words, but language is the vehicle that motivates and directs actions. Look at both the language and the actions of those who were leading the people. Terrorists have been equated with Islamic extremists not acknowledging the Ku Klux Klan and Jim Crow terror that African Americans have lived under in this country. One person aptly noted that one man's terrorist is another man's freedom fighter. Perhaps there is some lingering, subconscious or genetic sense of injury among Christian extremists still traumatized by the 14th. Century Crusades. Likewise, there are many in the Muslim world who are still burdened in their souls by the horrors of colonialism.

The Ottoman Empire was one of the longest lasting empires in history lasting for 623 years, but it was declining even before the western victors of World War I partitioned the remaining portion of Empire, leaving only Turkey itself intact. As early as 1830, Algeria had been ceded to French rule. Following the Russo- Turkish War (1877–1878) the Treaty of San Stefano of 1878 recognized Romanian and Serbian independence, as well as the establishment of an autonomous Bulgarian principality under nominal Ottoman protection. Austria-Hungary occupied Bosnia by default and Cyprus is occupied by Britain. In 1881, Tunisia became a French colony and in 1882, Egypt came under British protection. By the end of World War I the only parts of the Arabian peninsula that were still under Ottoman control were Yemen, Asir, the city of Medina, portions of northern Syria and portions of northern Iraq and these territories were handed over to the British forces on January 23, 1919.

The huge territories once ruled by the Ottoman Turks were divided into separate countries, each one under the colonial rule and leadership of Europeans and their proxies. The League of Nations, the predecessor to the United Nations, granted France mandates over Syria and Lebanon. It granted the United Kingdom mandates over Mesopotamia (Modern day Iraq) and Palestine (which was later divided into two regions: Palestine and Transjordan). Parts of the Ottoman Empire on the Arabian Peninsula became parts of what are known today as Saudi Arabia and Yemen. At the same time, the Balfour Declaration, promulgated by the United Kingdom, encouraged the international Zionist movement to push for a Jewish homeland in the Palestine region, which at the time had a small Jewish minority population living peacefully and secure within a vast majority Arab-Muslim population.

One significant statement of Balfour's declaration appears to be overlooked even today and that is: **"…it being clearly understood**

that nothing shall be done which may prejudice the civil and religious rights of existing non-Jewish communities in Palestine." The Stern Gang, a militant Zionist group, identified as a terrorist organization by Britain, through assassination and other terrorist acts, sought to forcibly evict the British authorities from Palestine, allowing unrestricted immigration of Jews and the formation of a Jewish state. Another overlooked fact in reference to the Holocaust is that Zionists, in many cases, lobbied in Washington and Europe, against assisting the Jews that were being persecuted because they felt it would take support away from establishing the Jewish state in Palestine.[3] Thus despite the understandable reverence toward the Holocaust and its innocent victims, the reality is that Zionists themselves facilitated it to further their own political ends of a Jewish state in Palestine.

Fast forward to the "war on terror" which was initially characterized as a *crusade*. Only the most naïve will believe that was a slip of the lip. That perception of a crusade was prevalent throughout America's military chain of command, from the commander-in-chief on down. General William Boykin described the wars in evangelical terms, casting the U.S. military as the "army of God." Kathryn Joyce pointed out in a Newsweek article that as late as 2008, there was still an evangelical military that saw spreading Christianity as part of its mission. She notes that in May, Al-Jazeera broadcast clips filmed in 2008 showing stacks of Bibles translated into Pashto and Dari at the U. S. air base in Bagram and featured the chief of the U. S. military chaplains in Afghanistan, Lt. Col. Gary Hensley, telling soldiers to "hunt people for Jesus." Mikey Weinstein, president of the Military Religious Freedom Foundation (MRFF) says a cadre of 40 U.S. chaplains took part in a 2003 project to distribute 2.4 million Arabic Language Bibles in Iraq.

The Bible initiative was handled by former Army chaplain Jim Ammerman, the 83-year-old founder of the Chaplaincy of Full Gospel Churches (CFGC) - an organization in charge of endorsing 270 chaplains and chaplain candidates for the armed services. Ammerman worked with an evangelical group based in Arkansas, the International Missions Network Center, to distribute the bibles through the efforts of his 40 active-duty chaplains in Iraq. A 2003 newsletter for the group said of the effort, "The goal is to establish a wedge for the kingdom of God in the Middle East, directly affecting the Islamic world."

The various military branches' 2,900 chaplains are sworn to serve all soldiers, regardless of religion, with a respectful, religiously, pluralistic approach. CFGC represents a conglomeration of independent Pentecostal churches outside established denominations. The group was accepted as a chaplain-endorsing agency by the Department of Defense in 1984, and since then, Ammerman's agency has violated numerous codes that govern chaplaincies, including a constant denigration of other religions, particularly Islam, Judaism, mainline Protestantism and Catholicism, but also non-Pentecostal evangelical churches. A 2001 CFGC newsletter asserted that the real enemy of the U.S. wasn't Osama bin Laden, but Allah, whom the newsletter called "Lucifer." A 2006 issue argued that all Muslim-Americans should be treated with suspicion, as they "obviously can't be good Americans." In a 2008 sermon, Ammerman called Islam "a killer religion" and Muslims "the devil." It is easy to see how this language could result in the many instances of rape, torture, and murder of Iraqi civilians.

Where does this extreme language originate? Is it primarily from the religious community once it becomes corrupted? The Honorable Elijah Muhammad taught from lessons given to him by Nation of Islam founder, W. D. Fard, that "they use his *(Jesus)* name to shield their dirty religion." Indeed, the very demagogues who perpetrate the most heinous acts on fellow human beings invariably invoke the name of G-d to justify their acts. On the continuum of behaviors toward fellow human beings, we find racism and apartheid ranking high on the scale of human cruelty and savagery, with ethnic cleansing and genocide at the extreme of that continuum. Today, just as in past history, extremists find support for their human cruelty in scripture.[4]

What has been described as the one of the most powerful and enigmatic themes in Judaism, the reference to the annihilation of the Amalek, is considered by some a *mitzvah* (*something commanded by God*) but questioned by others as a 'barbaric anachronism' and no different than the Holocaust. The Amaleks (Amalekites) were a marauding nation that picked off (Zanvu) stragglers as the Israelites *exodused* Egypt. The use of the word Zanvu (from Zanov-meaning tail) as opposed to the traditional word for ambush, emphasizes that it was the weak and the old that were picked off and plundered. Jeffrey Goldberg, in a New York Times article entitled "Israel's Fears, Amalek's Arsenal" in May 2009 wrote, "Amaleks, in essence, is Hebrew for *existential threat*-the undying enemy of the Jews. The rabbis teach that successive generations of Jews have been forced to confront the Amalekites: Nebuchadnezzar, the Crusaders, Torquemada, Hitler, and Stalin, which are all manifestations of Amalek's malevolent spirit." Now they have added the Palestinians and the Iranians to that list.

When Israeli prime minister, Benjamin Netanyahu, met with president Obama in Washington in 2008, he resisted the president's insistence on the establishment of a separate Palestinian state and a halt to expanding Jewish settlements on occupied Palestinian lands. His obsession was with the Iranian nuclear program and when Goldberg asked one of his advisers "to gauge for me the depth of Mr. Netanyahu's anxiety about Iran," his answer was "Think Amalek." The Zionist idea for Iran's elimination is driving its politics and influencing the American political landscape as seen from the Republican opposition to the Iran nuclear treaty. When leaders allow their political, economic and nationalist ambitions to be shrouded in religious language there is no difference between them and Al-Qaeda or ISIS.

12:9 "Slay ye Joseph or cast him out to some (unknown) land, that so the favour of your father may be given to you alone: (there will be time enough) for you to be righteous after that!"

Chapter 9

A Straight Lick with a Crooked Stick

Imam Mohammed (RAA) describes this attitude of "time enough to be righteous later," as the brothers' sin of moral or political expedience. The story of Solomon in the Qur'an teaches us not to accept the fly-by-night or instant success through jinn strategies of lying, cheating, and manipulation.[1] The brothers want the favor of their father to be for them alone. Dictionary.com defines jealousy as "resentment against a rival, a person enjoying success or advantage, etc., or against another's success or advantage itself." It is also described as a secondary emotion because it is sometimes a reaction to another primary emotion such as anger, fear, anxiety, sadness or negative thoughts and feelings of insecurity over an anticipated loss of something that the person values, particularly in reference to a human connection.

Envy (also called invidiousness) is best defined as an emotion that "occurs when a person lacks another's (perceived) superior quality, achievement, or possession and either desires it or wishes that the other lacked it." Envy can also derive from a sense of low self-esteem that results from an upward social comparison threatening a person's self-image. Allah tells us in the Qur'an to seek refuge with the Lord of the Dawn from enviers.[2] Prophet Muhammad (PBUH) said: "Keep yourselves far from envy; it eateth up and taketh away good actions, like as fire eateth up and burneth wood."

Many people are jealous of others who have imagination. In describing how this faculty is affected, as was Joseph (PBUH), by his relationship with his brothers, it is noted: in the *Metaphysical Dictionary, Charles Fillmore Reference Library Series*, that "While the imagination is a very necessary faculty and is powerful and productive, yet it is belittled and often derided and scorned by the other faculties of the mind while they are unawakened spiritually while they are functioning in intellectual consciousness instead of true spiritual understanding."

One of the biggest disagreement between our immigrant brothers and us is their insistence that we reject and disavow the Honorable Elijah Muhammad in order to be accepted and that we accept them as our leaders and interpreters of the Qur'an. How can they blame the Honorable Elijah Muhammad for the corruption and mistakes in our beliefs? It was the foreigner, W. D. Fard who set it all up, designed the Nation of Islam and the Lessons and gave them to the Honorable Elijah Muhammad, with the third grade, Georgia education. Toward the end of his mission and life, the Honorable Elijah Muhammad himself said, "Wisdom grows. I want to write the Lessons over again." (The Honorable Elijah Muhammad Table Talks, August 29th, 1973.) We're not going to disavow the Honorable Elijah Muhammad; we're not going to denounce him.

They are the one who have forgotten the message. We have been blessed with a reviver of the message, albeit through a roundabout way. G-d judges matters based on intention and the good intentions of both Elijah and Fard are evident. Are they any more guilty than Joseph's brothers who were eventually forgiven? Zora Neale Hurston, novelist, and anthropologist is one my favorite writers because of her down to earth, common soul, and her scholarly insight into the African American experience after slavery. She wrote in Jonah's Gourd Vine (1934), I think referring to this kind of moral and political expedience, "They is help if you knows how to git it. Some folks kin hit uh straight lick with uh crooked stick."

The Muslim world now has little advantage over the People of the Book who received Revelation and lost or forgot the message or went astray. Allah is the one who created us in tribes and nations and with different orientations,[3] and he has promised that the faith of the believers will always be rewarded despite our orientation.[4] The word that is used for tribes is from the same root of the word, *qabila*, used for *qibla* or *orientation*, the direction or point which one turns his face or attention. Allah has accepted us, and since we are the ones who have been blessed with the leader, I would say he has found us worthy. Imam Mohammed (RAA) said in his last interview on September 11, 2008, "If we become independent thinkers, we can make a contribution."

Imagination

In philosophy, imagination generally refers to three separate concepts: the imaginative, the imaginary, and mental imagery. Imaginativeness describes the faculty in which a person is able to think of things others cannot. It is considered a broader concept than just inventiveness or creativity. Imaginary refers to something that is unreal. Mental imagery refers to the ability to see things in the mind's eye and is related to the form of thought involved in perception. According to Charles Fillmore's "Revealing Word," imagination is "the faculty of mind that imagines and forms the power to shape and form thought; through this faculty the formless takes form. With our imagination, we lay hold of ideas and clothe them with substance." The body is the product of the mind. What man pictures or imagines in his mind will eventually appear in his body. In the communication of G-d with man, the imaging power of the mind plays an important part; it receives divine ideas and reflects their character to the consciousness. According to scripture, this is opening of the heavens and seeing the "angels of God ascending and descending upon the son of man."[5]

Charles Fillmore wrote, "Imagination gives man the ability to project himself through time and space and rise above all limitations." Sometimes this great power of man brings us immediate results and sometimes the results come from persistent and patient effort over long periods of time. But if it does take many years to materialize, as it did for Joseph (PBUH), we can be assured that the longer it takes to realize the results, the greater they will be when they do come.

Sensory Deprivation

In modern Western culture, the integration of the spiritual and material is often ignored. As a result, the role imagination plays in daily life has long been dismissed as useless, non-productive, even dangerous. In "normal" states of consciousness, we experience ourselves as existing within the boundaries of the physical body and, restricted by material reality, the limitations of time and space. The Message of truth and reality enables us to expand our life.[6]

Some primitive cultures believe in enhanced state healing and point to a wide range of conditions that can trigger the enhanced state, such as darkness, rhythmic drumbeats, social isolation, fasting, sensory deprivation, even fatigue or simple belief in the healing ritual. The picture of Joseph (PBUH) in the well presents images of these sensory deprivations. What is ironic is that we can have access to all of our senses and still be victims of deprivation when our senses are bombarded with excessive stimuli. (See Pollard, "Entertaining Ourselves to Death"). It may be that this overstimulation is a strategy to keep us in a material state of consciousness and not allow us to see within and get in touch with our higher forces.

12:10 Said one of them: "Slay not Joseph, but if ye must do something, throw him down to the bottom of the well: he will be picked up by some caravan of travellers."

Chapter 10

Whatever Doesn't Kill You...

We will find that the plan people make for evil is often turned to good, and whatever doesn't kill us, if we persevere and don't give up, will make us stronger. But don't expect that these other brothers or influences are going to help you if you're trying to do good. Look at how poor and struggling moral voices have been treated over time. Mother Theresa ministered to society's poorest and most rejected with little or no resources. The industrialists are saying, "right on, you're doing a wonderful job, she's a saint," but you don't see them committing much of their vast resources to solve the problem. Only a few, such as Bill and Melinda Gates, Mark Zuckerberg, have demonstrated that sensitivity where they recognize an obligation in their wealth to help.

One brother says of Joseph (PBUH), 'don't kill him.' He remembers G-d's word about the killing of one human soul.[1] Instead, let's confine him and restrict his life and his potential. 'Slay him not' may sound noble but often the alternative is even worse. Allah says, "Oppression is worse than outright slaughter."[2] In today's political climate, very few people have the courage to acknowledge that oppression can drive people to extremism. Though it's not justified, everything has its reason and its reaction.

Extremism

The exceedingly broad definition of terrorist activity as expanded in the USA PATRIOT Act and REAL ID Act, has led some, such as Bill Frelick - Human Rights Watch's refugee policy director, to suggest that the actions of a present-day George Washington would most certainly be covered as terrorist activity; yet we honor George Washington as a patriot and hero, a Founding Father. We demonize others who fought for the same freedoms. We should also remember that only a few short years ago, in my youth, and even some places today, the Ku Klux Klan, (KKK), and the White Citizen's Council who terrorized and lynched blacks were viewed as patriots.

Many who sought to change the status quo in favor of the oppressed, such as Dr. Martin Luther King Jr. have been called extremists. He wrote: "I have not said to my people 'get rid of your discontent.' Rather, I have tried to say that this normal and healthy discontent can be channeled into the creative outlet of nonviolent direct action. **And now this approach is being termed extremist.** But though I was initially disappointed at being categorized as an extremist, as I continued to think about the matter I gradually gained a measure of satisfaction from the label. Was not Jesus an extremist for love, 'Love your enemies, bless them that curse you, do good to them that hate you, and pray for them which despitefully use you, and persecute you.' Was not Amos an extremist for justice, 'Let justice roll down like waters and righteousness like an ever flowing stream.' Was not Paul an extremist for the Christian gospel, 'I bear in my body the marks of the Lord Jesus.' Was not Martin Luther an extremist: 'Here I stand; I cannot do otherwise, so help me God.' And John Bunyan, 'I will stay in jail to the end of my days before I make a butchery of my conscience.' And Abraham Lincoln, 'This nation cannot survive half slave and half free.' And Thomas Jefferson, 'We hold these truths to be self evident, that all men are created equal.' So the question is not whether we will be extremists, but what kind of extremists we will be. Will we be extremists for hate or for love? Will we be extremists for the preservation of injustice or for the extension of justice?" *Letter from a Birmingham Jail [King, Jr.]*

This "extremist" is the same Dr. King who, on January 3, 1964, appeared on the cover of *Time* magazine as its *Man of the Year* and later that same year on December 10, was awarded the Nobel Peace Prize; making him, at that time, the youngest person to be awarded the prize at age 35. He is also the same one who is now represented by a monument in our nation's capital.

Terrorism

The demonizing term of the day is "terrorist." There is no internationally agreed definition of terrorism. In the past, definitions tended to require some violence against innocent civilians. During the 1970s and 1980s, the United Nation's attempts to define the term foundered mainly due to differences of opinion between various members about the use of violence in the context of conflicts over national liberation and self-determination. Now, definitions tend to focus on a political or religious motivation and they tend to exclude violence by standing armies. The Organization of the Islamic Conference (OIC) also seeks to exclude, from the UN definition, resistance against foreign occupation. And the United States is still reluctant to describe the historical lynchings of African Americans, designed to terrorize and exclude them from political and social participation in the country, as terrorism.

The U.S. National Counterterrorism Center (NCTC) described a terrorist act as "premeditated; perpetrated by a subnational or clandestine agent; politically motivated, potentially including religious, philosophical, or culturally symbolic motivations; violent; and perpetrated against a noncombatant target." Under this definition, how could resistance in Iraq and Afghanistan be terrorism when it is directed toward the military occupying force? However, most other U.S. agencies have tended to eliminate the requirement that the violence be against civilians.

Nat Turner would be called a terrorist today, although it was the slave master who tortured, raped, and murdered the innocents. Turner was the resistance against terrorism and he was a man with imagination. Like Joseph (PBUH), he saw himself a free man, moving upon the spirit of G-d and capable of much more than his station in life allowed. In the "Confessions of Nat Turner - The Leader of the Late Insurrection in Southampton, Virginia," he described his childhood, his experiences and the inspiration that led him to lead a slave rebellion: "When I got large enough to go to work, while employed, I was reflecting on many things that would present themselves to my imagination and, whenever an opportunity occurred of looking at a book, when the school children were getting their lessons, I would find many things that the fertility of my own imagination had depicted to me before; all my time, not devoted to my master's service, was spent either in prayer or in making experiments in casting different things in molds made of Earth, in attempting to make paper, gunpowder, and many other experiments, that although I could not perfect, yet convinced me of its practicability if I had the means." When questioned as to the manner of manufacturing those different articles, he was found well informed on the subject. "I was not addicted to stealing in my youth, nor have I ever been, yet such was the confidence of the negroes in the neighborhood, even at this early period of my life, in my superior judgment, that they would often carry me with them when they were going on any roguery, to plan for them. Growing up among them, with this confidence in my superior judgment, and when this, in their opinions, was perfected by divine inspiration from the circumstances already alluded to in my infancy and which belief was ever afterwards zealously inculcated by the austerity of my life and manners, which became the subject of remark by white and black. Having soon discovered to be great, I must appear so, and therefore studiously avoided mixing in society, and wrapped myself in mystery, devoting my time to fasting and prayer. By this time, having arrived to man's estate, and hearing the scriptures commented on at meetings, I was struck with that particular passage which says: *Seek ye the kingdom of Heaven and all things shall be added unto you.* I reflected much on this passage and prayed daily for light on this subject. As I was praying one day at my plough, the spirit spoke to me, saying *Seek ye the kingdom of Heaven and all things shall be added unto you.*"

He was questioned: "What do you mean by the Spirit?" He answered: "The Spirit that spoke to the prophets in former days and I was greatly astonished, and for two years prayed continually, whenever my duty would permit, and then again I had the same revelation, which fully confirmed me in the impression that I was ordained for some great purpose in the hands of the Almighty. Several years rolled round, in which many events occurred to strengthen me in this my belief. At this time I reverted in my mind to the remarks made of me in my childhood and the things that had been shown me and as it had been said of me in my childhood by those by whom I had been taught to pray, both white and black, and in whom I had the greatest confidence, that I had too much sense to be raised, and if I was, I would never be of any use to any one as a slave. Now finding I had arrived to man's estate, and was a slave, and these revelations being made known to me, I began to direct my attention to this great object, to fulfill the purpose for which, by this time, I felt assured I was intended. Knowing the influence I had obtained over the minds of my fellow servants, (not by the means of conjuring and such like tricks, for to them I always spoke of such things with contempt) but by the communion of the spirit whose revelations I often communicated to them, and they believed and said my wisdom came from God."

Nat Turner spoke of imagining an ability to create things, of superior judgment in things that were perfected by divine Inspiration, and of living an austere life; devoting his time to fasting and prayer, until his confirmed belief that he "was ordained for some great purpose in the hands of the Almighty." He sounds more like a seeker, a visionary, than a terrorist. Years later Bob Marley would echo that sentiment in song: "But my hands was made strong...by the hand of the Almighty." And the Bible speaking of Joseph (PBUH) says, "his hands were made strong by the hands of the mighty God."[3]

12:11 They said: "O our father! why dost thou not trust us with Joseph,- seeing we are indeed his sincere well-wishers?"

Chapter 11

Trust Must Be Earned

We should not expect business, political or intellectual interests to be responsible for preserving society's ethical concerns themselves. If we trust the health and wholeness of the soul to the narrow interests of business, politics or intelligence, it's just a matter of time before they influence the spiritual development and bring the whole society down. Our destiny is for our moral nature to rise and influence the establishment of ethical society. The leadership of the world today has made great progress in analyzing systems of knowledge, but they have presented these systems as monuments to their own skill without acknowledging the origins of these systems in G-d's creation and his revealed Word. Prophet Ibrahim (PBUH) asked, "Why do you worship these things you carve with your own hands?" They were shamed in their stupidity.

Today we still create the things we worship and they are much more subtle than visible, material symbols. Anything we submit our devotional nature to becomes an idol for us. We say *Allahu Akbar meaning G-d is Greater*, but anything that we give part worship to is sharing the *Akbar*, or greatness. Sometimes we follow moral or political expedience for temporary benefit and we believe, for that moment, that it will get us farther than the righteous path. Noah's (PBUH) son said he wasn't worried about the rising waters. He felt that he would be secure in the world's great mountains of intellectual and material achievement amongst its powerful leaders.[1]

There is a difficulty when we come to a new knowledge with something else already firmly entrenched in our minds. Sometimes it's almost impossible to grasp the new. Sometimes the new concept has to be presented in drastic and earth shaking terms. We witness the great problems that have confronted man, some from his own digression from his noble dignity and others from his scientific advances ungoverned by ethical constraints such as global warming and environmental pollutants. All of these challenges will ultimately awaken the natural desire in man for cleanliness, orderliness, and beauty--the same environment of the garden where man's life started. It is that environment that will ultimately nurture the peace and progress he seeks. In our own psyches, we speak of it in terms of "peace of mind" and wholeness. In psychology, this is described as *cognitive consonance*, which means that our knowledge, our beliefs, and our actions are in accord. When they are, our garden of consciousness feels whole, fulfilled, and at peace.

The other problem, one against which we have to guard our children, is the tendency of the secular world to discredit religion and faith. The whole concept of secularism itself is represented in scripture as the devil transformed into light-that tendency to rebel and reject G-d's Will in favor of our own rationalizations. The forbidden fruit in Christian theology is from the Tree of Knowledge (of Good and Evil). Though the Qur'an does not name the tree as such, we are nevertheless warned not to approach it.[2]

It is hard to criticize knowledge because it is light and it is attractive and seductive. But the professors, like the sheiks and muftis, want students and disciples for themselves and in order to do so, they subtly and openly tear down belief in G-d. Albert Einstein wrote, "We should take care not to make the intellect our god; it has, of course, powerful muscles, but no personality." Students learn new disciplines, such as philosophy, which question everything, and they are so enamored with the value of their own judgments and created systems, (idols) that it's hard to reach them with root knowledge. They want to know your source and when you say nature, you look primitive in their sight. When you say Scripture, you look naive.

We have to exist in the system and we also have to have educated children. Sometimes we have to listen to our parent and know that they are wrong, but be silent out of respect. The teacher is legally identified as *in loco parentis*, or Latin for *in the place of a parent.* Allah has thus given us advice even in these situations.[3] We have to show our instructors respect while at the same time recognizing the source of the knowledge, which is Allah's Creation, the limitations of that knowledge, and having a context (i.e. doing for self, remaking the world) as to how we will use it. The brothers reverse this logic to get Jacob (PBUH) to entrust his beloved son Joseph (PBUH) to them because they have their own idea of how they will use him.[4]

12:12 "Send him with us tomorrow to enjoy himself and play, and we shall take every care of him."

Chapter 12

A Spirit Weak for A Good Feeling

'He's disposed toward sport and play, entertainment.' That's the image they cast of the African American: a descendant of Cain, the physical man and his descendant Jubal, the maker of instruments - the spirit of jubilation. Yes, we like to play but sometimes we play too much. And we like to get excited and fall out in church but we are of no use to G-d or ourselves unconscious. And there's nothing wrong with feeling good.

Science tells us that both exercise and sports produce chemicals that make us feel good called endorphins. Properly called *endogenous morphine*, these are the body's natural feel-good chemicals that function as neurotransmitters during exercise, excitement, pain, consumption of spicy food, love and orgasm, and they resemble the opiates in their abilities to produce analgesia - a feeling of well-being. This science may explain why African Americans are stereotyped as the consummate entertainers and sports celebrities. They are all doing the happy, feel good thing, and we are encouraged to follow that model (i.e. thank G-d it's Friday, living for the Weekend, let it All Hang Out, and Shake Yo' Booty). This carries over into other behaviors and areas of our lives--instant gratification from promiscuous sex, with no responsibility, getting high, and other at-risk behavior. The enemy of man's development exploits the natural urges and appetites of man.[1]

It is hard to find positive images of Black men in the public media and when you do, the media, in the name of journalism, cooperates in giving the bigots and detractors equal time. Nevertheless, these positive self-images help fuel an optimism that enables us to move forward past any obstacles. Today the African American is overcoming those negative stereotypes and is presenting a vision of the future.

On the eve of President Barack Obama's first inauguration, 69 percent of black respondents told CNN pollsters that Martin Luther King's vision had been "fulfilled." Nearly two years later, as America prepared for the 2010 midterm elections, blacks shared little of the disenchantment that had overtaken many whites. African Americans were more likely than whites to say that the economy was sound, found CBS News. And nearly half (compared with 16 percent of whites) thought America's next generation would be better off.

Ellis Cose wrote in Newsweek magazine article, May 15, 2011, even before President Obama's second election entitled, "Meet the New Optimists" and points out that "*Despite all the problems facing the U.S. these days, one group is surprisingly upbeat: African Americans.*"

The Obama presidency, of course, has had a lot to do with this. When I was a child the highest aspiration of my family for me, like many of my era, was to be like Jackie Robinson. Now a new generation of African Americans can truly see themselves as potentially the Leader of the Free World. Then there are his detractors who complain that he has not solved the plethora of Black issues, those issues that before, they were waiting for the Second coming of Jesus Christ (PBUH) to solve. If you ask them, though, "What have you done for yourself since his presidency to solve your own personal or community problems" in most cases you'll get only flashes of anger.

But this is why it is so important for us to write our own history and define our own value. When we don't we are left with an image that the public media and popular culture presents to us. Why would they present you the image of the scientist, the businessman or the leader so you can compete with them? No. You're going to get that fake super stud stereotype so that you expend your energy and your resources chasing something superficial. The brothers didn't say, "send him (Joseph) with us tomorrow so he can learn our business, how we trade, and how we interact with the world." They said "send him with us so he can play."

12:13: (Jacob) said: "Really it saddens me that ye should take him away: I fear lest the wolf should devour him while ye attend not to him."

Chapter 13

Every One Behaves According to His Own Disposition

Jacob (PBUH) knew that this was not Joseph's (PBUH) disposition and he also knew the potential for man to get so absorbed in satisfying animal needs that it will kill the spiritual life. He remembers the scheme that was attributed to him earlier of tricking his brother Esau out of his birthright by appealing to his hungry stomach. It saddened Jacob (PBUH) that his son would be *taken away.* The words "taken away" are from the Arabic, *thahaba - you (p) go/you go away/you take away.* We should also be aware and saddened by seeing our youth taken away in the direction of different *mathhabs.*

Mathhabs

Mathhab comes from the word *thahaba,* which means to travel, and in Islam, it refers to one of several Schools of Thought. It is said that the *hayyati dunya* or *life of this world* is just a vehicle for us to get to the *akhira.* If we are trying to travel to Detroit, we are not going to be satisfied just getting into the vehicle or comfortable at just seeing the signs along the way. If Detroit is 280 miles away, are we going to get off at every exit that says Detroit 240 miles, Detroit 180 miles? No. We stay on the road until we reach our destination and the destination is the hereafter. Your maththab is not the destination, and for us here, we have to recognize a greater destiny than the Muslim world in general envisions today. Why is it that some of us are afraid we are traveling on a unique interpretation of the Qur'an by an inspired man, Imam Mohammed (RAA)?

We don't like to be seen as sheep because we don't like to be seen as meek or docile, but we are quick to follow any fascinating ego that presents itself to us. All he has to do is come wearing a strange headpiece or speaking with a different accent and we're done; hook, line and sinker. We easily find fault in each other, but will accept a stranger with no questions. That's why it's so easy for some of us to get hung up in different sects and mathhabs. We're fascinated by the attraction of the unlikeness. How are they moving and how are they traveling if they are stuck in an interpretation that is itself locked in another geographical place and another chronological time?[1] Imam Mohammed (RAA) noted that some of the best scholars of the Muslim world today are only repeating the rules from dead scholars. That is why Imam Mohammed (RAA) stressed that "we can't stop now." We can't stop moving.

There are Muslims today in some sects who like Christians, are waiting for the return of Christ Jesus (PBUH) in physical form. Jesus (PBUH) was not the only Christ. W. D. Fard spoke of the return of the Mahdi. Minister Louis Farrakhan's official news organ, the Final Call newspaper, still publishes a section, "What We Believe" in which they expect the return of a divine figure in flesh, not realizing that he has already come and that the knowledge he brought was the only divinity about him. The message Imam Mohammed (RAA) brought was that we, as a community, are the flesh body that Divine knowledge is to be expressed or manifested through.

Wolves Will Devour You

Jacob (PBUH) feared that the wolf would devour his son, and rightfully so because we can lose our sons and ourselves to a loyal attachment to a passion, instinct or emotion. An elder Cherokee Native American man was teaching his grandchildren about life. He said to them, "A fight is going on inside me. It is a terrible fight and it is between two wolves. One wolf represents fear, anger, envy, sorrow, regret, greed, arrogance, self-pity, guilt, resentment, inferiority, lies, false pride, superiority, and ego. The other wolf stands for joy, peace, love, hope, sharing, serenity, humility, kindness, benevolence, friendship, empathy, generosity, truth, compassion, and faith. This same fight is going on inside you and inside every other person, too." They thought about it for a minute and then one child asked his grandfather, "Which wolf will win?" The man simply replied, "The one you feed."

The appetites are called carnal because they bring about gratification to the body or flesh (from Latin *carn-, caro* flesh). The society fuels and encourages these appetites. The low-level agents of the scheme do it for the money while the schemers behind the curtain do it as part of a plan to prove the human being unworthy of G-d's commission to him. We as men come out of the womb, out of the darkness where we controlled no part of the environment, into the light of day. We eventually stand up and evolve to our full maturity. Allah tells us to reverence the wombs that bore us, so we respect society. He also says that men are the maintainers and protectors of women, so at some point, we have to stand up and remove the corruption and poison from the environment.

In these last of days, the most prevalent vehicle for controlling the ignorant populations is through manipulation of their natural urges and appetites. Satan said, "I will approach them from before and behind them, from the right and from the left." So he and his class of organized conspirators try to influence us through our natural motivations, our passionate drives, our moral sentiments.[2] The main strategy today is sex and as any advertiser or marketer will tell you, 'Sex sells.' Just as our unchecked appetites lead us astray, the control or mastery of the appetites will be the key to our success. This is true even for those who are not turned on by the moral and social concerns but are sensitive to the practical and productive benefits and want to get ahead in the world. "Whether through asceticism, ideology, religion, advertising or other means. Whether consciously or not, elites in all societies manage desire—the starting point of wealth creation" *Revolutionary Wealth, Alvin and Heidi Toffler, p.15.*

12:14: They said: "If the wolf were to devour him while we are (so large) a party, then should we indeed (first) have perished ourselves!"

Chapter 14

The Innocent-The Last Man Standing

Innocence

The inherent goodness in the human being will survive all these other important developments. It is our innocence that is responsible for that goodness. Allah blesses that human innocence to rise and expand and it is fed by the heavens and the Earth so that we grow in knowledge and in our sensitivities. We are again in a womb of growth and development, but it is the bigger womb of Mother Nature now. If we saw Imam Mohammed (RAA) in his true light, we would see him as a model of humility and innocence; born into a society, the Nation of Islam, America, and the world, and reviving it. In the progression of social development, the spiritual evolves first, then the intellectual, the material, and the political.

The Bible and the Qur'an describe the current state of the world as the last days of G-d's plan for people on the Earth. There is nothing else to come, which is why everyone is being given the freedom to make their own decision as to their future. The discernment between right and wrong, intelligent and ignorant, decent and indecent is made clear. The last bastion of Satan in this time would be in the sanctuary, in the mosques, and in the synagogues.[1] The ones who persevere in their innocent inclination become the leaders. They rise above corruption and are fed directly from heaven.[2] The political leaders and the religious leaders know that the innocent servant of G-d will be the last man standing.

It was the environment created by Imam Mohammed (RAA) for over 30 years in the spiritual arena -breaking the hardened soil, planting the seeds, and enriching the plant with the light of knowledge and the gentle nourishing rains - that made it possible for the words of Barack Obama to resonate in the political arena. But we have had to come a long way, through many trials and tribulations to get to this point.

The murder of Emmett Till in 1955 was a catalyst for the Civil Rights Movement. Emmett was a 14-year-old African American teenager from Chicago visiting Mississippi when he was kidnapped, tortured, mutilated, killed, and his body dumped in the Tallahatchie River by white racists. His mother, Mamie Mobley Till, wanted to show the world the brutality of the killing so she insisted on a public funeral service with an open casket. Even though more than 500 African Americans had been killed by extrajudicial violence in Mississippi alone since 1882, Till's innocence seemed to be the reason his death resonated with so many right-minded people. What crime had a child committed to deserve such savagery? Years later the same satanic mentality would lead to the bombing of a church in Birmingham Alabama, killing four innocent Black girls. In each case, the killing of these innocents had a profound effect on the conscious of right-minded people throughout the world and brought many of them face to face with their own demons. That innocent life is in G-d's Hands and you can't kill it. You only kill a part of your own human soul.

12:15 So they did take him away, and they all agreed to throw him down to the bottom of the well: and We put into his heart (this Message): 'Of a surety thou shalt (one day) tell them the truth of this their affair while they know (thee) not.'

Chapter 15

We Shall Overcome

Imprisonment/Restriction/ Limitation

In the ancient Middle East, old dry wells were often used as prisons. The Arabic or Qur'anic term for bottom is *ghayaba* from *ghaba* meaning secret, hidden or unseen. This refers to a situation wherein there is no light, no guidance, and no hint as to how to escape or to get out of that situation. It also alludes to a potential within something that might be unperceived. As we shall discuss later in chapter 17, there is also a meaning implied in the word to slander or backbite. The restriction of freedom for a human being is one of the gravest punishments one can inflict.

Today prison should also be seen as a metaphor, not only for social limitation but also those self-imposed restrictions due to perceived inferiority. James Allen wrote in his well-known book *As A Man Thinketh*, "Man is manacled only by himself; thought and actions are jailors of fate - they imprison, being base; they are also the angels of freedom - they liberate, being noble." Muslims recognize Prophet Muhammad (PBUH) as one who came to break the unjust bonds that weigh down or crush the people. This alludes to slavery, but we know that it is not just the physical slavery of people on plantations. Imam Mohammed (RAA) pointed out that this enslavement also refers to the "enslavement of the faculties of the human mind and soul, denying us the opportunity to develop and enjoy the growth of our potential and the capacity of our potential. It is the enslavement of our created energies to a small space that cuts you off from roaming the earth and the universe with our intelligence and our hearts." Joseph (PBUH) was imprisoned, but much more than his physical confinement, we see the restriction and limitation of the use of his G-d given gift or his creative energies. Nevertheless, G-d uses Joseph's (PBUH) confinement in fulfillment of His Divine plan.

A key to our success is the awareness that G-d put the potential for attaining all our aspirations right within us. He created us as a plant and all the characteristics for complete development of the tree is within the seed.[1]

Too often we look outside ourselves for something we can acquire or something we can buy to fulfill us. The commercial society has built its wealth, not on satisfying legitimate human needs, but on satisfying perceived inadequacies. The health, beauty, and pharmaceutical industries are perfect examples. It promises to make us young, beautiful, healthy, and we don't have to make any change in our thinking or our lifestyle; just buy their product. Satan threatens you with poverty - the lack or the absence of something. That insecurity is what motivates the search for satisfaction through external factors. Most of us believe all of our problems would be solved if only we had more money. We should read the case histories of the many lottery winners who will testify that their sudden windfall of wealth only brought more misery into their lives. If your inner problem is low self-esteem and you are in the habit of self-medicating yourself with drugs to ease the pain, an unexpected jackpot is only going to help you finance your treatment. A better house or car is G-d's blessing to us, but if our happiness and wellbeing is tied into that then we are guaranteeing ourselves frustration and disappointment. Our happiness is inside ourselves. That concept is liberating because it empowers us and puts us in charge of our own happiness.

When Joseph (PBUH) was put in the well, it removed him from all external stimuli. Similarly, we are sometimes forced to look within and once we find that light, it will illuminate our perception of everything on the outside. The very thing that was designed by his enemies to imprison and restrain him was the thing that liberated Joseph (PBUH). We can't come out of those circumstances and get so excited that we forget the whole purpose of our suffering and sacrifice. One of the biggest keys to our success is the ability to delay our gratification until we have completed our mission. Too often we get so excited just to be in the competition that we forget what the object is. There are scientific studies that point to the ability to defer rewards or gratification as a sign of higher intelligence. Allah tells us that the latter will be better than the former. The history books and record books are full of great accomplishments, but none of them are recorded for making a good start. Few recount the triumph of attaining second place. They all are for races completed or competitions won.

For many years, Jews were confined to restricted quarters in Europe's ghettos. They used that experience to develop the potential within. They studied in secret, in the dark. When they were finally freed into the broader society, they exploded in knowledge and power across Europe.

Some of us are really mad at G-d. We can't understand why He would allow us to be made slaves and endure the treatment that we did. The person of faith, however, knows that whatever injustice a soul endures for G-d's sake, his reward is with his Lord. But as long as we continue to look at the white man or white America as the source of our problem or as the solution to our problem, our Lord should leave us to depend on whoever we are serving besides him.

Here in the well Joseph (PBUH) is awakened to the intuitive grasp of his mind. With no external stimuli or information, he nevertheless knows through his heart that "he will see them again." We see no indication of fear, uncertainty, doubt or terror in the terrible situation he's been put in. This deprivation of sensual perception in the well also provided Joseph (PBUH) with the quiet he needed to perfect the concentration, meditation, and prayer required to attain a state of higher consciousness - a consciousness not limited by time or space and that functions on all levels and in all directions at once.[2] Thus Imam Mohammed (RAA) notes: "Joseph represents the ideal follower or believer of G-d, the ideal person in religion; that he depended upon intuitive grasp or vision; that he saw eleven and also the sun (rational knowledge) and the moon (interpretation) bowing to him; and one who not only shares his material wealth with hungering people, but one who shares his knowledge with those thirsting for wisdom."

Deconstruction

I believe there is an effort to deconstruct the history of the African American Muslim community here. Dr. Martin Luther King Jr., Honorable Elijah Muhammad, and a whole line of leaders before them led a movement for real freedom, justice, and equality for the African American to reach the full potential of his intellect and the full evolution of his soul. This movement was successful. They did not bring about a perfect society, but rather one that was much better than the one they found. The people were energized and the citizens were engaged. People throughout the country and the world were watching the struggle of African Americans on the newly invented technology of television. At the same time the rulers of the society, recognizing this movement in the soul of the people, developed their scheme to maintain control and they did it by interpreting the concept of freedom. Freedom to many became the freedom to do whatever one wanted to do with no restriction and no responsibility.[3] True freedom is not "freeing the dumb," but instead "freeing the dome."

Many today did not experience the Nation of Islam but still think they know what it represented. They invoke Honorable Elijah Muhammad in support of their late message of Black Nationalism. But the essence of that message was misunderstood as early as the 1960s. A new leadership emerged that thought the movement was all about being superior as blacks and obtaining money and power. They went after the things of this world and lost their own souls, as the scripture says. In the Nation of Islam, Imam Mohammed (RAA) did the same thing that the Prophet Muhammad (PBUH) did. He removed the yokes that burdened the people; the first burdens being ignorance and mythology. Then he put the responsibility for supporting community life into the hands of the people. They had a right to make their own decisions about their individual life and about their leadership. That's the nature of responsibility. That's the right of the people but they must also own the consequences.

But the interpretation of some of the leaders, volunteer agents and some paid agents was the same as that of the enemy: "We're free; we can do as we please; we have no responsibility. We're not obligated to do anything now. We don't have to sell Muhammad Speaks Newspaper anymore. We don't have to donate to the Temple. We don't have to support the community's programs." Imam Mohammed (RAA) was insistent that he would not, nor would he let anyone else dominate the following. He let each individual make his own decision as to what he would obligate himself to. Nevertheless, our own good sense and conscience should have dictated to us to follow the best leadership available and to keep moving toward establishing community life.

Let's Put Him in the Well

Imam Mohammed (RAA), like his father Honorable Elijah Muhammad, guarded our cultural heritage as a distinct community of African American Muslims. Isn't this the way of G-d himself when he dedicates a community to Himself, a virgin more or less, that has not been touched by the seed of any man's knowledge?[4] African Americans knew nothing except what we were told.

Every community or tribe has its own distinctions. Consider the African: "The hero concept - the belief in the individual who is different from his fellowmen - is [also] almost totally alien to African life; and, as an extension of this, the hero in contemporary African fiction is for the most part non-existent. The hero is almost nonexistent in contemporary western literature too, but his descendant, the anti-hero, the isolated figure, is a force to be reckoned with. This is not true for African fiction, however. Rather it is the group-felt experience that is all important; what happens to the village, the clan, the tribe." *Heroic Ethnocentrism: The Idea of Universality in Literature, The American Scholar 42(3) (Summer), 1973.Charles Larson*

Historians, such as E. U. Essien-Udom, in his landmark book, Black Nationalism--The Search for an Identity, recognized that the true value of the Nation of Islam was in its establishment of a cultural identity. Many African American Muslims who did not come from that cultural experience do not understand that value and as such have been enamored by the presentation of Islam by immigrants. It is hard for them to conceptualize membership in the universal *ummah* of Muslims and at the same time appreciate the unique contribution of the 'Black' Muslims. Many of them do not appreciate the value of the independent view of the Qur'an and many of them are not comfortable in the exercise of their own intelligence. Many of them have grafted cultural influences of immigrant Muslims onto an African American mind.[5]

And many of them have not yet been liberated from the plantation ghost of accepting leadership from anywhere except black. Many of them fear not being accepted by the worldwide community of Muslims and their leaders. This rejection of any uniqueness among African American Muslims by immigrants in many cases is intentional and insidious.[6] Part of the strategy in this effort is the suppression of the Nation of Islam's contribution to the establishment of Islam in America and the establishment of an independent interpretation of the Qur'an by the community of Imam Mohammed (RAA). We have all heard the charge uttered in hushed tones and in private that we were not real Muslims. There were outright calls for Imam Mohammed (RAA) to denounce his father, Honorable Elijah Muhammad, throughout his teaching and in some cases, these calls were tied to promises of material assistance. Isn't it curious how the oil-rich countries, including the Saudi Arabia, did very little to help us promote Islam in our communities through our efforts? They would convert strays from our community to their schools of thoughts under their sheiks, but no help was available if it enabled us to remain independent. One notable exception was Sheik Al-Qasimi (RAA) of Sharjah. He assisted this community financially with no strings attached and no ulterior motives. Even W. D. Fard had ulterior motives.

Imam Mohammed (RAA) however, always upheld the good intentions and success of his father and W. D. Fard, even when he had to criticize their strategy and personal failings. He affirmed that Fard's intent was to bring us to the correct idea of G-d. If he had succumbed to their efforts, and if we do so today, then history will show that Islam in America among African Americans only began with immigrant Muslims. The redemption of the human being and society itself would be credited to late-comers to the struggle. The previous sacrifice of our great leaders and our pioneers would have gone for naught. Our history would be lost, but Allah says he will never cause the reward of the righteous to be lost.

In what is called a Brief History of Islam in America, that is disseminated throughout the internet by various Muslim Student Associations and on college campuses,[7] it reads in part, and I am adding critical analysis in parentheses and italics:

"…beginning in the '50s… An influx of Muslim professionals settled in this country. The black movements, *[They don't credit the Nation of Islam, but instead lump them all into 'black movement groups'. It ignores the period of 30's, 40's and 50's which developed the Nation of Islam]* the back-to-Africa groups, had come into

flower by this time. Great numbers of Muslim students from all parts of the world also began to arrive in this country. This was the period which saw the formation of the early Muslim communities and mosques in such places as Detroit, Ann Arbor, Gary (Indiana), Cedar Rapids (Iowa), Sacramento, and the like."

These areas had Muslim communities long before then. W. D. Fard set up the Temple of Islam #1 in Detroit in 1931; He and his Chief Minister, Elijah Muhammad left there and came to Chicago, where they established Temple #2 in 1934. Elijah Muhammad's son, Elijah Muhammad II remembers them driving a 1933 Chevy from Detroit that stayed in their backyard and rusted out after his father went on the run from his enemies. While in Chicago, they'd drive back and forth to Milwaukee, where they established Temple #3 in 1934. While Muhammad was on the run, he set up the temple in Washington, DC with Brother Benjamin around 1935. It didn't get its number, #4, until 1943 or 1944, when Muhammad came out of prison. Minister Asbury served time in prison with Honorable Elijah Muhammad and was released before him.

Asbury set up Temple #5 in Cincinnati in about 1943 or 1944. Temple #6 was set up in Baltimore, also around 1943 or 44, after Isaiah Karriem came out of prison in Terre Haute, Indiana where he served time with Brother Sultan, who was named head minister. Muslims were meeting in Lynchburg also and Minister Karriem set up temples throughout Virginia and the Appalachia mountains. Temple #7 in New York, which became the base of Malcolm X's support, was established by Lynn Karriem, Supreme Captain Raymond Sharrieff's brother-in-law. This continued until Honorable Elijah Mohammed's death in 1975 when there were hundreds of temples throughout the country. These early converts were characterized by the media as convict - converts, but most of those imprisoned were done so unlawfully. Honorable Elijah Muhammad was too old for the draft when he was imprisoned in Milan, Michigan and, at least, two older members, Tadar Hazziez and Brother William, a field minister and brother of Elizabeth Hassan, had wooden legs. In their zeal to minimize African American contributions, these commentators destroyed the accomplishments of their own immigrant brothers. In Detroit, after Elijah Muhammad had met and accepted W. D. Fard as his leader, Wallace D. Mohammed (RAA) was born in 1933 on Yeman street - a street that had been named after Muslim immigrants years before.

The article continued: **"It was this period that also witnessed the formation of national Islamic groups, such as the Muslim Students Association (MSA) of the United States and Canada, later to be replaced by the Islamic Society of North America (ISNA) and their supporting institutions. Regional and national conferences of Muslims for the discussion of issues of common concern were streamlined during this period. Many Muslims who had never practiced their religion now found their way back to their roots and began, for the very first time, to appreciate the value of their faith."** Most of these communities did not openly practice Islam until Imam Mohammed's (RAA) leadership of the Nation of Islam. Friday Jumuah began to be observed broadly only after he courageously established it. In fact, in reality, the immigrant community here made very few converts. Moreover, many of them abandoned their religion and their culture. Elijah Mohammed II remarked on many occasions how "in those early years of the Nation of Islam, you could go through the phone book and you'd find only a few Muhammads or other Muslims names and most of those would be our Nation of Islam members. They (the immigrants) changed their names to sound more American. The Shamsiddins were calling themselves Sam, and Jamils had become Jimmys." This explosion of population in the immigrant community and outward display of Islam really did not come about until after 1975 when Imam Mohammed (RAA), through presenting his universal view of Islam, and its compatibility with American ideals, made our presence here hospitable.

"For a time the movement flourished, but later, with the exposure of Mr. Muhammad's sexual improprieties, it began to whither and fade." It is a fact that Malcolm was the main catalyst to the public awareness of the Nation of Islam during this period, because of his tireless work and his affinity for the media, but the Nation of Islam, in fact, made its most progress and established its most prominence after Malcolm's demise.

I would be guilty of the same wrong of the immigrants if I fail to note the most recent scholarly research, which documents W. D. Fard's Ahmadiyyah roots and their early efforts to introduce Islam in America. An exhaustive study by Dr. Fatimah Abdul-Tawwab Fanusie has served to document these Ahmadiyyah efforts as early as 1887 and to demystify the origins and methodologies employed by W. D. Fard.[8]

The Prophet (PBUH) said, "It is a serious evil for a Muslim that he should look down upon his brother Muslim. All things of a Muslim are inviolable for his brother in faith; his blood, his wealth and his honor." And I have heard Imam Mohammed say that had he depended solely on the teachings and influence of the immigrant Muslims or the Islamic world to bring him to the true path of Islam, he would not have arrived. He would have chosen another path. He said specifically, "It is not the Qur'an and the Sunnah that made this Imam. It is my desire to live the best of my social nature and to follow the best aim in this social nature so that our people and I will be helped by my existence. Elijah Muhammad, my father, turned that on in me."[9]

In Dr. King's "Letter from a Birmingham Jail", he also alludes to the restraint in thinking that religion had fostered. He asked the profound question, "is organized religion too inextricably bound to the status quo to save our nation and the world? Perhaps I must turn my faith to the inner spiritual church, the church within the church, as the true *ekklesia* and the hope of the world." The heart or conscience is that inner spiritual church and it is there that G-d put the message that Dr. King preached and activists sang, "We Shall Overcome." It is the same message that Allah put in Joseph's (PBUH) heart, "you will live to tell them the truth of this their affair"[10] – "you will overcome this." These conditions were at best, a temporary abode and Allah inspired Joseph (PBUH) with this awareness.[11]

12:16: Then they came to their father in the early part of the night, weeping.

Chapter 16

Religion is Sincerity

In the criminal world, the conventional wisdom is to wait until the cover of darkness to do your wrong. Liars appeal to the emotional, not the well-lit consciousness. But the soul will necessarily confess one day. We say "in broad daylight" meaning someone had the nerve to not even try to hide his or her scheme in the darkness.[1] W. D. Fard acknowledged that he came to North America under the cover of darkness, meaning he came outside the view of the ruling authorities, with a dark scheme, to a people in the dark.

Africa

For many years Africa, particularly Sub-Saharan, was called the *Dark Continent*. This could refer to many things: the dark skin of its inhabitants, the darkness of the land under the thick canopy of jungle or the darkness of intelligent progress the continent descended into after the rise of the European west.

The word *Afri* was associated with the Phoenician word *afar* meaning *dust* and was used as the name for the society of people living near Carthage (an ancient city near Tunis) in northern Africa. Their existence was first noted during the Punic Wars between 264 and 146 BC. These three wars were the largest of their time, fought between the Roman Empire and Carthage. They were a battle over space between the well-established Carthage and the ever expanding Rome. Rome was ultimately victorious. When this happened, Carthage became the capital of the Roman province of Africa (which was, in part, made up of the coastal section of Libya). The Roman suffix to denote a country was *-ca* and this was thus added to *Afri.* The Arabians of that time converted this name to *Ifriqiya* in Latin. In Algeria, this name still exists, as is evident in such areas as Ifira and Ifri-n-Dellal. Consider also the Qur'an reference to the Ifrit.[2] Whatever origin we choose to accept we do know that coinciding with the rise of European dominance and white supremacy, Africa came to be seen in a negative light.

Romulus and Remus

Western civilization claims its origin from Rome, and according to Roman mythology, the founders of Rome were the twin brothers Romulus and Remus. They were the supposed sons of the god Mars and the priestess Rhea Silvia, who were forbidden to marry. The boys were abandoned in a remote location - a form of infanticide tolerated in many ancient cultures, and reminiscent of the Arabs' habit of burying their infant girls in the sand.[3] The boys were found by a she-wolf who, instead of killing them, looked after them and fed them with her milk. The she-wolf was helped by a woodpecker that brought them food.

Upon reaching adulthood, Romulus and Remus killed their uncle Amulius and reinstated Numitor, their grandfather, as King of Alba Longa. Then they decided to found a town of their own. Romulus and Remus chose the place where the she-wolf had nursed them. Romulus began to build walls on the Palatine Hill. Remus jeered at his brother because the walls were so low and leaped over them to prove it. Romulus, in anger, killed him. Romulus continued the building of the new city, naming it Roma (Rome) after himself. Its first citizens were outlaws and fugitives; to whom Romulus gave the settlement on the Capitoline Hill.

©2007 Sunbird Photos by Don Boyd
#2701_LS07

The photo above depicting the she-wolf nursing Romulus and Remus was a gift to the southern Georgia, USA City of Rome and stands at the entrance of its Municipal Building. A plaque commemorates the gift and its inscription is translated: "This statue of the Capitoline wolf, as a forecast of prosperity and glory, has been sent from Ancient Rome to New Rome, during the Consulship of Benito Mussolini, in the year 1929."

Photo by Don Boyd, courtesy of Sunbird Photos, copyright 2007.

Based on their mothering by the she-wolf and the wolf's natural characteristics, Romulus and Remus became the archetypical symbols of social life and of the predator nature in the history and mythology of the ancestors of western civilization. They are the grandchildren of Mars, the Roman god of war. They are nursed by nature's foremost predator. And when Romulus finally did establish his social order, he populated it with convicts and derelicts. It is no wonder that when the Christians appeared centuries later, the Romans found great pleasure and sport in watching lions tear the Christians' flesh apart. The early Christians, in converting the Romans, absorbed theirs and many others' pagan dispositions and practices into the rituals and beliefs that persist in their genes today.[4]

The Christians were given a poor, slaughtered dead body, Jesus (PBUH), as an image of god and an object of worship, who was mocked as the King of the Jews. While it looks apparently like the Romans crucified the Jewish nation, in reality, the script has been flipped on them too. It is the Romans' Christian descendants who are killed spiritually and socially by worshipping such an image of death.[5]

"How a god may reflect the character of his people, and may develop with his people's growth, is well seen in the case of Mars. There are two things," says Mr. Warde Fowler (Roman Festivals, p. 65), "which we may believe with certainty about the Roman people in the earliest times; (1) that their life and habits of thought were those of an agricultural race, and (2) that they continually increased their cultivatable land by taking forcible possession in war of that of their neighbors." Mars represented this double character. As the guardian god of the fields and herds of a small rustic community, dwelling among hostile neighbors, Mars was also the ideal "strong man armed" keeping his palace. The first month of the old Roman year, dedicated to him and named after him, was the occasion of the yearly enrolment of the newly grown-up Roman youths in the military forces of the city. It was celebrated by well-known agricultural New Year rites, as well as by the ritual dances of the priests of Mars, who patrolled the city bearing the sacred armor of the god from station to station. As the circle of the Roman territory spreads outward and successive conquests gradually made Rome the center of dominions, which covered almost the whole area of the then known world, the character of the patron-deity kept pace with the expansion of his people, and the rustic guardian of the ox and the plough was elevated into the god of battles of a world empire." *Handbook of Folk-Lore, Charlotte Sophia Burne, Senate, 1995 p.92*

And in witness that these origins are recognized even in the popular culture, Rapper Brother Ali in his song, "Uncle Sam Goddamn," sang: *"King of where the wild things are, daddy's proud, Cause the Roman Empire done passed it down."* Unfortunately, both sides of the story of social origin are passed down.

Uncle Remus

It is a well-known joke about Hollywood movies that the Black character always dies first. In the Romulus and Remus narrative, Remus is killed and Romulus goes on to found a great civilization. The same narrative creeps into the language and psychology of Western civilizations. In America's South, they identified the "natural wisdom" as coming from *Uncle Remus*. Uncle Remus is a collection of animal stories, songs, and oral folklore collected from Southern United States' blacks and recorded by Joel Chandler Harris. Many of the stories are similar to those of Aesop's fables. The 1946 Walt Disney movie "Song of the South," presented a blend of live action and animation based on Uncle Remus. One of the more popular stories is that of the "Tar Baby." The Tar Baby was the second of Uncle Remus' stories and was originally published in *Harper's Weekly* by Robert Roosevelt; years later Joel Chandler Harris wrote of Tar Baby in his Uncle Remus stories. A similar tale from African folklore in West Africa has the trickster *Anansi* in the role of Br'er Rabbit. Although the fox is historically the clever one in the natural animal kingdom, in the fables, Br'er Rabbit is a trickster who Br'er Fox hates because he always outwits the fox. He "succeeds by his wits rather than by brawn, tweaking authority figures and bending social mores as he sees fit."[6]

In Tar Baby, Br'er Fox constructs a doll out of a lump of tar and dresses it in some clothes to trap Br'er Rabbit. When Br'er Rabbit comes along, he addresses the tar baby amiably but receives no response. Br'er Rabbit becomes offended by what he perceives as the tar baby's lack of manners so he punches it and in doing so he gets stuck. The more Br'er Rabbit punches and kicks the tar baby out of rage, the worse he gets stuck. Now that Br'er Rabbit is stuck, Br'er Fox ponders how to dispose of him. The helpless, but cunning, Br'er Rabbit pleads, "but do please, Brer Fox, don't fling me in dat brier-patch," prompting Fox to do exactly that. As rabbits are at home in thickets, the resourceful Br'er Rabbit escapes. In modern usage according to Random House, *tar baby* refers to any "sticky situation" that is only aggravated by additional contact. More commonly, the expression tar baby is used as a derogatory term for black people (in the U.S. it refers to African Americans; in New Zealand it refers to Maori), or among blacks as a term for a particularly dark-skinned person.

As recent as August 3, 2011, *Christian Science Monitor* staff writer Patrik Jonsson reported, "the specter of two national Republican figures apologizing for calling President Obama, the first African American president, alternately a *tar baby* and *boy* gave new fuel to speculation that, underneath much of the criticism of the president and his policies lurks the shadow of racism."

Rep. Doug Lamborn (R) of Colorado said on a Denver talk radio show, "Even if some people say, 'Well the Republicans should have done this or they should have done that,' they will hold the president responsible. Now, I don't even want to have to be associated with him. It's like touching a tar baby and you get it, you're stuck, and you're a part of the problem now and you can't get away." Other Republicans, including Sen. John McCain and Former Massachusetts Gov. Mitt Romney, have in recent years apologized for using the phrase *tar baby*. Former GOP presidential candidate and MSNBC contributor Pat Buchanan, in a one on one with the Rev. Al Sharpton, referred to Obama as *your boy*. "My what?" Sharpton shot back. "My president, Barack Obama? What did you say?" Mr. Buchanan hinted that he was using a boxing analogy, replying that the president was "your boy in the ring."

Political Code Words and Illegitimacy

Many of us believe that racism is alive and well, but I'd prefer to think or, at least, hope that it is on life support. Billionaire Donald Trump, who I have no doubt was influenced by master promoter Don King, more recently became the most famous promoter of *birtherism* - the assertion that Barack Obama wasn't really born in the United States and therefore, is ineligible to be president. Many saw that claim and that movement as merely an "insidious new form of 21st-century racism," as Clarence B. Jones, scholar in residence at Stanford University, wrote on Huffington Post.

While we might have dismissed Trump's presidential campaign as self-promoting hucksterism, TV host David Letterman, speaking of Trump, observed, "It's all fun, it's all a circus, it's all a rodeo, until it starts to smack of racism." Psychologist Jack Brigham of Florida State University, an expert in racial attitudes research, told USA Today that "the results strongly support a role of racism in the birther movement."

Brad Knickerbocker, Slate.com Staff writer/April 30, 2011, quotes David Remnick, editor of The New Yorker magazine and author of an Obama biography: "To do what Trump has done is a conscious form of race-baiting, of fear- mongering." The cynicism of the purveyors of these fantasies is that they know very well what they are playing at, the prejudices they are fanning. Let's say what is plainly true, these rumors, this industry of fantasy, are designed to arouse a fear of the *other* - of an African American man with a white American mother and a black Kenyan father." He noted the comment of Mark Potok of the Southern

Poverty Law Center (best known for fighting the Ku Klux Klan and other racist organizations) that even if birthers are not racists, "they are shameless opportunists perfectly willing to exploit racism for their own personal benefit, proponents of a second Republican 'Southern strategy.' The continuing conspiracy theories about Obama - from his country of birth to his religion to his relationships with the radical left - come from people who are essentially motivated by antipathy toward black people."

Trump, the master promoter, must have discovered a significant sympathetic ear to his demonizing of 'all those other than like us,' when he decided to campaign for the Republican nomination for President. His popularity grew the more he attacked anyone other than ethnic whites—immigrants, Mexicans, Blacks, Muslims, the handicapped and anyone seeking political correctness.

A Today article reported on a study designed to gauge the level of prejudice and attitudes toward President Obama. 295 students were asked a series of questions used to gauge prejudice. Questions addressed Obama's performance as president as well as his *Americanism.* Those with a greater tendency toward racism rated Obama lower. The results pointed to the conclusion that latent racial prejudice may be at the heart of, or, at least, an important element in, the birther movement? "Many in the media have speculated that current criticisms of Obama are a result of his race, rather than his agenda," the study concluded. "We believe that the current results are an empirical demonstration that this is sadly the case." These false and sometimes irrational ideas are given credibility by news sources such as FOX News. They give cover for those who harbor these ideas and it feeds the already disturbed psyches of those who would act out violently. America now seems to be fixated on the violence spawned by extreme religious beliefs to the neglect of that violence spawned by their own extreme political beliefs. They are creating a monster they will not be able to control.

The Seeds and the Bloom

In August 2010, Anders Behring Breivik, a Norwegian, killed 76 young people in Norway. Anne Applebaum, on Slate.com, pointed out what the Norwegian mass murderer and American *birthers* have in common: "In contemporary America, we also have people who are - and I am inventing this word here—illegitimists: They believe that the president of the United States is illegitimately elected, or that the country is ruled by a cabal that is in turn controlled by some other sinister force or forces." She points out that the racism, white supremacy, and anti-Islam, accompanied the "insane conviction that his own government was illegitimate." These are things that reside just below the surface of consciousness of many Americans despite their outward display of empathy.

12:17: They said: "O our father! We went racing with one another, and left Joseph with our things; and the wolf devoured him.... But thou wilt never believe us even though we tell the truth."

Chapter 17

Thou Shalt Not Bear False Witness

Racing is a competition and those in the worldly interests, business, politics, education, and culture can get so absorbed in competing for the good things of this life, they neglect their vital concerns assuming that goodness will take care of itself. Though it will over time, in the short run, it enables those who seek only the benefit of the world to prevail and even deny the power of goodness. Joseph's (PBUH) brothers say, while we were competing for the *dunya* (material world), the influences of the world corrupted the innocence of society. That is the lie they tell, but we know thou shalt not bear false witness.

Ham-Cursed Son of Noah

The Biblical story of Noah's punishment of his son Ham by a curse on Ham's son Canaan was originally used to justify the Israelites' extermination and enslavement of the Canaanites. Ham was supposedly cursed black by the sun because he laughed at his father's nakedness.[1] The curse later took the form of *ugly* blackness and perpetual slavery (Drake, 1990, pp.15-23). Drake, St Clair, *Black Folk Here and There* Los Angeles, 2 vols. 1987- 1990. During the middle ages, this was interpreted to define Ham as the ancestor of all Africans. According to Edith Sanders, the sixth-century Babylonian Talmud states, "the descendants of Ham are cursed by being Black and depicts Ham as a sinful man and his progeny as degenerates." Both Arab and later

European and American slave traders used this story to justify African slavery. Early Islamic scholars debated whether a curse had any connection to skin color. Ibn Khaldun pointed out that the Torah makes no reference to the curse being related to skin color and argued that the differences in human pigmentation are caused entirely by climate and environmental determinism and not because of a curse, rejecting any racial interpretation of the curse.

After the death of Joseph Smith, Jr., founder of the Church of Jesus Christ of Latter-day Saints (Mormons), Brigham Young, its second president, taught that people of African ancestry were under the curse of Ham, and that the day would come when the curse would be nullified through the saving powers of Jesus Christ. Negroes were banned from the Mormon Priesthood until 1978 when Spencer W. Kimball received a revelation that extended the Priesthood to all worthy males. Mormons also believe in this emergence of a second coming of Christ, as Mitt Romney said, in his campaign for President, "The Church says that Christ appears on the Mount of Olives and splits the Mount of Olives and appears in Jerusalem and then over a thousand years, the millennium, the world is reigned in two places: Jerusalem and Missouri." I'm not picking on Mormons. This idea has permeated the whole world, and anywhere you go in the world you find signs of this attitude toward Black people and the perception of them being cursed.

The Real Curse

Yes, there is a curse but it has nothing to do with skin color. The real curse is the fall from the heavens of knowledge and scholarly pursuits. There is a natural progression and rotation of leadership that is inherent in social development, and any people can disqualify themselves from 'a turn at the wheel.'[2] Africans deserted the lofty principles of their previous history and leaders. They left their honorable traditions and the guidance of G-d. Similarly, as soon as we African Americans, got our freedom, instead of pursuing our G-d given potential, we followed the same path of our ancestors; so happy to be free, to dance and play, and show off. That is a curse when any people abandon intelligent behavior, and it has nothing to do with skin color. There is only a small percentage of the people who will keep themselves worthy. The majority don't understand.[3] Christians also speak of a select number of people who will be saved and sing of them as saints marching into heaven.[4] We are not the only ones cursed. The Muslim ummah today is also cursed. Most of the learned leaders in the religion are not guiding the people to the unlimited freedom of spirit and intellect that G-d intends for them. They are instead holding the people under their influence and you have to accept them as mini-gods before they share the knowledge.

12:18 They stained his shirt with false blood. He said: "Nay, but your minds have made up a tale (that may pass) with you, (for me) patience is most fitting: Against that which ye assert, it is Allah (alone) Whose help can be sought".

Chapter 18

Lies Have to Be Supported by More Lies and False Evidence

The word *qamis*, is defined in the Hans Wehr Arabic dictionary defines as a *shirt, dress, gown; covering, cover, wrap, envelope, jacket; (Chr.) alb, surplice, rochet; incarnation.* It is also from the root word of *taqmis* and *taqammus*, which means the transmigration of souls or metempsychosis. *Metempsychosis* is defined as the passing of the soul at death into another body; either human or animal. Its origin is late Latin, from Greek *metempsychōsis* from *metempsychousthai* to undergo metempsychosis, from *meta-* + *empsychos* animate, from *en-* + *psychē* soul - more at psych-. Its first known use was in 1591. See also metamorphisis.[1]

This *shirt* has been variously interpreted in Christian tradition. According to the Authorized King James Version, Genesis 37:3 reads: *Now Israel loved Joseph more than all his children, because he was the son of his old age: and he made him a coat of many colors.* The Hebrew phrase *Kethoneth passim* is translated here as *coat of many colors*, but some have suggested that the phrase may merely mean a "coat with long sleeves" or a "long coat with stripes." The Septuagint translation of the passage uses the word *poikilos*, which indicates "many coloured"; the Jewish Publication Society of America Version also employs the phrase "coat of many colours."

Scripture tells us that Jesus (PBUH) wore a himation over a tunic to the crucifixion. The soldiers tore the himation into four pieces, but because the tunic was woven in one piece, with no seams, they couldn't divide it and cast lots for it.[2] They wanted to divide it into four parts, one for each soldier. Business, politics, education and culture all use the soldier to advance their domination of the human being. It was said of the colonization of Africa that they came to the Africans first with the Bible and then with the gun.

If they could have torn the tunic, they would have had cover for each of their major influences. Today business, politics, education, and culture don't even pretend to be influenced by any innocence or morality. It is said of Satan's schemes: if he tries to cover his feet, his head will show and if he tries to cover his head, his feet will show. Dr. W. D. Fard taught in his lessons that "they use his name (Jesus) to shield (clothe, hide) their dirty (corrupted) religion which is Christianity."

Generations before this, ancient people found metaphors for the human circumstance in the heavenly bodies. The story of the *coat of many colors* was used to describe "the variegated beauty of the forest in November, 4,000 years ago. This beautiful coat excited the envy of the 11 other months (the other *brothers*). Joseph was sent into Egypt by falling below the intersection of the equator and ecliptic, and by his "passing" into another month or his "fall," he symbolically lost his coat to the other brothers.[3] This ancient description of the coat that covers the earth or the body with a beautiful array of colors that literally transforms it, continues its symbolism in the description of Joseph's coat. The same word is used in Arabic to describe transmigration and is adopted in the mystical Christian rituals involving the alb - a white linen tunic worn by priests in Catholic services said to symbolize self-denial and chastity. The priest, in putting on the alb, says this prayer: "Purify me, O Lord, from all stain, and cleanse my heart, that washed in the Blood of the Lamb that I may enjoy eternal delights." He is then considered transformed from his gross, worldly, material being into a spiritual being. Under this analysis, we can see how this shirt that is so prominent in Joseph's (PBUH) history could represent his inherent innocence and purification from animal passions.

When the brother's took Joseph's (PBUH) shirt stained with false blood to his father Jacob (PBUH), he recognized immediately that it was not the true nature (al-Fitr) of his son. That beautiful garment that was stained by the 'blood' (passions, immorality) of the culture was only a garment. He knew that the brothers were only concerned about the material world and its material gain, thus his comment: "that story may be good enough for you" (*that's all you have the capacity to recognize*). When he maintained his righteousness in the face of temptation, Joseph (PBUH) proved that his soul and any transformations were not tied to his garment. There in the chambers of Aziz' wife, he is in another shirt and although that shirt too is used to incriminate him, it actually exonerates him. It is "torn from the back."

Is there, in fact, a disposition toward passion and emotionalism among people of the African diaspora? Charles Larson found contradictions to this stereotype while teaching English literature to high school students in Nigeria. He discovered how African attitudes toward love and nature were very different from Western ideas. Larson wrote from a context of literature: "I can think of no contemporary African novel in which the central plot or theme can be called a love story, no African novel in which the plot line progresses because of the hero's attempt to acquire a mate, no African novel in which seduction is the major goal, no African novel in which the fate of lovers becomes the most significant element in the story. No African novel works this way because love as a *theme in Western literary sense is* simply missing. Romantic love, seduction, sex –these are not the subjects of African fiction."[4]

The Europeans "flipped the script" so to speak. The very idea of erotic or passionate disposition that they accuse us of is called Romantic love (from Rome). By staining his coat/shirt with animal blood, as proof that Joseph (PBUH) had been killed, they were accusing Joseph (PBUH) of having his spiritual life killed by animal passions. This is the charge that they make today against descendants of Africans. A popularization of Afrocentric culture today is the word *Afrique*, which, in its very phonetics, says *a freak*. They present the image of the African American as the oversexed 'Mandingo,' akin to the brute, close in line to the sex-obsessed simian primates. In slavery, one rationale that they used to justify separation of the races and continued subjugation of the race was that we were prone to rape their white women. When a white woman was raped an irrational frenzy erupted in their psyche that fueled lynch mobs and justified the lynching of "any nigger" to atone for the crime.

On May 30, 1921, the arrest of a young black man on a questionable charge of assaulting a young white woman in Tulsa Oklahoma sparked the deadliest race riot in U.S. history. Whites charged through the black community in retaliation, leaving an estimated 300 people dead and another 10,000 black residents homeless. Thirty-five city blocks, including the successful business district known as Black Wall Street, were in ruins. Booker T. Washington, who had lectured in Tulsa, was the first to call the district "the Negro's Wall Street." Many white Tulsans, who referred to the district as "Little Africa," were not happy about the growth and prosperity of the black community. In the summer and early autumn of 1919, alone, in a period referred to as Red Summer, hundreds of African Americans were killed in riots across the United States. Chicago was one of the few places in which African Americans fought back.

Once this demonization of a race is accepted, terror and persecution easily follows. In a July 18, 2011, editorial, Eugene Robinson, a Washington Post opinion writer, referring to the black Republican presidential candidate, urged readers to "Stand up to Herman Cain's Bigotry." Cain had fed into the targeting of Muslims by conservatives and extremists in much the same way Ben Carson, another black candidate would do on behalf of Republicans later in 2015. "This demonization of Muslims is not without precedent," Robinson wrote: "In the early years of the 20th century, throughout the South, white racists used a similar threat - the notion of black men as sexual predators who threatened white women - to justify an elaborate legal framework of segregation and repression that endured for decades."

The righteous have always been subject to false charges. It is recounted in the Qur'an Commentary of Yusuf Ali in Note 2962, in reference to the Prophet Muhammad's (PBUH) own wife Aisha: *The particular incident here referred to occurred on the return from the expedition to the Banu Mustaliq, A.H.* 5-6. *When the march was ordered, Hadhrat 'Aisha was not in her tent, having gone to search for a valuable necklace she had dropped. As her litter was veiled, it was not noticed that she was not in it, until the army reached the next halt. Meanwhile, finding the camp had gone, she sat down to rest, hoping that some one would come back to fetch her when her absence was noticed. It was night, and she fell asleep. Next morning she was found by Safwan, a Muhajir, who had been left behind the camp expressly to pick up anything inadvertently left behind. He put her on his camel and brought her, leading the camel on foot. This gave occasion to enemies to raise a malicious scandal. The ringleader among them was the chief of Madinah Hypocrites, 'Abdullah ibn Ubai, who is referred to in the last clause of this verse. He had other sins and enormities to his debit, and he was left to the punishment of an unrepentant sinner, for he died in that state. The minor tools were given the legal punishment of the law, and after penitence mended their lives. They made good.*

False rumors had been spread about Aisha (RAA) and both her and the Prophet (PBUH) were distressed. Finally, she met face to face with the Prophet (PBUH), her mother and her father, Abu Bakr. The Prophet (PBUH) said: "If you did something, tell me so that you can repent. If you did it, do tawbah so that you can meet Allah (azza wajal) repenting." Aisha denied having done anything. Her mother and her father told her the same thing and she finally became angry as her tears dried and her heart became hard. She asserted that by Allah, she could only say what Jacob, the father of Prophet Joseph (PBUH), had said: "Patience is beautiful, and Allah is my protection against what you describe" (Joseph 12/18). She realized that only Allah Himself could establish her innocence and vindicate her of the slander levied against her. Allah then revealed to the Prophet (PBUH) the following verses of Qur'an, Sura 24, ayat 11-20, condemning those hypocrites who had doubted Aisha's innocence and who had slandered her honor: *"Since you received it with your tongues, and repeated what you did not know anything about with your mouths, you thought it was a trifle, but in the sight of Allah it is serious. Why, when you heard it, did you not say: 'It is not for us to repeat this, Glory be to You (O Allah), this is a serious slander.' Allah warns you to never repeat anything like this again, if you are indeed believers!"* After saying those words, Aisha felt relieved and knew that Allah (azza wajal) would declare her innocent. She was finally able to sleep. She said that she no longer worried about her situation but instead the situation of her parents because she thought they would die from worrying about the slander.

Jacob's (PBUH) words in this ayat also give us another lesson: sometimes even when we know someone is lying, we avoid accusing them without proof. Jacob (PBUH) recognized the lie right away. Allah says in Qur'an that they know this (message) to be the truth just like they know their own sons. Jacob (PBUH) knew his son and knew that he had not given up his excellent human character to animal passions, but he had nothing but false evidence in front of him. In that case, all he had was patience and the knowledge that at the end of the day only Allah could assure truth and justice.

12:19: Then there came a caravan of travellers: they sent their water-carrier (for water), and he let down his bucket (into the well)...He said: "Ah there! Good news! Here is a (fine) young man!" So they concealed him as a treasure! But Allah knoweth well all that they do!

Chapter 19

Human Innocence-Priceless

We place value on many things in our lives, but nothing touches our soul or elicits love, compassion, and hope like the sight of a newborn baby.

Good News

The word *Bashir*, which they use to describe Joseph (PBUH) as "good news," also has reference to our skin, the outer surface of our body. The skin is our most sensitive organ and scientists tell us that the touch of parents and rubbing the skin communicates love to children and helps them develop socially. Allah says in Qur'an, I am making a mortal (*Bashirun*) from clay, meaning a sensitive human being - a creature with feelings and sensitivities. This type of person is also good news to the world. It is the type of person we need in the world now - one who is sensitive and not proud and selfish. In a cold, rational society, like we have today, it is this type of person, a person of human innocence, that is priceless.

In the desert, survival itself is dependent on finding water. But the caravan announced "good news" finding a young man in the well instead of water. He was obviously as valuable as the water they sought. He may have been the very type of innocent soul that was lacking in Egypt or something of tremendous value there. This may also explain why Joseph (PBUH) was ultimately put over the Aziz' possession. As the Bible describes it: "And he (the master) hath committed all that he hath to my hand, Genesis 39.8. There is none greater in this house than I." Genesis 39.9. The same language is used when Joseph (PBUH) is put into prison[1] and later when Joseph (PBUH) is freed.[2] See also 12:31 where the Ladies of the city say, "This is no mortal," using the same word 'bashir.'

Our Prophet Muhammad (PBUH) was identified as *Basheer*, a good news bringer. Part of the good news was his example of pure human sensitivities that could not be corrupted by the world.[3] The world gives us sensitivities but these are burnt off by the fires of hell on earth and replaced with another and another so that we stay in hell.[4]

In America, they have made their free enterprise system their god but when the material interests lack human sensitivity, it becomes a source of oppression over the people. When you look at the tobacco industry, the gambling industry, the alcohol and sex industries, and the gun industry, they all cause both physical and spiritual death to the people. There is so much money though to be made in these industries that it ends up being a calculation or a formula in which a numerical value is put on the individual life and it is weighed against a profit to be made. Any of the vital influences in man's society will become oppressive if there is no human sensitivity.

Even knowledge without mercy punishes people.[5] When the intellectuals of our society advance their studies and research without regard to its potential human harm, the people suffer.[6] America prides itself on the freedom and support it has given to its commercial society. Innovation, along with much technological and industrial advancement, has been brought about by this attitude. But today it has become the dominating force in the society. Their atomic research will result in bigger and more lethal bombs. Their botanical research will result in more profitable and genetically modified food with less nutritional value. Businesses operating with no regulation have polluted the environment and poisoned the air and water, although some believe that the solution to society's problems is to give business more power.

We often have something very valuable that we don't even recognize until someone else comes along and sees the value in it. This was the case with the Prophet Joseph (PBUH). A caravan of travelers, maybe similar to a convoy of slave traders, traveled over land or sea with commodities for sale or barter. The travelers concealed Joseph

(PBUH) as a treasure. Another translator says they concealed him as merchandise. In either sense, they hid him as something of obvious value. See also 12:88, 12:65, and 12:62. By contrast in the next ayat we see the brothers recognizing no value in Joseph (PBUH).

12:20 The (Brethren) sold him for a miserable price, for a few dirhams counted out: in such low estimation did they hold him!

Chapter 20

Things Only Have the Value that We Give Them

Joseph's (PBUH) brothers did not respect the same quality that the water bearer respected. Frederick Douglass, the father of the freedom movement, recognized how hard it is to see people in their true value and outside of our preconceived stereotype. "Though the colored man is no longer subject to barter and sale, he is surrounded by an adverse settlement which fetters all his movements. In his downward course he meets with no resistance, but when his course is upward, he is resented and resisted at every step of his progress. If he comes in ignorance, rags and wretchedness he conforms to the popular belief of his character, and in that character he is welcome; but if he shall come as a gentleman, a scholar and a statesman, he is hailed as a contradiction to the national faith concerning his race, and his coming is resented as impudence. In one case he may provoke contempt and derision, but in the other, he is an affront to pride and provokes malice." Frederick Douglass[1] Although written over 100 years ago this sounds exactly like the right wing's response to President Barack H. Obama. And this observation which was true in the time of Joseph (PBUH) and still holds true today, was written more than 400 years ago: "Things only have the value that we give them."[2]

Many whites throughout the south and in other parts of the country have maintained an attachment to the Confederate flag, the same one that the South fought under to divide the Nation in the Civil War.

Yet these same ones profess such patriotism now to the American flag. They have put so much value in that Confederate symbol that many of them have let it warp their human character. Some of them just have a dark heart like Dylan Roof, a white supremacist who, in June 2015 killed nine African American Christian worshippers in a Charleston, South Carolina church, hoping to ignite a race war because he felt "blacks were taking over the world." Are blacks taking over the world just because they no longer want to be seen as somebody else's property? Shortly thereafter, the South Carolina legislature voted to remove the Confederate flag from the State Capitol but work still needs to be done to remove the symbol from the hearts.

Corporal Price Lambkin of the First Black Regiment in the Civil War, organized by lecturer, writer and abolitionist, Thomas Wentworth Higginson,[3] appealed to fellow ex-slave soldiers, urging them to patriotism, under the American flag and rejecting the Confederate flag, despite them having been considered no more than currency as slaves: "Our mas'rs dey hab lib under de flag, dey got dere wealth under it, and ebryting beautiful for dere chilen. Under it dey hab grind us up, and put us in dere pocket for money. But de fus' minute dey tink dat ole flag mean freedom for we colored people, dey pull it right down, and run up de rag ob dere own." (Immense applause). "But we'll neber desert de ole flag, boys, neber; we hab lib under it for eighteen hundred sixty-two years, and we'll die for it now."

It was easy for white America to view their African slaves as currency but to see them now as brothers, as equals, that was hard. If the Prophet Muhammad (PBUH) had not said himself that he heard Bilal's footsteps ahead of him in the paradise, many people today, even in the Muslim world, would have Bilal lingering somewhere in the spirit world until his black soul had been purged.[4]

Bilal

Bilal was an African who lived in Arabia and had become a slave. We have a connection with Bilal as a Muslim and as an African ancestor. His freedom was purchased by Abu Bakr and he was appointed by Prophet Muhammad (PBUH) to call the people to worship. That's also what we have been asked to do. Imam Mohammed (RAA) recommended that we accept being identified as *Bilalian* as opposed to a skin color, which tells you nothing about a person's origin or character. It only makes sense if we are going to identify with something, it should be identifying with something that has human meaning, and something that represents the best in our background and our most noble and honorable achievements.

Ancient Foundation of Modern Civilization

It's hard sometimes to share the credit for our success. Nevertheless, all civilizations are built upon those that came before it. An honest scientist recognizes this. Albert Einstein noted: "A hundred times every day I remind myself that my inner and outer life depend on the labors of other men, living and dead, and that I must exert myself in order to give in the same measure as I have received and am still receiving."

The Romans civilization preceded the western civilizations of today and the Greek civilization that preceded it was built in large part on the accomplishments of the Africans in Egypt.[5] Shriners and the elite in the Christian Sciences know that even before Egypt, human sciences came from Mecca.[6] Egypt however, corrupted the sciences and used them for controlling the masses.[7]

Bekka is the ancient name of Mecca. Rebecca is the sister of Rachel, Joseph's (PBUH) mother. In the Bible, we have Rachel (spiritual sciences) pouring water (concepts) for Jacob (PBUH). It says Rebecca is crying in the wilderness. Why? Because her sciences had been polluted, abused & stolen. But with the advent of Prophet Muhammad (PBUH), she stopped crying and became Mecca. It is maintaining the purity of G-d's message and selfless sharing of knowledge with the people that has justified receiving G-d's Favor over time.

12:21 The man in Egypt who bought him, said to his wife: "Make his stay (among us) honourable: may be he will bring us much good, or we shall adopt him as a son." Thus did We establish Joseph in the land, that We might teach him the interpretation of stories (and events). And Allah hath full power and control over His affairs; but most among mankind know it not.

Chapter 21

Make No Small Plans

History

According to the research scholars of the Bible, Prophet Joseph (PBUH) was born around 906 B.C. and the incident with which this story begins happened in or about 890 B. C. The well he was put in was near Dothan, to the north of Shechem according to Biblical and Talmudic traditions, and the caravan, which took him out of the well, was coming from Gilead (Trans-Jordan) and was on its way to Egypt. The historical account of Joseph is always subject to corruption but the story in the Qur'an is the Word of G-d; it is that account that is important to us.

Ibn Kathir wrote: "The Egyptian who purchased Joseph (PBUH) was Aziz, a vizier in Egypt over the treasury. Ibn Ishaq says: His name was Potiphar b. Ruhayb. The king in Egypt in those days was Riyan b. Al-Walid. He was an Amalekite. The wife of the vizier was called Ra'el bt Rua'el. Others say her name was Zulaykha, but it is apparent that this was her nickname [laqab]." *Prophets in the Quran: an Introduction to the Quran and Muslim Exegesis*, Brannon Wheeler.

"At that time, Memphis was the capital of Egypt, whose ruins are still found on the Nile at a distance of 4 miles south of Cairo. When

Prophet Joseph (PBUH) was taken there, he was 17 or 18 years old. He remained in the house of Aziz for three years and spent nine years in prison. He then became the ruler of the land at the age of 30 and ruled over Egypt independently for 80 years. In the ninth or tenth year of his rule, Prophet Joseph (PBUH) sent for his father, Prophet Jacob (PBUH), to come from Palestine to Egypt with all the members of his family and, according to the Bible, settled them in the land of Goshen, where they lived up to the time of Prophet Moses (PBUH). The Bible says that before his death, Prophet Joseph (PBUH) bound his kindred by an oath: "when you return from this country to the house of your forefathers you must take my bones out of this country with you. So he died a hundred and ten years old, and they embalmed him."[1]

The City

The word used in this ayat for Egypt is *Misr,* from the root word *Masara*, meaning to milk with the tips of the fingers or build. *Massar* means to build towns and *Egypt* is also defined as the chief town of a kingdom. "The chief function of the city is to convert power into form, energy into culture, dead matter into the living symbols of art, biological reproduction into social creativity." (Lewis Mumford (1895-1990), U.S. social philosopher. The City in History, Ch. 18 (1961).) In an eloquent acknowledgment that G-d taught man through nature[2] Lewis Mumford wrote: "The social functions of the beehive, the termitary, and the ant-hill-structures often imposing in size, skillfully wrought - have indeed so many resemblances to those of the city, even the division of labor, the differentiations of castes, the practices of war, the institution of royalty, the domestication of other species, and the employment of slavery, existed in 'ant-empires' millions of years before they coalesced in the ancient city."[3]

Egypt is juxtaposed against the wilderness - desert uncultivated land - and since we should see Egypt more than just a geography, we should likewise see the desert as uncultured, uncivilized society. The city, particularly Egypt, is symbolic of the evolution into the major influences in society, business, politics, education and religion from the simple social structure of the garden. It represents the historical and philosophical growth from an agricultural society to industrial. "Go ye down to any city, and ye shall find what ye want!" *Holy Qur'an 2-61 (Al-Baqara [The Cow])* It is translated "any city" but it is not referring to any generic city. It says go to "any Egypt." It is referring to a model society, which is fully developed but in which the people are slaves - not necessarily chattel slaves - but a people with no authority over their own life and future. In that environment, citizens can readily trade real freedom for small comforts and condiments.[4] Note that the city is also specifically referenced later as *Madina, (12:30, ladies in the city)* and we know that *Madina* represented Prophet Muhammad's (PBUH) establishment of the model city or community life.

The Valley of the Nile, in which Egypt is situated, evolved from a tribal, self-contained village culture to a centralized, urban culture dominated by the temple and the palace. The people brought in their combined knowledge and experience from the wilderness to the city, from their farms, and from their herds. They realized that if they contributed their specialized labor to the whole, under one system and leadership, their wide variety of needs would be provided. Ralph Waldo Emerson wrote: "The city is recruited from the country. In the year 1805, it is said, every legitimate monarch in Europe was imbecile. The city would have died out, rotted, and exploded, long ago, but that it was reinforced from the fields. It is the only country which came to town day before yesterday, that is city and court today."[5]

In ancient Arabia, the Bedouins in the desert were considered to have preserved the pure language of Arabic and when parents wanted their children to learn the language, they sent them to the desert Bedouins to learn it.

The most enduring symbol of Egypt is the great pyramids, symbols of engineering and industrial advancement. The pyramids, "built to illustrate the most perfect principles of astronomy, mathematics, geometry, and the spiritual side of man which we know under the general term of religion should be forever free from the erroneous idea that this massive structure was erected merely as a huge royal sepulcher."[6] Honorable Elijah Muhammad understood the power of magnifying human energies to project the big vision and feed aspirations. He understood the view of renowned Chicago architect, Daniel Burnham, who famously said, "Make No Small Plans... they have no magic to stir men's blood." Because of this, our passion has to be excited and focused. Our psyche is empowered much more when we're working with things of higher value. In the Nation of Islam, we were asked to expand our work to broader and broader venues and as a result, we were well-primed to grow in our capacity.

Individual Successes

Conversely, this communal energy and release of explosive powers is often focused on individuals such as our successful African Americans. We have our Oprahs, our Jay-Zs and Beyonces, our Will and Jada Smiths, and our Barack Obamas. We will always have signs of the potential of the whole community or race[7] but at best they are just symbols. In a time in which slaves were considered less than human, the race produced the foremost thinker of its time – Frederick Douglass and the dreams, aspirations, and spirit of the whole race were crystallized in that one person.[8]

Sometimes those images are not bright enough and not powerful enough to bring about significant change in the masses of the people. Why? Because to be effective, each of our successes must be magnified and projected through the lens of community as a whole. We advance the community by acknowledging our own success, but also by crediting the source of the blessing; by recognizing and testifying as Jesus (PBUH) did that "I in you and you in me." The same potential G-d put in me he put in you. But the potential does not necessarily mean actualization, which implies an expression and realization of our capacities. Everyone has their own destiny, but we advance as a people by presenting the best of these examples as our models and leaders.

The city, as an institution, served as a container, a comfortable womb, for the development of the self, and the expansion of human powers. This "earliest of complex power machines was composed, not of wood or metal, but of perishable human parts, each having a specialized function in a larger mechanism under centralized human control. The vast army of scientists, engineers, architects, foremen, and day laborers, some hundred thousand strong, who built the Great Pyramid, formed the first complex machine, invented when technology itself had produced only a few simple 'machines' like the inclined plane and the sled, and had not yet invented wheeled vehicles. Even speed was not lacking in this homo-mechanized economy. While the cathedrals of the Middle Ages often required centuries for completion, many an Egyptian tomb was finished in the lifetime of the pharaoh whose mummy was destined to be placed in it, sometimes within a single generation. No wonder the central authority that set such machines in motion seemed authentically godlike." *The City in History*, Lewis Mumford, p60.

America too was formed as a womb of development. It has been called an "experimental democracy," and its Constitution was designed to accommodate its evolution. Our freedom was essential to that evolution. Although we know historically of the cruelty of slavery, the majority of the slaveholders viewed his slaves as a financial asset – something of benefit. The wife of the Aziz said the same thing about Joseph (PBUH) that Pharaoh's wife said of Moses (PBUH): "Maybe he will bring us much good, or we shall adopt him as a son." *yanfaAAan[a] aw nattakhi[th]ahu waladan.*[9]

Saba/Sheba/Shabazz

The Qur'an translator Abdullah Yusuf Ali in his commentary of *ayat 27:22* identifies Saba with Sheba in the Bible. (1 Kings x. 1-10). Sura 34 in the Qur'an is entitled Saba (Sheba) and in Arabian tradition, she is called Bilqis. Saba was a city in Yemen that in ancient times was a very prosperous country. The Queen of Sheba is reported to have ruled over Abyssinia (present Ethiopia), named after the Habasha tribe, which originated in Yemen. Between the two countries is the narrow straits of the Red Sea. Trade, exchange of language and culture has taken place for centuries. Thus, Sheba has connections with both Arabia and Africa. "3264. ...Abyssinians possess a traditional history called *The Book of the Glory of Kings (Kebra Nagast),* which has been translated from Ethiopic into English by Sir E.A. Wallis Budge (Oxford, 1932). It gives an account of the Queen of Sheba and her only son Menyelek I, as founders of the Abyssinian dynasty."[10]

Some Muslims, in ignorance, portray Christians and other People of the Book as *kafirs* or disbelievers. The early history of Islam on the Arabian Peninsula gives us a model of what our relationship should be with our Christian neighbors. After the persecution of his followers by the pagan Quraish in Mecca, Prophet Muhammad (PBUH) advised his followers to migrate to the country of the Christian ruler, Negus of Abyssinia, who was reputed to be just and kindhearted. Ten Muslims left Mecca for Abyssinia and a total of eighty-three persons later fled to Abyssinia. (Ibn Hisham, Vol. Pp. 320-21) The news that the Muslims were living in peace in Abyssinia reached Mecca and angered the Quraish. They sent their emissaries to get the exiles back from Abyssinia. King Negus did not believe in forsaking those who had sought his shelter and he summoned the Muslims to his court and asked them: "What is this religion for which you have forsaken your people and neither accepted my religion nor any other?"

Jafar Ibn Abi Talib (May Allah be pleased with him), the cousin of Prophet Muhammad, (PBUH), responded by acknowledging that his people in the past had been living in the *Jahilliyyah* – a period of ignorance – and worshipping idols and violating decent and intelligent behavior. He spoke of the Prophet's (PBUH) noble birth and his noble character and the message that he had been given from Allah. Negus listened and then asked for something of the message that had been brought by the Prophet (PBUH). Jafar (May Allah be pleased with him) recited the opening verses of Surah Maryam (19th Chapter) and Negus wept until his beard was wet. His bishops sobbed until their scrolls were moistened with their tears. Negus acknowledged that this message along with what Jesus (PBUH) had brought were both revelations from G-d. He refused to send the Muslims back; treated them with honor and pledged his protection to them. (Ibn Hisham, pp. 334-38).[11]

W. D. Fard identified Africans in America as the lost found tribe of Shabazz (a play on Sheba). I believe he did his best to embed truth into every lesson that he gave us. This identification connected us with our Christian tradition and our Islamic and African heritage. It also connected us to a brother who had been sold into slavery by his jealous brothers. I believe the plan was for us to retain the best of all those traditions. The vast majority of Nation of Islam members transitioned into "proper Islam" under the leadership of Elijah Muhammad's son, Wallace Deen Mohammed (RAA). Admittedly, the changes were momentous: no more man-god, no apocalyptic destruction of America by a futuristic "mother plane," no easy identification of the devil based on black or white skin, and no hierarchy of discipline. We were forced to look in the mirror at self and its capacity. That "self" identity was defined as "righteous Muslims." We were also given a "self," or a cultural identity that tied us together, genetically and culturally, in a bond that could never be broken.

12:22 When Joseph attained His full manhood, We gave him power and knowledge: thus do We reward those who do right.

Chapter 22

The Strong Get More, While the Weak Ones Fade

The Qur'an refers to a point at which, "Joseph attained his full manhood" and it has also been translated as "attain the age of full strength." Commentators described this full manhood as forty years old. We don't get the blessing of power and knowledge until we are ready for it. We start with four, which is a balance of the major influences in human life and this four is multiplied by 10 when we reach the completion of universal dimension or full strength and manhood.[1] Until the evolution is complete, circumstances force the soul's growth. It is confined and imprisoned. We must look within to the ideal – the vision of our highest and best self – and develop the resources that will expand us beyond the limiting environment of prison. As a youth, Joseph (PBUH) told his father of his dream and Jacob (PBUH) was the only one who understood its meaning; now Joseph (PBUH) himself is able to interpret others' dreams and events.

The Strong Get More

It is a long and tortuous journey in arriving at one's ideal, which may be called *nafsi mutmainna* (the soul at rest), or one's authentic self or the destination of one's life journey. We are staying away from sin and receiving G-d's Mercy. There is a synergy that builds once a person commits to that path and the angels assist along the way. Malcolm Gladwell writes in *Outliers-the Story of Success*, of a phenomenon by which, through fortuitous circumstances, those better situated, at the right place and the right time, will over time accumulate based on those initial advantages. He points to what sociologist Robert Merton called the "Matthew Effect," after the New Testament verse in the Gospel of Matthew:[2] "For unto everyone that hath shall be given, and he shall have abundance. But from him that hath not shall be taken away even that which he hath." It is those who are successful, in other words, who are most likely to be given the kinds of special opportunities that lead to further success. It's the rich who get the biggest tax breaks. It's the best students who get the best teaching and most attention. And it's the best biggest nine and ten year olds who get the most coaching and practice. Success is the result of what sociologist like to call "accumulative advantage."[3] Both Gladwell and Merton basically mirror the observation made in Billie Holiday's famous rendition of the song, "God Bless the Child," written by Holiday and Arthur Herzog Jr., where she sang: "Them that's got shall get, Them that's not shall lose, so the Bible said and it still is news. Yes, the strong gets more, While the weak ones fade…"

Affirmations-Staying Strong in the Face of Adversity

We all have our flashes of brilliance and our moment of strength but staying strong in the face of adversity is the real test. Aaron (PBUH) represents the fifth level of social development. The Bible reports that Moses (PBUH) took Aaron (PBUH) and Hur with him to the top of the hill as his followers battled the Ameleks. As long as Moses (PBUH) held up his hands, his army was victorious in the battle. When Moses (PBUH) got tired of holding up his hands, Aaron (PBUH) and Hur assisted by holding them up for him. They helped Moses (PBUH) keep his hands uplifted until nightfall, and Joshua (PBUH) was able to overcome the Ameleks in battle.[4] Moses (PBUH) asks Allah in the Qur'an for the assistance of his brother Aaron(PBUH) to confirm and strengthen him and Allah says: *"We will certainly strengthen thy arm through thy brother"*[5] Dr. Ponder interprets Moses' (PBUH) hands upraised by Aaron (PBUH) as our need to employ affirmations to keep ourselves strong in the midst of difficult battles.[6] I believe Aaron (PBUH) also represent the strong supporters of leadership among the people. In the Qur'an, it says Moses (PBUH) assigned Aaron (PBUH) to "act for me amongst my people."[1] This is the leadership among the people that was so remarkable in the Nation of Islam's First Experience. They upheld the leadership and they kept it strong. When you saw any one of us in the street you saw the Honorable Elijah Muhammad.

Political

We all have a political nature in us. We all have the responsibility for governing our individual selves and contributing to the governance of our communities and countries. When this instinct exceeds the bounds of spiritual and moral consciousness, it manifests as an appetite for vanity. Instead of wanting to **be** acceptable, we want to **be seen** as acceptable.

The novelist, folklorist, anthropologist, and bright star of the Harlem Renaissance, Hurston was an independent thinker and her work captured the cultural traditions of African Americans. In her book, *Moses, Man of the Mountain* she retells the story of Moses (PBUH) as one who leads a slave nation from captivity to the freedom of a 'Promised Land,' the wise prophet who brings law and government to an unruly and divided people. She points out that variations of the concept of Moses (PBUH) appear in cultures throughout the world. She adds: "Wherever the children of Africa have been scattered by slavery, there is the acceptance of Moses (PBUH) as the fountain of mystic powers." There are many parallels in Hurston's depiction of this Biblical saga – it's critique of the leadership that is supposed to support the leader and the people, and even the uncertainty within Moses (PBUH) himself, just as today in an African American elite, as to whether he was Egyptian or Hebrew. But she also explores the nuances of both Moses (PBUH) and his brother Aaron's (PBUH) character. Hurston portrays Aaron as a self-absorbed "under-boss" to whom power meant: clothes, ornaments, and titles; one who never truly supports the mission of the G-d appointed brother Moses, (PBUH) and, in fact, acquiesces in the children of Israel's idolatry when Moses (PBUH) goes up into the mountain to commune with G-d.

Some Imams in the following of Imam Mohammed (RAA) complained he was undermining their leadership by criticizing them. That mirrored so clearly the passage from Hurston's book. After returning from the mountain with the law, Moses (PBUH) finds the children of Israel have slipped into idolatry and had begun worship of the calf they had fabricated from their ornaments. Moses (PBUH) berates Aaron (PBUH):

"Aaron," he said, "what on earth did these people do to you to make you bring such a sin on everybody like you did?" Aaron tried to back off but Moses had him by the whiskers and wouldn't let him go. Aaron lifted his hand as if to break Moses' grip on his beard, but the eye of Moses forbade him. He winced and said, "You oughtn't to hold my whiskers like that, Moses, the people are looking at us, and me being a leader..." "The people are looking at you naked and capering around like an old goat, too. Let's forget about that while you answer me."

Aaron wasn't embarrassed by his bad behavior; he was embarrassed by Moses (PBUH) calling him out on it. Similarly, in the Qur'an, Aaron (PBUH) complains of being chastened in front of the people and how they will look at him.[7] In Hurston's account Aaron (PBUH) has his own "beard boy," whose sole job was to look after his whiskers. In the Qur'an, Moses (PBUH) drags Aaron (PBUH) by the very hair he loves preening over. In Hurston's story, Aaron (PBUH) reveals his true heart with the attitude expressed by many Imams, even while Imam Mohammed (RAA) lived: *"It's your time now; be mine after a while."*

Energy (Physical Vitality)

We can direct our energy into any of the four vital functions of life. The ability of runners and other athletes to go beyond their own perceived limitations and to find and function within a zone is well known. Allah says, He blesses this kind of focus with additional unseen forces.[8] There are forces of another dimension that come into play when we reach the epitome of our own best efforts and then will to excel beyond that.

Money

Money is one of those vital resources of life that has a profound effect on every other area of our lives: our health, our time, our creativity, our family and our spiritual pursuits. Richness or wealth, while commonly referring to the accumulation of money, is more broadly seen as an abundance of any of the vital resources. We say *he's led a rich life*, or *he has a wealth of experience*. There is an overlap between these vital resources. Some who invest all of their time into making money find that they have irreparably harmed their health beyond being able to remedy it with any amount of money. Some find that they have neglected their families to the point of its disintegration. And some will lose their souls.[9] "Riches are not from an abundance of worldly goods but from a contented mind." Prophet Muhammad (PBUH)

"Whatever is potent for us, whatever elicits strong emotions or seems to 'hold on to us' in life has the power to bring forth our greatest strengths and most remarkable qualities. Our relationship with money calls on us to wake up, to see how we are handling all kinds of energy – not only money, but time, physical vitality, enjoyment, creativity, and the support of friends – and to use those lessons to enrich every aspect of our lives." *The Energy of Money*, Maria Nemeth, PH.D.

Many people's self -image and even health are tied into their possessions. If you perceive your life force as being the flow of money, you may become physically ill and your health decline with a decline in your financial fortunes. When you hold a poor image about yourself and money, it's almost impossible to attract enough of it into your life. And even if you have used your talent and enormous energy to earn some big money, a poor image will do everything it can to sabotage your wealth. There are many well-known athletes and celebrities who are proving these truths right now. When you are physically organized and good at managing your schedule, you make the most of your time, space, energy, and money.

Joshua

In Christian theology, the name *Joshua* not only means "Jehovah's help, salvation, triumph, victory and deliverance," it also means "Jehovah makes rich." Joshua was the son of *Nun*, a name which means "durable prosperity" or "eternal increase." Joshua was born of the tribe of *Ephraim*, which means "very productive" or "doubly fruitful." Ephraim was the son of Joseph (PBUH), who received a tribe's portion of the twelve tribes blessing. The prosperous significance of the name of Joshua is further shown in the fact that Joshua in Hebrew is identical with the name Jesus (PBUH) in Greek. In Islam, Joshua is identified as Yusha ibn Nun. He is not mentioned directly in the *Qur'an* but in a number of authentic narrations, the Prophet (PBUH), identifies Yusha ibn Nun as the attendant of Musa referenced in Qur'an.[10] – See for example 3/124 and 55/613 of *Sahih Al-Bukhari*. Joshua can thus be seen as related to at least these three levels of development represented by Prophets Moses (PBUH), Jesus (PBUH), and Joseph (PBUH).

As a leader, Joshua was also Moses's (PBUH) successor, but whereas, "Moses helped teach the Hebrews that they had a power within them that would deliver them from their bondage and wilderness experiences, it was Joshua who helped them externalize that inner power and use it in a universal way." Dr. Catherine Ponder

Scripture says that Joshua caused the sun to stand still.[11] I became aware many years ago, that I was letting my life and schedule be run by external clocks. Like many others, I found myself looking at my watch every 90 seconds, just like some people today can't tear themselves away from their cellular device. I saw that hurrying and rushing was a manifestation of fear; fear that I would be late or that I would not have enough time to do what I had to do. When I recognized this, I stopped wearing a watch, realizing that we are all on Divine time; I stopped rushing. Now I am consistently on time and have time for everything I need to do.

As we said earlier the sun is a symbol representing higher knowledge of human life or of material life. We say the sun is the symbol of freedom because it's available to everybody. It shines on the poor and the rich. It shines equally on the wicked and the righteous. It is the higher knowledge of mathematics, social science, chemistry, and all of these subjects that help make a good life for human beings. Joshua was able to keep that knowledge from going down on his people. Imam Mohammed (RAA) pointed to the symbolism of our prayers: "Muslims are told to watch the prayers of the midday for the same purpose. Don't let the sun of enlightenment go down on your society. Pray to G-d to keep the sun of enlightenment high in the world. Keep it at its peak. When you gain intellectual strength and superiority in the earth, pray to G-d and guard over that with more giving of yourself, with more sacrifice, with more devotion, with greater commitment than that you would give to protect your worldly or earthly treasures. Because the knowledge can bring back the material wealth, but the material wealth cannot bring back the knowledge."

The British once boasted that the sun never set on their Empire, but history shows their Empire was short-lived and the sun did set on it. Its knowledge was limited and it was based on material power and not freedom for all people. There is another knowledge--the interpretation of scripture – divine understanding—that the sun never sets on. This is our full strength. Joseph (PBUH) did not acquire his power until he attained his full strength, around age 40. But this is not a literal age. It is when we have harnessed all of our latent potential, our vital energy. You're really no threat before that point, but it is then that that lady of the house tries to seduce you.

12:23 But she in whose house he was, sought to seduce him from his (true) self: she fastened the doors, and said: "Now come, thou (dear one)!" He said: "Allah forbid! truly (thy husband) is my lord! he made my sojourn agreeable! truly to no good come those who do wrong!"

Chapter 23

Everybody Loves a Lover

Ibn Kathir wrote: "in Bukhari and Muslim on the authority of the Seal of the Prophets: "There are seven people whom God will cover with shade on a day when there is no other shade: a just leader, a man who remembered God when alone and his eyes shed tears, a man whose heart is attached to the mosque so that as soon as he leaves he wants to return to it, two men who love each other for the sake of God, a man who gives out alms secretly so that his left hand does not know what the right hand does, a youth who grows up in the service of God, and **a man who when summoned by a beautiful woman say: "I fear God."** *Prophets in the Quran: an Introduction to the Quran and Muslim exegesis*, Brandon Wheeler.

Man has to understand and respect his lawful and natural mate. Joseph (PBUH) was a lover of mankind and understood love on a higher plane than carnal passion. "Males traditionally, historically have supported females by going out of the house into field. Going out in the field and getting food and providing the needs for the home has engaged his intellect. And his heart was mated with the creation itself, the field, the land that produced the food. And the sky that he needs to have rain come down to help his crop. And the sunlight that he needs to be warm and to shine on his crop. So his devotion connects him with earth and sky and in time he falls in love with this beautiful world he becomes a philosopher, beautiful thinker."[1]

That's the man on a higher plane. Strong and 'hard' in engaging the world, and his 'heart' in the right place. When you don't have that aspiration that your nature craves, though, you find your manhood, only in the physical hardness. You find your fulfillment only in the male animal satisfaction of sex. And that part of it is good if you're natural and if you're normal. But we are not designed to live there. G-d says in the earth is our livelihood and our dwelling place. Too many of us find our life full of thorns and thistles because we've consigned ourselves to a diet (plants of the field- Genesis 3:18) for wild animals. Too many of us are merely thumping our chest and boasting of our animal prowess. Over time, I discovered that America's leadership wasn't afraid of the militancy of the Black Panther's or even the then Nation of Islam. America boasted that she could destroy the world several times over with her weapons. She wasn't afraid of the blustering and threatening Black man, responding to his hurt or his anger. What she was afraid of was the Black man coming into his full strength (40 acres and a mule) which would evolve him into the independent thinker.

The signs are before us. Black on black crime--we are angry so we attack the closest ones to us. But the source of the anger is our unwillingness to look at our own soul, acknowledge its shortcomings, and live up to its potential. Gang warfare—we want to belong to something strong and powerful. We have to satisfy a social nature but we try to find it in the thug mentality because the world has made righteousness seem lame. Our nature cries out for social responsibility but we don't even want to start out with the basic responsibility of marriage.

12:24 And (with passion) did she desire him, and he would have desired her, but that he saw the evidence of his Lord: thus (did We order) that We might turn away from him (all) evil and shameful deeds: for he was one of Our servants, sincere and purified.

Chapter 24

I See Where This is Going

Joseph (PBUH) is put to his first test of whether his purity and innocence was authentic or whether the charge of his brothers was true. But even in his confined quarters Joseph (PBUH) still did his best to distance himself from temptation. He knew to not even go near it.[1] He could have tested himself, pretending he was so strong and approach the temptation, feeling like he'd be able to turn it down. But Allah says: "he saw the evidence of his Lord." That evidence was in his very nature *(and he would have desired her)*. So he didn't try to test himself or challenge his natural urges. When faced with these temptations, we will almost always be able to say, "I See Where This is Going." Of course, he passes the test but look at where he could have gone. He could have let passions consume his good sense – from a sincere servant expressing spiritual purity--to one going through the motions and just reciting empty platitudes.[2]

Restraint

Restraint whether imposed from without or within can have the benefit of strengthening us. Just like straining the muscles against iron in the gym strengthens them, exercising our willpower makes it stronger in restraining our appetites.

We have to choose however to extract the benefit from limiting conditions. We can rant and rave and revile the injustice of life and our circumstances. It is the spiritual perception that comes from faith enables us to benefit from those circumstances. When Joseph (PBUH) was put in the pit, he never displayed the slightest fear or uncertainty. Allah tells us this by saying, "We put it in his heart that he would see his brothers again and they would not know him." He knew he was not going to die from his experience. It is maintaining this elevated state of mind that kept him in the beautiful shape and mold that the merchants recognized when they found him in the well and exclaimed, *Bashir* – Good News--(Beautiful Human Model)

There are consequences of losing this beautiful mold (model). If people ignore the important things in religion and intelligent life and follow their own impulses or whatever fad or whim comes to their mind, they will regress in their nature to that of animals. We are given this warning in Qur'an 2:65: *"And well ye knew those amongst you who transgressed in the matter of the Sabbath: We said to them: "Be ye apes, despised and rejected."*[3] They became unconscious of their shame; unaware that their behavior was below their dignity as human beings.[4] Shame is defined as "the consciousness or awareness of dishonor, disgrace, or condemnation" and these people had fallen to a level of apes or monkeys since they, like these animals, did not possess reflective awareness or consciousness.

The earliest English uses of the word 'ape' are tied closely to human behavior on the level of animals or which imitates animals. Apes were noted for their ability to imitate humans and presumably, the word came to identify the reverse tendency in humans. That characterization continues to this day as we use the phrase, "*go ape*." *Qiradatan,* used in the Qur'an for apes, comes from the root word *Qarada*, which means, to cling to the ground or lie in the dust, so it clearly points to a people that have not overcome the gravity of materialism.

We have to make a conscious effort to keep our thoughts and desires from feeding on the dust.[5] "Spiritual achievements are the consummation of holy aspirations. He who lives constantly in the conception of noble and lofty thoughts, who dwells upon all that is pure and selfless, will, as surely as the sun reaches its zenith and the moon its full, become wise and noble in character and rise into a position of influence and blessedness."[6]

In a passage that closely mirrors the story of Joseph (PBUH), Allen also writes: *"Your circumstances many be uncongenial, but they shall not remain so if you only perceive an ideal and strive to reach it. You cannot travel within and stand still without. Here is a youth hard pressed by poverty and labor. Confined long hours in an unhealthy workshop, unschooled and lacking all the arts of refinement. But he dreams of better things. He thinks of intelligence, or refinement, of grace and beauty.*" Prophet Muhammad (PBUH) himself described Joseph (PBUH) as "The embodiment of half of all beauty."[7]

12:25 So they both raced each other to the door, and she tore his shirt from the back: they both found her lord near the door. She said: "What is the (fitting) punishment for one who formed an evil design against thy wife, but prison or a grievous chastisement?"

Chapter 25

Race Toward the Good

The culture of our past should not be held against us. It is not our fault that we perceived G-d incorrectly and called him by the wrong names. The slave master introduced us to Christianity, its doctrines, and its images. At that time, there was a plan in place to dominate all Christians.[1] Then as Muslims, Professor W. D. Fard gave us a corrupted language. G-d is going to judge the matter based on our intentions and if our intention was to cry out to our Creator, our Lord, and our Redeemer, He is going to respond as if we called Him by His Proper Name.

Here in this passage is another story of the shirt, that is torn or damaged and is used to accuse Joseph (PBUH) of a sin. But here the condition of the shirt bears witness to Joseph's (PBUH) innocence. Just as animal blood was obviously out of character for Joseph (PBUH), so too is the shirt torn from the back – evidence that his true character was fleeing away from the sin and not toward it.

If we are going to race toward something, it should be towards good. Running away is sometimes considered cowardly, but wise people realize that removing themselves physically from temptation can often be the most courageous action to take.[2] There is a hadith that addresses this need and, while primarily focusing on the issue of repentance, it also provides a great lesson on the concept of distancing ourselves from the place of sin. Here, the sinner was advised to accompany his repentance with a change in his physical environment.

Referring to a very wicked man who was guilty of many sins including murder, Abu Sa`id Al-Khudri (RAA) reported that the Prophet of Allah (PBUH) said: "He was directed to a monk. He came to him and told him that he had killed 99 people and asked him if there was any chance for his repentance to be accepted. He replied in the negative and the man killed him also, completing one hundred. He then asked about the most learned man on the earth. He was directed to a scholar.

He [the murderer] told him [the scholar] that he had killed 100 people and asked him if there was any chance for his repentance to be accepted. The scholar replied in the affirmative and asked, 'Who stands between you and repentance?' Go to such-and-such land; there (you will find) people devoted to the worship of Allah. Join them in worship, and do not come back to your land because it is an evil place. So he went away and hardly had he covered half the distance when death overtook him, and there was a dispute between the angels of mercy and the angels of torment. The angels of mercy pleaded, 'This man has come with a repenting heart to Allah,' and the angels of punishment argued, 'He never did a virtuous deed in his life.' Then there appeared another angel in the form of a human being and the contending angels agreed to make him arbiter between them. He said, 'Measure the distance between the two lands. He will be considered belonging to the land to which he is nearer.' They measured and found him closer to the land (of piety) where he intended to go, and so the angels of mercy collected his soul." (Al-Bukhari and Muslim)

Similarly, in reference to changing one's place or position, The Prophet (PBUH) said, "When one of you becomes angry while standing, he should sit down. If the anger leaves him, well and good; otherwise he should lie down." [Abu Daud; Book 41, No. 4764] Scientists have supported this advice with research that indicates that taking insults lying down may hurt your pride but it is less likely to make you angry. Richard Alleyne, a science correspondent, reported in August of 2009 on research that showed those who took personal insults while upright exhibited brain activity linked to attacking, but this urge disappeared when they took the same insults lying down. Eddie Harmon-Jones, a cognitive scientist who led the study at Texas A&M University, said, "In the upright or leaning forward state one might be more likely to attack." Tradition further advises: "come near to earth, as you have been created of earth. Thus, make yourself calm like the earth. The cause of wrath is heat and its opposite is to lie down on the ground and to make the body calm and cool." Here we have the change in physical position or space facilitating a calmer condition. Even from a practical standpoint, when a standing person sits he decreases his mobility and consequently his ability to act on his anger and likewise when he lies down, it is decreased even more.

Consider also the causes of anger. Isa (Jesus Christ) (PBUH) was once asked, "What thing is difficult?" He answered "God's wrath." Prophet Yahya (John the Baptist) (PBUH) then asked, "What thing takes near the wrath of God?" Isa responded, "Anger." Prophet Yahya (PBUH) asked, "What thing grows and increases anger?" Isa (PBUH) answered "Pride, prestige, hope for honour and haughtiness."

These attitudes have historically and physiologically been associated with a rigid erectness, i.e. *stiff-necked, nose in the air.* Isn't this the same pride and arrogance of Satan and that of the many of the rich and powerful-"I am better than he."?

Brian Alexander, msnbc.com contributor, wrote on August 10, 2011, "Psychologist and social scientist Dacher Keltner says the rich really are different, and not in a good way. Their life experience makes them less empathetic, less altruistic, and generally more selfish. In fact, he says, the philosophical battle over economics, taxes, debt ceilings and defaults that are now roiling the stock market is partly rooted in an upper-class ideology of self-interest.

We have now done 12 separate studies measuring empathy in every way imaginable, social behavior in every way, and some work on compassion and it's the same story," he said. "Lower class people just show more empathy, more pro-social behavior, more compassion, no matter how you look at it." Poor people were first. Adam (PBUH) had access to everything in the Garden but the picture that we have of him in his original creation is nakedness. This is not to condemn wealth or those who attain it. That is a blessing from Allah, but He also tells us in the Qur'an that the poor have a right in that wealth and that we must purify ourselves by giving of that wealth in charity to avoid it corrupting us.

Garments of the Prophets

The shirt and the garments play a prominent role in describing man's outer personality, as opposed to his inner character. The garment is what the public sees of us and it covers whatever defects we may have on our body. Adam (PBUH) listened to the whispers of Satan and not only lost his place in the Garden, but also was stripped of his garment. He recognized his nakedness, meaning he was then without culture or development. Joseph's (PBUH) shirt is torn from the back. African Americans have similarly had their past culture and development torn from the pages of history, and if we listen to the whispers of Satan today and follow the world we'll lose our connection with a great past and greater future.

12:26 He said: "It was she that sought to seduce me - from my (true) self." And one of her household saw (this) and bore witness, (thus):- "If it be that his shirt is rent from the front, then is her tale true, and he is a liar!

Chapter 26

Our Deeds Will Speak for Themselves

Allah says in the Qur'an, 36:65: "That Day shall We set a seal on their mouths. But their hands will speak to us, and their feet bear witness, to all that they did." Just as the hands of the mechanic will absorb the grease and the grime of his tasks, so also will the face of the hater, the lips of the smoker, the eyes of the intoxicated, and the behavior of the pork eater, reflect their deeds. Similarly, our surroundings and our garments will make a statement about us. The Nation of Islam could be seen as a cultural garment – a container or an environment – that provided structure, teaching, discipline, and represented independent thinking. The first sign of the civilized culture is putting clothes on. And conversely, the first sign of the deterioration of civilization is when we start taking our clothes off in public. The garment covers our physical (animal) body parts. Passion is a natural human urge but when it is not contained in rules, discipline and refinement, we take on the image of the savage.

The Evolution of Culture

Prophet Idris (PBUH) is the archetypical figure for cultural development. Some scholars identify Idris (PBUH) as the Enoch of the Bible, referring to him as one who "walked with God" (Gen. 5:21-24) and "God took him" (Gen. 5:24). He was a man of truth and sincerity, a prophet held in a high position among the people. The elementary Biblical interpretation is that he attained immortality having been taken up without passing through the portals of death. A more reasonable interpretation is that the *immortality* alluded to refers to his position as the Fourth level in the permanent hierarchy of human and community development.[1]

Idris (PBUH) is considered to be the first person to write with the pen, the first to sew garments, and the inventor of the balance to prevent deception in commerce and trade.[2] The word *Idris* itself comes from the root word *darasa*, which means to study, read with attention, and disappear (trace). *Dirasatun* means attentive study. It is said that Prophet Idris (PBUH) was so named because of his great learning. "The word Hanuk (Enoch), used in the Bible and Idris (PBUH) closely resembles each other in their meanings and significations." *Dictionary of the Holy Qur'an.* The ancient Greeks suggested that Enoch was also the same person identified in their mythology as Mercury/Hermes. Hermes likewise is credited with inventing the alphabet and numbers and, he personified mental quickness, communication, and fluent use of the word. Curiously, the 1998 action movie, Mercury Rising starring Bruce Willis and Alec Baldwin, depict an evil plot to murder innocent people to protect a top secret code, pointing to the supreme importance of information (letters, number, words, and codes) to today's society.

Healing-Writing

If we accept that *al-Qur'an* is al-Shafi (the Healer), then we can see the Qur'an also as the source of medical science. Some scholars believe that even the art of medicine was originally revealed through the Prophet Idris (PBUH). We can also see that writing, if we consider words of truth, can be a healing for the unenlightened mind and a healing for the soul. "Writing comes into being to retain information across time and across space."[3]

Weaving garments is very much like writing. Sewing together – with various parts of speech, nouns, verbs, conjunctions etc., like thread – words into sentences and sentences into paragraphs and paragraphs into books and essays – that convey broad ideas and concepts. We use the expression "weave a tale" to describe the process of putting the different elements together into a story. When that story is false we describe it as *fabrication* or made from *whole cloth.*

Information

Writing soon became the primary vehicle for the spread of information, but since that time, science has forced us to recognize more and more new technologies. When they were announced to the world, no one knew the changes they would bring about. "Bell Telephone Laboratories announced the invention of a tiny electronic semi-conductor [that] may have far-reaching significance in electronics and electrical communication." Claude Shannon, credited with founding the field of information theory, writing in *The Bell System Technical Journal* in July and October 1948, in an article entitled "A Mathematical Theory of Communication," introduced the *bit* – a fundamental unit of measure for information. Today most information in the world is transmitted through this language. Even biology has become an information science, a subject of messages, instructions, and code. Genes encapsulate information and enable procedures for reading it in and writing it out. Life spreads by networking. The body itself is an information processor. "Memory resides not just in brains but in every cell."[4]

Richard Dawkins, whose scientific theory we will discuss later, wrote: "What lies at the heart of every living thing is not a fire, nor warm breath, not a 'spark of life,' it is information, words, instructions."[5] "As scientists finally come to understand information they wonder whether it may be primary: more fundamental than matter itself."[6] Imam Mohammed's (RAA) first message to the followers of Honorable Elijah Muhammad was "Words Make People."

This information is composed of words, ideas, and concepts. All physical manifestations begin with a word and proceed from the mind of their *creator*.[7] Thus begins John's version of Christ Jesus (PBUH) story. We should also look at the scheme of domination through hiding this truth. John goes on further saying the Word became flesh and dwelt among us.[8] Under this same analysis, that reading should be seen as saying that the *concept* was brought into *physical manifestation*, not that the Creator of the heavens and earth assumed a physical body.

12:27 "But if it be that his shirt is torn from the back, then is she the liar, and he is telling the truth!"

Chapter 27

We Pray to Cover Our Faults

We are often snared by the appeal to the subconscious. We are also burdened by past memories and hurts or what Imam Mohammed (RAA) once referred to as "plantation ghosts." We are responsible for what we do consciously. We are not responsible for a culture that was imposed on us and we should not keep responding to those spirits. One of the books Imam Mohammed (RAA) recommended to his followers many years ago was *Subliminal Seduction* by Wilson Bryan Key. In this book, Key described how the commercial society sells us many products by bypassing our conscious minds and appealing directly to our subconscious with primal images embedded in advertising. If external forces can influence us through our subconscious, we should be able to direct ourselves the same way. It begins with the words we use and thus Imam Mohammed's earliest lesson was "Words Make People."

Commanding the Subconscious Mind

While our conscious mind may perceive only a small percent of the stimuli to our senses, the subconscious records it all. How powerful would that be if we were able to access all of that information at will? Thinkers and those classified as genius are known to be able to get more information from their subconscious minds than the average person. The ability to take full control of all facets of man's mental being has been an objective of the thinker from the beginning. The power of commanding the subconscious mind starts with the words we use. When we condition our subconscious mind with positive ideas and concepts, we develop a consciousness of success.

Much of what resides in this dark realm of consciousness are things that have been embedded since our early being; childhood and even before. Some are painful experiences that can cause self-sabotage, low self-esteem, bad habits, and a host of other unwanted behaviors. Because these instructions are deeply buried in the subconscious, we often don't even know what is really driving our behavior. We do know this, though. If you want to improve your life, you need to improve the instructions which govern it. Although we like to think of ourselves as independent agents, we're not. Everything we know came from somewhere and we are the ones who decide where we "eat" from. Both prayer and meditation are known to provide a direct line to the subconscious. When you pray, you release a potent spiritual vibration or force. G-d says He gave everything He created something of his *Ruh* or spirit. Through prayer, we unleash a divine energy within and around us that works for and through us producing right attitudes, reactions, and results.

We are obligated first to respect the conscious mind, so in our preparation for prayer, we must first make *Niyat* or intention, so that we know exactly what prayer we are performing. The rituals should present messages to our subconscious mind at the same time. We also must not have our mind confused or obscured with anything. We say in the *athan*, our call to prayer, *Hayya ala salah, Hayya ala falah*, come alive to prayer, come alive to success. Although we commonly understand *hayya ala falah* as *come to success, prosperity and safety both in this life and in the hereafter*, the word *falah*, actually comes from *falaha*, meaning to till the earth – as in cultivation. *Falah* is the farmer. He plants seeds in the dark subconscious (underground) of the earth. "Falah, therefore, consists in the working out of our latent faculties to our best ability, whatever of noble and good hidden in us must come out and whatever is in the form of potentiality in the human mind must be converted into actuality." *Dictionary of the Holy Qur'an.*

What are some of the things that are hidden? Arabic lexicons, such as Edward William Lane's Arabic-English Lexicon, defines jinn not only as spirits, but also anything concealed through time, status, and even physical darkness. *Jinn* derives from the Arabic meaning *to hide* or *be hidden.* Prophet Muhammad (PBUH) said he made his jinn a Muslim.

The subconscious mind can help us solve problems, but we have to trust that it can bring us help from a higher level than the one on which we normally function. This level has been downplayed by psychologists; perhaps because the society wants us to give up control of this realm so they can control it. It was considered to be the lesser part of our consciousness, but since everything we experience is recorded there, we want to have the benefit of that vast storehouse of information. Many creative people, artists, and inventors point out common techniques for accessing this part of the mind. Many recommend rhythmic or repetitive tasks to access this part of us. In Islamic tradition and practice, there is a ritual of devotion known as dhikr, which involves the rhythmic repetition of the Names of G-d, His Attributes, short phrases or prayers, recited silently or aloud. The creative people also stress the need for an ongoing and intense motivation toward solving a particular problem. We have to preserve our interest over a long period of time. Answers and success don't come without patience and persistence. We will sometimes come to a point when we don't have the answer. Then when we are stymied or blocked, the advice is "do something else." Many times when we step away from the problem, we'll find our thoughts clarified, the line of reasoning worked out, and our problem solved. As Gospel artist Donnie McClurkin advises in his song "Stand:" What do you do when you've done all you can… you just stand.

To be effective in reaching the subconscious mind, the conscious mind should not know that a message is being sent. In a way, it is a form of deception. A good demonstration as to how this works in the mental realm is its operation in the physical. Jaden Smith, the son of actors Will and Jada Pinkett Smith, starred in a remake of the classic movie Karate Kid. Just as in the original movie, the young martial arts neophyte wanted to jump directly into the training of various offensive and defensive fighting techniques. The master emphasized that "Kung Fu is life" and the life lesson that the boy needed to learn most was respect for his mother. The entire regimen of his training, therefore, involved him picking up his jacket off the ground, hanging it up, putting it on, and taking it off repetitively. After doing this thousands of times he finally became frustrated with the routine and rebelled.

The master confronted him in fighting mode and the boy realized that the physical routines he had practiced, while not directly related to combat, had actually developed the same muscles and the same skill set required in combat.

12:28 So when he saw his shirt,- that it was torn at the back,- (her husband) said: "Behold! It is a snare of you women! truly, mighty is your snare!"

Chapter 28

There Are Degrees of Guilt

Joseph's (PBUH) master was wise enough to know that when the culture itself has imposed certain circumstances on the people, they should be considered less guilty. The American legal system recognizes degrees of culpability; *misdemeanor* means exactly what the word implies – a "wrong attitude." It's not so serious that it can't be adjusted. The word *felony*, on the other hand, originates from the word meaning "wickedness" or "sin." It is a much more serious offense than a misdemeanor and in most states, punishable by a year or more in prison.

Some of us are guilty of seeking out the wrong. How many times have we heard it said: *'I'm gonna go out and get tore down tonight – wasted,'* or as the popular singer Pharrell Williams sang on his featured appearance on the group Daft Punk's Grammy-winning song, *Get Lucky*: "She's up all night to the sun. I'm up all night to get some. She's up all night for good fun. I'm up all night to get lucky." Allah says, "They make the prayer for wrong instead of good." Then there are some who just slip. Adam (PBUH) slipped but had no firm resolve to sin. Rather he got caught in a snare or trap – interpreted two ways: one, he was not strong enough in his resolution. He was able to function obediently in the simple Garden, the creation before man's rationalizations. But once he evolved intellectually into industry, the world, overwhelmed by Satan's influence was too big for him. Two, he had no strong inclination toward sin – he had been created *hanifa,* "innocent and upright."

Orphans – Motherless Child

Some people are less guilty because they've just been put into bad circumstances through no fault of their own. The orphan, generally speaking, is simply one who is in difficult circumstances. Of course, the more technical definition is a child without parents. We live in a society where there's a disconnect between us and the first mother – nature – and a society moving further and further away from a natural lifestyle. We cannot manifest our intellectual capacity without being connected to mother earth. Allah told the man, Adam (PBUH), "Get you down from here altogether into the earth; there you will find your activities that you are trying to carry on up here and there you will have a situation for the fulfillment of all of your aspirations."[1] G-d created the earth for our comfort – our bodily comforts of course, but more importantly to grow our intellects. It is food for our thoughts and a place to express our spirit. As sounding clay, we were created as a vessel for expression. Subconsciously, we will always express that spirit.

Transplanted and enslaved Africans longed for the mother land, Africa. They found some comfort in the rural south. They sang in the old Negro spiritual: *Sometimes I feel like a motherless child...a long way from home.* As agricultural slaves, we had contact with the earth and nature. We were identified as Uncle Remus because he talked to and gave voice and personality to the animals; also because he was the childish brother (of Romulus) who was killed because he wasn't qualified for the serious business of civilization building. Remus was a man much like Booker T. Washington, who would sit in the forest and learned to emulate the sounds of all the animals in the forest. Washington became an archetype of African American leadership, advocating self-help and racial solidarity. He was a mentor of George Washington Carver who similarly shared a relationship with nature. Carver studied the peanut until it revealed its utility to him. He did the same thing with the earth, which enabled him to revolutionize agriculture. He was also a confidant of Henry Ford and developed other products as a pioneer in the plastics industry. After inventor Thomas Edison died, Henry Ford said Carver had "taken the place of Edison as civilization's greatest inventive genius." Today, history tends to marginalize his contribution as just the "peanut" – a little bitty thing, just as they referred derogatorily to President Jimmy Carter as a peanut farmer.

When you are disconnected from nature, how do you receive the guidance or signs that G-d created in everything? As individuals and as a group, our soul yearns for that reconnection. Our ancestors sang in their song, *When Its Sleepy Time Down South*: "Dear old Southland, with it dreamy song, take me back where I belong, I'll find shelter in my mother's arms." *When it's sleepy time down South* represented the time during slavery where social isolation forced African Americans into a group consciousness. Just as important as the group consciousness is the leadership of the group and that is the father.

Fatherless Child

A truly involved father figure, particularly in today's society, is necessary for a child to have a full life. Children of unmarried mothers of any race are more likely to perform poorly in school, go to prison, use drugs, suffer from poverty, and have their own children out of wedlock. Dr. Natalie Carroll, an obstetrician practicing in Houston, encourages her patients to get married. "The girls don't think they have to get married. I tell them children deserve a mama and a daddy." In the black community, 72% of children were born out of wedlock in 2008, eclipsing that of most other groups: 17% of Asians, 29% of whites, 53% of Hispanics, and 66% of Native Americans. We are handicapping ourselves, on many levels, for generations to come. We should consider the advice offered by Imam Mohammed (RAA) of encouraging our youth to get married when we see that they are experiencing sexual drive toward each other. Then we should help them continue their schooling and develop a foundation in life.

Between the incarcerated, the missing in action, and those on the corner in a substance-induced stupor or on the way to being incarcerated, the African American male is noticeably absent in the community; another strategy of social control.[2] Social service workers will acknowledge how their agencies aggravated that absence by policies to ensure that there were no men, visible or standing in our communities. The social workers used to visit the homes of aid recipients and search the closets and under the beds for men's shoes and clothes. They'd check the size of any men's shoes found and if they were a children's size, you could explain them, but if they were size 11 or 12, you ran the risk of being cut off from assistance. These policies, in addition to chronic unemployment among African American men, succeeded in making black men invisible in their own community. And if we're going to allocate guilt, who is more guilty – the one who finds himself in bad circumstance or the one who helped put him there?

12:29 "O Joseph, pass this over! (O wife), ask forgiveness for thy sin, for truly thou hast been at fault!"

Chapter 29

Forgive and Overlook; Everything Is Not a Battle

Allah's promise is a *Garden of Paradise*--a heavenly state in which he removes any lurking sense or injury or rancor.[1] Since we all want an unburdened heart here on earth too it stands to reason that we can have no peace of mind until we have given one thing in exchange for something else: *"Give-up"* our hurt, pain, and anger *"For"* forgiveness and peace of mind. Without this, there is the lurking sense that we have not received justice. That sense belies the belief in G-d's perfect justice, that dictates whether it is today or in the final accounting, we will not be wronged in the least. In telling Joseph (PBUH) to pass over this, the master is saying, in essence, you cannot realize your own potential if you are going wallow in your past hurts forever. We tell people all the time "you need to let that go." The danger of not letting go is that over time we can develop a victim mentality that manifests itself in a range of different behaviors. It can manifest in the habit of blaming others for situations we have some responsibility for; failing to take responsibility for our own actions; ascribing negative intentions to other people; seeking pity or sympathy and believing that others have been blessed with all of the advantages. Just because he no longer carries the burden of injury in his heart doesn't mean that the society is absolved. In the same ayat, the master is telling the guilty party to pray for his/her own forgiveness.

Whites often respond to African American's real or imagined feelings of oppression with statements like: "I had nothing to do with enslaving your ancestors." What they don't understand is that, just by virtue of their white skin, they have benefitted from American slavery. Many are unaware of how many better-qualified African Americans may have been passed over for jobs they've gotten. Many haven't seen disinvestment in their neighborhoods. Many of them haven't felt the deep-seated scorn and rejection of African Americans. They haven't experienced their sons being stereotyped as violent and angry, thereby precipitating violence against them.[2] They may not know that African Americans with similar and superior income and credit are charged higher interest rates than whites and that excess burden sabotages their children's education and future. They may not know that African American students in U.S. public schools are expelled at 3 times the rate of white students. In some of these so-called zero-tolerance schools and districts, students are expelled for minor infractions such as a young girl expelled for saying "Bless you" out of turn, when another student sneezed. These students enter what some call the *school-to-jail pipeline.* So my response to them is, "I can get over it when you stop doing it."

And then I'd like for you to acknowledge what you've done. My heart is healed because I know that the justice for America's treatment of her once slaves is in G-d's Hands and I see it manifesting every day. But I will never forget. The memory is in my genes and in the collective conscious of the race. I will never let my descendants forget because their ancestors made too many sacrifices and suffered too much for them to have opportunity today. I know though that you cannot move forward in life carrying the burden of your past hurt in your heart, but don't be in denial and lie. Instead of repenting, there is this movement now to re-write history. In Texas and other southern states, textbooks used in schools have completely omitted mention and history of slavery, Jim Crow, lynching or the Ku Klux Klan.Instead, they imply that slaves voluntary migrated to this country to find work. Not only does that delay the necessary healing process, but to distort history and reality to that extent in the classroom sets the stage for raising a whole generation of idiots. I pray to Allah that my children and my people not be among them.

12:30 Ladies said in the City: "The wife of the (great) 'Aziz is seeking to seduce her slave from his (true) self: Truly hath he inspired her with violent love: we see she is evidently going astray."

Chapter 30

To Appreciate the Thing Is to Recognize Its Value

There is a popular line from the Shakespeare's play, *Henry the VI*: "The first thing we do, let's kill all the lawyers."[1] It appears to suggest that the surest way to revolution is killing off the commercial interests and their legal protection and the saying has been used to deride the legal professional. But what it was actually saying was 'let's remove the guardians of the people's liberty.' Indeed, it points to an age-old strategy for domination of the common man. The best way to establish tyranny is to remove the protection of independent thinking.

When they claimed to have crucified Jesus (PBUH), before the crucifixion, they tortured him and mocked him by fashioning a crown of thorns and pressing it onto his head. On many of the depictions today of the crucifixion, you'll see on the cross the letters *INRI*, which means, "Jesus of Nazareth, King of the Jews." The message is 'this is what we do to your kings.' Those thorns pressing into the brain are a perfect metaphor for the killing of any of our brain cells that might present a spark of independent thinking. In the Qur'an, a queen who is commonly identified as Sheba or Bilqis, remarks of Prophet Suleiman's (PBUH) invitation to leave idolatry and submit to the One G-d: "Kings, when they enter a country, despoil it, and make the noblest of its people its meanest thus do they behave." *Holy Qur'an 27:34*

The ones who would dominate human life must first convince the people to distrust good guidance and instead put their confidence in the common run of the society. Today people say: "Everybody's doing it" so consequently it must be alright. We live in an artificial construct that is bad and made to look good and attractive. The things that are good, like rational behavior and clean living, are made to look lame. Long dresses that cover the female body below the knees are ridiculed as *granny clothes.*

The photo above shows the nuns, who taught me at Holy Angels grammar school from grades K through 8—covered heads, arms, and legs. Middle photo are sisters of the MGT (Muslim Girls Training) at the Annual Muslim National Convention, 1970—covered heads, arms, and legs. Today, women who cover themselves, instead of being praised for their decency, are ridiculed and demeaned. Covering their bodies is portrayed as an imprisonment and deprival of their freedom. Yemeni

TawakkulKarman, at the time, the youngest Nobel Peace Winner in 2011, when asked by journalists about her hijab, a head covering used by some Muslim women, and how it was not proportionate with her level of intellect and education, replied, "Man in the early times was almost naked, and as his intellect evolved he started wearing clothes. What I am today and what I'm wearing represents the highest level of thought and civilization that man has achieved, and is not regressive. It's the removal of clothes again that is regressive back to ancient times." Today a growing segment of the public (Muslim women) have chosen to demonstrate that same modesty and reverence by covering their bodies as in the photo below. At the same time a narrow (in numbers and in mind) segment of the public choose to stigmatize and demonize these women. Above photo of nuns at Holy Angels School courtesy of Burke and Dean photographers, CPC_01_C_0243_004, Chicago Photographic Collection, University of Illinois at Chicago Library, Special Collections.; Middle photo by Waliakbar Muhammad, as part of his first assignment as staff photographer for Muhammad Speaks Newspaper's newly opened printing operation at 26th. & Federal in Chicago, Illinois. Bottom photo by Tristan Savatier courtesy of Fotomoto.

The word *niswatun* is translated as *ladies* and is derived from the words *anisa* and *insun*, which imply the *social person.* Some scholars derive the word from *nasiya,* meaning to forsake or forget. Prophet Muhammad (PBUH) said, "Paradise is at the feet of the mother." The Bible too advises: *"Train up a child in the way he should go and, when he is old, he will not depart from it."* G-d emphasizes the importance of the woman, the mother, but this society has made her no more than a sex object. To appreciate a thing, we have to recognize its value and if we want a future for our people, for civilization as whole, we have to appreciate the value of the woman as a foundation of society.

The wife of the Aziz loved Joseph (PBUH). She saw in him the ideal man that all women want to see their sons grow into. But in such a commercial construct she saw more value in him as a commodity than as a spiritually evolved soul. In our society today, much of the social progress this country has made has been in response to the human sensitivity that African Americans have represented and advocated. America and the Founding Father's vision was not a reality during slavery and Jim Crow. It did not begin to manifest until it recognized the human worth of all people, including the country's ex-slaves. But even today, we are viewed as a market—a ready outlet for their goods, services, and ideas. Even immigrants coming to the American dream arrive looking to exploit this market.

We must begin to see ourselves in a better light. We must see ourselves as tomorrow's scientists, artists, educators, adventurers, inventors, and leaders. Even the most commercial mind recognizes the long terms benefits of *good.* The better forces in society want human and social progress. They recognize that all of society's is dignified by the upliftment of any of its members.[2] Our true self is a better self and not one that is a slave to our appetites and emotions. They should serve us like slaves but sometimes the influences in society, particularly in our urbanized environments, seduce us from our true self.[3] The society doesn't expect this kind of authenticity, this sensitivity, in normal human beings. They elevate people like that to saintly or angelic beings. Instead of that characteristic being natural, they see it as abnormal. But perhaps the female recognizes and respects this sensitivity better than the male. This kind of vision is rarely produced from the seats of power so it helps to have that kind of person nearby. Eleanor Roosevelt was well known as the wife of President Franklin Delano Roosevelt and she noted that: "The future belongs to those who believe in the beauty of their dreams."

While President Roosevelt was a pragmatist and politician, Eleanor was seen more so as the moral conscience of the administration. She was a Civil Rights advocate and close friend and confidant to great Civil Rights' icons, Ida B. Wells Barnett, and Mary McLeod Bethune. Mrs. Roosevelt, along with Secretary of the Interior, Harold Ickes, was responsible for the great African American contralto singer Marian Anderson's Easter Sunday appearance on the steps of the Lincoln Memorial before an audience of 75,000 on April 9, 1939. Ickes was a visionary, too. Introducing Anderson, he said, "In this great auditorium under the sky, all of us are free. When G-d gave us this wonderful outdoors, and the sun, the moon and the stars, he made no distinction of race, or creed or color." Anderson had sought to appear at the Daughters of the American Revolution-owned Hall, but a clause in its contracts restricted the Hall to "a concert by white artists only, and for no other purpose."

It was in large part Eleanor Roosevelt's courage that brought about a higher social consciousness in the administration of President Roosevelt. Her belief was "You gain strength, courage, and confidence by every experience in which you really stop to look fear in the face. You must do the thing which you think you cannot do." But the leadership did not feel the country was ready for her kind of human sensitivity and the African American continued in restricted circumstances "for a time."

12:31 When she heard of their malicious talk, she sent for them and prepared a banquet for them: she gave each of them a knife: and she said (to Joseph), "Come out before them." When they saw him, they did extol him, and (in their amazement) cut their hands: they said, "Allah preserve us! no mortal is this! this is none other than a noble angel!"

Chapter 31

They're Not Standing on Anything

It is easy for us to invite other negative influences into our lives once we open the door. The ladies malicious talk was gossip, which circulates just like any other troublesome social currents. The saying "birds of a feather flock together" speaks to the belief that if you entertain fearful thoughts, they will invite doubtful thoughts to feast off of and devour the good thinking in your mind. The influences and attitudes that are corrupt (malicious talk) can be curtailed when they see the image of the ideal man. We all need examples we can identify with. The ladies extol Joseph's (PBUH) beauty and cut their hands or curtailed their deeds.[1] When you cut your hand, you bleed and bleeding is a break in the circulatory system. Memory is made up of circuits constantly connecting via chemical and nervous reactions and those more emotionally charged or memorable events form habitual circuits of travel. Thus, we can curtail such influences by way of the natural functioning of the brain. By consciously breaking the circuit (cycle) of those memories, influences, attitudes or reactions that produce negative responses we can interrupt (short circuit) those responses by remembering the image of that noble *angel*—the positive image of the ideal mind.[2] This causes new grooves and circuits to be formed.[3]

Jesus (PBUH) described the magnetism that we see in Joseph (PBUH) with his words "Lift me up and I will draw all men to myself."[4] Dr. Catherine Ponder, in "The Dynamic Laws of Prosperity," suggests an affirmation that accesses this attractiveness or magnetism. She wrote: "I am an irresistible magnet, with the power to attract unto myself everything that I divinely desire, according to the thoughts, feelings, and mental pictures I constantly entertain and radiate. I am the center of my Universe! I have the power to create whatever I wish. I attract whatever I radiate. I attract whatever I mentally choose and accept, I begin choosing and mentally accepting the highest and best in life. I now choose and accept health, success, and happiness. I now choose lavish abundance for myself and for all humankind. This is a rich, friendly Universe and I dare to accept its riches, its hospitality, and to enjoy them now."

This reminds us that not only is this great friendly Universe, ready and anxious to serve our needs, but there are dimensions of this same system we don't see that will come to our service. The angels and all the forces of nature are operating all the time and can assist us and operate on our behalf. We just have to believe in the power of these unseen forces.[5]

It was the ladies *niswatun* in the city that saw him as a noble angel *(malakun karim)*. They saw that kind of moral purity and beauty as being on the level of an angel. Of course, we can be *angelic* in our behavior because we have all the properties of every creature below us, plus a potential spirit that will place us above the angels.[6] But they see this beauty as a separate class of being; so holy that they levitate inches above the ground when they walk. Sometimes they get so holy that they float many feet above Earth and acquire halos. Their feet never get dirty and don't touch the ground, so you can't see what they're standing on. That's the vision of holiness when you come from that kind of society.[7] Notice it wasn't the men who saw him like that. The thinking minds (men) are looking for rational bases for things. They want to know what he's standing on. They want understanding.

We are meant to get our feet dirty. There's a saying about work that you're not working if you're not getting your hands dirty. Similarly, you're not walking on the horizontal path in the material earth if you're not getting your feet dirty, so washing the feet is part of our ablution *(wudu)* ritual. Jesus (PBUH) told his disciples to wash each other's feet and he showed them how to do it by washing theirs.[8] First, we have to clean up the disciplines that we stand on and fulfill the need for establishment, then we can clean up the influences in society.

12:32 She said: "There before you is the man about whom ye did blame me! I did seek to seduce him from his (true) self but he did firmly save himself guiltless and now, if he doth not my bidding, he shall certainly be cast into prison, and (what is more) be of the company of the vilest!"

Chapter 32

A Continuum from Restricted Life to Superman

Social Controls

We should look at prison not only as a literal experience of confinement but also as a metaphor for broader mechanisms of social control. Once these mechanisms have been applied, they can become pathological and the controlling agent doesn't even have to exercise direct influence at all. They can throw up their hands and point to the apparent free will of the victims. They can also wash their hands and insist they had nothing to do with our condition. In the Gospel of Matthew,[1] Pontius Pilate, the fifth prefect of the Roman province of Judaea, when Jesus (PBUH) is brought to trial before him, washes his hands to show that he is not responsible for the execution of Jesus (PBUH) and reluctantly sends him to his death.

The Aziz's wife threatened to imprison Joseph (PBUH) with the vilest offenders, what we see today as inmates of "super-max" prisons, but when the men decided to confine him, he ended up in prison with the elite – the king's servants. In fiscal year 2010, the Illinois Department of Corrections (IDOC) spent nearly $1.2 billion in prison expenditures with an additional $566.1 million spent in prison-related costs outside the department's budget.[2] The average annual cost per inmate is $38,268. Michigan spends $35,000 a year to keep one inmate in prison, which is more than the cost of educating a University of Michigan student. The 50 states and the federal government spend $69 billion a year to house over two million prisoners, with a significant number of these inmates charged with minor drug offenses. In the general population, substance abuse accounts for more deaths than aids, breast cancer, and traffic accidents combined. Moreover, many of the other criminal offenses resulting in incarceration are drug related. Although only 12-13% of the American population is African American, they make up 40% of the almost 2.1 million male inmates in jail or prison (U.S. Department of Justice, 2009). Since the incarcerated have no voting rights, limited job potential, and economic mobility, it's obvious they pose no threat or competition to leadership in the society as a whole.

Former Attorney General Eric Holder endorsed a plan to reduce sentences for certain drug offenses, which he says could reduce the federal prison population by more than 6,500 inmates in five years. Recently, it was reported that prison reform might one of the few issues that the Republican Congress and President Obama may be able to pass in his last year in office. The United States is home to 4.4% of the world's general population but houses 22% of the world's prisoners. This points either to a higher level of criminality among Americans or the use of prison as a mechanism for social control. In order to garner broad support for his initiative, the attorney general presented the economic implications of widespread incarceration. He noted, "This overreliance on incarceration is not just financially unsustainable, it comes with human and moral costs that are impossible to calculate."

"An exorbitant amount of money is dedicated to incarcerating people," said Nancy La Vigne, director of the Justice Policy Center at the Urban Institute. "There are ways you can go about reducing the number of people incarcerated. The best way to help them successfully integrate into society and become independent, law-abiding citizens is to make sure they get a job."

Michigan has been able to trim their prison population by about 15% over the last four years, yielding more than $200 million in annual savings. Analysts say many prison systems could do the same thing, but the prevailing economic model favors incarceration over re-entry programs, substance abuse treatment, and job training. What is not addressed is the moral component—a realistic view of how we fall into criminality in the first place. [3] There is an impressive list of people that survived prison to become great leaders: Mahatma Gandhi, Anwar Sadat, Dr. Martin Luther King, Jr. Malcolm X, Honorable Elijah Muhammad, and Imam W. Deen Mohammed (RAA), among others. Prison does not necessarily have to become a lifelong handicap. In fact, sometimes confinement can help us figure out our path to destiny. But if we must face prison it should be because of standing on right and righteousness and not because of a moral breakdown.

12:33 He said: "O my Lord! the prison is more to my liking than that to which they invite me: Unless Thou turn away their snare from me, I should (in my youthful folly) feel inclined towards them and join the ranks of the ignorant."

Chapter 33

Why Bad Things Happen to Good People

Like Egypt and America, the Nation of Islam was established as a container – a womb or social construct for the magnification and projection of power. In this container, individual components and ingredients were ingested into a womb that provided energy for an economic engine. As a womb, there was also protection and restriction. We voluntarily accepted those restrictions, as we were taught, "the restricted laws of Islam are our success." The protection was against the cultural influences of the outer society. When we stepped outside that womb we lost our protection. Imam Mohammed (RAA) reminded many older Muslims that Honorable Elijah Muhammad used an identification card that was given to all members of the Nation of Islam and that identification card said if the police arrested a Muslim, a member of the Nation of Islam, "this bearer of this card is a righteous Muslim. If the bearer of this card is found otherwise, take this card from him and punish him."[1]

Joseph (PBUH) recognized that there was a greater imprisonment in being confined and restricted by the whims and fads of a corrupt society than accepting the voluntary restrictions, more to his liking, of righteous discipline. There is a restriction of the development of our own soul when we give freedom to the urges that bring it down.[2] Prison should be seen, not only as the restriction of personal freedom but also the restriction of personal abilities and capacities. Allah says he does not want to give us difficulty but to purify us.[3] The greater our destiny, the stronger we must be and we gain this strength by struggling over obstacles.[4,5]

For some, prison forces a look within. Dr. Martin Luther King expressed in his *Letter from a Birmingham Jail* that he might need to turn his faith to the inner spiritual church, the church within the church.

Anwar Sadat, in what the late Stephen R. Covey describes in his book, *The Seven Habits of Highly Successful People*, as a "rescripting process" evolved his thinking toward Israel while in prison and later was able to initiate a peace agreement with Israel. Nelson Mandela, the first South African president to be elected in a fully representative democratic election was an anti-apartheid activist and the leader of the armed wing of the African National Congress (ANC). From an early age, Mandela was exposed both to prosperity and learning, but much of his lessons were obtained by listening and watching. He observed Chief Jongintaba, the regent of the Thembu people, lead the people. He sat in the council meetings that were held to discuss new edicts issued by the British magistrate, property disputes, and other matters important to the tribe. All male members, whatever their station or rank, were free to attend and speak. Mandela listened as some made succinct arguments and others rambled. He noted how some sought to appeal to intellect and others to emotion. In 1962, he was arrested and convicted of sabotage and other charges and sentenced to life in prison. He served 27 years in prison, many of those on the notorious Robben Island. Following his release in 1990, Mandela led his party in the negotiations that led to multi-racial democracy in 1994 and his election as South Africa's President.

In a 2011 interview with National Public Radio, Lee Myung-bak, former President of South Korea, tells of his crushing poverty as a child. He was taught never to seek handouts and was primarily responsible for establishing Hyundai into a global giant. He describes his imprisonment during his years of student activism as a "time of both physical and spiritual renewal." Why is it that these great men had to endure such hardship in order to realize their human potential? G-d allows us to endure these things because these circumstances strengthen us, purify us and prepare us for our destiny.

12:34 So his Lord hearkened to him (in his prayer), and turned away from him their snare: Verily He heareth and knoweth (all things).

Chapter 34

Take One Step Toward G-d and He Takes Two Steps Toward You

It is said if you take one step toward G-d, He takes two steps toward you. Joseph (PBUH), responding to his upright nature, made that step, indeed many steps, in fleeing from temptation. G-d's steps toward him were rewarding his uprightness with an even higher level of conscience development. What are these levels of development? Note 5810 referencing Sura 75, Al-Qiyamat, Verse 2, of Yusuf Ali Qur'an translation describe them:

Our doctors postulate three states or stages of the development of the human soul: (1) Ammara (xii. 53), which is prone to evil, and if not checked and controlled, will lead to perdition; (2) Lawwama, as here, which feels conscious of evil, and resists it, asks for Allah's grace and pardon after repentance and tries to amend; it hopes to reach salvation; (3) Mutmainna (lxxxix 27), the highest stage of all, when it achieves full rest and satisfaction."

Imam W. Deen Mohammed (RAA) also noted how the three sons of Noah are symbolic of the three Nafs, spirits or aspects of the soul/features of human nature.[1] *Mutmainna* is when we have arrived in the promised garden of fulfillment of our aspirations. W. D. Fard called for laborers in his work and taught "there's a wide open field for the wide awake man to work out in." Allah (G-d) says He will give us a field to work in whose width is the heavens and the earth.[2] If we could travel to the edge of the known universe and look out past what we might think is its edge, we would see more of the same universe. And yet we know that it is created matter so it has a limit. It had a beginning and an ending. The universe looks like it is unlimited and this tells us that our potential is limited only by depth of our own perception. Our destiny is to compete on the world stage materially and intellectually, but also the garden of spiritual consciousness. Allah says when we enter, we will be pleasing to him and pleased with ourselves.[3] If you wonder why some African Americans' behavior is sometimes regressive and self-destructive, it is because, in our very soul, we know we are not measuring up to our potential and thus are not pleased with ourselves or pleasing to G-d.

12:35 Then it occurred to the men, after they had seen the signs, (that it was best) to imprison him for a time.

Chapter 35

Let's Restrict Their Potential for A While

Modern Uses of Incarceration

We don't just limit ourselves; we get a lot of help from a sometimes hostile society in restricting our potential. The United States has the highest documented incarceration rate in the world. The prison population grew by 700% from 1970 to 2005, a rate that is outpacing crime and population rates. About 2 million Americans currently live behind bars in jails, state prisons, and federal penitentiaries, with millions more on or having been on parole or probation. The incarceration rates disproportionately impact men of color. African Americans make up only 13% of the total U.S. population, but comprise half of all prisoners.[1] 1 in every 15 African American men and 1 in every 36 Hispanic men are incarcerated in comparison to 1 in every 106 white men.[2] In recent decades, the U.S. has experienced a surge in its prison population, quadrupling since 1980, partially as a result of mandatory sentencing that came about during the "war on drugs." It is just recently that both political parties are beginning to take a look at criminal justice reform.

Most African Americans will suffer life-long social and economic restriction by having a felony conviction on their record. In *The New Jim Crow: Mass Incarceration in the Age of Colorblindness* (Washington Journal interview) Michelle Alexander said: "Once labeled a felon, you can be subjected to all forms of discrimination that once applied to African Americans during the Jim Crow era. You may be denied the right to vote, you're automatically excluded from juries, and you're legally discriminated against in employment, housing, access to education, and public benefits, relegated to a second-class status much like your parents or grandparents may have been."

There is another side of this phenomena that we must address also and that it the reality of black on black crime within our own communities. At the annual convention of the NAACP in 2016, Former President Bill Clinton, while campaigning for his wife's Democratic nomination campaign for President, apologized for signing the Violent Crime Control and Law Enforcement Act in 1994, which had a devastating impact on African American incarceration rates. "I signed a bill that made the problem worse. And I want to admit it... In that bill, there were longer sentences, and most of these people are in prison under state law, but the federal law set a trend. And that was overdone; we were wrong about that."

That did not satisfy many in the Black Lives Matter movement who confronted the former President on the campaign trail. At an April 7, rally, he engaged protestors and addressed his wife's 1996 characterization of some criminals as super-predators.

"I don't know how you would characterize the gang leaders who got 13-year-old kids hopped up on crack, sent them out onto the street to murder other African-American children," Clinton said. "Maybe you thought they were good citizens. She didn't. You are defending the people who kill the lives you say matter. Tell the truth. You are defending the people who cause young people to go out and take guns." If unfortunate that our own leaders often do not have the courage to tell us the cold hard truths about accepting some responsibility for our own actions and our own communities.

Innocents Incarcerated

More oppressive than those legitimately imprisoned is the significant number of incarcerated that are innocent or imprisoned for minor and non-violent offenses. The New York Times reported on September 17, 2010, the latest in a long line of cases in which innocent defendants have been exonerated after spending decades in prison. Philip Bivens, 59 and Bobby Ray Dixon, 53, were serving life sentences for a rape that was later found to have been committed by another man. Larry Ruffin, who was convicted with them, died in prison eight years ago. The

Innocence Project of New Orleans pressed for the men's release after examining the forced confessions and lack of evidence. No one knows how many other innocent men have been killed and have languished and died in prison for crimes they did not commit.

Many cases in the south are well known, where officials knew they had arrested the wrong person but insisted on going to get them 'some nigger, any nigger' to atone for the crime. In the north, the same scenarios are still taking place. Former Illinois Governor George Ryan made a courageous moral decision in 2003 and commuted the sentences of 167 death row prisoners due to what he described as "the demon of error" in the capital punishment system. He was prompted by numerous cases of Illinois death row inmates being exonerated and reports of widespread prosecutorial and police misconduct.

In Chicago, former Police Commander Jon Burge was implicated in dozens of cases where confessions were obtained by torture. Burge was convicted in January 2011, not for the torture itself, but for lying about it under oath in another case. Recent DNA testing has proven the innocence of 10 men from Cook County, Illinois who were forced to confess as children to crimes they didn't commit. Some of them have been imprisoned for nearly 20 years. Despite the overwhelming genetic evidence, which has linked the crime to the real killers, state officials have refused to recognize their innocence. In September 2010, another one of Burge's innocent victims walked free at 39-years-old after 20 years of imprisonment. "Victor Staffold said he confessed to two murders only because he was tortured by...Burge's underlings"[3]

In New York, Jonathan Fleming was exonerated of murder after almost 25 years behind bars. Fleming was on a family vacation in Disney World when a friend was shot dead in Brooklyn in 1989. Prosecutors had evidence proving his innocence but failed to present it. Fleming is among more than 1,350 inmates exonerated nationwide in the last 25 years. Most of them face challenges adjusting to life. There are children they have never met, children who themselves are incarcerated because they had no male figure in their lives. Many have outlived their families, and many others have had their families die while they were in an environment where they could not show emotions such as grief. As hard as it is for us to adjust to a rapidly changing world, it's a whole new world on the outside for them.

This harsh regime effects all age groups. While the U. S. is critical of the criminal justice system in many palaces in the world, it also has the harshest punishment regime for children in the world. In 2012, 79 youth under 14 were serving life imprisonment terms without possibility of parole. And the percentage of these youth imprisoned for killing a white is twice that for the killing of an African American.

Debtors' Prison

An October 2010 report by the American Civil Liberties Union (ACLU), The Rise of America's New Debtors' Prisons revealed that courts across the United States routinely disregard the protections and principles the Supreme Court established in *Bearden v. Georgia* over 20 years ago. In the wake of the recent fiscal crises, states and counties now collect legal debts more aggressively from men and women who have already served their criminal sentences, regardless of whether they are able to pay these debts. In the report, *In For A Penny: The Rise of America's New Debtors' Prisons*, the ACLU presents the results of its yearlong investigation into our modern-day "debtors' prisons." The report shows how, day after day, indigent defendants are imprisoned for failing to pay legal debts they can never hope to manage. In many cases, poor men and women end up jailed or threatened with jail though they have no lawyer representing them. These sentences are illegal, create hardships for men and women who already struggle with re-entering society after being released from prison or jail, and waste resources in an often fruitless effort to extract payments from defendants who may be homeless, unemployed, or simply too poor to pay.

Incarceration as a Path to Lifelong Poverty

There are many reasons for the churning incarcerations. Colorlines, the publisher of the Applied Research Center, explained in its 2009 "Race and Recession" report, one big problem is that ex-offenders struggle to get a fair shake in the job market. That's particularly true for African Americans. Bill Quigley, Legal Director for the Center for Constitutional Rights, broke down the numbers in a 2010 Huffington Post essay. "Even when released from prison, race continues to dominate," Quigley wrote, "17% of white job applicants with criminal records received call backs from employers while only 5% of black job applicants with criminal records received call backs."

In an October 8, 2010, article entitled *Toxic Persons*, Sasha Abramsky detailed new research that shows precisely how the prison-to-poverty cycle does its damage. "Forty years after the United States began its experimentation with mass incarceration policies, the country is increasingly divided economically. In new research published in the review Daedalus, a group of leading criminologists coordinated by the American Academy of Arts and Sciences argued that much of that growing inequality is linked to the increasingly widespread use of prisons and jails. "In devastating detail in Daedalus, the sociologists Bruce Western of Harvard and Becky Pettit of the University of Washington have shown how poverty creates prisoners and how prisons in turn fuel poverty; not just for individuals but for entire demographic groups. Crunching the numbers, they concluded that once a person has been incarcerated, the experience limits their earning power and their ability to climb out of poverty even decades after their release. It's a vicious feedback loop that is affecting an ever-greater percentage of the adult population and shredding part of the fabric of the 21st century American society."

"In 1980, one in 10 black high-school dropouts were incarcerated. By 2008, that number was 37 percent. Western and Pettit calculated that if current incarceration trends hold, fully 68 percent of African American male high school dropouts born from 1975 to 1979 (at the start of the upward trend in incarceration rates) will spend time living in prison at some point in their lives." Slate's Timothy Noah provides startling statistics in "The United States of Inequality" and points out that the income inequality here exceeds that of many so-called developing countries such as Venezuela, Nicaragua, and Guyana. He noted, "The main difference is that the United States is big enough to maintain geographic distance between the villa-dweller and the beggar."

From Poverty to Depression

While the link between poverty and incarceration may be clear, the connection between poverty and even more social and emotional problems should be explored. In evidence of a troubling cycle, more than half of babies in poverty are being raised by mothers who show symptoms of mild to severe depression, potentially creating problems in parenting and in child development, according to a new study which links poverty to depression among mothers.[4] In what was described as the first detailed portrait of its kind, researchers reported that 1 in

9 infants in poverty had a mother with severe depression; typically breastfeeding their children for shorter periods than other mothers who were poor.

"A mom who is too sad to get up in the morning won't be able to take care of all of her child's practical needs," said researcher Olivia Golden, who co-authored the paper with two colleagues at the district-based Urban Institute. "She is not able to take joy in her child, talk baby talk, play with the child - those are features of parenting that brain development research has told us contribute to babies' and toddlers' successful development." The study said that even severe depression goes largely untreated among low-income mothers of infants, with just 30% speaking to a professional about their mental health problems during the year, before the survey was conducted. Thus, the wisdom of Prophet Muhammad's (PBUH) words is clear, "If you help a woman, you help many." Moreover, his advice to help your mother goes beyond the need to support our biological mother but points to the need to protect and maintain the woman and society as a whole.[5]

12:36 Now with him there came into the prison two young men. Said one of them: "I see myself (in a dream) pressing wine." said the other: "I see myself (in a dream) carrying bread on my head, and birds are eating, thereof." "Tell us" (they said) "The truth and meaning thereof: for we see thou art one that doth good (to all)."

Chapter 36

I in You and You in Me

Self-image refers to both a conscious and subconscious way of how we see ourselves. It is an emotional judgment we make about our self-worth. Most people form their self-image through interaction with others, taking into account their reactions to them and the ways they categorize them. Yet Allah asks us to consider the inherent value that He put into His human creature.

Bread

We have two fellow inmates of Joseph: one is a person with knowledge (bread) on his head instead of in his head where his life and behavior would be influenced by it; the other is the person with difficult circumstances but still manages to extract spiritual lessons from them.

Bread and its symbolism have very ancient origins. It is among the most popular foods in the world and occupies an important place in almost every culture. In the East, it is the primary diet; other articles of food being merely accessory. In the West, meat and other things chiefly constitute the meal and the bread is secondary. It has exceptional nutritional value and as a nearly perfect product for human nourishment, it can be consumed by itself. In today's culture *bread* is a colloquialism for money, but it has always been used to refer to something valuable or necessary to life. The production of bread and farming, in general, had a profound effect on the religious beliefs of agricultural communities and the symbolism of wheat is deeply associated with the symbolism of bread. Since the Neolithic period, mythology and ritual representation have tended to be identified with plant life because the mystery of human birth and death was, in many respects, similar to the life cycle of plants. Allah says in the Qur'an, "we created man as a plant."[1]

Grown in Mesopotamia and Egypt, wheat was likely chewed before anyone discovered that it could be pulverized and made into a paste. Set over a fire, the paste hardened into a flat bread that kept for several days. It did not take much of a leap to discover leavened (raised) bread when yeast was accidentally introduced to the paste. The growth of settlements, which ethnologists refer to as the "great turning point for humanity" was indirectly inspired by the search for bread and helped to define social and economic institutions (the growth of property rights, the use of wheat as a form of exchange value, and so on). Planting and harvesting, as well as the events that endanger crops (flood, drought), were key events in agricultural life.

Bread and wine were used to represent abstract ideas and concept at times when the majority of ordinary people were not able to read or write and printing was unknown. Early in scripture bread is used as a symbol for a body of knowledge or the word of G-d.[2] Jesus (PBUH) is reported to have said: "Take this bread in remembrance of me, my body" and this symbolism is continued throughout the New Testament.[3] The New Testament's lord's prayer request of G-d to "Give us this day our daily bread" means not merely loaves, but truth and knowledge-the sustenance for spirit, mind and body.[4] I understand this sustenance (substance) to also mean the essence and reality of things – that which stands under or forms the foundation of things.

Unleavened bread is that made without yeast or leavening. If bread represents a body of truth in its sincerity, then what is the leavening? It is blowing up the bread with air, making it bigger than the reality of its substance. We have an old expression to describe when someone is exaggerating, perhaps not to the level of lying but blowing something up bigger than it really is and that is "putting yeast in it" or "yeasting it up."

Why now, in the bakers dream, is bread stuck on his head instead of it being distributed to the hungry. We find this metaphor of feeding bread to the poor prevalent in scripture. Prophet Muhammad (PBUH) is reported to have told the early companions, as soon as you learn and understand and are able to apply One Line, go and inform another one of that. He didn't tell them to wait until you know the whole Book. He didn't even have the whole book revealed to him at that time. He didn't tell them to wait until you've become a scholar. Allah condemns selfish and greedy people who hoard knowledge because they want to stand over others and dominate them, especially religious people who hide the substance of the word or only give the people a child-like or watered-down version of it.

Wine

Wine and other alcohols are also referred to as spirits. Catholic doctrine accepts the concept of "transubstantiation," which means by the blessing said over the bread and wine it actually turns into the body and blood of Jesus (PBUH). Most Protestant groups believe the bread and wine are not actually changed, but rather a symbol of Jesus' (PBUH) body and blood. National Public Radio's Fresh Air host Terry Gross interviewed Seth McFarland (creator of animated comedy TV shows Family Guy, American Dad, and the Cleveland Show) who recalled how, even at a young age, he was confounded by the dichotomy of the concept. "I would go to church on Sundays," he said. "I was weirdly fascinated by the communion ceremony; there was something about it that just struck me as so odd. I remember turning to my mom and saying O My God, they said they're drinking blood. Is that really blood? That's disgusting! She said, 'oh, no, no, that's wine.' There's just something bizarre about that ceremony."

Christian writer, Charles Fillmore provides a much more rational interpretation of this metaphysical process. "The wine of life or vitality of the organism, must be available in large quantities before a blending of thoughts or of soul and body (wedding) can be made successfully. When the new Christ life comes into a mind, where old beliefs concerning the body have been held, the body is transformed into its innate spiritual perfection." *Revealing Word, Charles Fillmore.*

We should try to read, even Christian Scripture, in light of rational human life and in light of the corrective prescription of the Qur'an.

Jesus (PBUH) is reported to have said: "14:20 At that day you will know that I *am* in My Father, and you in Me, and I in you. 14:21 He who has My commandments and keeps them, it is he who loves Me. And he who loves Me will be loved by My Father, and I will love him and manifest Myself to him." *John 14:20-21* We know that Jesus (PBUH) never taught of a Godhead of which he was part and he always made the distinction between himself as creation and G-d as Creator. What he is saying here is the same thing that was taught later by Prophet Muhammad (PBUH). "*I am in my Father*" is simply saying that I am still in that excellent mold that G-d created me in-[5] that body of knowledge and that spirit that forms me. "*You in me,*" tells us that your human make-up is the same as mine. "*I in you,*" says that the same potential for this excellence that is in me is also in you. You have the same capacity as I do to accept that divine knowledge and spirit. *Whoever has my commandments and observes them is the one who loves me; and whoever loves me will be loved by my Father.* This humanness of the prophets has historically been a basis for their rejection by disbelievers. The chiefs of the Unbelievers among Prophet Muhammad's (PBUH) people said, "We see (in) thee nothing but a man like ourselves."[6] The Prophet said in the hadith of Anas, "Whoever loves me will be with me in the Garden." He also said, "No, by him in whose hand my soul is, (you will not have complete faith) till I am dearer to you than your own self." *Bukhari Volume 008, Book 078, Hadith Number 628.*

Wine in popular interpretations is narrowly seen as spirit– emotional content just designed to give us a momentary happy feeling. Wine is pressed or extracted from grapes. In the ancient world, one type of wine press was a large basin where men would hold onto ropes above them and stomp the grapes. "They press the grapes with their feet (soul) to get the juice (juz- is also one of thirty parts of equal length into which the Quran is sometimes divided)." The juice would run into containers on the sides of the large basins. The same pressing that produces the wine is the same struggling that will give us freedom and life, even from difficult circumstances. Joseph (PBUH) was required to extract the benefits from whatever situation he found himself in and we are required to do the same.

'Asara' means to press, squeeze, wring, withdraw a thing from, thus, we have here the word 'asiru' meaning 'I am pressing' and *'asr'* meaning juice. From the same root, we get the word *'Asr,* which bears

the connotation of "the passing of time or time that can never be recaptured.[7]

The use of intoxicants is forbidden in Islam and we know that their use and sale has caused innumerable deaths, broken families, and broken lives. But there are distillers, grape growers, and distributors making so much money that the society will not forbid it. We have to oppose it, first by not drinking or using intoxicants ourselves and second by not being anywhere in that chain of commerce. Though use of wine is haram, understanding its origin enables us to make the best of a bad situation. The Baker's destiny was death while the wine presser survived. The wine presser was the one who, regardless of the circumstances, was able to press on, persevere, and squeeze the benefit out of whatever situation he found himself in. This is a mindset within us all that we have to recognize and embrace.

In reality, most people in society today are on something. It may be an illegal or legal substance; it may be an extreme emotional ride or it may be an ego trip. Any of these, however, takes us out of our rational minds. It is in our nature to survive but we allow things to take us out of that nature and we entertain fear, doubt, and uncertainty. However we see ourselves is our reality and is guaranteed to come to pass. The Bible notes: "that which I have feared, desired or either fixated on will eventually materialize."[8] Man has the power to control his own thinking. Allah says when a thought from Satan attacks our mind, bring Allah to mind and we'll see right. Norman Vincent Peale, in *A Guide to Confident Living*, notes that we can't govern the thoughts that come into our minds, just as the inmate baker couldn't control the birds flying over his head. But Peale also noted an old saying, "You cannot keep the birds from flying over your head, but you can keep them from building nests in your hair."

Vine

Grapes, from which wine is made, grow on a vine, which also represents the archetypical symbol of social connections. i.e. *I heard it through the grapevine.* This meaning may be even more significant in this modern era of social networking–the vine being recognized as a botanical organism that grows its fruit from common roots and not individual roots as many plants do. It points to a natural dynamic in the popular culture. The grape vine also was used in the Old Testament as a symbol of Israel and as a symbol of blessing and fertility. The Celtic meaning of the vine in druid lore is ripe with the same symbolism such as regeneration, continuation, opportunity, connection, expansion, fertility and bounty. In the Druid perspective, the vine earned its symbolism from its growth patterns. They recognized the vine grows opportunistically and would dig in wherever feasible in order to gain a strong foothold to assure its own growth. This is a powerful metaphor of *going with the flow* or *growing where you are planted*. In other words, it is a message that when we observe the best of our environment/situation and stay in a relaxed, flowing state of mind, we will likely gain our highest advantage.[9] In a negative context, the vine can also represent the ego trying to rise on someone else's back.

Goodness

Even the fellow inmates acknowledge that Joseph (PBUH) is one who does good. This goodness is inherent in the human being, whose destiny is to rise and prevail. Ibn Kathir, in a report about the Prophet's (PBUH) Night Journey, says: "I passed by Joseph and he had been given half the goodness." What is the nature of this goodness? Addressing the topic *Goodness is on the rise*, Imam Mohammed (RAA) pointed to the example of then presidential candidate, Barack Obama. He said, "what he has done to sensitize African Americans, Hispanics, poor Whites, rich people, everybody high and low cannot be erased or removed. Allah has enthused into the human world a power pack of energy for renewing this whole planet. Whether you want it or not, you are going to get better because of the rise of Barack Obama. Whether you want it or not, you are going to become a better human being." He also said that Obama represents the Hajj and we understand the Hajj to be symbolic of the coming together of all people as one human family.

This is part of the address of President Barack Obama to the Muslim world on June 4, 2009, from the Major Reception Hall at Cairo University in Egypt. Speaking of the conflict and the tensions that were created by the 911 attacks and the subsequent military conflicts, he said in part:

"Violent extremists have exploited these tensions in a small but potent minority of Muslims. The attacks of September 11th, 2001 and the continued efforts of these extremists to engage in violence against civilians has led some in my country to view Islam as inevitably hostile not only to America and Western countries, but also to human rights.

This has bred more fear and mistrust. So long as our relationship is defined by our differences, we will empower those who sow hatred rather than peace and who promote conflict rather than the cooperation that can help all of our people achieve justice and prosperity. This cycle of suspicion and discord must end. I have come here to seek a new beginning between the United States and Muslims around the world; one based upon mutual interest and mutual respect; and one based upon the truth that America and Islam are not exclusive and need not be in competition. Instead they overlap and share common principles – principles of justice and progress; tolerance and the dignity of all human beings." He reminded us of G-d's words, in the Qur'an: "Be conscious of God and speak always the truth."

The U.S. government has gone to court to protect religious accommodations for Muslims and to punish those who would deny it. There should be no doubt that Islam is a part of America. I believe that America holds within her, the truth that, regardless of race, religion or station in life, all of us share common aspirations: to live in peace and security; to get an education; to work with dignity; and to love our families, our communities, and our G-d. This is the hope of all humanity. Many of us have reservations about lifting the President up so high and consequently lifting our expectations beyond his ability to deliver. This is of particular concern after his election when we saw conservative, right wing, neo-conservative, neo-liberals and Islamophobic forces aligned against any progress he would like to make. And we have seen him make, what I would describe as politically expedient decisions such as the recognition of same-sex marriages. But he is still a politician and he is the President of all people of the United States not just the G-d conscious.

Imam Mohammed (RAA) made the point in an address that it was not he, Imam Mohammed (RAA), who was lifting Obama up. He said: "Allah has lifted him up that high." Scripture says, "As one man is falling who thought he could go it on his own, making decisions by himself, brought all of us down and causing all of us to lose sight on G-d's Plan in our lives, so will one man coming back into his innocent nature, and speaking from and acting from his innocent nature, can cause all of us to rise again." *Imam W. Deen Mohammed (RAA), First Sunday Address, May 4, 2008.* Imam Mohammed (RAA) was such a man and so is Barack Obama.

12:37 He said: "Before any food comes (in due course) to feed either of you, I will surely reveal to you the truth and meaning of this ere it befall you: that is part of the (duty) which my Lord hath taught me. I have (I assure you) abandoned the ways of a people that believe not in Allah and that (even) deny the Hereafter."

Chapter 37

Eating Ourselves to Death

Symbolically, food is whatever we put into our minds, our hearts, or our consciousness as well as our body. Joseph (PBUH) put knowledge and spiritual food before the inmates feeding their bodies. It is reminiscent of his father Jacob (PBUH), who in the biblical account tricked his brother out of his birthright because of Esau's obsession with satisfying his physical (creature comfort) needs. This indulgence of our material appetites extends to the diet. In May 2012, David Brown reported on a study published in the *American Journal of Preventive Medicine* that said a third of Americans were obese and it is projected that by 2030 that number will rise to 42%. Obesity- related ailments – diabetes, heart disease, and kidney failure – consume at least 9% of healthcare spending in the United States. We are urged by Prophet Muhammad (PBUH) to take care against sickness while we are healthy[1], but unfortunately, most of us procrastinate until we get sick and then are unable to help ourselves.

Procrastination

An important principle that many of us neglect when we are seeking our success is overcoming procrastination – putting off the things we know we need to do now for a later time. The important things pile up and soon overwhelm us. The old adage is *never put off until tomorrow what you can do today.* There is also a saying that helps us remember to do this: "If the first thing you do when you wake up in the morning is eat a live frog, then nothing worse can happen for the rest of the day!" That *frog* is the most unpleasant or difficult issue that we have to face on any given day, but it is also the one we're most likely to avoid. We're conscious of it because our soul tells us that we should take care of it; so it stays in front of us even though we're avoiding doing it. Every time our conscience reminds us of it, we either take care of it or we don't. If we don't take care of it, we give it power and it becomes bigger and even more intimidating to tackle. If we do take care of it, it gives us power and confidence and the rest of the day becomes easy. In some cases, procrastination can be sinful. "Procrastination (delay) in paying debts by a wealthy man is injustice."[2]

Giving Freely

It is truly giving that makes the world go around. Joseph (PBUH) did not try to negotiate some kind of power over his fellow inmates. He didn't try to mystify the knowledge and encrypt it so that only he could issue it out or seek access to it. He gave freely. Nature itself instructs us in this. The winds give of themselves to scatter fertilizing seeds throughout the earth and to drive clouds to land that is dry and dead. The clouds become heavy with water vapor until the water descends from the sky and gives us water to drink and revive the earth after its death. The earth's produce then gives of itself, nourishing man and beast. The humble plant, being blessed with neither intellect nor mobility, gives nevertheless. It may give food to man and animals. It may provide food or a home for insects. It may only provide peaceful beauty to someone looking upon it. In any event, even the smallest and most humble of G-d's creation fulfills its purpose of giving in His grand scheme. We know that Satan makes a scheme too and the theme of his scheme is selfishness. It was Iblis' exaggerated view of himself and his rejection of a diminished role, that caused him to reject G-d's plan in the beginning of man's creation. Today we find again it is still selfish vanity short-circuiting G-d's Plan and keeping man from his role in the giving scheme.

It is in our very nature to give, but that nature has been corrupted by an attitude in the society of selfish gratification. Adam (PBUH) was made a "Khalifa," trustee of the great material creation and we, as his descendants, inherit that responsibility. But we have to remember then the role of trustee. He is not the owner of a thing; he is the agent of the owner. Adam (PBUH) found himself in a Garden that was already abundantly furnished and supplied all of his needs. He had created nothing that he could fall in love with and become proud and arrogant about. He knew the source of his blessings.[3] This recognition is important because it works subconsciously to cleanse selfish and proud tendencies that we may not even be aware of. It also works to empower us and reinforce our understanding of our role as Khalifa. If we realize that we have been given everything, then we become aware of our obligation to give. The Bible says, "It is better to give than to receive." Our Prophet Muhammad (PBUH) has likewise taught us that "the hand above is better than the hand below."

Yusuf (PBUH) told his companions in the prison that before any food comes to them, he would tell them the interpretation of their dreams. Social evolution, knowledge, and interpretation has to be established before we can appreciate or benefit from the material establishment. For all of the successes of the Nation of Islam under Honorable Elijah Muhammad, they were at best a symbol and not the foundation on which we could build real community life. Joseph (PBUH) placed the priority on satisfying their need for knowledge and understanding above satisfying their physical appetite. Satisfying the natural appetites are normal instincts, but how they can go awry. In her book *Supernormal Stimuli: How Primal Urges Overran Their Evolutionary Purpose*[4], Deirdre Barrett, Harvard Evolutionary psychologist explains how our once-helpful instincts got hijacked in our modern world:[5] Our instincts – for food, sex, or territorial protection – evolved for life on the savannahs 10,000 years ago, not in today's world of densely populated cities, technological innovations, and pollution. We now have access to a glut of larger-than-life objects, from candy to pornography to atomic weapons – that gratify these gut instincts with often dangerous results. Animal biologists coined the term "supernormal stimuli" to describe imitations that appeal to primitive instincts and exert a stronger pull than real things, such as soccer balls that geese prefer over eggs.

Barrett applies this concept to the alarming disconnect between human instinct and our created environment, demonstrating how "supernormal stimuli fuel dangerous excesses" and are a major cause of today's most pressing problems, including obesity and war. She also reminds us that by exercising self-control, we can rein them in; potentially saving ourselves and civilization. Even the scientists acknowledge 1) that our appetites can be corrupted by too much stimulation; 2) that overstimulation brings about disaster; 3) that our survival depends on controlling our natural appetites.

12:38 And I follow the ways of my fathers,- Abraham, Isaac, and Jacob; and never could we attribute any partners whatever to Allah: that (comes) of the grace of Allah to us and to mankind: yet most men are not grateful.

Chapter 38

He is High Above the Partners They Attribute to Him

Ibn Kathir cited a report: The Prophet Muhammad (PBUH) was asked: "Who is the most noble of the people?" He said: "Joseph, the prophet of God, son of the prophet of God, son of the prophet of God, son of the friend of God." *Prophets in the Quran: an Introduction to the Quran and Muslim exegesis*, Brannon Wheeler.

Abraham (PBUH) is described as a friend of G-d that represents the balance of faith and intellect. G-d commands of us that we have faith, but He also reminds us through Prophet Muhammad (PBUH) that the intellect was the best thing He created in the whole universe. He requires rational religion and rational behavior of us. If we look at the things that mankind has worshiped over time and look at the things they worship today, they would embarrass intelligent human beings. Allah says, "He is high above the partners they attribute to him."[1] G-d also asked, through Prophet Abraham (PBUH), "Do you take idols for gods?"[2]

Joseph (PBUH) tells his fellow inmates how he arrived at this knowledge–the source. He followed the ways of his fathers, Jacob (PBUH), Isaac (PBUH), and Abraham (PBUH).[3] He describes the way that he follows: *sirat al-mustaqeen* – never attributing any partners whatever to Allah and belief in one true G-d, the source of all grace and beneficence. G-d did not forget Abraham's (PBUH) prayer to Him[4] and He did not forget His promise to Abraham (PBUH). Abraham (PBUH) shamed the idol worshippers by pointing out that the idols they worshiped had no power to bring them either harm or good and that they really shamed their own intelligence by worshipping them.[5]

How then are we misled? Sometimes others set up objects of worship for us.[6] Other times, we worship the objects of our own imagination. We see a continuation of the wisdom of Joseph's (PBUH) father Jacob (PBUH), in his conversation with the inmates. Jacob (PBUH) had already discovered that you couldn't give your appetite sway in your decisions. Allah says, "many do mislead (men) by their appetites unchecked by knowledge." What exactly is the birthright that we sacrifice because of our appetite? Since Adam (PBUH) is our first father, that birthright is dominion over the Garden and the destiny that G-d intended for man.

12:39 "O my two companions of the prison! (I ask you): are many lords differing among themselves better, or the One Allah, Supreme and Irresistible?"

Chapter 39

Logic Develops from the Generalities to the Specific

Allah gives us the logic in the Qur'an of how to respond to those who deny the concept of absolute obedience to one G-d. In our own personal experiences, we can attest to the frustration in the workplace where, as the saying goes, "we have too many bosses." One boss tells you to do one thing and another tells you to do something else. Even in our family life, our children know instinctively how to play one parent against the other when they find that the parents are not on the same page. So, Allah speaking through His Prophet Joseph (PBUH), gives the fellow inmates clear and simple logic for the "One G-d, Supreme and Irresistible."

From Diversity to Oneness

To the unenlightened, the concept of *Tauheed*, or *the Oneness of G-d* might seem contradictory to the diversity that we find in the creation. All the beautiful things in different places, with different properties, leave us in awe. Men devote their whole lives to study in one field – biology, geology, chemistry, astronomy, etc. But we are not to fall in love with and worship that field of knowledge or what we have produced from it; like the mythical character Pygmalion, the sculptor who fell in love with a statue he had carved. No matter how much study we give in any field, we find that there is a relationship to a whole. There is a consistency. There are common principles. There is a oneness. There is one set of rules that governs it all and this leads, logically, to the conclusion that there is one Architect and Creator of it all. This great freedom that Allah has given us–to grow and expand our minds to the furthest reaches of the universe and beyond–is a blessing for the human intellect. It has its purpose and that is to guide us back into the unified system that encompasses it all and the one Lord Creator of it all. This acknowledgment then gives us the ultimate freedom. We can no longer then accept any other object of worship. Anything else that is put before us demanding our devotion we can put in its place.

Now with all of this intellectual potential to reach out and conquer the vast systems of knowledge of the material creation, we should ask ourselves why we cannot think ourselves out of the small geography of a depressed community; why we can't think ourselves into a bigger garden or think ourselves into solutions that improve our lives of and the lives of our neighbors.

We tend to get stuck on our differences and neglect the bigger picture. Diversity has to be respected because it is by the principle of differences that we have come into existence. We multiply by differences (by co-functioning opposites). Allah says in the Qur'an, "the male is not like the female." In the African American community, there is this tendency to blame the opposite sex for our problems. They say "men are missing in action" (MIA); they say "the mothers are not raising the children." But creation, (in this context, healthy, functioning individuals, and healthy prosperous communities), takes both the male and the female. Both the male and the female are from one soul, so even this creative principle points toward oneness. The same logic that applies to the creation of our physical and social lives applies to everything that G-d created.

The thinker studies his own life and the world around him to make sense of it and most often concluding that there is one consistent system. It is whole, and that in itself points to one Designer and one First Cause, not a committee or a collaboration of creators.[1] This recognition in itself gives us peace and forms the basis of Tauheed.

Even so-called primitive thinkers understood these concepts. Black Elk was a leader of Native Americans. Though they are not commonly seen as a monotheistic culture, he noted the same conclusion from being in touch with nature. "The first peace, which is the most important, is that which comes within the souls of people when they realize their relationship, their oneness with the universe and all its powers, and when they realize that at the center of the universe dwells the Great Spirit and that this center is really everywhere, it is within each of us."[2] Although many of the scientists of the world today present themselves as rational thinkers, they are very different than Abraham (PBUH). Abraham (PBUH) stayed with his interest to its end. In true scientific fashion, he followed his observations to their logical conclusion. Imam Mohammed (RAA) pointed out, "Every thing, every effect, has a cause. The thinker respects his intelligence and he won't give up his logic that has been responsible for him getting as far as he's gotten with his studies. He's not going to stop and say 'well at this point the effect has no cause.' That's the *kafir (disbeliever)*; he wants to come to that conclusion so he can continue to be independent of any authority over him, so the Quran says, 'Do you think that there is no authority over you?'"

We must recognize this authority over us in order for our soul to grow.[3] The soul is the seed of our life. G-d put everything that we need in that seed and there is a progression for the soul. Like all of life, it evolves and matures. We should see the sign in the fig and the olive as to how our knowledge should evolve. Both have seeds within them and both seeds represent a particular phase of knowledge development. The fig, however, is full of many seeds, while the olive only has one seed and that is the main difference between the two.[4] This illustrates how our logic develops from the generalities to the specifics and also how our observations of all the diversities in nature still point toward a oneness in its Creator and its creation.

12:40 "If not Him, ye worship nothing but names which ye have named, ye and your fathers, for which Allah hath sent down no authority: the command is for none but Allah: He hath commanded that ye worship none but Him: that is the right religion, but most men understand not."

Chapter 40

The Most Progress Made by Humanity Over Time Has Been by Civilizations that Believed in One G-d

Any fancy of our own imagination that we give part worship to is bound by its very nature of limitation to fail us.[1] We are obligated, as rational creatures, to follow the leaders in knowledge, but we are also obligated to reject their leadership when it leads away from belief in G-d.[2] There is a movement among Black Studies programs in universities and high schools to discredit Islam and I believe it is part of a broader scheme to eliminate G-d from our higher education. It is said in the Qur'an that when you have seen yourself, you have seen your Lord. This does not mean that we are like G-d--He is One, He is Alone in His Rule, He is Unique, and there is nothing like Him. Rather what this means is that we come to know ourselves through living our life and interacting with G-d's creation. At some point, we come to recognize our own limitations and our own potential. We ask ourselves, what is it that moves us beyond our limitations? What is it that sustains us? Do we create the food we eat or the air we breathe? Do we cause the life that we see coming from dead matter? Of course not! All these things exist beyond us, beyond our control, beyond our limitations. These things are in G-d's control. So Allah says, "why do you question My Nature when you can't even explain your own?"

As African Americans, we are all in this confinement together. Many activists will continue to appeal to the spirit and emotions of the people and their intentions may be good. Then there are others who indirectly serve the interest of slave masters—modern day Pharaohs who want us to see them as gods. They serve this interest by attacking Islam. There are now, and there have been, forces to lead African Americans away from the religion of Al-Islam.

During slavery, there was direct physical force, torture, and execution of slaves attempting to practice their religion. During the subsequent years of Jim Crow and segregation, the African American mind was conditioned to outright rejection of any independent thought. Efforts to introduce Islam to African Americans by Noble Drew Ali and others met with limited success.

With the rise of the Nation of Islam, Islamic terminology, and fundamental principles began to spread over broad areas of the United States. It was a foreign doctrine to most and because of its syncretism,[3] it was quite foreign even to orthodox Muslims. It was just this strangeness, this 'unalikeness' that attracted African Americans, but perhaps as important was the fact that it represented an independent thinking that had never been encouraged or even allowed among the ex-slaves. W. D. Fard knew Islam very well but felt that the best strategy to reach the African American with Islam was to incorporate into his teachings, Christian concepts with which we had already been indoctrinated and the best traditions of our own leaders over time.

The Nation of Islam survived and by the 1940s members of the Nation of Islam were being imprisoned during World War II and viewed as a direct threat to America during its war. The movement grew thereafter and high profile members such as Muhammad Ali and Malcolm X gave it national and international visibility. Both paid and volunteer agents were enlisted by the United States government, and put in place, just as they had done with Marcus Garvey's movement but they were never able to undermine the Nation of Islam progress while Elijah Muhammad was alive. A new generation of leaders that had not been taught and raised by the ruling order emerged.

America, like most ruling orders with potentially powerful minority populations, hand picks our leaders. In most cases they present those leaders for us who are weak and flawed. The plan is to kill off or co-opt their independent thinkers.[4] Even today, immigrant Muslims, along with leading scholars on Black campuses, minimize the work of Honorable Elijah Muhammad. They favor Malcolm X as a leadership symbol because as powerful as he was, he was a break in the chain of the Divine Plan to establish independence in the African American. He correctly noted that Honorable Elijah Muhammad was not practicing correct Islam, but the leadership of the Muslim thought, the Reviver of true Islamic practice in modern time, W. Deen Mohammed (RAA) had not yet emerged. It would have defeated G-d's Purpose for us to be liberated from white America just to come under the new domination of a political "ism" or an Arab Islam.

Afrocentrism soon became the tool to steer the African American away from Islam and when it was presented with any theology at all, it was usually Christian or animist.[5] Those that hold up animism as a valuable cultural tradition ignore the intellectually honest truth that the most progress made by humanity over time has been by civilizations that believed in One G-d. A popular Afrocentric theme is that Al-Islam, like Christianity, led to the destruction of African civilization; and that Islam is a religion/way of life/philosophy created by Arabs for the advancement and edification of Arabs and their culture.

The single most important figure in the development of what is now called Afrocentric thought is the Senegalese historian Cheikh Anta Diop.[6] Diop, born in 1925 and died in 1989, was a Senegalese physicist, historian, anthropologist, and politician who promoted that all African history emerged out of its prototype *Kemet*, renamed Egypt by the Greeks. While Diop, a Muslim, was disciplined in his scholarship, subsequent scholars, while building on his research, lost their objectivity.

The key ingredient to uncorrupted scholarship, indeed rationality itself, is that the prejudices of the observer must not interfere with the observation. Allah tells us this in the Surah An-Nur, in which He says the flame doesn't touch the oil. That surah starts out addressing the sin of adultery and continues addressing adulteration of the truth.[7] The understanding of this is that our own passion for knowledge and the brightness that we hope to project from the flame should not burn the pure oil or absolute truths. To do so is intellectual dishonesty.

Dr. Chancellor Williams, author of *The Destruction of Black Civilization*, builds on Diop's research and attributes the fall of "Black Civilization," to Arab intrusion. "These Arabs confused African leaders everywhere, increased the tensions and tribal wars among them, and helped mightily in destroying the independence of African states. These Arabs actually served as slavery middle men in Eastern Africa, capturing and selling four times more slaves than the Trans-Atlantic slave traders did!" Here again, we have a basis of truth, "that Arabs were involved in slave trade,"[8] but it ignores the broader truths: that the Islamic kingdoms such as Mali, Songhay and Ghana represent the heights of civilized development and Islam's influence is felt throughout the continent and throughout its history. We should remember that Prophet Muhammad's (PBUH) first Muezzin, (the man who calls Muslims to prayer) Bilal, was an African, and it was the African kingdom of Ethiopia that first welcomed Muslim refugees from persecution in Mecca. It was Muslim North Africa that brought about the successful conquest of Spain, the 700 years of Muslim rule there and ultimately the Renaissance of Europe. The Arab influence in this history is purely incidental. Islam is now the fastest growing religion in America, the fastest growing religion in the world, and the fastest growing religion among Africans. It is the largest religion in Africa-accounting for 1/4 of the world's Muslim population of 1.6 billion.

Dr. John Henrik Clarke (January 1, 1915-July 16, 1998) was a Pan-Africanist-American writer, historian, professor, and a pioneer in the creation of Africana studies and professional institutions in the late 1960s. His basis of truth was the same one addressed by the Honorable Elijah Muhammad and later by Imam Mohammed (RAA) in his formation of CRAID[9] (Committee for the Removal of All Images that Attempt to Portray the Divine) committees throughout the country, through which he questioned the racial images of divinity prominent in religion. Similarly, Clarke wrote, "My main point here is that if you are the child of God and God is a part of you, then in your imagination God is supposed to look like you. And when you accept a picture of the deity assigned to you by another people, you become the spiritual prisoners of that other people." As Muslims, however, we perceive the imaging of G-d in any flesh identification, not just un-Islamic but un-Christian as well, and the substitution of a black image over a white image is just a blind, emotional reaction that does not advance our cause toward intelligent religion at all.

Clarke addressed the Arabization of Islam and how Africans must remove the Arab connotations from Islam and identify with the spiritual aspects of the religion. This is an issue that has been addressed since the time of the prophet (PBUH) even giving rise to the Ahmadiyyah movement.

These issues have constrained the inclusion of Islam as part of African American history[10] and expression of solidarity between peoples of African descent, and other oppressed people, Arabs or Muslims. In 1967, support expressed for Palestinians and Arabs caused SNCC, (Student Non-Violent Coordinating Committee, one of the most important organizations of the American Civil Rights Movement in the 1960s) to lose much of what remained of its already dwindling White and Jewish American support. When SNCC members published a fact sheet about Zionism and Israeli colonization of Palestine, it caused a furor; major American newspapers ran stories decrying SNCC's 'anti-Semitism', and Jewish groups subjected it to prolonged public attack. The American Jewish Congress called the move 'shocking and vicious anti-Semitism.'

Molefi Kete Asante, a professor and considered a contemporary scholar, went even further than most Afrocentrics by suggesting that there was something inherent in the nature of people from the African diaspora that is incompatible with Islam. He wrote that the "Adoption of Islam is as contradictory to the Diaspora Afrocentricity as Christianity has been."[11] I must reflect back to the inmate's dream in Chapter 36 where in the imprisoned baker's dream he saw himself "*...carrying bread on my head, and birds are eating, thereof.*" Birds also represent *bad omens.* They eat bread wherever they find it and they don't care whether it's fresh or spoiled or what. In this case, we can see them eating bad food from the head of this inmate and I have no doubt that these bakers and their body of knowledge will eventually die. That body will be crucified like the baker because it has no rational basis or balance.

We Need to Be G-dcentric

It was G-d, even when we did not have a correct picture of Him, that brought us over the troubled waters of our history in America. None of these philosophies or movements in and of themselves can claim to have been the sole source of our liberation. Nor can we deny the 'Hand' of G-d in each of them that blessed good intentions and brought good out of whatever the circumstances were. I believe that many proponents of militancy, Black Nationalism, and Afrocentrism are sincere. But I also know that many of them did not have the courage to follow or even acknowledge the Honorable Elijah Muhammad while he was alive. Many today are young and simply do not know the history. I see both them as having missed the bus and now running behind it inhaling the toxic 'black' fumes of its exhaust.

The author, with Kwame Touré, (June 29, 1941– November 15, 1998), formerly known as Stokely Carmichael, during a visit to Libya in the 1990s. Touré, a leader in the Civil Rights Movement, became an icon of the more militant wing of the movement. He was chairman of Student Non-Violent Coordinating Committee (SNCC) in 1966, taking over from John Lewis, who later was elected to the US Congress. He also served as the "Honorary Prime Minister" of the Black Panther Party, and finally as a leader of the All-African People's Revolutionary Party. Touré graduated from Howard University and in his first year at the university, in 1961, he participated in the Freedom Rides of the Congress of Racial Equality (CORE). He was frequently arrested and jailed, once in the infamous Parchman Farm in Sunflower County, Mississippi, along with other Freedom Riders. My late uncle, Luqman Ziyad (John D. Spight Jr.) worked as the Muslim Chaplain at the Parchman prison until his passing in 2009. Touré, along with Jamil Abdullah Al-Amin, formerly known as H. Rap Brown, (currently serving a life sentence for murder following a 2000 shootout with two Fulton County, Georgia Sheriff's deputies), another chairman of SNCC in the 1960s, were an inspiration to me during that time as they presented to me a more viable alternative to the non-violent philosophy of Dr. King and other mainstream Civil Rights leaders.

12:41 "O my two companions of the prison! As to one of you, he will pour out the wine for his lord to drink: as for the other, he will hang from the cross, and the birds will eat from off his head. (so) hath been decreed that matter whereof ye twain do enquire."

Chapter 41

Every Decision is a Matter of Life and Death

Joseph's (PBUH) story is described as "the most beautiful of stories." (*Holy Qur'an*, 12:3) I believe one reason why it is so beautiful is that it presents human behaviors in such contrasts that it's hard not to see, with clarity, humanity in its best and in its worst light. In verse 22 of Chapter 12, Allah refers to "those who do good," and in the very next verse to "those who do wrong." In verse 26, Allah says (either), "he is a liar" and in the next verse (or) "she is a liar." In verse 17, the brothers lie and say "we went racing with one another" and in verse 25, Yusuf and the wife of the Aziz "both raced each other to the door."

Here within the same verse, we have the ultimate contrast of life and death. One fellow inmate of Joseph lives and the other one dies. I believe we can also see these inmates as two contrasting dispositions within the same psyche. In all aspects of life except the final transition, we make the choice, as to whether we live or die. Even there we can bring on catastrophic consequences that result in sudden death. Our future is very much as we ourselves see it. Every decision we make in life is a matter of life and death. The consequences of a decision might be in the distant future but each step, each decision-large or small-is a step on the path in either direction. The pack of cigarettes that some smoke a day begins with one. That one is a step towards physical death.

We might say, "well it'll take a lot of them to kill me" or a "little bit won't hurt," but just going down that path is a step toward death. That habitual sin that we commit began with one; that one was a step toward spiritual death. To knowingly accept a false or irrational premise is a step toward intellectual death. In the short-term we can also relate attitudes of optimism and pessimism to life and death. The optimist is inspired and motivated while the pessimist always has a burden on his head. Look at how pessimistic the whole Christian doctrine is, of man being born into the original sin of our first father, Adam (PBUH). You start out hopeless. It's no wonder they are so comfortable with the symbol of the cross-crucifixion and death.

The well-known martial artist and actor Chuck Norris made a statement prior to President Obama's election to a second term that U.S. Citizens would face "1,000 years of darkness" if President Obama was re-elected for a second term. There is an audience out there that he is addressing and we should look closely at the subtext of his statement. I could easily see him speaking to one audience saying that if the Black man returns to power after centuries on the bottom, he will rule for a thousand years. I could also see him saying that (blackness) innocence and human sensitivity will take over from dry rationality and materialism and will stay in power for a millennium. Allah reminds us that he is the one with the power to make the night or the day perpetual over us. *(Holy Qur'an 28:71-27).*

The artist Madonna, at a Washington concert, said of President Obama, "For better or for worse, all right, we have a black Muslim in the White House, okay?" Sally Quinn wrote in the Washington Post, referring to the 16% of Americans that believe he is a Muslim: "For many of those, Muslim is code for black. Madonna managed to sum up among the worst fears of the Obama campaign in two words." Here again in code, we have an acknowledgment that the Muslim nature of innocence can be related to black or darkness. The community that G-d wants began in darkness among unlettered people led by the unlettered Prophet-people who had only strong faith and human innocence. They were blessed with enlightenment that has enabled the material and intellectual progress that we see today. G-d promised that even the Muslim world would go into darkness and rise again. We should also remember Imam Mohammed's (RAA) advice to "stay piously devoted to Allah's cause always and He will preserve your civilization, your order for society. The sun will never set on you, the sun of enlightenment will never go down, it will be with you always." I also know that there is some subconscious fear and maybe a little collective guilt among some of the white population. As soon as President Obama's poll numbers increased and it looked like a real possibility he could be re-elected, gun sales soared. On the surface, they express concern that his administration will erode 2nd Amendment rights to own guns. There are also those out there who fear that, should Blacks rise to power, there will be payback for whites' 400 years of oppressing them.

The presidential election of 2012 brought optimism and pessimism into stark contrast. While both Democrats and Republicans claim to have the best vision of America for the future, they represent two very different visions of that future and they utilize two very different strategies. As the Chuck Norris statement illustrates, the Republican view is one of pessimism – doom and darkness. It plays on fear and ignorance. This promotion of pessimism caused dissension even within the ranks of Republicans. Candidate Mitt Romney's consistent theme throughout the country has been pessimistic – things are bad and getting worse. In the very important electoral state of Ohio, things were actually better, presenting a conflict with Romney's pessimistic narrative. The statewide unemployment rate in Ohio had fallen to 7.2%, a point below the national average. In bellwether central Ohio, home to the capital city of Columbus and its thriving suburbs, the jobless rate fell to 5.9% in August. Republican Gov. John Kasich's of Ohio, a Republican candidate for president in 2016, is a big booster of his state and at a campaign event in conservative Owensville, CNN reported that Kasich boasted, "Ohio is rocking" moments before turning the microphone over to now U.S. House of Representatives Majority Leader, Paul Ryan, who proceeded to issue dire warnings about Obama's economic policies. Democrats led by President Obama continued the theme of hope and optimism.

The 2016 election presented the same contrasts. The rise of the candidacy of Donald Trump shocked and amazed everyone but his slogan, "Make America Great Again," carried a message to many people. Given the support for his "anti-everybody" rhetoric, it meant to me, "Make White America Superior Again." To me, America is now greater than it has ever been. The contrast is glaring. In February 2016, Lindsey Cook, writing in U.S. News & World Report, penned an article entitled: "Trump, Cruz, Rubio and the Power of Negativity in the 2016 Race"

"Using debate transcripts, data scientist Alex Petralia calculated the sentiments of both Republican and Democratic presidential candidates, looking at whether their language during the contests was positive or negative. Donald Trump was by far the most negative candidate, dipping to even 13 percent in one debate, meaning only 13 percent of the phrases he used were positive. "Trump's negativity, at this point, is his identity," Petralia says. 'He would certainly lose popularity if he became more positive because that is not the Donald Trump we know.'" Nothing about their presentation inspires, but we should be aware that the opposite of inspire is expire and thus this group is embarking on a path that leads to death.

And this is not just figurative death. Recent research has uncovered an alarming statistic that shows Middle-Aged White Americans Are Dying. We invest our life force into many different avenues and streams and when there is a loss in that stream sometimes we lose our life. The life force of the white supremacist ideology in America has been shattered and now we see middle-aged white Americans, who have traditionally held power under a belief in white supremacy, dying at increasing rates.

A study, co-authored by Anne Case and Angus Deaton, analyzed death rates for men and women aged 45 to 54 in the United States, a range often categorized as "middle-age." The duo, both economics professors at Princeton, then compared the data to those death rates found within other domestic racial categories and those seen in similarly wealthy nations. Those with less education were more likely to die in middle age due to suicide or alcohol and drug poisoning, the authors note. The study links the increase in mortality to a slew of problematic issues seen throughout American society, including an increase in drug and alcohol abuse and an increase in suicide rates, and white men had the highest suicide rate of any demographic in 2013 according to the Centers for Disease Control and Prevention.

The concept of inspiration and its relation to the attitude of optimism can be seen in the context of spirit. As to the destiny of the one inmate, Allah says, "he will pour out the wine for his lord to drink." Wine is *khamr* and refers to alcoholic drinks or what we call *spirits*. Many credit the struggle of African Americans for human dignity and civil rights as the *inspiration* for the movement for freedom and democracy in the world today. As that model evolves, I believe it will represent more and more clarity of vision for man. The first meaning of the word Khimar is to *cover, conceal, veil.* But it also means any intoxicating thing – anything that befogs the mind or causes us not to think clearly. All alcoholic drinks are Khamr. All illegal drugs are Khamr. The Prophet Muhammad (PBUH) said, "Every intoxicant is khamr and every khamr is haram." Umar, the second Khalifah, confirmed the Prophets words, declaring from the pulpit of the Prophet, "Khamr is that which befogs the mind." Similarly, in Hebrew, is the word, chemer, corresponding to the Aramaic chamar. It is defined as "wine" and the word "conveys the idea of 'foaming,' as in the process of fermentation or when poured out. It is derived from the root hamar, meaning to boil up."

In the Qur'an Allah instructs women when they go out in public "that they should draw their veils over their bosoms and not display their beauty except to their husbands, etc." *(Holy Qur'an 24:31).* The word used is *bikhumurihinna* from *Khimar,* not Hijab. It's understandable why Satan pushes fashions that expose women's bodies in the public. He does this to cover, cloud or veil the moral and intellectual senses of man. Man can become drunk with passion and in that state, he's not fit to pray or to accomplish much else. Some thinkers say that everything must be covered except the face and hands. While this is generally accepted as not required, Imam Salim Mu'min interprets this, saying: "we should not hide our character and our work in the public." We are well advised to avoid all forms of intoxication, including spiritual drunkenness and the reward from Allah, will be purity and clarity.

In many European countries, the issue of Muslim women's right to cover themselves has become prominent. Roberto Maroni, the Italian Interior Minister, commented, on Italy's Parliament debated laws banning veils in public saying, "If the Virgin Mary appears wearing a veil on all her pictures how can you ask me to sign on a hijab ban law?" We should be aware that much of the Muslim world has let their own cultural prejudices and western colonial influences color their perception of Islam. Covering everything on the woman except openings for the eyes has little to do with Islam. We know the real meaning of hijab is a wall or partition in the home, sometimes just a sheet or cloth that separates visitors from the private quarters of the home and keeps women from being exposed to the view of the company. This was prevalent in the south among African Americans and many brought the custom here to the North when they had to squeeze large families into small tenement dwellings. There is no magic to an Islamic scarf, nor to a prayer rug. Look at the phenomena of many young Muslim immigrant women who are wearing the tight Gucci jeans and then sanctifying the outfit with a hijab. Yes, the hair is covered but the real body parts that are exciting men today are on display.

Looking again at optimists and pessimists, we could also draw parallels to survivors and those who go extinct. There is support for the proposition that the very ones who have been socially and economically confined (fellow inmates) may ironically be the ones most optimistic. In an article in Newsweek entitled *Meet the New Optimists* by Ellis Cose in May 15, 2011, he made the point that despite difficult circumstances, the spirit of African Americans remained high, as compared to whites. "Over the past few years, pollsters repeatedly have corroborated the phenomenon. Whereas whites are glum, blacks are upbeat, which is remarkable since the economic crisis has hit African Americans with particularly brutal force." Cose continued, "even before Obama came on the scene, optimism was building; most notably among a new generation of black achievers who refused to believe they would be stymied by the bigotry that bedeviled their parents. Obama's election was, in effect, the final revelation – the long awaited sign that a new American age had arrived." *Adapted from The End of Anger: A New Generation's Take on Race and Rage by Ellis Cose.* To be published by *Ecco, an imprint of HarperCollins Publishers, Copyright © 2011 by Ellis Cose.*

We need to have spirit—energy and enthusiasm to survive. W. D. Fard gained freedom from British colonial thinking in his native India. He pursued a missionary quest among Africans here in America, using a common strategy that Fatima Fanusie has described in her dissertation, *Fard Muhammad in Historical Context: An Islamic Thread in the American Religious and Cultural Quilt* as "religious syncretism," which I would describe bluntly as presenting Islam with a flavor of the local culture. Distillers and vintners will acknowledge that the spirits and wine they manufacture retain the local flavor and influence of whatever grain or grapes are grown in the area. Fard drew heavily on the African American history and culture and served up a doctrine that was both veiled/concealed and intoxicating. We should be grateful to be survivors and to be still hopeful and optimistic toward the future.

Crucifixion

The person without that spirit is dead or dying. It is reported in the Bible that when Jesus (PBUH) was supposedly crucified, before his death, he called out with a loud voice, "Father, into your hands I commit my spirit." When he had said this, he breathed his last.[1] The Qur'an states that Jesus (PBUH) was never killed physically.[2] It is the membership[3]of the Christian church, recognized even today as the Body of Christ, that was crucified.[4] No one has been as mocked, tortured, hanged and crucified as much as the African American. The following of Jesus (PBUH) went from a socially orientated message to a spiritual-only orientated message that was separate from the world.[5] In this chapter, the baker is hung from the cross, and in an ironic twist, the very product of his efforts, is being eaten from off his head. He who accumulates knowledge (bread) on his head and does not use it to benefit the people may be following a vertical path of spirituality, but he is not extending along a horizontal path that is benefitting society. He has no balance and either extreme will cause him to die or be crucified by losing his balance, like a tree whose growth is stunted or the tree with no base, or roots.

Responsible leaders teach their knowledge and this elevates not only those whom they are teaching but also themselves. When they don't, their following and their descendants digress and become inferior. American society never tried to give its African American citizens social or scientific knowledge. In fact, they have ruled over the poor and ignorant by giving them irrational Christian theology and continuous playtime activities. This is where we are at today. One deprived group with optimism and a view toward a brighter future and another group who did not share who see only gloom and doom. That is why Dawah (Propagation) is stressed so much in Islam, and why our Prophet, Muhammad, (PBUH) said when you learn one ayat go and teach it.

Birds

Few things cause the soul to soar like watching birds in flight, moving effortlessly, their wings lifted by the air. Aerodynamics is that study of the way air moves around things. It involves the four forces of flight: lift, weight, thrust, and drag. These are the forces that enable the flight of birds[6] and it is the force of nature that man had to subjugate to enable the flight of airplanes. The ability to fly has made birds, from ancient times, symbolic of the soul flying free from the earth-bound body and seeking the heavens. They represent a passage between the physical world and spiritual worlds and thus freedom. A bird with a broken wing can represent the loss of freedom or a painful handicap. Predatory birds, like the eagle or hawk, are often associated with rulers. Perhaps this association was reinforced by the fact that the upper classes could afford to have trained hunting birds. Pigeons have a less lofty reputation nowadays, but they used to be associated with loyalty and bravery. They were used as messengers and homing pigeons were known to overcome incredible odds to bring a message home; flying through battle zones and terrible weather.

The peacock, on the other hand, is known for its beauty because of its vividly colored tail and feathers. The tail spreads out to display feathers that form a semi-circular fan over an angle of more than 180 degrees and sometimes to a height of five feet or more. They are something to see, walking around with their chest out, perhaps oblivious to everything but their own splendor. They are also considered a symbol of vanity, conceit, and pride, as described by the common expression *proud as a peacock*. But alas, despite its apparent beauty, its pride is unwarranted because as the Arab proverb points out, it has ugly legs. The conclusion is that everything has its flaws. Only G-d is Perfect.

Aesop

The great and ancient wise man Aesop extracted and articulated the signs in animals and nature. He taught that "birds of a feather flock together." But perhaps no one in historical tradition is more respected, more subtly denigrated, or more persistently obscured than *Aesop*. Most scholars believe that he was African. His name, Aesop, is the Ancient Greek word for *Ethiop*, the archaic word for a dark-skinned person of African origin. His fables, usually involving personified animals, are well known throughout the world and are still taught as moral lessons; such stories as *The Fox and the Grapes* (from which the idiom "sour grapes" was derived), *The Tortoise and the Hare*, and *The Boy Who Cried Wolf*. It is also said that Aesop spoke up for the common people against tyranny through his fables.

Aesop lived from about 620 to 560 B.C. in Ancient Greece, but beyond that, much of the rest of his existence is mired in mystery. He was mentioned by Aristophanes, Plato, Xenophon, and Aristotle and was known to have been a freed slave. The obscurity shrouding his life has led some scholars to deny his existence altogether. In the Villa Albani in Rome, he is represented in a sculpture, but just as is today, the European standard of beauty was dominant and he is depicted, as in contemporary legends, as ugly and deformed. The wise Aesop tells the story of the Peacock's encounter with a Crane. A Peacock, puffed up with vanity, met a Crane one day and to impress him spread his gorgeous tail in the sun. "Look," he said "what have you to compare with this? I am dressed in all the glory of the rainbow while your feathers are gray as dust!" The Crane spread his broad wings and flew up toward the sun. "Follow me if you can," he said. But the Peacock stood where he was among the birds of the barnyard, while the Crane soared in freedom far up into the blue sky. The moral: the useful is of much more importance and value than the ornamental.

Luqman

Aesop was a well-known figure in Arabia during the time of Prophet Muhammad (PBUH). Some suggest that the Sura, in the Qur'an titled *Luqman*, was referring to Aesop. Luqman is described in the Qur'an as "one to whom Allah brought wisdom."[7] The one criticism that I have ever heard of commentator Yusuf Ali's translation was made by Imam Mohammed (RAA) who pointed out Ali's reference to Luqman as merely a *sage*, as opposed to a *prophet.* Opinion was sharply divided between those who thought that he was a prophet and those that maintained that he was just a black slave whom Allah rewarded for his faith by giving him wisdom and a long life.[8]

The implication is that his status as a slave and an African precludes him from being a prophet. If that is the case, I think we can say that racism has influenced the mosque as well as the sanctuary and the synagogue. I was blessed to have an uncle, Luqman Ziyad (RAA), who was very active and very much well-loved in the Memphis area and other areas of the South.

Even more shrouded in mystery is whether Luqman and Aesop were one in the same. In Arabic literature, 49 animal fables are attributed to Luqman; all but two identical to fables in the collection of Aesop. It is obvious that either the Greek fables are translations from the Arabic or that the Arabic fables are translations from the Greek. Luqman, like Aesop, dispensed practical wisdom about politics, women, class differences, poverty, planning, and reputation. This is considered the most famous story about Luqman:

Luqman, while he was still a slave, was summoned by his master and ordered to slaughter a sheep. He did so, and his master said, "now give me the best part of it." So Luqman removed the tongue and the heart and prepared them for his master's supper. The next evening, he was again summoned by his master and ordered to slaughter a sheep. He did so, and his master commanded, "Now give me the worst parts." Again Luqman prepared the heart and tongue of the sheep for his master's supper. His master grew angry and said, "When I ordered you to prepare the best parts of the sheep for me, you gave me the tongue and heart, and now when I order you to give me the worst parts of the sheep you again serve me the tongue and heart." Luqman responded: "There is nothing better than them when they are good and nothing worse when they are bad." Paul Lunde, Aesop of the Arabs, *Saudi Aramco World*, pages 2-3, March/April 1974.

The same story is told about Aesop by the Greeks. Another revealing anecdote is related by the great historian at-Tabari. One day while Luqman was sitting at a social gathering talking with important people a man came up to him and said:

"Aren't you the guy that used to herd sheep with me?"

"Yes," replied Luqman.

"Well how in the world did you end up here, hobnobbing with professors?"

"By telling the truth and keeping quiet about things that don't concern me," answered Luqman. *Aesop of the Arabs, Paul Lunde.*

Chickens Come Home to Roost

The traditional understanding of this adage is that bad deeds or words will always come back on you. This idea may have originally included curses coming back to haunt their originator and is long established in the English language. It was expressed in print as early as 1390 when Geoffrey Chaucer used it in The Parson's Tale: *"And often tyme swich cursynge wrongfully retorneth agayn to hym that curseth, as a bryd that retorneth agayn to his owene nest."*The allusion that was usually made was to a bird returning to its nest at nightfall. Other references to unwelcome returns include the Elizabethan play The lamentable and true tragedie of Arden of Feversham, 1592: "For curses are like arrows shot upright, which falling down light on the suters [shooter's] head." Reference to the birds as chickens was made in the 19th century when a fuller version of the phrase was used as a motto on the title page of Robert Southey's poem The Curse of Kehama, 1810: "Curses are like young chicken: they always come home to roost." The belief that the evil that men create returns to their own door also exists in other cultures. Buddhists are familiar with the idea that one is punished by one's bad deeds, not because of them.[9]

Malcolm X

In more modern times, Malcolm X popularized the term "Chickens Coming Home to Roost" in referring to the assassination of President John F. Kennedy. It is obvious that he too intended to refer to the recompense of evil deeds returning to the doers as the statement traditionally is understood. All deeds carry with them their own consequences. Honorable Elijah Muhammad, recognizing both the sensitivities of the American people and respecting our own position as Americans, informed all of his ministers not to make any statements after the assassination. This was well before the 9/11 attacks and the subsequent resentment and abuse that was directed against Muslims in America. I have no doubt Honorable Elijah Muhammad remembered the abuse his followers suffered during World War II because they were different. After Malcolm's statement that the assassination was "chickens coming home to roost," he was ordered not to make any public appearances outside of his Temple in New York. He disobeyed that order and was suspended. During that 90-day suspension, members in the national leadership, who were envious and jealous of Malcolm X's popularity, quickly began to undermine and discredit him in the eyes of the membership.

Prior to this break, Malcolm X was a prime motivator of the members of the Nation of Islam. Imam W. Deen Mohammed (RAA) has said that Malcolm was the best worker the Honorable Elijah Muhammad ever had. He challenged the leadership to step forward and perform while challenging the following to support the leader and his programs. One of those he motivated was Honorable Elijah Muhammad's son, Elijah

Mohammed II. Elijah II remembers the great contributions of Malcolm as well as many others whom Malcolm motivated in and outside of the Temples of Islam. "My father bought Malcolm a 1955 Chevrolet and he burned it up going from the East coast to the West coast. He traveled around the country building support for the Honorable Elijah Mohammed and the Nation of Islam. He went along the East coast, along with Captain Yusuf Shah, from New York to Miami, setting up Temples everywhere there were black people. There were others who came around that time: Ali Rashid in California, Husain Shabazz in New Jersey, and Malcolm's brother Philbert Omar who set up Temples throughout the state of Michigan. Isaiah Karriem did the same thing and he picked it up from Malcolm."

In those days, we were just a network of storefront temples where the Minsters would come out and teach Yacub's teachings and there was no activity. "My father went to Minister Lemuel's house one morning at 7:00 and he was still in the bed. My father told Sister Eva, his wife, to go and get him up. He said, "Brother, you should have been up. The followers have been up and they're out there working, supporting you." Malcolm picked that work ethic up and put it in his own words and took it across the country. By 1961, Malcolm was speaking from both the Honorable Elijah Muhammad's teachings and the emerging teaching of Imam Mohammed (RAA), as demonstrated in his 1959 address in New York, *The Man Who Introduced Malcolm X.*

Elijah Mohammed II recalls that Malcolm X had been influenced toward a break long before the Kennedy statement. He remembers that Harry Belafonte, Ossie Davis, Ruby Dee and others met with Malcolm often in Amherst, Massachusetts encouraging him to break from the Honorable Elijah Muhammad. Their position was that Malcolm was young and charismatic and that the Honorable Elijah Muhammad was old and becoming increasingly sick. The late commentator, Mike Wallace did much to publicize Malcolm. He asked Malcolm once what it was he wanted, no doubt expecting some of the same outlandish demands that were made by the Honorable Elijah Muhammad, such as separate states for Black people, but Malcolm answered simply, "Ask yourself that question, it's the same thing." All people in their best nature have the same human aspirations. Mike Wallace also fed the desire in Malcolm to break away and go on his own. He told Malcolm, "We have your number" apparently meaning Malcolm had become enamored by the media lights and attention and that this could at some point be used to undo him.

Imam Mohammed (RAA), Elijah Mohammed II, and other top officials all assert that the Honorable Elijah Muhammad had nothing to do with Malcolm X's assassination. In an interview, Imam Mohammed (RAA) said, "I don't believe that my father ordered Malcolm's assassination. He would never do that. It's true that he was very much dissatisfied with the turn in Malcolm's life – his going outside the disciplines of the Nation of Islam to try and get support from other nations to help us with our problem here in America." This was a departure from the need within the African American community, even today, to do for self. To have the respect of the Nations of the earth, to have dignity within our own souls, we have to do exactly what Elijah Muhammad urged us to do and that is "Do For Self."

2:42 And of the two, to that one whom he consider about to be saved, he said: "Mention me to thy lord." But Satan made him forget to mention him to his lord: and (Joseph) lingered in prison a few (more) years.

Chapter 42

How Soon We Forget

Imam Mohammed calls this a great, mystical, and beautiful passage of Joseph (PBUH); one that we should take hints from "to strengthen and tighten up your own life and your own situation."[1] *Forgetting* refers to the apparent loss of information already encoded and stored in an individual's long-term memory. As opposed to ignorance, this is something that we knew and possessed at one time. Our Arabic scholar, Imam Salim Mu'min, notes, in a scriptural context that man (mind) "has the ability to receive abstract perceptions from material manifestations. Within the illuminated perceptions, he has the tendency to forget." He notes that the Qur'an references communities that forgot their covenant with Allah. The Bible also references the same phenomena.

According to Abu Hurayrah, Prophet Muhammad (PBUH) said, "God was merciful to Joseph for if he had not spoken the words 'Mention me to your lord,' it would have (been) no time that he lingered in prison. God shows mercy to the oppressed if they seek refuge in God alone. God sent no prophet after him without the wealth of the people." *Prophets in the Qur'an: an Introduction to the Quran and Muslim exegesis*, Brannon Wheeler.

Sometimes we forget our own capabilities. The Honorable Elijah Muhammad, in his work of exciting us to accomplish bigger and better things as a people, taught that we should never fear that we don't have whatever we need to get the job done. G-d has given us what we need. The keys to our liberation are always at hand. We focus on our lack of resources instead of the resources that we do have.[2] Then we become fixated on the lack – the abyss – as Nietzsche describes.[3] There is a part in each of our psyches that allows for fear of inadequacy. The Qur'an says, "Satan threatens you with poverty (loss, not enough, or inadequacy)" and that is a vulnerability. When we allow that fear, doubt or uncertainty to take hold, we linger in our confinement. We forget that if Allah wills, we can have it all despite the giants (big obstacles).

Imam Mohammed (RAA) made the point many years ago in response to some African American claims that they were in a prison here in America. He noted that even if we wanted to see ourselves in a prison, we are sitting there in a cell, where jailer that has become old and infirmed, and the door to the prison is rusting off the hinges. We could push the door open, walk on out, and go on about our business if we chose, yet we're sitting there in our prison cell complaining.[4] President Obama tried to point out to us the harsh reality, that we needed to accept more personal responsibility and he was criticized for stating that truth.

Since both the baker and the wine steward served in the court of the king, they obviously had some high rank in the society. Yet both of them ended up in the same confinement as Joseph. (PBUH) I think this points to a shortcoming of African American intellectuals also. Many of them rise to high positions, attain great knowledge and wealth but they sometimes forget us. What good is the power, wealth and knowledge if it cannot be used to liberate self. Unfortunately, when the dominant society allows you to have success, it usually means success in serving their interests. Our educated African Americans contribute much to the country's economic system but many, instead of thinking independently, "carry the water" for the ruler's oppressive system.

Men in Islam

I believe one of my mentors, Elijah Mohammed II, as an organizer and longtime Captain of the Fruit of Islam, exemplifies the expression of the last man standing. To this day, he still tries to encourage men to uphold the unity and progress of the community.

Elijah Mohammed II was born June 29, 1931, in Detroit, Michigan. He was the sixth child born to the Honorable Elijah Mohammed and

Sister Clara Mohammed and the older brother of Imam Mohammed (RAA). He mentioned to me on many occasions that his prayer to Allah was that he be able to recognize his father's enemies. He spent his childhood not seeing his father, but seeing his father's enemies lying in wait outside his house. Thus, security became the single focus of helping his father's work and security to him meant protection of the leader, his message, and his programs.

The family moved to Chicago when he was four years old and he spent his early years growing up on Chicago's Southside. Those early years were years of struggle for the believers. For several years, from 1934 to 1941, the Honorable Elijah Mohammed was on the run from his enemies within and outside of the Nation of Islam. Honorable Elijah Muhammad's wife, Sister Clara Mohammed, with the support of strong and loyal pioneer believers such as Ephraim Bahar, held the family together and kept his presence and laws in front of her children. Elijah Mohammed II recounted those depressed years: "We lived at 5308 Wabash. Ephraim Bahar would bring us a chicken and we kept it in our yard. Me and my brother Herbert (Jabir) would feed it buttermilk and cornbread to get it fat. We ate one meal a day in Ramadan. Otherwise, we ate three bowls of bean soup and most times it was sour because we didn't have no ice. My brother Ayman (Emmanuel) used to get tomatoes from a garbage can behind the grocery stores." For several more years, until he was fifteen, Elijah II's father was imprisoned with other believers for their objection to the draft. He noted: "I didn't really know my father until 1945." His childhood was that of a normal young man of his time, although he always carried a bigger responsibility than most youth. He had young friends from the neighborhood of 61st & Michigan, who rode the streetcars, went to the beach, and hung out in Washington Park. He went to the Tivoli Theater on Cottage Grove and was always teaching his little group of friends that Allah was God; that Jesus (PBUH) was not G-d.

He worked a lot of odd jobs in the city, Oxford Electric at 39 & Michigan, Ideal Furniture Company on 63 & Vernon, and at drug stores and hotels on the Southside and Northside. He sold the Chicago Defender on street corners. But when his father came home in 1945, he found his real job and his real mission. He started helping his father, riding around with him and helping him in the businesses. He was always most comfortable working with and around the Fruit of Islam (FOI). But even that respected body of pioneers and soldiers were not always the effective machine that the media liked to project in later years. It was Elijah II, along with strong and loyal soldiers here in Chicago, that established the FOI as a true paramilitary unit with discipline, obedience, and dedication to the leader and his programs.

Those men, like Lieutenants Quentin, Walter, Russell, Louis, Bobby, and Theodore Bey, were responsible for the organization, training, and transformation of the FOI. Elijah II became its Assistant Supreme Captain and led the men in establishing the physical part of the Honorable Elijah Mohammed's program. Later, with Assistants such as Imam Ibrahim Pasha of Atlanta, Karriem Bey, and a staff of young officers that included myself, Imam Qasim Ahmed, Bashir Asad, and others, Elijah II presided over the soldiers of the modern Nation of Islam. He was involved in the purchase and the maintenance of dairy, cattle, and produce operations on farms in Michigan, Georgia, and Alabama; securing the many industrial, commercial, and residential real estate holdings in Chicago; the training of the new FOI; and the distribution of *Muhammad Speaks* Newspaper.

His friends of early years make the same comments as we of today do. "He doesn't talk about anything but Islam. He is a loyal friend. He is free." His most proud accomplishments have been working with those successive generations of men who belong to Islam. Elijah II's hope for the future is that these same types of leaders among men will step forward in this time, in cities across the country, and establish the legacy of Imam Mohammed (RAA) and make their mark in the history of Muslim society.

The Captain's Office—Assistant Supreme Captain Elijah Mohammed II's last staff of Lieutenants, Secretaries and Helpers.
Photo bottom left: l-r, Elijah Mohammed II, Nuri Madina, and Imam Ibrahim Pasha
Photo bottom right: l-r Elijah Mohammed II, Zakee A. Madina, and his father Nuri Madina

12:43 The king (of Egypt) said: "I do see (in a vision) seven fat kine, whom seven lean ones devour, and seven green ears of corn, and seven (others) withered. O ye chiefs! Expound to me my vision if it be that ye can interpret visions."

Chapter 43

Withered Ears Can't Hear

We see the manifestation of the King of Egypt's vision in our society today. There are those who have evolved upon material power and material wealth and have been in control of lives and resources. But now circumstances have changed. Society has been shaken. The climate has changed. The earth itself has shifted. And those who felt self-sufficient before now find themselves with nothing to stand on. Now they feel the insecurity that those of lean means have felt over time. Those who have evolved without material fatness are better situated than most now because, when everyone has to start over, the playing field is level again. We, in fact, have an advantage. If we choose, we can build on a foundation of reality, rooted in material creation (realty), not false perceptions, false doctrines or prejudices. We have an advantage of a new paradigm and new opportunities. Through this vision, Allah points us to the concept of a charitable social order that shares its knowledge and material resources with the poor. Here He describes seven ears of corn and, earlier in the Qur'an, He uses the same symbol of corn to illustrate the 700 fold rewards of charity.[1]

"The good action will be rewarded and increased from ten to seven hundred times," from the first oration delivered by the Prophet Muhammad (PBUH) at the mosque of Medina on Friday, 1 A.H.

Throughout scripture, G-d's reference to *seven* represents the potential for the development of man's human and community life.

Joseph (PBUH), in his very name, represents increase and abundance. His interpretation and understanding of this dream indicate that he understood the laws of giving and the laws of abundance. Many times we miss the blessings of our giving because we violate an important principle of giving and the importance in everything of the *niyat* or *intention.*[2] We often give with the expectation of a certain return or response. We have made a bargain and the recompense of our giving is whatever we've bargained for. It may be some advantage or domination over the recipient or even a simple thank you. In either case, that expectation is the only thing we have coming. Sometimes we will get it and sometimes we will not. Whether we do or don't, we have neglected the bargain Allah invites us to.

Corn also represents knowledge. Originally, corn was not referred to as yellow, it was called golden. Yellow is weak or diluted knowledge. Gold stands for wisdom. It took Imam Mohammed (RAA) to point out, through the various stages and types of corn, what the enemy has done to our soul and how he reveals his scheme and mocks us with it.[3]

Historically the Pharaoh has been the ruler of Egypt but Pharaoh is not mentioned in the surah of Joseph (PBUH). There is reference to the king and one scholar suggests that the translator misunderstood the historical time frame in which the dynastic Pharaohs ruled. It is Allah, however, the Author of Qur'an, Who does not mention Pharaoh. This may be due to the fact that in the evolution of Egypt as a cultural center, the function of the ruler changed also. Pharaoh, as mentioned in other parts of the Qur'an, is an oppressive ruler. He is the prototype of the Dictator who stands over and controls the life of the common people and his mindset is seen in the story of Iblis. Just as the nature of the Civilization in Egypt evolved so also did the nature of its ruler.

Rise of the City-Rise of the King

"The walled city in Egypt was an early form, whose military features disappeared once the great Pharaohs had established a universal order and a unified command, resting mainly on religious belief and voluntary support, rather than on physical coercion." *The City in History, Lewis Mumford*, p81. This transition is reminiscent of the change brought about in the structure of the FOI when Imam Mohammed (RAA) became the leader. He made it clear that there would be no compulsion on the brothers to sell *Muhammad Speaks Newspaper*, but we knew that it was the financial arm of the Nation, so the brothers who understood this continued to sell the paper. Now 40 years later we still struggle to get support for the successor propagation arm of this Muslim community, Muslim Journal. At that meeting with the Captains of the Nation of Islam in Chicago, when Imam Mohammed (RAA) said that we didn't need Captains anymore, he also said: "What we need is Doctors of Psychology." These Captains were recognized as leaders in the movement for freedom, justice, and equality and his wish was that we should pick up exactly where we had left off under his father.

But we needed a new set of skills for a bigger job. Our role was to move the material part of the Honorable Elijah Muhammad's program. As such, we directed the legs. We motivated the body. But we did so with rank and authority. Then we were taught in our very first lesson, that "Man means Mind." We now had to use the newly developed mental skills to uphold the material part of the program. To be Doctors of Psychology, we had to study the mind, starting with our own. Prophet Jesus (PBUH) said "Physician heal thyself." So our first task was to grasp the understanding of our history, our mission, and our religion--the medicine that was intended to make us mentally healthy.

Then we were to tend to the members. We still needed to motivate the body and direct the legs. In order to do that, we needed to learn how to make the man want the best for himself of his own free will--make him understand the value of his leadership so he would strive, as the Holy Qur'an says, "with his life and his possessions," to establish that leadership. Everybody must have a leader in their lives. It's in the devotional nature of the human being. Even popular culture recognizes this. The musical artist, Bob Dylan wrote: "You're gonna serve somebody."

In Egypt, the king served that important function. "The most important agent in effecting the change from a decentralized village economy to a highly organized urban economy was the king or rather the institution of Kingship – one of the attributes of the ancient Egyptian god, Ptah. As revealed in a document derived from the third millennium B.C. that he founded cities, is the special and all but universal function of kings. In the urban implosion, the king stands at the center; he is the polar magnet that draws to the heart of the city and brings under the control of the palace and the temple all the new forces of civilization." *The City in History, Lewis Mumford*, p 35

We can see then how as the city evolved, the king evolved into a Pharaoh – a leader with absolute power over the people and whom we will later see maintained that control by keeping human knowledge from the people. As advanced as the city may become, all seven levels of that advancement will wither and dry up if it does not share the wealth and the knowledge with the people.

12:44 They said: "A confused medley of dreams: and we are not skilled in the interpretation of dreams."

Chapter 44

Unintended Consequences and Other Absurd Results

If we look at the history of mankind we see its evolution and progress as well as its infirmities and diseases over time. But by the token of time, we are sometimes allowed to see, in close contrast to each other, both of these processes. And man's real loss is the loss of his vision of the way and path to his destiny.

A medley is a mixture of dissimilar or unlike things that would normally not be seen in the same context. This is the description of the dream or vision that the leadership had during Prophet Joseph's (PBUH) confinement. Honorable Elijah Muhammad, spoke of a "Time and What Must Be Done..." and I believe he was speaking of just such a time as this, in which we will see the best of times and the worst of times, at the same time. He also called it the time of Manifestation of All Defects. His son, Imam W. Deen Mohammed (RAA) interpreted the confused medley of events that face the world as we try to move forward in it, as an independent people. He also identified this time as the Yaum-Mi-Deen--the Day of Religion or Day of Accounting.

When leadership pursues a strategy of expediency instead of guidance by a moral compass, the time always arrives when the price of their bargain must be paid. In the meantime, a confused medley of *unintended consequences and other absurd results* is bound to occur.

At the 2012 GOP Presidential Convention in August 2012, city legislators in Tampa, Florida passed an ordinance that prohibited spray bottles and water guns from the site of the convention, but a curious integration of that ordinance with Florida State Law allowed real guns to be brought onto the site. More recently President Obama encouraged Congress to enact sensible restrictions on gun purchases in response to the spate of mass shootings. One irony that surfaced was that even some of the same people who were on Homeland Security's "no-fly" list developed to protect airline passengers from bombs and hijackings, were not restricted in any way from purchasing guns.

In trying to locate a particular book, I had occasion to visit Chicago's main public library, the Harold Washington Library, in downtown Chicago. The Library was named after Chicago's first African American mayor. I asked for help in finding my book and in conversation with the librarian, discovered that books being stolen was a common and a growing problem. What was curious though was the type of books stolen.

The most frequently stolen item was the Bible, which ironically, individuals and religious groups are giving away on street corners. But why would a person, seeking moral and spiritual guidance, try to obtain that guidance by stealing it? Success and positive mental attitude themes are also frequently stolen; but what would make a seeker of positive principles think they could affect self-improvement through a negative deed? Another popular theft subject is books on secret societies; but what would make one think he could find keys to a *secret* society in a *public* library? Which brings to mind the fitting lyrics from recording artist, Lauryn Hill's song *Doo Wop (That Thing)*. *"How You Gon' win when you ain't right within?"*

Sometimes this medley of circumstances and events reveals stunning contrasts and sometimes it reveals blatant hypocrisy. On a visit to Masjid An-Nur in Minneapolis Minnesota, I had occasion to attend Jumuah there and visit two friends and longtime members of the indigenous African American community there, Arlene El-Amin, an administrator and Abdul-Karim Bilal, a tireless propagator in the city.

There in the state of Minnesota was another strange juxtaposition. It is the home of Congressman Keith Ellison, the first Muslim to be elected to the Congress and one of only two current Muslim members, and at the same time the home of Congressman Michelle Bachmann, who is leading the crusade for investigating Muslim influence in the U. S. government and who appears to truly believe that Muslims are evil.

The Imam at Masjid An-Nur, Makram El-Amin, delivered the Khutbah (sermon) in which he very rationally and eloquently condemned the recent violent demonstrations and death, in Benghazi, of the American Ambassador to Libya, Christopher Stevens and three others. The assembled crowd consisted of many races and nationalities--indigenous African American Muslims, Somalis, Arabs, Indians-including the media. He reminded us of the history of the Prophet (PBUH), in which he accepted much personal abuse and still showed nobility and concern for his attacker. He reminded us of our love for the Prophet (PBUH). And he reminded us of how bullies intentionally do things to make us react emotionally and control us. The Minneapolis StarTribune was present at the Masjid and reported on the Khutbah in its Sunday edition, and noted the question that the Imam had asked us to ask ourselves, as Muslims in responding to any provocation: "What would Muhammad do?"

It was first reported that the attack was in response to a video that was derogatory toward Prophet Muhammad (PBUH). Although the video offended the sensitivities and the sensibilities of most right minded people, public officials emphasized the importance of the concept of freedom of speech and freedom of expression. We too respect those concepts, even more than most. If G-d allows Satan himself the freedom to express his will and plan, who are we to force anyone to our religion or viewpoint? Allah emphasizes in Qur'an, 'Let there be no compulsion in religion.' The world's governments announced that they were powerless to do anything to the perpetrators of the film or do anything to curtail its dissemination.

Nevertheless, in another curiously hypocritical contrast, in a timeframe that could only have been set by Allah Himself, during the same week, topless photos of the Duchess of Cambridge were disseminated across the internet. A French court ordered a magazine publisher to hand over all digital copies of the photos within 24 hours and blocked further publication of what was called a "brutal display" of William and Kate's private moments. So William and Kate are *royals* or what some might consider *lords and patrons*. No one mentioned freedom of speech and freedom of expression then. They have been set on a pedestal of honor and nobility where a court would protect them from being defiled and disrespected. Prophet Muhammad (PBUH) didn't warrant that same protection.

The King in Egypt during Joseph's (PBUH) time acknowledged that he could not interpret dreams or visions. The leadership today likewise has no vision; they can see some things but only from a narrow perspective and they have ruled thus far because, in the land of the blind, the one-eyed man is king. Despite its great sciences and material accomplishments, neither Egypt's leaders nor its masses had the gift of interpretation. *Ta'wil*, the word used for interpretation, also implies *to return, to come back to, or to be before*. It will be the neglected brother, that was put in restricted circumstances, but blessed with the gift of interpretation, that they will have to come back to; that will have to tell them the meaning of today's events.

12:45 But the man who had been released, one of the two (who had been in prison) and who now bethought him after (so long) a space of time, said: "I will tell you the truth of its interpretation: send ye me (therefore)."

Chapter 45

What Were You Thinking

Creativity vs. Habit

Dr. Carolyn Myss wrote in Anatomy of the Spirit: "Creative energy breaks us out of habitual patterns of behavior, thoughts, and relationships. Habit is a hell to which people cling in an attempt to stop the flow of change. But creative energy defies the repetition of habit."[1] I could add to her observation that habit can also be seen as a prison. Because Divine energy is inherent in our biological system, every thought that crosses our minds, every belief we nurture, every memory to which we cling translates into a positive or negative command to our bodies and spirits."[2,3] Our energy and motivation come from listening to our inner voice. If there's something missing in our life, it's more than likely something we're not seeing right in front of our face or even closer.

Allah says he will not change the condition of the person until they change what is in their heart (soul). We can have whatever we desire. That which we need and that which we want is already within our grasp, it's just a matter of recognizing that. Often when we need a resource, it dawns on us that we know the person that can provide it but have forgotten them or lost contact with them. Our lives are dominated by the daily demands of our responsibilities and we are distracted by the allurements of the popular culture. The work begins within. The answers are inside us, but we need to listen to them and act on them to achieve the goal or dream that we desire. *Emerson* asked: "What is a weed? A weed is a plant whose virtues have not yet been discovered."

If his ability to interpret dreams and visions is a valuable aspect of these resources operating within his psyche, one of all of our valuable possessions, then Joseph (PBUH) had the power within him to free himself all the time. Despite his imprisonment, he still had a vital resource powerful enough to save himself-possibly creativity, the ability to interpret, or support of friends (social esteem in high places). But it was only after such a long time, he realized: "I am *now* qualified to administer the storehouses, or resources of all the society because I know their value."

Allah said that He created everything in pairs (opposites). In nature, he shows us that it takes both the positive and the negative elements working together to make motion (energy). Our task has always been to harness that energy. Even that which we might perceive as an obstacle or an enemy can be brought into our dominion. The jinn nature or jinn people cannot be rulers of the earth, according to Allah's Plan, but that is not to say they don't serve a purpose. Prophet Muhammad (PBUH) said that all humans had a jinn (nature) within them, but that he had made his jinn obedient to him.[4]

Creativity

Allah said to Adam (PBUH) after He had created him and created all of the adornments of the material world, "Tell them their natures." To the scientist, that means to reveal your utility to me. This is an inherent ability in every human being but it is also a blessing and a mercy, and we often take this ability for granted. We have signs in nature of the human beings lacking this power. Oliver Sacks a renowned neurologist, psychologist, and writer describes such a condition in his book, *The Man Who Mistook His Wife for his Hat.* In his book, he describes a case study in which a patient lost his ability to recognize and identify common objects.[5] His patient had *visual agnosia* – the inability of the brain to recognize or understand visual stimulus. The patient had normal visual functioning and could see but was unable to interpret or recognize what he was seeing. Dr. Sachs treated him by retraining the man's mind so that sound or music was his primary tool of perception.

The Honorable Elijah Muhammad, in advising his laborers on how to reach the *Lost Found (his term for the so-called Negro who had lost knowledge of his true self),* African American people, said, "Speak to the Ear that's alive in the person." Businessmen and professionals are trained to bring the forces of nature, physical science principles, into the service of man. Booker T. Washington learned the language of creation through its creatures and his protégé, George Washington Carver studied the peanut until it communicated its utility to him. David Philpot is a Chicago artist who carves staffs and other objects from trees. His work has been displayed in the DuSable Museum and elsewhere. He has said in choosing to carve a piece from a tree, "The tree talks to me." So all of creation speaks to man; and there is an ear that is always alive in the person, that Allah has preserved so His creation is never lost.

The media understands its power through Adam (PBUH) to name things. But its labels are sometimes designed to hide the truth and to mislead. We are very familiar with the Civil Rights Movement and its role in securing the rights of African Americans, but I reject that term *Civil Rights* for two reasons: First, it disconnects us from the broader *Freedom Movement*, which began when the first slaves rebelled before Dr. Martin Luther King Jr. and others began fighting for rights based on our American citizenry. Those slaves were fighting for their human right to be free. I'm not going to discard Nat Turner and his struggle just because he might not have had the best tool to work with at that time. Dr. King was also fighting for those same G-d given, inalienable rights that Thomas Jefferson, referenced as being endowed by our Creator. Secondly, it disconnects African Americans' struggle from the broader movement in the world for human rights. Frederick Douglass was not just an African American leader. He was the foremost spokesman for human rights in the world during his time.

Every child is born with creative imagination. Allah says that He is the Best of Creators, which tells us that there are others. This creative power can be increased by applied effort. As with any muscle or faculty, when we don't use it, it atrophies. That's why children bring such awe and inspiration to our lives. Everything is new to them so they see these things with fresh eyes. We see things in the way that we have always seen them and we do things in the way we've always done them. We do ourselves and society a grave disservice when we get so busy and occupied that we don't find time to spend with children.

We have to be willing to go to different places and do different things that stimulate the imagination. The benefit of the fishing trip is not how many fish you caught, but the time you spent in the natural undeveloped environment. It is the time you spent staring at the water and seeing how the least little disturbance makes a ripple that spreads in every direction. It is the sounds of natural life that we never hear in the urban environment. It is hearing the birds and small animals chirping and recognizing the pattern in their speech. It is the time we give to our subconscious mind to work on problems while our conscious mind feeds on the quiet.

Attraction

The tremendous power of creativity also has a downside. We picture in our mind what we want and that picture unites with the creative power and attracts it. The same power, however, will attract what we fear or resent. It operates just like a magnet. Once it has a clear picture of what we want, it automatically begins to attract to us the things, resources, opportunities, circumstances, and people that we need to produce it in the material reality; that vision that has already become real in our mind. This power of the mind is impersonal and non-discriminatory. It has been commanded to operate in a certain way. We are the ones that have to plant the proper seeds in it to produce the fruits-the results that we want. Whatever it was that we got, came from the bloom of some seed of thought. How often have we asked ourselves and even others, after doing something so obviously dumb, "What were you thinking?"

Unfortunately, fear is equally magnetic to our thoughts. In the book of Job 3:25, Job says, "For the thing which I greatly feared hath come upon me, and that which I dreaded hath come to me." That is why we are told to fear no one but Allah. This frees us from coming under the domination of any other person, thing or circumstance. It also makes us aware of the need to constantly look within ourselves to clear our minds of incorrect mental or emotional pictures and not allow ourselves to become disturbed, anxious or fearful. Through conscious living, we either increase or diminish that spirit or *Ruh*, which we are blessed with by our Creator, by our way of life--manifested by every act of thinking, desiring, and acting. This powerful energy source operates just like a battery-self-contained and not requiring any external outlet.

The more powerful this sustained thought becomes, the greater it's drawing force and the more it attracts. It also, like a battery, can be charged and discharged. Faith energizes our imagination and creative power. Fear, doubt, and uncertainty discharges it.

Focus

It is said that you cannot have any more than one thought in your conscious mind at one time. In scientific terms focus is the point where rays of light meet or where an image is its sharpest and clearest. Similarly, in human activity, it means concentrated action or attention. In artistic or athletic endeavors, it has been called *in the flow* or *in a zone*. It is a place of angels and another spirit.[6] It represents a state in which all of our mental activity and conscious efforts are directed towards a single pursuit and we become aware of our own command of the situation as well as the flow of energy and insight from unseen sources. To think is to be alive and conscious as a human and, to think with a particular focus, with a particular interest, seeking certain rewards or certain benefits, profits you and society. Indeed, Allah says that thinking on him is the greatest power for producing results.[7] It dawns on man at some point that 'I am the creator of these circumstances and I know exactly how I got here.'

12:46 "O Joseph!" (he said) "O man of truth! Expound to us (the dream) of seven fat kine whom seven lean ones devour, and of seven green ears of corn and (seven) others withered: that I may return to the people, and that they may understand."

Chapter 46

The Present is Fleeting; Take Ownership of the Past, and Live for the Future

Few people are blessed to know the future. Allah says, "No man knows what he will earn tomorrow and no man knows what land he will die in." Joseph (PBUH) was blessed to see a part of his future; a future in which he would survive his present circumstances and see his brothers again under different circumstances. Confucius said, "Study the past, if you would divine the future." Sometimes that past will give us no idea of what the future brings and sometimes it will be clearly laid out in our dreams and visions. There is a saying, *Live in the moment* because the present moment is fleeting. It is gone by the time we can think about it. All we can really do is to take ownership of the past. We did what we did and the consequences are ours. Now we learn from that and live for the future. That is the way to have a different history.

In the Hebrew, seven ([b'v, - Sheh'-bah) is from a root word meaning to be complete or full. This can be clearly seen from the first time a variant of the word is used in the Bible.[1] *Al-Fatihah*, which consists of seven verses often called the "seven oft-repeated verse,"[2] is the first surah of the Qur'an and one of the earliest portions of the Qur'an revealed to the Prophet Muhammad (PBUH). It is also said that whole of the Qur'an is within Al-Fatihah. The Arabic word *fâtiha* indicates an *opening*, *beginning* or *commencement*, and is derived from the root *f-t-h*, which mean *to open, unlock, reveal, conquer.* The idea of *opening* or *beginning* is significant in several ways: first, this is the opening verse of the Qur'an, secondly, this is said to be the first complete surah that was revealed to the Prophet Muhammad (PBUH), but, more importantly, this name also symbolizes the fact that the Grace of Allah has opened the doors of life to us. As we begin to live our lives in harmony with the ways of Allah, the heart truly begins to open allowing us to let the spirit of Allah consciously manifest openly through our daily lives.

Here we have sevens, green ears and withered ears of corn, fat and lean 'kine'. Kine is an archaic word for cow, but more specifically the mature female cow.[3] The cow in many cultures is symbolic of Mother Earth. It has been a symbol of fertility, nurturing, and power. If seven represents a completion of evolution, we can say that in his vision, Joseph (PBUH) saw both the best and the worst of societies.

In many areas of the world, the cow is the primary dairy animal. Its production of milk makes it a symbol of gentle, nourishing motherhood, abundance, and fertility. Because it provides milk for humans, the cow in a way is the nurse mother of humankind. The legs of Nut, Egypt's *Celestial Cow* are mythically the four quarters of the earth. Even though the cow is a very earthy symbol, her crescent-shaped horns make her an ancient symbol of the moon. Many lunar and mother 'goddesses' around the world wear cow's horns on their heads. The moon personified is sometimes pictured riding the skies in a chariot pulled by a cow. Look at how they've taken this important symbol and codified their scheme for dominating man. The cow looks pitiful and dumb, but he's really very smart. Man puts a lot of hard work into planting hay and the cow stands around all day and eats it up. The religious establishment is most readily identified with the cow. They get the contributions from their congregations, they get tax free status, and they contribute nothing to the society. We have more trouble in the world now than ever before and at best you may get two hours of refuge from these troubles in the church on Sunday. After that, they provide no help. The people that are helped by religion most are those who recognize their own spirituality and don't seek it in the establishment of religion.

Cows eat the grass-the surface covering of the earth-which represents the common knowledge that's available to everyone. People don't get to eat this knowledge that should be available to everybody, the cow eats it. The priesthood class eats and all we get is what's left-dung; what they mockingly refer to as cow pies. The cow tricks society;

it eats the good stuff and gives us milk instead. If you don't keep it cold, that milk breaks up into water, some curd or cheese, and fat. Our intelligence and spiritual makeup are all broken up in the same manner, going its own way. We see a vision of a society where a new order of people with little common knowledge (lean, because they've only been fed foolishness) are now devouring cows, (the elite) who've gotten fat in the past. This is a picture of the change in the order of society. In 2016, Presidential candidate Bernie Sanders came virtually out of nowhere and challenged the apparent nominee Hillary Clinton for the Democratic nomination, calling himself a 'Democratic Socialist.' That term would have meant instant political death in the past, but today he has struck an apparent chord with many, particularly young people in society. His policy rails against Wall Street, corporate control, big banks and the domination of the existing establishment.

Control Through False Spiritualism-the Cow

Imam Mohammed (RAA) analyzed how the symbol of the cow has been used by a wicked group of people as a blueprint for a religious ideology to control the people: "Go again back to Egypt and look at the sacred cow symbol in Egypt and you will find that it has a three figured symbol, all on its body standing for this Trinitarian doctrine that they didn't invent. They just went to Egypt and dug up the thing and made it work and gave it to us."[4] This cabal lied on Jesus (PBUH), Moses (PBUH), and all of the Prophets (PBUT) and gave the public weak and corrupt images of G-d's messengers.[5]

We came from under a Nation of Islam mythology in which the rebellion against G-d's word, His Plan for man, and the origin of evil, are represented by the evil scientist Yacub. In the transition to true scriptural interpretation from that 'theology', a model of that wickedness is seen in parallel language, in Jacob's (PBUH) story in the Bible. We know that Jacob (PBUH) was a righteous prophet of G-d, but we also know that the language of the Bible was corrupted to hide the true message of G-d. These masterminds are rational human beings who, like Satan himself, believe they are doing the work of G-d by proving the mortal obedient human unworthy of G-d's Favor. The origins of this corruption of scripture were uncovered for us, the common people, by Imam Mohammed (RAA).

He coined the term *Jahcubite*, not to be confused with the *Jacobites* of history, to describe people who have tried to imitate Satan. He said, "I was thinking of the cub lion. You know lion and jah is a name for god, hence jah-cubs – cubs-lion, Jahcubite. In other words, the little lion of god – the little cubs, not the big lion. Actually I was thinking of people who try to imitate the big Satan and do a worse job than they would if they consulted the big Satan. I would call Jahcubites reckless people with scripture, reckless people with cultural knowledge.[6] This type is condemned in the Qur'an. And both Scriptures, Qur'an, and Bible tell us that there were renegade Jews, devils, who were notorious for that.[7] History tells us that these Jews were disowned by their own Jewish community. 'The word "Yacub" inspired me to search for a people who would be Jacub or Jacub-like and give them a new name so that we wouldn't be hung up in this (Nation of Islam) Yacub story. I started using the term Jahcubite to identify people who experiment and play with divine things and do reckless things in the world, in the life of man. I wouldn't want them to think that when I use Jahcubite I'm talking about the Jews. I've tried to correct that several times."[8]

There is a lesson here that we must accept some sacrifice and some difficulty in order to be prepared for the future. That future is a future of Truth and Reality. This world of deception, confusion and lies has run its course. Truth has to unravel the past, in our history, and in our subconscious. But once that is done we can move forward.

12:47 (Joseph) said: "For seven years shall ye diligently sow as is your wont: and the harvests that ye reap, ye shall leave them in the ear, except a little, of which ye shall eat."

Chapter 47

Save Something for Tomorrow

There's a bigger *seven,* a social order that's bigger and more important than my individual intellectual and spiritual development. There are seven archetypical human personalities represented by major prophets that are brilliant lights of guidance for our smaller, personal evolutions. They maximized the human potential and as such, qualified as guidance for all of us that follow after them. There is no excuse today for those who claim they don't know what they should follow. Follow something that doesn't represent the flaws and imperfections that you have. There is no excuse today for those leaders who claim they don't know how society should be structured to best serve the needs of the people and seemingly exhaust themselves trying to come up with a better model.[1] That seven model is complete and perfect.

Nature evolves in cycles so we can't expect that everything is always going to go along swimmingly. Scripture says that there will be wars and rumors of wars[2] and the poor will always be among us.[3] If we hold fast to those examples though and the benefits they have brought to society over time, we can weather any storms. We have to preserve all of these higher developments in structuring our lives and society. Allah says in Qur'an, that Hell has seven doors too, but those superstars of the firmament show us how to avoid those doors.

Prophet Muhammad (PBUH) said, "Live today as though today is going to be the end of you. Live as though you are never going to die." It is possible to do both at the same time. I am to live my best life today, so if I do not return to this life in the morning by Allah's Grace, I will have done all I can do. At the same time, I recognize that my good work is for the future. I may not see the rewards of my work today, but Allah has told me that what is with Him is what endures. Truth, Reality, Charity, Knowledge are with Him.

There is a western expression, "Do not put off until tomorrow what you can do today." There is scientific research that finds that people who make plans for the future are more intelligent than those who live from day to day. Consider also that if a man's average life span is 80 or so years, you can only accomplish so much within your temporal physical existence. Through our children, we can extend that to 160 or even a 1,000 years or more. But the key to that span is a broader concern-for our people and their future. We have to stop living the life of a happy seasonal animal and establish a foundation for future generations; that involves sacrifice and putting investment forward. The farmer understands this better than most. Instead of exploiting all of his land to maximize his crops and his profits, every seventh year he saves a portion of his land and lets it lie fallow. This land is plowed but is left unseeded for a season or more. Another meaning of the word fallow, which is not in common usage anymore is *talents,* creative energies that have gone uncultivated or an idea/state of mind that is undeveloped. The process allows the farmer to rest that land so it can regain its productivity. Allah says, "Let every soul look to what (provision) he has sent forth for the morrow."[4] That's investing in your soul.

When we plant trees or build institutions, we know we are not going to reap the benefits of these things today, but yet we have faith that the results will materialize in the future. Businessmen invest and have faith even though they work in the rational realm. They have to have faith just like the spiritual man does. He has to believe in his skills, in his customers, in his product, and in the principles that govern business. When he has faith in all those things, he moves forward with his investment. Even then he has to trust that G-d will give him the results of his efforts. Check your insurance policy and you'll see that even the business world recognizes that there are things they have no control over. They all have a clause that protects them against "acts of God."

We should be reminded of the ayats in the Qur'an about the two men who had gardens side by side. They both sowed and they both expected a harvest, but the one with faith recognized that on top of all his best efforts, his success depended on Allah. The other looked at his garden, prideful in his efforts and his accomplishments, thinking them permanent, and when Allah's forces intervened he was lost.[5]

We don't have to look far to see gardens that have lost their water. In April 2015, California Governor Jerry Brown imposed strict rules on water consumption as his state experienced its worse drought in 1,200 years. Governor Brown made his announcement at the snowpack in Phillips California. Snowpacks store water that falls during the wet season and release it during the summer. The Governor remarked, "We are standing on dry grass and we should be standing on five feet of snow." At the same time, the Boston area saw 108.6 inches of snow, one inch more than the previous record, which was set in the 1995-1996 winter, according to the weather service. The region broke other records that winter, with a peak of 46 inches of snowpack at the Blue Hill Observatory in Milton, the deepest in the past 130 years. It has also been the second-longest stretch of days with more than 20 inches of snow on the ground. February, with nearly 65 inches of snow in 28 days, marked the snowiest month ever recorded in Boston — by more than 21 inches.

We can't take our resources for granted. We all have physical energy, moral and intellectual forces, and while Allah tells us to seek the Garden of the hereafter with all of these resources, He likewise reminds us to use these talents to claim our part of this earthly paradise.

12:48 "Then will come after that (period) seven dreadful (years), which will devour what ye shall have laid by in advance for them, (all) except a little which ye shall have (specially) guarded."

Chapter 48

Where There is No Vision, the People Perish

The leadership (head) sits atop the society and advances it, but sometimes it can become blind (the blind leading the blind).[1] There is a blindness resulting from the lack of light (enlightenment) and there is a blindness resulting from too much light too suddenly. In either case, there is no vision and as the Bible says, "Where There is No Vision, the People Perish." [Proverbs 29:18]

Both the new world (unable to adjust to quickly emerging science and popular culture) and the old world (unable to apply revelation and tradition to modern problems[2]) can perish. The leader in Egypt had a vision that he did not understand, but he was wise enough to reach out to someone who could interpret it for him. Joseph (PBUH) had a vision in his youth, which defined his ideal. His circumstances within the family were such that he was the younger of jealous brothers and traditionally would not have been favored over the elder brothers. He was plotted against, put in a well or a pit, and sold into slavery. Even this couldn't destroy his broader vision. The limitation of the pit couldn't hold him for long because the traders recognized his value as *basher-good news*. Being separated from home and family also presents him with a wider view of the world and a larger scope. The opportunities soon grow to fit the scope of his expanding powers, as he rose to power in the house of the Aziz.[3] His vision refused to be confined by its present time and space and eventually, that time and space had to expand to accommodate the vision.

Time and Space

Scientists today are recognizing that to understand even material reality we need more than the concepts of time and space. Dictionary.com defines *space* as "the unlimited or incalculably great three-dimensional realm or expanse in which all material objects are located and all events occur." Everything, including space, has its beginning, its ending, and its limitations.

Dictionary.com also defines *place* as, "a particular portion of space, whether of definite or indefinite extent. Space and place can sometimes be used interchangeably. In common language, a person's place is sometimes referred to as their living space. We raise our children to respect their personal belongings and their personal space with the hope that they will go out into the world and respect the broader space and evolve to become trustees of the environment.

"The stronger our spirits become, the less authority *linear time* can exercise in our lives." *Anatomy of the Spirit, Dr. Carolyn Myss, p* 173. The Honorable Elijah Muhammad had a vision, a mission, and a keen insight into time and space. As a social reformer, he was in touch with the sentiments of the people and as a politician, he knew how to manipulate the levers of power within the system. Those early years of the Nation of Islam were years of struggle for his followers. They were depression years when food was scarce and local grocers in the neighborhood helped keep the family fed. Before his passing, his vision began to manifest and he had established a network of business enterprises in Chicago that was mirrored in major cities throughout the country. This included: Two supermarkets in Chicago, a fish house, a bank, 3 bakeries/coffee shops, sales and office buildings, over 40 schools nationally, an import operation and store, clothing factory, cleaners, transportation department that included: 10 dry bed and refrigerator tractor trailer trucks, a slaughter house, 111,450 acres of farmland in Georgia, Michigan and Alabama, cattle sheep, chickens, and another 400,000 acres in British Columbia, production and distribution of over 40,000 pounds of meat per month, over 500,000 eggs; real estate development managing 42 homes and housing for 200 families, weekly production and distribution of 800,000 copies per week of Muhammad Speaks Newspapers,

When he returned to Allah, he was described by *Readers Digest* as "the most powerful Black man in America." How did this struggle evolve into that success? He knew what time it was. After being released from prison, he went about building the 'Nation' on the teachings, principles, and lessons that had been left with him by W. D. Fard. By 1959, he recognized that it was time for something else. He ordered all the lessons to be confiscated. The ministers were no longer to teach Yacub's history, the making of the white man, and the other esoteric teachings. Instead, they would emphasize the material promises of the teaching – money, good homes, and friendships in all walks of life. He would begin building businesses, proving the success of self-help, getting some land, and providing for black people's needs – the material success that we found upon his passing. But signs pointed to a transition towards a different time.

Angels and Birds

Angels and birds have similar symbolic meanings. The most likely reason for this linkage is the idea of communication and message delivery.[4] Birds' songs and angel's tongues both seem to have the same goal – the revelation of something important, something otherworldly, something perhaps divine to the mortal. With such an emphasis on birds' ability to communicate, it seems pretty obvious that in a dream, the bird may represent communication of some form. The bird may be a herald, bringing news about something that may soon come into being.

I personally observed signs of the transition from an industrial to an informational society. On the morning of December 23, 1986, astrologer Irene Hughes noted: "Mercury was in a dangerous [conjunction] with [Scorpio]." Mercury, she stated, is related to transportation and communication. Allah and Prophet Muhammad (PBUH) condemned the belief in heavenly bodies influencing human behavior, but that does not say they cannot influence the material creation that does not possess free will. We know, at the very least, that they are signs that may mark fixed periods of time.[5] For example, the sun and the earth influence a plant's growth, as in heliotropism and geotropism. The sun, through solar storms, can blast massive clouds of material called a coronal mass ejection (CME), into space and if these clouds of plasma and charged particles hit the Earth head on, they can cause geomagnetic and solar radiation storms that can knock out satellites in space and power grids on the ground. On that day in 1986, a major blackout occurred in Chicago, shutting down vast sections of the city and affecting transportation and communication (commerce). On that same day, the American space capsule Voyager completed the first flight around the world without refueling – another feat of transportation and communication – linking the world.

The book *Future Trends* chronicles society's evolution from an industrial society to an informational society with transportation and communication being the vehicles of information. Decades ago, cultural observers said that the telegraph – a major vehicle of communication – was "annihilating time and space."[6] Today we can say the same thing about the Internet and cellular connectivity. Everything that we think we know about the world and how it works is changing. It is being devoured[7] by a new paradigm of social development.

12:49 "Then will come after that (period) a year in which the people will have abundant water, and in which they will press (wine and oil)."

Chapter 49

He Speaks and Lives Are Changed

Joseph (PBUH) understood that putting him in charge of the storehouses of the land was necessary for individuals and communities to evolve to the heaven (seven) on earth and how they similarly degenerate from that high development. That's why he was able to speak and change lives.

We all hope and pray for abundant water to nourish our gardens and to revive our dead land. When we get it, we can't forget the devotion we had when we were in need and praying for relief. It is that time – once we have been relieved of our burdens and struggles – that we should show even more devotion.[1] Once our moral and spiritual lives are established, we will have fewer struggles.[2]

Cultivation-Socialization

Culture is defined as "the quality in a person or society that arises from a concern for what is regarded as excellent in arts, letters, manners, scholarly pursuits, etc." The term originally meant the cultivation of the soul or mind as seen by Roman philosopher Cicero in his series *Tusculan Disputations*, where he wrote of a cultivation of the soul or *cultura animi*. The Arabic language confirms this meaning in its word *falah*, which literally is defined as a farmer who cultivates the soil, but is used throughout the Qur'an to refer to the cultivation of the soul or what we could describe as the conversion of the soul's potentialities into actualities (notice the similarity between soil and soul, and the fact that the human soul, Adam (PBUH) was made from earth *soil*). (2:189, 3:130, 3:200).

Human infants are born without any culture.[3] They come into the world naked. Their parents, teachers, and others transform them into cultural and socially adept animals. The general process of acquiring culture is referred to as socialization. During socialization, we learn the language of the culture we are born into, as well as the roles we are to play in life. For instance, girls learn how to be daughters, sisters, friends, wives, and mothers. In addition, they learn about the occupational roles that their society has in store for them. Humans also learn and adopt cultural norms through the socialization process. Norms are the conceptions of appropriate and expected behaviors that are held by most members of the society. Anthropologists also use the term *enculturation* for the process of being socialized to a particular culture. Socialization is important in the process of personality formation. While much of human personality is the result of our genes, the socialization process can mold it in particular directions by encouraging specific beliefs and attitudes, as well as selectively providing experiences.

Supreme Wisdom

What Yusuf (PBUH) saw in his dream was the exact destiny that Allah created for Adam (PBUH). Allah says in Qur'an, "*Sakhara lakum maa fee al-Ard—He* has subjected to our (use) everything on earth. All resources in the heavens and the earth have been created for the service of mankind, thus Joseph's (PBUH) vision of eleven stars and the sun and the moon making obeisance to him. Obeisance means (a movement of the body expressing deep respect or deferential courtesy, as before a superior; a bow, curtsy, or other similar gesture) –another word for prostration or sajdah (sajdah being the position in the Muslim prayer ritual, Salat, in which the forehead, the nose, the palms, the feet, and knees, your toes in front or your feet on the ground--eight spots touch the earth.)

W. D. Fard organized the Nation of Islam and organized us, the FOI, under those same symbols – the sun, moon, and star. He put them in front of us on our national flag and we wore them on our head, on our fezzes, on our uniforms, and carried them on our shoulder. He gave us "knowledge" of their origins, their size, weight, and distances. We owned them. He was a Professor and his object was for his students to try to answer the lessons and expand our minds in the process. Imam Mohammed (RAA) went to the head of the class and answered the lessons and questions of W. D. Fard 100% correctly. Fard called his teaching *Supreme Wisdom* and with that wisdom came a mission of leadership; the resurrection of the African American people. We were born from that womb of the Nation of Islam and we will always reverence that experience.[4] That mission was expanded under Imam Mohammed (RAA) to the remaking of the whole world through the proper representation of Al-Islam.

This focus on the heavens has an important purpose since heavens means leadership. The sun gives light and represents the knowledge that rules the earth. When the sun goes down, that light is reflected by the moon-the prophets. Man has always identified with nature and heavenly objects. Many of us want to be *superstars* and we are all still in the garden of material creation.[5] Abraham (PBUH) was promised his offspring would be as numerous as the stars in the sky. The vision, therefore, has to be bigger than the material dominion. The stars are bodies of light and guidance and even the ancient or primitive man understood this.

We might consider primitive man's identification with certain animals and objects quite backward but look at the modern phenomena of sports competition and the symbols and mascots of these teams. Both the competitors and the spectators are living vicariously through the Bears, Wolves, Gators, Eagles, etc. But what we should also look at is the logic behind these identifications. We are just today trying to find a better relationship with these fellow earth-citizens and a rapidly depleting Mother Earth. "The same ideas of the interdependence, the interchangeability, the essential unity, of all forms and manifestations of life, which appear in the folklore of plants, underlie much of the folklore of animals." *The Handbook of Folklore – Traditional Beliefs, Practices, Customs, Stories and Sayings*, by Charlotte Sophia Burne, 1914. p 40.

G-d said to Adam (PBUH), "Tell them their names." The things existed then just as they do today but the language to name things is still evolving and our understanding of things that feed that language is still evolving. Primitive man thought in pictures just as we do today. These early pictures eventually were reduced to symbols that grouped together to become letters, then words, then sentences, and formal language was born. But there was language there all the time. Charles Babbage, the

19th-century mathematician, and mechanical engineer noted: "In tree rings he saw nature encoding messages about the past. A profound lesson: that a tree records a whole complex of information in its solid substance. Every shower that falls, every change in temperature that leaves in the vegetable world the traces of its passage; slight indeed, and imperceptible perhaps to us, but not the less permanently recorded in the depths of those woody fabrics." [6,7]

In the 1600's, Isaac Newton struggled to find words to describe nature's laws. Language had not caught up with the reality or perception of the material universe.[8] Galileo, in 1611, saw that it was language that was actually holding science back. He said, "Names and attributes must be accommodated to the essence of things, and not the essence to the names, since things come first and names afterward.[9] There is a need for a new paradigm. "The time is close at hand when the scattered members of civilized communities will be as closely united, so far as instant telephonic communication is concerned, as the various members of the body now are by the nervous system."[10]

As this brave new world evolves, we are challenged to extract from whatever circumstance, whatever technologies arise, the spiritual and intellectual benefits. One of the greatest benefits is the universality of language and communication. The social unrest in many parts of the world reflects this. Circumstances will bring out more true spirituality, more wisdom, and a greater social sensitivity. Oppression and ignorance can't be hidden anymore. People are arriving at an understanding that the earth belongs to G-d, and the trustees that have been put over it have an obligation to assure that G-d's blessings accrue to all people. The one who has this perspective is the one that should be taken to the king. "In his hands he holds the cords of gigantic responsibilities; he speaks and lives are changed; men and women hang upon his words and remold their characters."[11]

12:50 So the king said, "Bring ye him unto me." But when the messenger came to him, (Joseph) said: "Go thou back to thy lord, and ask him, 'What is the state of mind of the ladies who cut their hands'? For my Lord is certainly well aware of their snare."

Chapter 50

You Can't Put New Wine in Old Bottles.

What will this new paradigm in society look like? First, let's look at the old one. The decent person or the man of truth trying to get his point across ends up on network TV looking less than respectable. They laugh at him saying, "He wants us to stop promiscuity and only have sex in marriage. Ha, ha, ha. We watch all these network TV shows and reality shows. There's nothing wrong with promiscuity, as long as you use a condom. He wants us to get serious about life but life is just for fun."

Sa'id ibn al-Musayyab and Abu 'Ubayd reported from Abu Hurayra that the Prophet (PBUH) said, "If I had remained in prison as long as Yusuf remained and then the summoner had come to me, I would have responded to him." I supposed I would have jumped out of the door myself. But I can understand Joseph (PBUH) too. "You people have some problem out there and you want me to help you but you are not willing to change anything about your behavior."

The society is always looking for sacrificial lambs – redeemers on whom it can focus its transformation and live vicariously through. The concept that Jesus (PBUH) died for our sins enables one who believes that to do anything they want because the price for the sins has already been paid. I have had Christians tell me that Islam is too harsh for them. They have been cleansed in the blood of Jesus (PBUH) so they can do whatever they want. Joseph (PBUH) sent a message to the king saying, "It's not enough for you to just release me; you have to clear me of these false charges. I never was a part of your society's corruption." This is reminiscent of Jesus' (PBUH) assertion that you can't put new wine in old bottles.[1] Joseph (PBUH) represented a new language and a new spirit in leadership; one that focused on the common person and opening up the knowledge to the masses. It was already said that the ladies in the city cut their hands when they saw him. Now society has to be ready for change and real change requires new social structures and institutions. W. D. Fard and the Honorable Elijah Muhammad recognized this so they provided, in the Nation of Islam, a completely new social construct. We had our own teachings, our own laws, and our own diet, and our history, destiny, and our survival depends on us not being seduced by the trends of the society. Once we overcome our dependency, indeed our addiction to the ruling society, we open the way for a new culture, a new garment, and a new container for a pure spirit.

12:51 (The king) said (to the ladies): "What was your affair when ye did seek to seduce Joseph from his (true) self?" The ladies said: "Allah preserve us! no evil know we against him!" Said the 'Aziz's wife: "Now is the truth manifest (to all): it was I who sought to seduce him from his (true) self: He is indeed of those who are (ever) true (and virtuous)."

Chapter 51

How Do You Establish Normal Civilian Life Surrounded by Land Mines?

We live in a world today that has literally been turned on its head. Logic and rational behavior has been placed on the ground as something to be kicked around or mocked and fads, ignorance, and immorality has been elevated to honorable status. Take for example the latest entertainment news. The names don't matter; they're interchangeable. The subject is the same. Who's sleeping with whom? Who's got a gay a partner? Who's cheating on whom? Who's gotten naked or exposed their body? Who's in the latest sex scene in a movie? All of the interest is below the belt.

If we follow the flow of the *common lot* we will miss the whole purpose of our existence here and all the abundance that G-d intends for us.[1] Everything we need and could want is given to us in abundant measure, but if we look around us today we see broken homes, broken communities, and broken lives leading us to wonder where the abundance lies. Our physical environment is what feeds our senses and our perception. Everything that we ever eat will come from this material creation. Everything that we will ever know comes from G-d or through His Creations: His prophets, His Revelation to His prophets or inspiration to us.

That original environment of the Garden was designed to feed man's senses, nourish him, and enable him to grow to evolve his society and accomplish bigger and better things. What has happened? We've been tricked. Satan is known as the *ghuruu* – the one responsible for all of the deceptions in the creation.

Allah created the beautiful institution of marriage and sex, and Satan interprets them now as a *lifestyle choice* or *unrestricted freedom*. We have the beautiful food that G-d put in this Garden to keep us healthy, but try to get a child to eat a slice of whole wheat bread or raisin bran cereal. Most of what we eat is processed food infused with sugar, salt, and fat. We perceive this food as making us young and beautiful but the reality is, it puts us on the path to obesity and hypertension. Allah created us in tribes and nations so we would grow in knowledge from our interaction with each other but instead, we see each other as racial groups and nationalities. The object is to seduce us from our true self-our true reality.

The earth is supposed to be an enriching environment but you can't truly grow from the experience for having to dance around the land mines that are placed at every step of the journey. There is a scientific concept called environmental enrichment that involves the enhancement of an animal's physical or social environment. In 1947, researchers found that rats raised as pets performed better on problem-solving tests than rats raised in cages. Later, research found that growing up in such enriched environments increased and improved brain activity and enhanced learning capacity. This enrichment for the rats involved housing them in groups to increase social contact and adding stimulating, novel objects into the immediate environment. In contrast, other rats were raised under conditions of isolation, housed singly in cages; thus the concept of enriched environment versus the impoverished environment. Scientists did not put the term *impoverished* on the deprived environment by accident. As human beings, we have a choice. We have the power to create our physical environments and we can enrich them with good things – parks, playgrounds, trees, beautiful homes, businesses, clean streets, etc. But if we don't actively work to do this, the popular culture, and our subconscious, where Satan holds sway, will create an environment for us.

We have to recognize that everything has been changed. It's not natural and it's not nourishing anymore. If we have an impoverished environment within, if our soul is empty, if we are uninspired, if we don't have the energy to spread this great message of Truth, as given in the Qur'an and the example of our Prophet (PBUH), then we are living a life of poverty and it's going to reflect in our outer environment – our homes, our neighborhoods, our businesses, and our community life.

12:52 "This (say I), in order that He may know that I have never been false to him in his absence, and that Allah will never guide the snare of the false ones."

Chapter 52

You Can't Connect Nonsense to Material Reality

There are many currents flowing through society and they take many different forms. Most of them are like air or wind – they come and go and leave nothing but a good feeling or, as with violent winds, death, and destruction. A fad is a behavior that occurs in the population with no logical origin and quickly fades. It can be driven by the mass media but can also take on a life of its own. Allah addresses these fads and behaviors in the Qur'an 4:56: *"Those who reject our signs, we shall soon cast into the Fire: as often as their skins are roasted through, we shall change them for fresh skins, that they may taste the penalty: for Allah is exalted in power, wise."*

Those fresh skins are new fads and when they burn that one off, we'll get still another. And that's hell when your life is miserable and you go from one nonsense behavior to another and you never get a chance to establish your life. I pray that this behavior of the sagging pants, parading their butts and underwear that is so popular now among many of our young men wears out and eventually they realize the uncivilized behavior that it represents.

A fetish, which comes from the word meaning *false* or *artificial*, refers to an object of irrational reverence or obsessive devotion. It originally meant a material object believed to possess magical powers. Perversion is the alteration of something from its original state, although it also refers to a sexual behavior that is considered abnormal or unacceptable.

Unfortunately, every generation redefines perversion according to the whims of the masses. The common thread of all these behaviors is that none of them have a rational basis; none of them is rooted in anything natural. You just can't connect nonsense to material reality.

If you wonder why many of us have no place in the economic picture of America, it is because we have neglected to connect with the earth, with productive activity, and with reality. We have become content with functioning in the illusions of pop culture. We put all of our energy in and seek identity through things of no substance leaving us exhausted with nothing to show for it. We are warned to save ourselves and our families from the fire.[1] In our first experience (First Resurrection) in the Nation of Islam, when we were put out of the temple for a major sin, it was called class *F*, which meant the *fire*. If the Judgment came before you got back in the temple, you were just burnt up.

Translator and Qur'an Commentator, Abdullah Yusuf Ali, offers two constructions for this verse: one in which the Aziz's wife makes the statement and the other in which Joseph (PBUH) does. I prefer the latter construction and that of the majority of commentators because there appears to be no context in which the wife would be saying "I have never been false to him in his absence." She, in fact, is the one who had been false to her husband in his absence when she tried to seduce Joseph (PBUH).

Also, Joseph (PBUH) would have been the one most likely testifying that "Allah will never guide the snare of the false ones." It was his escape from that snare, his character, and his life, that qualified him to make that assertion. Joseph (PBUH) referenced their "trap" in 12:50 and picks it up again in this ayat after the wife confesses, "It was I who sought to seduce him from his (true) self." Here he conditions his own release on their (the ladies) acknowledgment of his innocence. Yusuf (PBUH) asserts his truthfulness; that he is never sneaky or false even when his master is not present.[2] Many of us demonstrate exemplary conduct when it is on display. We pray as Allah says, "to be seen of men." We give in charity to be seen as the "big man." But in our private quarters, when there is no external payoff, we waver. We do a cost-benefit analysis. What am I to gain from this act? That is, unfortunately, the antithesis of faith. Yusuf (PBUH) however is the same when he is not being seen and he accepts being right even when there is no logic and objective force requiring him to do so. Allah says He did not create two hearts in man and that's a sign that we cannot present one face to the world and another in our private life. When we do find ourselves in error, as we all will do, we have to accept responsibility for our own acts and not blame others. I tell people all the time when they complain about something they should be doing or are not doing, "Maybe the aliens will release you one day." That illogical premise that something foreign or outside of themselves is controlling their actions seems to wake them up to the fact that they are responsible for their own choices and their consequence.

12:53 "Nor do I absolve my own self (of blame): the (human) soul is certainly prone to evil, unless my Lord do bestow His Mercy: but surely my Lord is Oft-forgiving, Most Merciful."

Chapter 53

I Am Where I Am Because of My Own Choices

We all have to take ownership of our choices and that includes our sins, mistakes and errors. We use the expression *own up to* meaning to take responsibility for our actions and in the Nation of Islam teachings we were told, "Excuses, mistakes or pardons of any nature are not considered on the law books of Islam." That might seem harsh but the teaching of *unalike attracts* of the Nation of Islam provided a rigid and unflinching structure in contrast to the moral laxity and injustices of the *dead world.* The message was very clear and the spirit was to encourage us to stop making excuses and placing blame on others. We all have to be able to look in the mirror and say, "I am where I am because of my own choices."[1,2] Prophet Muhammad (PBUH) said, "Verily your deeds will be brought back to you as if you yourself were the creator of your own punishment." We must also accept responsibility for every thought and desire, for Allah says that every act of thinking or feeling will be inquired about on the day of judgment.[3]

Abdullah ibn Masud (Radiallahu Anhu) has narrated that he heard the Messenger of Allah (PBUH) say, "Each one of you is a shepherd. And each of you will be asked about your flock. A ruler also is a shepherd and he will be asked about his flock. And every man is a shepherd to his family. And every woman is the custodian of her husband's house and his children. Thus, each one of you is a shepherd and each one will be asked about his flock." [Sahih Bukhari and Muslim][4]

We all have the capacity to repel evil and to fulfill these responsibilities. Muslims reject the idea that human nature is gross matter, a situation for sin. Rather it's a tendency in the soul to want to do its own thing as opposed to obedience. That's what gets us in trouble; not some original sin. Scripture says that G-d made everything and it was all good.

Human nature is the base that supports everything else. The whole life of the animal world is ruled over by the drive to overcome hunger – the drive of the flesh for something to satisfy it. If you can control that very powerful drive, it not only gives you the power to withstand the flesh, but it helps you in every way because everything in the universe is related. The body affects the mind, the mind affects the body, and thereby, morality is affected; all these things influence each other. There is also an influence of the jinn from within and from outside of us – a reasoning, questioning and doubting capacity. That jinn that is outside of us must exist in another human being.

Man has the power to animate the dead material world and make it speak to us, engage our rational mind, communicate to us; even answering questions and talking back to us and making us come to a conclusion. We live in a society that wants to give extraordinary power to these natural influences as a way of absolving the individual from blame. The African American Comedian Flip Wilson did a well-known skit in his television show in which he would do something ridiculous or irrational and then say, "the devil made me do it." Of course, all the humor of the skit would have been lost but what he should have said is, the devil whispered a suggestion to me and I obeyed it.

By thinking on God's great wonders, we are kept powerful and very much alive. Our mind is awakened and it makes us stand up independent of the outer body. We have to strive to rule over that outer body, sometimes deny its cravings in order to live in the higher realm. This is what Joseph (PBUH) is acknowledging here—that tendency to want to be in charge and do it our own way. The popular culture recognizes this and speaks to that nature. It tells us, *"Have it your way," "Obey your thirst," "Just do it."* Many of us are unable to step outside of the outer environment and look within. Even more difficult is listening to the voice within us. We all have voices within us, but we are taught and conditioned to ignore the one that gives us the best guidance. We sometimes ignore our intuition and the adage that says *follow your first mind.* In the old cartoons, the character would often be shown with an angel on his right shoulder and an *imp* or devil on his left shoulder. The angel, which would always give the character good guidance, would either be ignored or brushed off by the devil and the character would then go on to get into trouble. It has been said by learned Imams in this religion that "The best victory is victory over yourself." The best conquest is the management of your own impulses or urges. Prophet Muhammad (PBUH) said, "to achieve self-control is the best Jihad."

12:54 So the king said: "Bring him unto me; I will take him specially to serve about my own person." Therefore when he had spoken to him, he said: "Be assured this day, thou art, before our own presence, with rank firmly established, and fidelity fully proved!"

Chapter 54

I Will Be What I Am, and I Am Already What I Shall Be

The King offered to bring Joseph (PBUH), "to serve about my own person." This appears to be the same type of position that the baker and the wine steward had. And how did it work for them? They both ended up in prison and one ended up dead. The goal was not to be a personal servant. Joseph (PBUH) was not looking to serve the personality, but as we see from the next verse to serve the needs of the people.

Serving the Pharaoh or King was the popular reward in this type of society. The leaders who rule based on secret knowledge promise to bring you into their inner circle. The Pharaohs would bring their ministers, sorcerers, staff, and servants all into the tomb with them when they died so they could still serve them in the afterlife. So really the promise that was made was a promise of death.[1]

While it may take time and circumstances to establish our worth in the eyes of the public and the leadership, the value is always inherent in us. Imam Mohammed (RAA) described this awareness saying: "I recognize that G-d created me with that that shall place me where I should be in the future. But I have to discover it. When I discover what G-d has endowed me with, enriched me with as a special creation of His, I will discover what will put me where I am to go. I may be a lost savage eating with animals and living like an animal, but when I wake up to what G-d has made me I will separate myself from the animals and from the savage. I will pursue the course that G-d designed for me when He designed me. I will be what I am, and I am already what I shall be."

We started in our creation in an excellent mold and our journey is to get back there. T. S. Eliott wrote: "We shall not cease from exploration and the end of all our exploring will be to arrive where we started and know the place for the first time." He continued, "What we call the beginning is often the end. And to make an end is to make a beginning. The end is where we start from."--*"rank firmly established and fidelity fully proved."* When we reach this state of peace and satisfaction, the mind and the body become faithful servants of the soul; it is at rest because they are established in obedience and will not cause it to stray.

Nature

Al-Islam is the religion of nature. I have always been fascinated with nature. My own path to Islam began in trying to find a natural way of life or, as it was expressed at that time, "getting in tune with the universe." It is more than just accessing your internal alarm clock – affirming to yourself, that you are going to awake at a certain time and having your body obey and wake you up at that time. It is more than having the birds wake you up at the time for fajr prayer. It is appreciating the beauty and the power of the sun, the moon, the stars, the plants, and the air. It is finding your true self-your best self.[1] During that time, I stopped smoking, drinking and eating pork. I studied the book Back to Eden, by Jethro Kloss and adopted healing and healthful practices. I studied with a lady herbalist on Cottage Grove Avenue near Bowen Avenue in Chicago, who still collected, processed plants, and sold botanicals and incense. I studied nutrition and went on extended fasts under Dr. Alvenia Fulton, who had also counseled Dick Gregory. Phil Cohran, the venerable musician, was my mentor and his Affro Arts Theater became the focus of culture in Chicago. Everyone involved in the movement had spoken or performed at that Theater – Stokely Carmichael (Kwame Toure), Fred Hampton, Rahsaan Roland Kirk, etc. It was there that I met Wallace D. Mohammed (RAA) who was teaching an Arabic class there. I investigated Orisha Vudu culture because of its personification of and belief in accessing forces of nature. In both Christianity and in pagan history this universal concept of returning to original nature has been clothed or influenced by pagan ideas. It is seen in primitive cultures and even in the rituals of Christmas and Easter.

I grew out my natural hair when this was seen as a symbol of *African-ness* or naturalness; before it was called an Afro and made into a popular style. I recently saw an interview on YouTube where Kathleen Cleaver, who was very involved in the Student Non-Violence Coordinating Committee and the Black Panther Party in the 1960's and 70's, explained the natural hair to chants of "Black is Beautiful" in the background: "This brother here, myself, all of us were born with our hair like this and we just wear it like this because it's natural. The reason for it, you might say, is like a new awareness among Black people that their own natural appearance, this physical appearance, is beautiful and is pleasing to them. For so many, many years we were told that only white people were beautiful, only straight hair, light eyes, light skin, was beautiful and so Black women would try everything they could to straighten their hair, lighten their skin to look as much like white women. This is changed because Black people are aware."

There is a powerful force in embracing the natural; a recognition that the world as it is ordered by man, is not conducive to our health and success. We all start with this original nature or pattern.[2]

The word *fitraa* describes the original pattern of our creation, and *Din al-Fitra* is the religion or way of life that complements that original pattern and nature. The observance and the disciplines of our sacred month of fasting – Ramadan – is designed in part to bring us back to that original, obedient state.

This is opposite of the ideology or theology that G-d wants you to be good, but in order to be good, you can't be yourself. You have to go outside your nature to be good. That is going to create a perverted creature – a person at war within himself. Your nature is urging and telling you one thing while your desire to be good is pulling you another way. That is textbook schizophrenia. These teachings say that man must first die to his own nature. The truth is that if you must die, then die to your own sin and your own foolishness. Then you can live in the truth. This removes fear, inspires courage, and allows us to begin to live.

Though nature is the beginning of our growth and development, it is not enough. Nature is a good beginning toward man's full potential but Revelation then has to come to show man his purpose on this Earth. The proof that nature is the good base for establishing excellence for man in society is Prophet Mohammed (PBUH). The more I traveled in that direction, the more I realized peace and Islam is the religion of peace. I may not have known where I was headed but I knew that following my best nature would get me there.[4]

A popular song during this period of freedom protests in the 60s and 70s was by a group called the *Fifth Dimension*, which sang "This is the dawning of the age of Aquarius." So whereas many of us recognized a need for the real freedom that G-d intends, the majority of society was flooded with morally undisciplined freedom – Aquarius the water pourer, drowning the people in their own ignorance; a strategy for retrogressing and retarding the individual nature and corrupting the concept of freedom.

There has to be a rejection of the world once we make the decision to get on the right path. The Nation of Islam presented some of the same philosophies and disciplines that I had already accepted, including militancy, Black Nationalism and eating to live. I also found resonance in the Nation of Islam with the moral precepts I had been raised with in my youth. When I came into the Nation we had to cut off the naturals. We got a short haircut just as they do in the American military. I think what that actually represented was a trade-off – the individual symbol of rebellion and rejection of the dominant white society, in favor of a common symbol of the same rejection. We all looked and acted like Elijah – neat, clean, serious, respectful, bow tie, or as we described ourselves-"quick moving, fast thinking, right down to modern time."

W. D. Fard's Strategy

Imam Mohammed (RAA) described Fard's strategy in converting the African American to Islam. That strategy was trying to bring the community to Jah. Jah represents the natural motivation, natural human drive, natural human sentiment, and natural human aspiration. Fard came to awaken and stimulate that nature.

The pagans said to the Prophet Ibrahim (PBUH), "we know these idols are not really G-d, they are our *illah* (deity) or *Elijah* – a means for reaching G-d. They knew the idols were objects, not Almighty G-d who created the heavens and the Earth, but *Jah.* W. D. Fard (Master Fard Muhammad) wasn't trying to bring this community called the

Nation of Islam to G-d. He was pointing us in that direction and putting us on the path. The Honorable Elijah Muhammad told us many times that his job was to clean us up for the next one who would teach us the religion? Most of us went through that difficult, patient process called the Nation of Islam and arrived at the planned Destination.

The popular Reggae artist Bob Marley sang in his song, *Forever Loving Jah,* of "shedding no tears, having no fears, never being blue, being patient regardless of what stages, rages, or changes we go through" and he points to the bigger purpose at the end of those trials:

> What has been hidden
> From the wise and the prudent
> Been revealed to the babe and the suckling
>
> Cause just like a tree planted
> Planted by the rivers of water
> That bringeth forth fruits
> Bringeth forth fruits in due season;
>
> Everything in life got its purpose,
> Find its reason in every season,

Although on the surface joining the Nation of Islam in 1968, may have looked like a momentous change in belief and lifestyle, in reality, it was just a natural and a logical transition for me. A lot was happening in 1948 when I was born and by 1968 the world was undergoing another sea change. New nations were emerging and gaining independence: India, Pakistan, Israel, Palestine. In the midst of all of this was our own freedom movement. The words that I remember that influenced me most, in coming into the Nation of Islam, was in a quote from the Qur'an that was carried in Muhammad Speaks Newspaper: "A people guided by Allah cannot be enslaved." That resonated with me and I understand now that it was the same spirit of freedom in me, the same spirit behind the freedom movement that was touched by that statement. That spirit is the spirit of truth because the truth will set you free. There was so much power in that one *ayat* that spoke to my human soul and I believe now that the search for the authentic self (soul) can be seen as a portal or pathway to the higher self. William James wrote: "Seek out that particular mental attribute which makes you feel deeply and vitally alive, along with which comes the inner voice which says, 'this is the real me,' and when you have found that attitude, follow it."

Fard created a satirical mythology designed to counteract the oppressive self-hate and white worship psychology that we had lived under for 400 years. It was also designed to give us some familiarity with Islamic language and ideas and to connect an isolated people to the worldwide community of Muslims. It accomplished all of these things and also pointed us in the direction of excellent Muslim life and the highest standards of Muslim behavior. When we finally would come into a mature and an enlightened understanding of scripture (Islam proper), we would recognize ourselves in a unique leadership role. That connection to each other and to other humanity satisfied a void in our social nature. That is why most of us honor him (Fard) and the Honorable Elijah Muhammad today and pray for their souls and pray that Allah grant them the reward of Paradise for the good intentions and efforts.

12:55 (Joseph) said: "Set me over the store-houses of the land: I will indeed guard them, as one that knows (their importance)."

Chapter 55

I Will Define Me

Once Joseph (PBUH) is freed and his worth is established, he tells the King, "Appoint or establish me over the treasure of the earth or treasury of the land or regard me (above) them." The treasury is where the nation's capital is. Capital comes from the word head. The nation's true head or leadership, its true value, is its moral excellence, its human innocence, and correct knowledge and you find these in the common people. It is accepted that information and particularly useful information or correct knowledge is the currency of the future. If we reflect back on Verse 12:19 Allah says, "They concealed him (Joseph) (PBUH) as a treasure." Joseph's (PBUH) assertion is that he knows or can distinguish (the importance of the treasures of the earth). This passage is reminiscent of two things: One is Allah's command to Adam (PBUH), 2:31 to 33 "Tell them their names." Another interesting parallel is the Bible passage: "They will beat their swords into plowshares and their spears into pruning hooks." Adam (PBUH) was given the power to identify everything in creation according to its utility to him. We define what the object is to be used for. Many of us have had to, at times, knock a nail in with a brick. Is wasn't designed for that purpose but that's what its utility was for us at that time. Now Joseph (PBUH) is seen as knowing his own value and that of valuable things.

We love gold, and it is a precious metal, but it is iron that is a more necessary component in our blood, needed for strength and to avoid anemia. The same iron is a key component of the tools of war.[1] The

Bible speaks of a time when the metal of those weapons would be seen and named in its positive value to man, as plows and pruning hooks for cultivation and the nourishment of humanity, instead of swords and spears. I do not believe that all wars and conflicts will end, but I know a time must come when civilized nations will allow the Word of G-d to judge between their disputes. President Obama ended the war in Iraq and is winding down the war in Afghanistan, although there is some inconsistency and consternation in his escalation of the drone wars. He does appear to recognize a greater value in the nation's treasury being used to build up the country, its infrastructure, and the education of its citizens instead of its vast military expenditures. His election symbolizes progress in many respects. Former Governor and Attorney General of New York, Eliot Spitzer, wrote in Slate online magazine the day after the election, in identifying one of the six obvious lessons from Obama's victory, "At a deep level, this election was about our notion of community in times of need." He was responding to a campaign theme advanced by the President that an individual did not build his business or his success by himself, without the help and support of the broader community and the government. He also points out the theme of inclusion in the Obama campaign, as opposed to exclusion and exclusivity.

The Romney campaign of 2012 relied more heavily on big money donors that enabled him to flood the media and influence those more susceptible to false perceptions and emotions than facts. Michael Isikoff wrote for NBC News, "A study Wednesday by the Sunlight Foundation, which tracks political spending, concluded that Republican strategist, Karl Rove's super PAC, American Crossroads, had a success rate of just 1% on $103 million in attack ads–one of the lowest returns on investment (ROIs) of any outside spending group in this year's elections." Of the eight candidates supported by casino billionaire Sheldon Adelson, the biggest single donor in political history with tens of millions of dollars in contributions to super PACs, none were victorious on Tuesday. In contrast, Obama recognized the value of individuals despite their race, gender, and orientation. He appreciated the value of human capital and was thus qualified to be set over the treasury. The first value we should recognize is that of our human self.

We begin our life with a divine script written for us by our Creator.[2] Then we come into a physical and social environment and begin to live those scripts that have already been written by someone else – our parents, our peers, our spouses, our bosses, our nations – and many times we live our whole life having existed but never having truly lived. The life fully-lived requires that we step outside these roles and write our own script. Though this takes courage and self-esteem, this is the only way to truly liberate ourselves. We are as we see ourselves, so when we are asked to describe who we are, we, by default, identify ourselves by our professions. I am a lawyer. I am a doctor, etc. We have to see ourselves in our real personhood and that is primarily as a human soul. The person with human sensitivity is the one who should be in charge of the country's resources. Looking at the Muslim world today, it is obvious why the people are revolting all over it. There are kings and their family and elites who control all of the wealth of the country. And in many of those places, the common people don't even have sanitation and pure water to drink. In other places, there are sheiks and others who control and hide the knowledge while the common people can't even read and write.

Many times we don't even recognize or appreciate our own resources. As a community, too often we have lived lives of the profligate in which we squandered our resources and have just as often allowed others to benefit from those resources to our own detriment. I was raised on Chicago's Southside in the mid-1950s. I grew up on 39th street (Pershing Road) near Cottage Grove Avenue. On 39th street, on just the one block on which I lived, there were 10 or more businesses owned and operated by African Americans. On one side of the street was Porter's Pharmacy where I worked for a time. There was also Tasker's Barber Shop and a shoe shine parlor, where my mother used to take me to get my haircut, and the patrons would inquire about my progress in school and have me read articles in the newspaper to see how I was progressing. On the other side of the street, there was Mrs. Thomas' grocery store, Bo Diddley's variety store, and Smitty's Pool Room and Record Shop. On the ground floor of the building in which I lived was Mrs. Caldwell's Bakery and Grocery Store, where I'd stop and get a chocolate donut or long john on the way to school in the morning. This pattern was mirrored on every major commercial strip in the community – 35th street, 43rd street, 47th, 51st, Garfield Boulevard and 63rd street. This did not include the roving vendors that sold merchandise from wagons and carts, the mobile street merchants with carts-the milk man, the watermelon man, the ice man, the scrap man, the knife sharpener, and the door to door dry goods merchant. In those same communities today, we are dependent on others for all of those needs.

In the poem, *Invictus* by William Ernest Henley, he points out the need, in spite of whatever circumstances or tumult, to be in charge of self, and this self includes the broader self of community:

I am the master of my fate;
I am the captain of my soul.

James Allen wrote, "Man is buffeted by circumstances so long as he believes himself to be the creature of outside conditions, but when he realizes that he is a creative power and that he may command the hidden soil and seeds of his being out of which circumstances grow; he then becomes the rightful master of himself."[3] We have to find the circumstances that are conducive to our healthy growth and if we can't find them, we have to make them.

Compare the confidence Joseph (PBUH) displayed at this point, (defining his own value), with the position, when he was first taken into Egypt. In 12:21, the man in Egypt who bought him decided what his value was, i.e.: *"maybe he'll bring us luck or we'll adopt him as a son."* In our own community, we are reminded of the tension between us and our immigrant Muslim brothers at Imam Mohammed's (RAA) insistence that we have our own independent interpretation of the Qur'an. Imam Yahya Abdullah of Dallas, Texas, reminded us and them once in a speech, addressing our immigrant brothers, "You are our brother, not our daddy."

Many of these same mentalities tried to marginalize Imam Mohammed (RAA) early on by defining him as merely a spiritual leader. Community life is not just spiritual life. Imam Mohammed (RAA) was a leader of all community life, just as was Prophet Muhammad (PBUH)– the leader, Commander in Chief of the Faithful, the husband, father, and friend. We see from Joseph (PBUH), that it was not people who established him in the land. In fact, the people he came in contact with saw only his value to them. It was G-d who established him in his true value.

12:56 Thus did we give established power to Joseph in the land, to take possession therein as, when, or where he pleased. We bestow of our Mercy on whom we please, and we suffer not to be lost, the reward of those who do good.

Chapter 56

Power Concedes Nothing Without a Demand

Allah says He grants power to whom He wills and strips power from whom He wills,[1] and it is here that we see how Joseph's (PBUH) innocence and character brought him into established power in the land. For a powerless people, this should be a textbook strategy. Yet we struggle and strive trying to find a way. Let us remember Frederick Douglass' advice, "Power concedes nothing without a demand. It never did and it never will. Find out just what any people will quietly submit to and you have found out the exact measure of injustice and wrong, which will be imposed upon them, and these will continue till they are resisted with either words or blows, or both. The limits of tyrants are prescribed by the endurance of those whom they oppress." While the tone of this advice implies a different kind of resistance, in this time, we have become our own jailers. We have oppressed our own souls. The jailer's bars are open and all we have to do is walk into a new free space. But, we have to demand more of ourselves.

Joseph (PBUH) did not have to demand power from the King. It came to him because he demanded more of himself. He demanded the best of his human nature. He demanded that he always speak the truth and do good to everyone. He demanded that he guard his chastity and that he remain patient and persevere in spite of any trials. Because of this, there was no oppression that was able to touch his soul and it was just a matter of time before his body and mind were free. It is power over self first that prepares us for any other power. We get a glimpse of this power during our Ramadan fast and the blessed night that occurs within that month. Allah says in Qur'an that, "the night of power is better than a thousand months." A thousand months is the typical life span of the human so it means this one night is better than a lifetime in the world of our making. During the month of Ramadan, we die to the worldly temptations and struggles of the flesh and on this night the angels (pure light) descend, obeying every command of G-d. This *qadr* (power) is symbolic of the qadr we all have in common. That is why we strive for obedience during the last 10 days of Ramadan when this night occurs--thinking on the Qur'an, reading it, and trying to establish the radiance of our own pure soul.

The Five

Just as human innocence is a common property of all people, so is common sense, although in today's society it is more rare than common. Five represents these common properties and metaphysics is the study of that which is beyond what can be grasped by our five senses. There is a sixth sense, intuition, which involves perceptions obtained from all the senses working together. The word intuition comes from the Latin word *intueri*, which is often roughly translated as meaning *to look inside* or *to contemplate*. Although intuition has come to commonly refer to knowledge acquired without inference or the use of reason, it should not be seen as divorced from intellect or intelligent behavior. Imam Mohammed (RAA) wrote: "Mental energy bursts forth from previously unknown capacities because of determination – the persistent effort to realize the objective. The phenomenon of psychic intuition is the result of this persistence in the intellect." The five (senses) is vital to us and the foundations of our development and success. For example, we have five pillars of Islam. We call them pillars because they support the entire structure or establishment of the religion: (1) Shahadatain (the open declaration that there is no G-d but Allah and that Muhammad is his Apostle, (2) Salat (Five daily prayers); (3) Zakāt (Almsgiving), (4) Sawm (fasting during month Ramadan), and (5) Hajj (the pilgrimage to Mecca at least once in a lifetime.) Our ritual prayers five times a day serve to keep our five senses alive and to keep our establishment strong. Ten is a number representing the social plane – a whole cycle or completion of the order on the individual plan – so we have a mathematical system and an economic system based on decimals (ten).[2]

Prophet Muhammad (PBUH) said: "Take benefit of five before five: your youth before your old age, your health before your sickness, your wealth before your poverty, your free-time before your occupation, and your life before your death." W. D. Fard said think five times before you speak and then you might be right. If we use common sense (five senses) and consider how each decision we make will affect each of these five important areas, we are reasonably assured of making a right decision.

I am convinced that a wasting of any of these vital resources cannot occur in a vacuum and that such a misuse must necessarily cause a diminution or an impairment of all the other resources and the organism as a whole.[3] Many spend all of their time seeking wealth to the neglect of their souls. Allah says that the investment should be in our souls and he also says that *he loves not the spendthrift.* We are thus called on to master these forces, this energy, and to organize them so that they serve our needs and we maximize their benefits. Being physically organized and managing your schedule enables to you make the most of your time, space, energy, and money. The preservation of each of these elements requires one to pace themselves and develop patience.

Agricultural to Industrial Society

The farmer had patience naturally. He couldn't realize the rewards of his labor and his investment until its completion, its fulfillment-the harvest of abundance. He takes the dry seed that looks dead and lifeless and plants it in the same place where they bury dead things – in the cold, dark earth. Then he holds faith in unseen forces. Man has been doing this long before he scientifically analyzed the sunlight, the soil, and the air and discovered what nutrients were in them. The farmer was also forced to understand seasons; that things have to be done in time and on time and that there was a season and a time for everything.[4] He had to prepare the ground during a certain season and then plant. He had to attend to the plant during a season as it was growing and then harvest. You can't rush any season and you can't perform any of the processes out of time.

Today that knowledge is all but lost. In addition to the number of farmers who produced natural food for our consumption, we lost other things in the evolution from the Agrarian society to Industrialization. In 1870, the first year that African Americans were counted in the U.S. Census as people with a name instead of as property, farmers accounted for 53% of the U.S. labor force. By 1920, when African Americans began migrating to the North from the South in large numbers, farmers were 27% of the labor force. In 2011, the rural population in America accounted for 16% of the total population; down from 20% in 2000 and representing the lowest percent in history. I have read as recently as 2016 that the percentage of African Americans who own farms in the South has fallen below 1%. While we rightfully complain about the mega industrial food complex giants and the proliferation of genetically modified food, if they were not around, we probably wouldn't be able to eat anything. No one is disposed to the life of the farmer anymore. But we still need those lessons that we reap what we sow and that the latter will be better than the former.

12:57 But verily the reward of the Hereafter is the best, for those who believe, and are constant in righteousness.

Chapter 57

The Reward of Good is Good

The farmer is forced to have faith. He can prepare the ground. He can plant. But he has no control over the sun, the wind or the rain. Nor does he have control over the process of the seed maturing. Everything that the seed is to become is within it, but the farmer has to have faith in all those elements outside of his control. Today we live in the age of instant gratification. It's the age of multi-tasking, minute rice, and instant oatmeal. We want what we want right now and that attitude brings about impulsive behavior. The theme is, 'if it feels good, do it.' Nike has shortened this to "Just Do It!" The opposite of this behavior is called *delayed gratification*, another term for patience. This mentality has led a whole generation away from the idea of personal responsibility. *I have no obligation to my family, to my community. I am free. It's my life. What's in it for me?* We've heard it all. But the question is, is it rational or decent? And the problem is, if we just want to feel good right now at any cost, we find that we have created a hell for ourselves tomorrow by such shortsightedness today

This is not the natural progression of things. It is at a thing's maturity that we reap the most benefit. The latter situation will be the better one.[1,2] Life evolves from lesser to better. Matter and we, are created in a simple form and evolve into more and more complexity, more and more capability, of higher and higher vibration.[3] There are many evolutions for us to observe that prove this. Our own souls drive us to more progress and better circumstances. Human behavior evolved from savagery to civilization, although unfortunately, man's weapons of war also evolved from clubs to neutron bombs. The farmer has gone from back-breaking work behind a mule to air-conditioned combines. Transportation, communication and all forms of human activity have progressed. We've gone from hollering across the valley to communicate long distances, to instantaneous messages that are measured in fractions of seconds.

G-d shows us a progression in the prophets also from Adam (PBUH), who was ill-equipped to deal with the developed world to Muhammad (PBUH), whose guidance will last as long as the world endures. In our own history, we see the Nation of Islam as an early incarnation of community life, one that was designed from the very beginning to evolve into G-d's model community. As African Americans, we have to recognize and appreciate progress. I've told my children, when I've seen in them the tendency to be angry at the white man's past mistreatment of African Americans that, "I know the history of slavery and that mistreatment as well as anybody, but we have to honest that things are much better, and from your standpoint, in this modern time, you have it better than any generation of our people have ever had it. You have never felt a lash on your back." My grandmother told me many times about her hard conditions in rural Mississippi and Memphis, and the threat of assault and death that she lived under, but she never ended her story without acknowledging, "but I've had a good life."

My grandmother, rear, Edna McCann and mother, Louise Alexander in the back yard of our apartment building on 39th. Street in the mid-1950s.

I know that some of us feel powerless, like all of the important elements of our lives are in the control of others, but that is not our life today. That is the Palestinians life in Gaza. Our life has all of the freedoms that we have struggled for. We have access to education. We have access to economic empowerment. We have freedom of speech and freedom to worship G-d as our souls bid us. But if we look at the white man as the source of our power, and not G-d and the resources He has put within us, then G-d should leave us to whomever we have put before Him as our Benefactor. The reward of good is good. We are blessed today because we 'kept the faith.' We kept our good human character, under circumstances that have warped that of many people. The better state, the progress that we point to, did not come from the savage that retreated back into the caves. It came from the man who accepted knowledge and accepted the best guidance.

We see this progression in Joseph's (PBUH) life. James Allen gives us a beautiful picture of this archetypical Joseph (PBUH). "He conceives of, mentally builds up an ideal condition of life. The wider liberty and a larger scope takes possession of him; unrest urges him to action and he uses all his spare times and means to the development of his latent powers and resources. Very soon so altered has his mind become that the workshop can no longer hold him. It has become so out of harmony with his mindset that it falls out of his life as a garment is cast aside. And with the growth of opportunities that fit the scope of his expanding powers, he passes out of it altogether. Years later we see this youth as a grown man. We find him a master of certain forces of the mind that he wields with worldwide influence and almost unequaled power...Sun-like, he becomes the fixed and luminous center around which innumerable destinies revolve. He has realized the vision of his youth. He has become one with his ideal."[4]

12:58 Then came Joseph's brethren: they entered his presence and he knew them, but they knew him not.

Chapter 58

The Good, the Bad, and the Ugly

This is the fulfillment of Allah's promise to Joseph (PBUH) in ayat 12:15, "...We put into his heart (this Message): 'Of a surety thou shalt (one day) tell them the truth of this their affair while they know (thee) not'. *"You'll be able to tell them about themselves and they won't even recognize you."*[1] The words used in this verse for "he knew or recognized them" is *fa 'arafahum* –– and the words used for "they didn't know or recognize him" is *lahu- munkirun.* Both phrases provide a broader context of the nature of Joseph (PBUH) and his brothers relationship. Fa 'arafahum comes from *arafa* meaning to know or recognize, but it implies something recognized as universally good, respectable, elevated, and of the highest standard. Lahu-munkirun comes from *nakira*, which means unacquainted with or unrecognized, but it implies disliked, repugnant or strange to human nature. Munkar (from nakira) is the opposite of M'aroof (from a'rafa), and thus we have not only opposites of knowing and not knowing but also implications of the good and the bad.

After all he has experienced can you picture Joseph (PBUH) now saying, "Okay, guys, we both have been tested and had our worth established. G-d has shown the contrast between right and wrong, good and bad. So now I'll go ahead and follow you guys?" No. Rather he should be saying: "I've been blessed for my good; you are where you are at because of your bad, and what you did was ugly." African Americans should always maintain humility and be thankful for the blessing of having received G-d's guidance, especially when it has come through one from among ourselves. And it would likewise be the height of ingratitude for us to continue to act like we need someone from a foreign time or place or someone from a different tribe or race to lead us.

Consider how far out of sight and out of mind they must have put Joseph (PBUH) to the extent that now they don't even recognize their own brother. Ask yourself, who is it that came to America, recognized the poor condition of the African American, and told themselves, "Yes, this is my brother; he's been removed from his humanity for so long, but I know this is my brother from our father Adam (PBUH)." No foreigner saw this; no one said this except perhaps W. D. Fard. He saw our humanity and our nobility and he said, "I can stand on the top of the earth and tell anybody that the most beautiful nation is in the wilderness of North America."

There is much research, and particularly that of Imam Mohammed (RAA), that W. D. Fard had an ulterior motive. Yes, he expected that we would one day come into a true understanding of Islam, but he also expected that we would come under the leadership of his movement. Dr. Fatima Fanusie has also done extensive research pointing to Fard as a missionary of the Ahmadiyyah movement in this part of the world. Nevertheless, Allah has promised that His plan subsumes whatever plan we might have. We cannot escape the Divine Plan, and His Plan has always been to restore His lost property. The Bible asks the question, "Will a man rob God? It answers the question that you have robbed me of this whole nation.[2] Fard identified this nation, not as the historical Israel, but as the Lost-Found Nation of Islam in the wilderness of North America.

Today, we seek restoration. African Americans want to be seen and recognized in their true humanity. But we have to step outside the construct that has been provided us by Pharaoh. Pharaoh's response to Moses (PBUH) was, "We've raised you in our house – (society of Western civilization). We've taken care of you, educated you, and treated you like a son. And maybe one day you'll inherit our power. How dare you accept another God beside me. How dare you try to be responsible for yourself, how dare you want to be independent and make decisions for your own future." This is in essence what most of our people are hearing in their mind today and it explains most of their reluctance to consider Islam. They are afraid of accepting something that doesn't meet white America's approval. We have bought into this stereotype so thoroughly that our own brothers don't recognize us – our white brothers here in America, our immigrant Muslim brothers, our brothers in the monotheistic faith of Abraham (PBUH), our brothers from the continents of Asia, nor even our African brothers. We even find it hard to recognize each other as African Americans and live peacefully in our communities. We are the ones who have to first recognize ourselves as servants of only G-d, as noble descendants of Adam (PBUH) and brothers of all humanity. And we have to recognize ourselves as a favored nation who came into this favor because of our faith, long-suffering, and patience. Once we recognize ourselves, our brothers will recognize us too.

12:59 And when he had furnished them forth with provisions (suitable) for them, he said: "Bring unto me a brother ye have, of the same father as yourselves, (but a different mother): see ye not that I pay out full measure, and that I do provide the best hospitality?"

Chapter 59

There Are People Who Love People and People Who Love Things

It is possible that people may still not recognize us or respect us. There are always people who don't respect human value. There are really two types of people in the world. There are people who love people and people who love things. Right now the world is dominated by people who love things and we find that those people will always sacrifice the innocent to get the things they love.

The brothers put their own brother, Joseph (PBUH) in difficult circumstances. Is there no retribution due for this deed? Allah is the Lord of Power and Lord of Retribution. There is a Qadr, a fate or Divine Destiny that must be fulfilled. Qadr implies having power over something, as in the case of Creator over the creation. I understand Qadr to mean the Exact Measurement of Judgment. Al-Qadir is also one of Allah's attributes and means the One Who has the Complete power, Who is not frustrated by anything at all, and Who needs no means to do anything. His command is that whenever He decrees anything, He says to it: "Be!" and it is.[1] Is there any surprise that we now find the brothers in bad circumstances themselves?

I have never seen it fail. Whenever I've had an injustice done to me and I had no immediate redress, it may have taken many years and many circumstances to prove the fact to me, but I have always come to see that person again. I have seen the justice at work in their situation. And sometimes they will not even remember what they did, or know that what they are seeing in their life now is the compensation for what they did.

Joseph (PBUH), knowing them so well, gives them an offer he knows will appeal to their material nature. They are given provisions, which they later find are even more than what they had coming. We all know people who are never satisfied. You can give them the world and they complain because they didn't get the moon too. They don't recognize or appreciate their blessings. It's like the man who thought he was in bad shape because he had no shoes, then he met a man who had no feet. But this type feels entitled. They've done nothing to deserve the mercy and blessings they've received yet they are constantly demanding more. So instead of showing their gratitude, the brothers are going to be willing to risk the loss of another brother for more things. Joseph (PBUH) also speaks past their greed, as Allah has ordered us to do.[2] He speaks to their genetic disposition. He knows their father and their forefathers. There is also in this tradition the history of those who cheated.[3] When they were set to receive they demanded full measure but when they had the upper hand they put their finger on the scale to deprive the receiver.[4]

Consider the many immigrants who have come to America and found the freedom to worship as their soul demands and have prospered. Consider the many of them who have prospered off the backs of the African American communities – selling pork, alcohol, tobacco, drugs, and drug paraphernalia. They can feel the hurt of their own people back in the Muslim world who are under the oppression of cruel leaders and they demand justice for them. But they can't feel the same justice when it is the African American brother. Allah tells us to speak a word to them to touch their soul and this is what Joseph (PBUH) did. He knew it would reach them and would resonate with their father.

Joseph (PBUH) plans to bring his brother to him—the brother of the same mother and father. There is a closeness that this implies even in today's society. A good friend whom we've known most of our life or is extremely close to us is considered almost like a brother and sometimes called *a brother from another mother*. The relationship of brothers has a long and varied history as far back as Cain and Abel. Even then we see jealousy and hatred playing a part in the relationship.

In most cultures, siblings who have the same mother and father are considered full brothers while siblings with only one common parent are considered 'half siblings.' This distinction historically resulted in inheritance and other laws that accorded half siblings unequal treatment, although this view and interpretation has been abolished in the United States. I consider it backward but there is still the common attitude that siblings from the same mother are full siblings while those of the same father are not. Of course, this may be due to the fact that they give more weight to a shared mother and womb, and perhaps because children are usually raised by and have more interaction with their mother. The mother as a symbol of society and the socialization of its individuals seems to bear more importance to them than the leadership role of the man. In this culture, there is the tendency to undermine the contribution of the man and thus, we have today a society where nobody appears to be in charge.

Africans anywhere in the diaspora are from the same motherland, and particularly Africans in America, who shared the same womb of development, culture, and forming conditions. Nevertheless, we are not feeling each other; we have lost the sensitivities to each other's needs. We are not recognizing each other as brothers. And Pharaoh has killed off the males—the fathers and father figures. There's no leadership (the man in the house) and our community has to find its own way.

Joseph (PBUH) has no instinct to treat his brothers in any way less than as brothers. He reminds the brothers of his hospitality. The word for one who provides that hospitality, *munzilina*, comes from the root word *nazala*, which also carries the meaning of sending down of divine revelation. He appeals to their material interests, but at the same time, he's conditioning them for the acceptance of his inspired leadership.

12:60 "Now if ye bring him not to me, ye shall have no measure (of corn) from me, nor shall ye (even) come near me."

Chapter 60

Materialists Respond to the Threat of Material Loss

The story of Joseph (PBUH) presents many contrasts. The contrast of good and evil, the contrast of truthfulness and dishonesty, the contrast of greed and charity, and the contrast and juxtaposition that is shown here in the words of Joseph, [bring him] "to me," *bihi*, and if you don't, you won't get anything else "from me," *indī*. This scenario of Joseph (PBUH) and his brothers is reminiscent of the work and strategy of the Honorable Elijah Muhammad in building the Nation of Islam. There was the early history of the Nation when it had become dormant and seen as small temples locally, storefronts and followers who devoted their time to studying the esoteric and mythical lessons of W. D. Fard, and trying to solve the mathematical problems of the problem book which he left as a study guide for the followers. The focus was on the mythical aspects of the teachings, such as Yacub's history and the workings of the Mother Plane. Then Malcolm came along. Malcolm saw this situation and committed to motivating the leaders and followers across the country to step up. The Honorable Elijah Muhammad recognized this and in 1959, at a public address in the Uline Arena in Washington DC, he presented a new vision, a new direction for the Nation of Islam and shifted the focus to material progress. He gave orders that the lessons were to be confiscated and were no longer to be used in the teachings and his teachings began to focus on his philosophy of "We want some of this earth for ourselves;

Do for self, and the establishment of businesses." He recognized that African Americans had become over-spiritualized under the white man's Christianity. He criticized, as did his ministers across the country, the concept of suffering under the cross – a symbol of death – here on the earth while we lived, in favor of receiving a starry crown or some pie in the sky after we die. He utilized the principle from W. D. Fard's teachings, that unalike attracts, so he attracted these over-spiritualized African Americans with the philosophy *of let's get some of this earth while we're here.*

The Honorable Elijah Muhammad also said, "Speak to the ear that's alive in the person." In the turbulent years of the Civil Rights movement, militant activity, and social change, that message of "do for self" and "get some of this earth for yourself," resonated in the ear of African Americans. The people came into the Temples in waves and the message touched their hearts. We were being excluded from the white man's restaurants in the South during the segregation era so the message of establishing our own restaurants struck a responsive chord. We were being excluded from the white man's clothing stores, his grocery stores, and his society in general. So the message of creating our own Nation or society was heard in our hearts.

Most of us wanted to be a part of society. We wanted brotherhood. We began calling each other brother and sister. Many of us responded to the philosophy of 'fight with those who fight with you, but be not the aggressor.' This made more sense to us than turning the other cheek and following other non-violent philosophies.

The promise of W. D. Fard that was relayed to us by the Honorable Elijah Muhammad was, "Money, good homes, and friendships in all walks of life." That promise translated to the material benefits of the world and the social acceptance that we had been denied. But just like material comforts are attracted by those that don't have them, those that do have them want to keep them protected. It has always been ironic to me that Dr. Martin Luther King Jr. was assassinated when he went to Memphis, Tennessee to support the sanitation workers striking there. I think white society was much less threatened by his non-violent and moral preaching than there were by his threatening to impact their economy. Materialists respond to the threat of material loss. What Joseph (PBUH) wanted was his brothers with him and what his brothers wanted was more corn and material benefit. He lured them with exactly what he knew they would respond to.

12:61 They said: "We shall certainly seek to get our wish about him from his father: Indeed we shall do it."

Chapter 61

They Have Confidence in Their Schemes

Joseph's (PBUH) brothers agree to appeal to their father to release Benjamin to their care, and they don't express any doubt about their ability to do so. The words used to express "getting their wish from him", is from *Râwada*, the same root word that is used earlier meaning *to seduce*. They have confidence in their schemes: "Indeed we shall do it." They've got experience. They brought the same appeal to their father in reference to Joseph (PBUH), in verse 11, where they assure their father that "we are indeed his sincere well-wishers."

We would all hope that perpetrators of injustice would one day come to realize their actions; show some remorse or show some compassion. But in real life they seldom do until they are broken down. There's the old country saying that "you dance with the one that brought you." We commonly see this as requiring a commitment to the person that you've invited to the dance; you don't get there and get all excited about all the others young ladies and leave the one you brought there standing on the wall. It also points out that we're generally going to stick with the philosophy that we've established a relationship with, the strategies that have gotten us to a certain point. There is a natural comfort with them and a natural reluctance to try something new when we've been successful with something else.

The brothers are schemers and they've gotten their way with their father before. They've sacrificed one brother already to their selfishness, and it doesn't even occur to them that they are going down the same path. We know that Allah is the best schemer, but that never stops us from coming up with our own.[1] Nevertheless, our schemes are always subsumed in his.[2,3] Whatever it is we plan, we must believe in. That belief infuses our plan with a power and a magnetism that mobilizes nature's forces and resources for its manifestation. W. E. B. DuBois wrote in 1910: "There is, in this world, no such force as the force of a person determined to rise." This was the force behind W. D. Fard's scheme and the Honorable Elijah Muhammad captured that force. Muhammad's plan was successful. Mahasin Sadr Ali of Brooklyn, New York wrote of him: "This great American pioneer and hero who was the unmartyred leader of the only successful and enduring movement that came out of the Civil Rights Era. They did not assassinate him, permanently incarcerate him, extradite him, deport him, stamp him out or kill his movement. What he meant to do, he did." And that should tell us that it was also part of G-d's Plan.

12:62 And (Joseph) told his servants to put their stock-in-trade (with which they had bartered) into their saddle-bags, so they should know it only when they returned to their people, in order that they might come back.

Chapter 62

Ooh Look! Something for Nothing

Some of my fondest memories growing up is going fishing with my grandparents. My grandmother had a fishing buddy that she would go fishing with in the summertime. I would go to Lake Michigan with them at 39th and 47th Street, which was within walking distance of our apartment. I'd play with the minnows, dig holes or throw rocks while they fished. In those days, they allowed you to throw out trolley lines with several separate hooks on them and when you pulled them in, you might have your whole dinner on the line. When I got older my grandmother didn't want to be bothered with the worms so she'd have me bait her hooks. My grandfather worked in the steel mills in Indiana and in his 40 plus years working there, I never remember seeing him home on a weekday unless it was a holiday. I never remember him being late, calling in sick or taking a day off. On weekends, he would drive us to some of the farther off fishing spots; most of them along the Fox River in Chicago's western suburbs. We fished along the river at all the towns there before they became the big towns they are now – St. Charles, which had reform school where they sent the bad boys; Geneva, where they sent the bad girls; Batavia; and McHenry Dam.

Fishing is the ultimate test of patience. You have to have a certain frame of mind to sit on the river bank all day with no guarantee of catching anything and still come home refreshed and at peace. Then you talk to the older fishermen who fancy themselves 'fish whisperers' and talk about how to fish and where to fish just like they were in the fishes' mind. It seems to me that the main thing about the fish is that they get caught because they're trying to get something for nothing, like many in our present generation of instant gratification. The fish is impulsive. He sees something he likes and he's going to bite it. He's got it halfway down his throat before he realizes it's got a hook in it. They don't want to swim around chasing a worm or a minnow. 'Here's one just hanging there, and he's not even moving around.' So when you bait the hook you have to hide it. But there is nothing free in life. Even if we're not paying in the currency we bargained in, there's still no getting away from paying the price. Ralph Waldo Emerson, in his essay, *Compensation*, points out this universal law: "Experienced men of the world know very well that it is always best to pay scot and lot as they go along, and that a man often pays dear for a small frugality. The borrower runs in his own debt. Has a man gained any thing who has received a hundred favors and rendered none? Has he gained by borrowing, through indolence or cunning, his neighbor's wares, or horses, or money? There arises on the deed the instant acknowledgment of benefit on the one part, and of debt on the other; that is, of superiority and inferiority."

Joseph (PBUH) knew his brothers well. He knew they would be too excited to get home and find out they still had their stock in trade. He knew their reaction, "Ooh Look! Something for Nothing." When we go into the store and make a purchase and the clerk counts us out too much change, don't we give it back? There are some people who consider themselves righteous but when they receive something they are not entitled to, they justify it and say this must be G- d's Will. That's the type that Joseph's (PBUH) brothers were – lovers of things and supporters of principles only when those principles help them get more things.[1]

A young FOI, Edward 23X (right), with my grandfather, Walter McCann (center) and younger brothers, Rex Alexander (left), and Kipp Alexander (front)

12:63 Now when they returned to their father, they said: "O our father! No more measure of grain shall we get (unless we take our brother): So send our brother with us, that we may get our measure; and we will indeed take every care of him."

Chapter 63

They Still Love Things More Than People

The Appetite for Foolishness

It is said that there would come a time when there would be a famine on earth. This is not just referring to a famine of food. It was referring to a famine of the Word of G-d, indeed, any intelligent communication. Scan the airwaves of your local radio or TV station and try to find a broadcast of intelligent communication. Whatever we constantly put in our diet we eventually develop an appetite for and then popular culture exploits that appetite.

Look at the condition of the general population, with access to more information than ever before in history. Only one in four (¼) Americans can name more than one of the five freedoms guaranteed in the First Amendment to the U.S. Constitution, but more than one-half (½) can name at least two members of the Simpson's cartoon family. 22% of Americans can name all five Simpson family members compared to 1 in 1000 who could name all five (5) First Amendment rights. A 2012 national survey by FindLaw.com, a legal information website, found that nearly two-thirds of Americans are unable to name any of the nine members of the U.S. Supreme Court. In 1985, Andrew Postman, in his book *Amusing Ourselves to Death*, made this point: "TV is turning all public life (education, religion, politics, journalism) into entertainment; how the image is undermining other forms of communication, particularly the written word; and how our bottomless appetite for TV will make content so abundantly available, content be damned, we'll be overwhelmed by "information glut" until what is truly meaningful is lost and we no longer care what we've lost as long as we're being amused." The death that Postman is describing is of consciousness, the death of regard for important things, the death of intellectual capacity and curiosity. Now 20 years later, add to that information glut, content from computers, PDA's, smartphones, iPods, iPads, Facebook, YouTube, and instant messaging, and it will take a Noah's Ark to save us from the flood of virtual nonsense. Spiritual language – the language of intelligent behavior – is no longer reaching the public.

Pope John Paul II popularized the phrase *culture of death* in his Encyclical, Evangelium Vitae (April 1995): "While the climate of widespread moral uncertainty can in some way be explained by the multiplicity and gravity of today's social problems, and these can sometimes mitigate the subjective responsibility of individuals, it is no less true that we are confronted by an even larger reality, which can be described as a veritable structure of sin. This reality is characterized by the emergence of a culture which denies solidarity and in many cases takes the form of a veritable "culture of death". This culture is actively fostered by powerful cultural, economic and political currents which encourage an idea of society excessively concerned with efficiency. Looking at the situation from this point of view, it is possible to speak in a certain sense of a war of the powerful against the weak: a life which would require greater acceptance, love and care is considered useless, or held to be an intolerable burden, and is therefore rejected in one way or another."

Allah says in reference to death, "Die, that you may live. Die not unless you die in the state of Muslim [and that He] has made the earth as a place for you to die." This tells us that you can die right here on earth because of miscalculation or misconception of what our relationship is supposed to be with this world. And we must die to the dominance of the popular culture in our lives in order to truly live, which is in intelligent behavior and spiritual consciousness. When we face physical death, we pray to be in that consciousness. African Americans, having always been dependent on the dominant culture, more than anyone, are susceptible to the influences of the popular culture.

The cruel treatment of African Americans as slaves was justified by the belief that we were a people that did not have the capacity for serious thought or serious activity. This was the conclusion of the belief that we were inferior to the whites and thus, our life's activities and future should be controlled by the master. We like to think that this idea is long past but until the mid-20th century, it was taught in some of America's university that, because of the Africans inferior capacity, the slave master was actually doing us a favor with their enslavement. Many of us bought into this idea and accepted spending our lives in sport and play. But many more recognized their inherent motivation to excellence. They remained connected to the ancestors that built their human life upon a standard of excellence. It was just natural. All animals reject certain things. Our body seeks cleanliness and rejects impurity. Thus, the saying "cleanliness is godliness" or "cleanliness is next to godliness." It is our nature to reject ignorance and seek intelligence; reject hostility and show compassion. But here again, you have to be sensitive to the respect for human values and when you see youth killed for a pair of gym shoes, just because the media has convinced them that they must have this thing and their identity is tied into this thing, then we know that the system is broken. Here we see Joseph's (PBUH) brothers again put in a position where they may have to sacrifice a brother to get the things they want.

12:64 He said: "Shall I trust you with him with any result other than when I trusted you with his brother aforetime? But Allah is the best to take care (of him), and He is the Most Merciful of those who show mercy!"

Chapter 64

A Leopard Doesn't Change Its Spots

Despite our best intentions, a leopard doesn't change its spots and people generally don't change basic aspects of their character so Jacob (PBUH) recognizes the power of natural appetites to be subverted and the tendency of the social institutions to adopt expediency.

Subconscious and Natural Appetites

Imam Mohammed (RAA) interpreted for us Allah's prohibition in the Qur'an against approaching people, selling things to them and influencing them through their subconscious:[1] "Reach them through their brains," he warned, "respecting the temple. You're not respecting the temple when you communicate to the temple through its foot, arm, its skin, and it has a brain inside. You respect it when you address the boss. It's like a man coming into your house influencing your family and he gets attention away from what he is doing so he can talk to your little children. So he goes down and does not talk to the intelligence that is supposed to be governing in the house but he talks to the little children. He gets your little daughter or your little son and he influences them and destroys your respect in the family, that the family should have for you and he destroys your authority in your own house. The house that I am talking about is the government, the nature itself. Instead of going through the intelligence, the rational mind and letting people know what is happening to the community, no he goes in by the back door. We have people like that in and outside of our community that want to lecture us with baby teachings." Imam W. D Mohammed (RAA) 2003.

It's not just our Muslim community that is approached like this. The media floods us with appeals to our perceived inadequacies to sell us junk. And many of our own leaders pander to our hurt feelings. Instead of reminding us of our ancestors' contribution to spur us to more progress, they maintain us in a perpetual state of hurt feelings. Jacob (PBUH) knows his sons; he knows their shortcomings, their motivations and what they will resort to in order to get what they want.

Ego and Emotions

The common people are ruled by ego and emotions. They select leaders that accommodate those things in them-leaders that pander to their rancor, their bruised psyches, and their missing identities.

Business people, professional people, and scientists are rational thinkers. They must have rational scientific minds or they would not be successful. They operate on immutable principles. You will not be successful riding the roller coaster of emotional extremes. That's why when we visit the amusement park, we have fun then come back home to real life. You will not be successful letting your appetite, your subconscious or your subjective experiences color your reality. "To escape--or at least forget--what appears like chaos, millions turn to television, where "reality TV" fakes reality… Elsewhere, players of online games pay thousands of dollars in real money for virtual swords that their virtual selves can use to win virtual castles or maidens. Irreality spreads." "Revolutionary Wealth: How it will be created and how it will change our lives", by Alvin Toffler and Heidi Toffler

Corruption of the Natural Appetite-Overstimulation

Our youth is bombarded today with vast digits and bytes of information and stimuli from the media, school, and the World Wide Web. Information is not necessarily knowledge and unfortunately, most of what we get today is useless--entertainment directed at the carnal appetite. The fundamental principle of education, which is structured and useful knowledge, is that a framework is established in the formative years when information can be organized. The American

Academy of Pediatrics discourages television altogether for children under 2 years of age, recommending other activities such as reading, playing, singing, and talking with other children. It suggests limiting older children to no more than two hours per day of total media entertainment, preferably of high-quality programming.

Dr. Rahil Briggs, a psychologist, and director of the Healthy Steps Program at Children's Hospital at Montefiore in the Bronx said the fast-paced, fantastical sequences of some programs might actually prime the early childhood brain to "Not be able to pay attention to something that is not so fantastic. You may be priming the brain to be almost A.D.H.D.-like impulsive." The child's mind is like a sponge, and it seems that the producers of the popular children's TV show *SpongeBob SquarePants* is exploiting that tendency in our children. Researchers report in the September 12, 2011, issue of the *Journal Pediatrics* that 4-year-olds who had just watched the fast-paced fantasy cartoon, which follows the undersea adventures of a yellow sponge, did worse on tests of attention and problem-solving than young children who watched a slower-paced, educational program or spent time drawing. The natural property of the sponge is its extreme absorbency just as is the natural property of the toddler mind. SpongeBob lives in the ocean where he is completely saturated, yet he continues to absorb all of these extraordinary adventures. He never leaves the water to dry out, let the water evaporate or to restore himself. He thrives in the totally impulsive environment of water. It would be naive for us to think that these people, who are masters of the human psyche and human development, have done this by coincidence. The tests were administered immediately after the children watched the program and were designed to assess what is known as children's executive function, which underlies attention, working memory, problem-solving, and the delay of gratification. Any impairment in executive functioning skills can impact many important life skills and a child's future. It can impair an ability to stay focused on tasks, the ability to follow-through and complete tasks, the ability to plan and anticipate the organization of thoughts and materials, the ability to cope with unstructured situations, the ability to cope with changes in routine, and the ability to regulate emotions. These people will struggle academically with work completion, organization, and motivation for any task which is perceived as difficult, frustrating or simply unappealing.

Officials from Nickelodeon, the network that produces SpongeBob, dismissed the significance of the study, saying in a statement that preschool-age children are not the show's intended audience. SpongeBob is designed for 6 to 11-year-olds, according to the network, which questioned the study's small sample size of white middle and upper-middle-class children. Are we really to believe that the producers of this show, who invested millions of dollars into its research and production and stand to make millions from its airing and syndication, did all this without knowing everything there was to know about their market? Just as they knew it was designed for 6 to 11 years, they also had to know that it was not beneficial to children ages 4 and under. This begs the question; why would they do it? We could assume that the money motive was the overriding consideration, but behind every lover of dollars is a lover of control. The scheme behind this kind of project is to control the future of the people starting with the children. If this generation is ill prepared in executive functioning, then they'll be ill prepared as CEOs. If they are addicted to instant gratification, they will never be able to plan for their future. If they can't focus on undertaking and completing tasks they will not be able to reach the rewards of their labor. If they cannot regulate their emotions, they will always be controlled by other men.

12:65 Then when they opened their baggage, they found their stock-in-trade had been returned to them. They said: "O our father! What (more) can we desire? this our stock-in-trade has been returned to us: so we shall get (more) food for our family; We shall take care of our brother; and add (at the same time) a full camel's load (of grain to our provisions). This is but a small quantity."

Chapter 65

Always Pay; For, First or Last, You Must Pay Your Entire Debt

We've all heard the expression *freedom isn't free*, but I believe we'll find that nothing is really free. In *Compensation*, Emerson continues noting how indelibly our obligations are written into the accounting of life: "The transaction remains in the memory of himself and his neighbor; and every new transaction alters, according to its nature, their relation to each other. He may soon come to see that he had better have broken his own bones than to have ridden in his neighbor's coach, and that the highest price he can pay for a thing is to ask for it." We are needful creatures by nature, but there is also a nature in us, to first recognize the Creator and source of all things, and to ask, beg, and pray only to that One. When we do ask others, we ask in His name, fully aware that the one we are asking is only a conduit and that any good or lack thereof is from our Lord. Prophet Muhammad (PBUH) has said that the hand above is better than the hand below. I believe that this psychic relationship is what Emerson is referring to when he says, "A wise man will extend this lesson to all parts of life and know that it is always the part of prudence to face every claimant, and pay every just demand on your time, your talents, or your heart. Always pay; for first or last, you must pay your entire debt. Persons and events may stand for a time between you and justice, but it is only a postponement. You must pay at last your own debt. If you are wise, you will dread a prosperity, which only loads you with more. Benefit is the end of nature. But for every benefit which you receive, a tax is levied." This sounds very much like the *Day of Religion-* the Day of Accounting, Judgment, Reckoning, Recompense, or Faith. The word used for *religion* is *din*, which has its root in the word *dana*, meaning *to be indebted.* Thus Emerson statement: "first or last, you must pay your entire debt."

Emerson holds those unwilling to render what is due in low esteem, again pointing to Prophet Muhammad's (PBUH) reference to the hand above and the hand below: "He is base, and that is the one base thing in the universe, to receive favors and render none. In the order of nature, we cannot render benefits to those from whom we receive them, or only seldom. But the benefit we receive must be rendered again, line for line, deed for deed, cent for cent, to somebody. Beware of too much good staying in your hand. It will fast corrupt and worm[1] worms.[2] Pay it away quickly in some sort." Prophet Muhammad (PBUH) when asked what should be given in Zakat (charity) replied, "Whatever is beyond your own needs." Look at how many people in society today are undone by seeking the shortcut, the free ride, never realizing that they will have to pay somewhere down the line. The brothers show genuine surprise at finding their stock in trade in Jacob's (PBUH) presence only after they had returned. This undoubtedly helped them overcome Jacob's (PBUH) natural reluctance to trust their word, which he expresses in 12:64.

12:66 (Jacob) said: "Never will I send him with you until ye swear a solemn oath to me, in Allah's name, that ye will be sure to bring him back to me unless ye are yourselves hemmed in (and made powerless). And when they had sworn their solemn oath, he said: Over all that we say, be Allah the witness and guardian!"

Chapter 66

I'd Sacrifice All of You Together for That One

Jacob (PBUH) tells his sons that the only thing that will justify them not bringing his son Benjamin back is if they are all surrounded and made powerless. The word used for *hemmed in* (and made powerless), added by the commentator, is *yuhata*. This verb's trilateral root is ḥā wāw ṭā and its meaning is to watch, guard, protect or surround. It also has an implied meaning of to encompass, surround, comprehend (knowledge), and know. Today our lives are completely surrounded by commercial interests. I remember raising my older children during the age of attention deficit and there was a time when my voice wasn't getting through to them at all. If I wanted to be assured that they heard me, I would have to interrupt their television shows like an emergency weather report and tell them, "Turn around and give me your undivided attention." Then I could tell them, "I want you to do this or that or I want you to do this chore before you go out." I would be comfortable then that they had gotten the message. Today, it is the popular culture that has the undivided attention of the masses.

There is a time that is spoken of when a beast would rise up and would dominate the lives of the people; a beast with one eye. Ibn Umar narrated: Once Allah's Apostle stood amongst the people, glorified and praised Allah as he deserved. Then, mentioning Dajjal, he said, "I warn you against him (i.e. the Dajjal) and there was no prophet but warned his nation against him. No doubt, Noah warned his nation against him but I tell you about him something of which no prophet told his nation before me. You should know that he is one-eyed, and Allah is not one-eyed." Sahih al-Bukhari, 4:55:553

Commentators describe this time as one in which people have become faithless, irreverent, dishonest, and shameless. That beast, the *Dajjal*, has only one focus and dominates all of the vital forces--the sacred energies of the people. Dr. Fatimah Abdul-Tawwab Fanusie discusses the Ahmadiyyah Anjuman intelligentsia interpretation of Dajjal, as the Anti-Christ, represented by the Christian nations of the West. "In their religious attitude, in contradicting the teachings of Christ and the teachings of all of the prophets of G-d, they represented the Anti-Christ, while in their material power and materialistic tendencies they represented Gog and Magog."[1]

Everything in American politics and social policy revolves around money. The debate over the legalization of marijuana centers not on any moral or health considerations, but rather on the amount of the industry and the potential of taxing sales. As early as 1994, estimates in tax revenues were from $2.2 to $6.4 billion per year, comparable to the revenues currently raised through the federal tax on alcohol ($8 billion) and cigarettes ($5 billion).[2] The research that marijuana exposure during development can cause long-term or possibly permanent adverse changes in the brain carried no weight.

The debate on same sex marriages never addressed the clear prohibition of homosexuality in scripture, but rather on how much allowing the marriages would add to the economy. During research, the Williams Institute – UCLA School of Law noted, "The total spending on wedding arrangements and tourism by resident same-sex couples and their guests will add an estimated $88 million boost to the state and local economy of Washington over the course of three years, with a $57 million boost in the first year alone.

In Illinois, when debate occurred on the closing of some prisons in the state, the human and social costs of incarceration were downplayed in favor of the number of jobs that rural communities would lose as prison guards and ancillary employment. The controversy over the Affordable Car Act (Obamacare) was not based on the moral imperative that the society assures that all of its members be secure and healthy but rather on what it would cost.

This is the world we live in today, but there is one saving grace. There is one characteristic of human life that will survive and bring us back if we preserve it. It is the innocence and purity of human nature. It is Muslim nature. It is also the Christ-like nature. Whatever we choose to call it, it is in every human being and if we preserve it, we will never become lost to the world. I can understand the Prophet Jacob (PBUH) putting such a value on Joseph (PBUH) and his brother Benjamin. I can see him being willing to sacrifice all of his other sons, as long as that one with the pure innocent nature is preserved.

12:67 Further he said: "O my sons! enter not all by one gate: enter ye by different gates. Not that I can profit you aught against Allah (with my advice): None can command except Allah: On Him do I put my trust: and let all that trust put their trust on Him."

Chapter 67

Cast Down Your Bucket Where You Are

This ayat is pertinent to the condition of African Americans today because although we are not technically foreigners trying to get into an established society, in a very real sense, we have been stigmatized as different and excluded from America's business, political, and social life, just as any foreigner would be. A word that has rapidly entered the English lexicon is "otherness." It was given renewed life during President Obama's campaign and election as the media, pundits and Republicans implied that "he is not one of us." Even today they refer to him using his middle name "Hussein." In their political correctness, they used every symbol and metaphor they could find to imply his "otherness." And they kept the concept alive with Donald Trump's relentless "birther" movement, challenging Obama's birth and his qualification to be President. They stopped short of saying, "you are African American. Stay in your place," but they came very close. Now again the chickens are coming home to roost. All of that venom, anger and resentment has settled into a significant part of the Republican/ Conservative establishment. The media is reluctant to identify the real root of Donald Trump's support as the 2016 Republican Presidential nominee but if you look at his language, his rallies, and his supporters, you find that the bigots, racists, and xenophobes have found a leader to coalesce around.

Of course, we have individuals in the highest seats of power in all of America's business, political, and social life but most of them are there to represent Pharaoh, not themselves or their community. Allah tells all of us to work in our places.[1] Just as Jacob (PBUH) advised his sons on how to enter the different gates of society, Booker T. Washington did the same thing for African Americans in his time. He did not advocate beating on the main gate of the city or marching or protesting around the walls. He encouraged African Americans to "Cast down your bucket where you are."[2] In 1895, Booker T. Washington gave what later came to be known as the Atlanta Compromise speech before the Cotton States and International Exposition in Atlanta. His address was considered one of the most important and influential speeches in American history, guiding African American resistance to white discrimination and establishing Washington as one of the leading black spokesmen in America. Washington's speech stressed accommodation rather than resistance to the racist order under which Southern African Americans lived. He stated, "To those of my race who depend on bettering their condition in a *foreign* land, or who underestimate the importance of preservation-friendly relations with the southern white man who is their next door neighbor, I would say, 'Cast down your bucket where you are. Cast it down, making friends in every manly way of the people of all races, by whom you are surrounded." Washington's philosophy prevailed until the early 1900's when debate ensued between him and W. E. B. DuBois, who advocated social protest. DuBois later found, along with others, the Niagara Movement, which later became the National Association for the Advancement of Colored People (NAACP). From DuBois' time until the work of Dr. Martin Luther King Jr., DuBois' idea set the tone of the Civil Rights movement.

Both philosophies represented legitimate positions, and both were viable strategies or gates of entry into American society. The Honorable Elijah Muhammad's work more closely resembled Booker T. Washington's in its focus on hard work and self-reliance. Dr. King's work was much akin to organizations such as the NAACP. Both, however, have been essential to the progress of human rights. Whereas some might have picketed and demanded the right to patronize white facilities, others saw the establishment of our own facilities as the priority and a true freedom.

Freedom Riders

In the fight against segregated facilities throughout the South, Freedom Riders sought to integrate restaurants and waiting rooms in terminals serving buses that crossed state lines. These students and youth activists rode buses and other public transportation into the South in 1961. While racial segregation in these facilities was supposed to be outlawed, local authorities disregarded the federal law and police arrested riders for trespassing, unlawful assembly, and violating state and local Jim Crow laws. Often they stood by and allowed white mobs to attack the riders. These protests, most organized by Congress of Racial Equality (CORE) and some by the Student Nonviolent Coordinating Committee (SNCC), brought the issue of racial discrimination against Blacks to the attention of the public. After arrests in the state of Mississippi, Governor Ross Barnett sent some of the Freedom Riders to the notorious Parchman penitentiary, where my late uncle Luqman Ziyad (John D. Spight Jr.) (RAA) would later serve inmates as Muslim Chaplain.

On one trip on May 4, 1961, two small groups, one of which included Alabama native and U.S. Congressman John Lewis, left on a bus from Washington, D.C., on the first leg of a trip to New Orleans, Louisiana. In Anniston, Alabama they were attacked by vicious mobs. In Birmingham they were again attacked by a large crowd of whites, many belonging to the Ku Klux Klan and armed with pipes, chains, and baseball bats. Public Safety Commissioner Eugene "Bull" Connor informed Klan leaders that the police would delay their arrival at the bus station for 15 minutes and encouraged the Klan to attack the riders. They met the same violence in Montgomery and at each of the stops the public officials either failed to protect them or were complicit in mob attacks upon them, despite pleas from President John F. Kennedy and his brother Attorney General Robert F. Kennedy. President Kennedy ordered Federal Marshals into Alabama to restore order. Robert Kennedy, who was tasked with enforcing the Federal law, addressed the attack of Freedom Riders in Birmingham Alabama, in a Voice of America broadcast to more than 60 countries. He acknowledged the mistreatment of Blacks while at the same time noting that progress had been made. As far away as Czechoslovakia, nations called America out on her hypocrisy. There it was commented: "In the land of Ernest Hemingway, people still struggle for basic human rights." In a prescient statement that we should be able to appreciate today, Kennedy foresaw racial progress in the future noting: "There's no question that in the next thirty or forty years a Negro can also achieve the same position that my brother has as the President of the United States."

Diane Judith Nash was a leader and strategist of the student wing of the 1960s Civil Rights Movement. She was part of the first successful Civil Rights Campaign to desegregate lunch counters in Nashville, one of the Freedom riders, a founding member of the Student Nonviolent Coordinating Committee (SNCC), and part of the Selma Voting Rights Movement campaign. Mrs. Nash was one of the first people I met on my job with *Muhammad Speaks Newspaper* when I entered the Nation of Islam. It was all of these people, using all of these different strategies, that resulted in the progress we see today.

Barbarians at the Gate

The phrase, Barbarians at the Gate, evokes images of citizens looking out over the walls of their fortified city at foreigners attacking the gates of their city, trying to get it. In fact, the term barbarian used to simply mean 'foreigner' but it has also been used to imply a rival group of people, often deemed to be less capable, or somehow "primitive". And here we are today, with that scene playing out in countries across the world. Immigrants, many of them from countries we have destroyed with our bombs, seek entry into established nations-seeking freedom and new lives. That debate has been central to the Republicans 2016 presidential campaigns in America. The opponents of continued liberal integration policies seem to forget that the ancestors of the European Americans representing the ruling order today, came here as immigrants. Yet they came with power and weapons, and instead of living peacefully as good neighbors, dominated and nearly exterminated their hosts. When we say that America is the military leader of the world, aren't we also saying that that is a gate she has chosen to establish herself in human society? And if we say, whether we accept its truth or not, that Jews control the media or the financial systems, aren't we likewise saying that they have chosen those gates to establish themselves in society?

Look at the irony of the conditions of some of our inner city communities. Large swathes of vacant land cover the same areas where unemployment is highest and the people live in *Food Deserts*.[3] Couldn't these unemployed men be hired to cultivate these the miles of vacant property in Chicago's Bronzeville or West Garfield Park communities as urban gardens? Will Allen, CEO of Growing Power, Inc., a national nonprofit organization and land trust that promotes affordable food for all residents in the community through urban farms and local employment has proven it can be done. He is the author of the *Good Food Revolution* and recipient of a MacArthur Foundation Genius grant. His work is an example of working with what you've got or casting your bucket down where you're at.

No one demonstrates accessing these various gates as effectively as foreigners coming into America. The Chinese took back-breaking jobs building railroads in America until they earned enough to open laundries and restaurants in the urban areas. Today they have graduated into highly technical jobs and if you want Asian food, that restaurant will more than likely be Thai. An African American going out on the weekend will most likely fill their car up at an Arab-operated service station/convenient mart, go buy hair extensions from Southeast Asian women, get their manicure and pedicure in a Korean shop, and drive their Japanese made car to their destination. And if by chance they have an accident and require medical treatment, they can expect to be treated by an Indian doctor and Filipino nurse.

12:68 And when they entered in the manner their father had enjoined, it did not profit them in the least against (the plan of) Allah: It was but a necessity of Jacob's soul, which he discharged. For he was, by our instruction, full of knowledge (and experience): but most men know not.

Chapter 68

The Best Laid Schemes of Mice and Men

Even when we are successful in entering mainstream economic or social life in America, we still do not enjoy the freedom envisioned by the founding fathers, because we still carry a stigma-a race burden. We sit in its boardrooms of its top corporations, but if the same CEO was to drive into certain neighborhoods in a sweat suit and hoodie, he runs the risk of being brutalized and insulted before he can present his credentials. No matter how carefully a project is planned, something may still go wrong with it. The saying is adapted from a line in *To a Mouse* by Robert Burns: "The best laid schemes o' mice an' men / Gang aft a-gley" (Often go awry). The line is from a poem of Burns and was adopted in the Nobel Prize-winning author John Steinbeck's novella, *Of Mice and Men* about two displaced migrant ranch workers during the Great Depression. We all make plans, but G-d is the best planner and it is His Will and Plan that will prevail in the end.[1]

The Honorable Elijah Muhammad entered a gate of the city-the consciousness of America. Regardless of how one felt about him, no one could deny his significant impact on the lives of African Americans and America in general. Nevertheless, his accomplishments are still denigrated and trivialized. We uphold the students and ignore the teacher. He gave us Malcolm X, Muhammad Ali, Imam Warith Deen

Mohammed (RAA), and Louis Farrakhan. His counsel was sought by Dr. Martin Luther King Jr. and others seeking advancement of the African American. He popularized the identification of us as Black at a time when we were happy to just graduate from the terms colored to Negro, with a capital "N." He also popularized the reference of Black men and women to each other as brother and sister. That meant more then than the fad we find in the popular language today. It was a recognition of our shared experiences that bonded us together spiritually and culturally.

He put the black in Stokely Carmichael's *Black Power* and Bobby Seale acknowledged he and Huey P. Newton developed the 10-point program of the Black Panthers from studying the Muslim Program *What the Muslims Want and What the Muslims Believe* from the Honorable Elijah Muhammad's book *Message to the Black Man in America.* Jill Nelson, author of *Volunteer Slavery*, 1993 said, "I can think of no twentieth-century leader with anything like the impact of Elijah Muhammad whose life has been so profoundly unexamined." His impact is also documented in Imam Mikal Saahir's book, *The Honorable Elijah Muhammad: The Man Behind the Men.*

Perhaps Muhammad's best known convert and student was Muhammad Ali, although it is clear that the expanse of Ali's soul and spirit was beyond the narrow confines of the Nation of Islam. and its doctrines. At one time he was considered the most famous person in the world and he touched so many people that his recent passing brought grief and sadness to people around the world, from the common person who saw him as a truly "people's Champ" to heads of state, who respected his excellent human example. Ali transcended the boundaries of sport, country and even religion, and might have been the United States' greatest ambassador.

I remember my contacts with the Champ over the years and like many, many millions, he was always an inspiration to me. I remember in 1964 listening to Cassius Clay's (before he accepted the name, Muhammad Ali) 1st. fight with Sonny Liston on the radio with high school classmates. I followed his name change and relationship with Malcolm X, until Malcolm was killed in 1965.

His courage to stand up to oppression was his defining trait. At that time, I sympathized with all freedom movements and all things revolutionary—Fidel Castro, Che Guevara, Mao Tse Tung, Kwame Nkrumah, Jomo Kenyatta and Patrice Lumumba. I saw then what many are just now seeing and that is that most of America's interventions and military conflicts have been on the side of puppets and oppressors and against those fighting for freedom. I remember seeing pictures of the beleaguered and defeated French Army at Dien Ben Phu in Viet Nam, and I saw America's involvement there as merely an attempt to vindicate the defeat of their little brother.

I, like Ali, would have no part in it and in 1967, when Ali refused to be inducted into the U.S. Army and was stripped of his heavyweight title, he became an even bigger hero of mine. I can think of no other act that demonstrated his love of G-d more than that decision—at the height of his career, his prime and the pinnacle of his success. Allah says, in Qur'an, 3:92 "By no means shall ye attain righteousness unless ye give (freely) of that which ye love; and whatever ye give, of a truth Allah knoweth it well." Ali sacrificed all of that for a principle.

I remember hearing him speak out against the war at Northwestern University in Evanston, Illinois. Then he was vindicated by the U.S. Supreme Court and his stature continued to grow as one of 20th Century's greatest athletes and as an ambassador of the Nation of Islam. But he was never limited by any of those roles and the love he endeared worldwide was based more on his authentic love of all humanity.

Later, I would meet him and assist in promoting a charity exhibition with Chicago boxer and ex-convict, Jumbo Cummings in Chicago's Grant Park as part of the Muslim community's 4th. of July, New World Patriotism Day celebration. When I ran for office he donated to my campaign and when I got married I held my reception at his Hyde Park Mansion. Even after his retirement, his spirit never wavered. I remember him personally involved with his Manager Jabir (Herbert) Muhammad in building the Masjid (Mosque) Al-Faatir at 47th & Woodlawn in Chicago and his struggling to personally sign his name to Islamic propagation flyers. Later, in his characteristic sense of humor we would meet and he would perform magic tricks for my kids who were with me. In his passing, it seemed that the whole world recognized his character and nobility, and everyone with whom he came in contact would acknowledge that they saw him as trying to please G-d and get into heaven.

There were many other courageous people who, even though they did not follow the Honorable Elijah Muhammad, still respected the best intentions he had and his tireless work in uplifting Black people. Imam Mohammed (RAA) mentioned how the great artist James Brown, who inspired a whole generation of African Americans with songs such as "Say it Loud, I'm black and I'm proud," acknowledged that he had been inspired by the Honorable Elijah Muhammad. Former Mayor of Gary, Richard G. Hatcher, in declaring December 15-22, 1974 Honorable Elijah Muhammad appreciation week in the city of Gary, noted that for the past 43 years Muhammad had worked for the development of a positive self-image and self-determination of Blacks in America. He cited his establishment of an independent educational system, his economic program, and his success in avoiding being co-opted.

Jim Brown and his teammate, Walter Beach (known to his teammates as "Professor"), were also influenced by the Nation of Islam. Both were stars of the Cleveland Browns at the time when the Browns won the NFL Championship in 1964. Beach was actually confronted by management for reading *Message to the Blackman* and protested vehemently against having someone dictate what he should and should not read. He and other star athletes openly defended Muhammad Ali's stance refusing to be inducted into the Armed Service during the Vietnam War. Beach is now CEO of Amer-I-Can of New York, Inc.-a youth project and life skills management program founded by Brown.

The Reverend Jesse L. Jackson, speaking at the Nation of Islam's Savior's Day Convention the day after the passing of the Honorable Elijah Muhammad said, "I'm here today because I have been privileged by the Honorable Wallace Muhammad to be a part of this ceremony. Because I, like many of you, sat at the feet of the Honorable Elijah Muhammad and shared, and was taught. The single most powerful Black man in this country died yesterday. His leadership extended far beyond the membership of the Nation of Islam. For more than three decades, this prophet has been the spiritual leader and a progressive force for Black Identity and self-determination and economic development. He was the father of black consciousness, during our colored and Negro days, he was Black."

Paul Adams III is President of Providence St. Mel School (PSM) in Chicago. PSM, on Chicago's West Side, has the distinction for 37 straight years, of having 100% of its graduates accepted at 4-year colleges. And for the first time in 2015, 100% of PSM graduates were accepted at Tier One colleges and universities. Mr. Adams has maintained this exemplary record of accomplishment by insisting on Academic excellence and laying down strict rules, making gangs, drugs, gambling, graffiti, stealing and fighting grounds for expulsion. My youngest son, Abd-eljaami is a PSM graduate and currently a Junior, majoring in Chemical Engineering at the University of Notre Dame. What was really interesting to me, after my son started attending the school, was the Administration Office of the School. Mr. Adam's photograph is prominently displayed in the main office and in his hands is a copy of the Honorable Elijah Muhammad's "Message to the Blackman."

I had to interview him for this book and question him about Muhammad's influence on his work. In the 1970s, Adams operated a business next to the Nation of Islam's Your Supermarket on 83rd & Cottage Grove in Chicago. He remembered: "Your Supermarket was there, the Restaurant across the street, Salaam Restaurant; on 79th Street was the bakery." In 1976, as part of Imam Mohammed's (RAA) "spin-off" (privatization and decentralization) of the Muslim businesses, I, along with a business partner, Tiahmo Ra'uf, were given the opportunity to operate the Salaam Restaurant, which we reopened in that year as the "New Salaam Restaurant and Cultural Center."

Mr. Adams spoke of the Nation of Islam's influence on him. "I was just influenced by the fact that here were Black people doing so well; they were bringing fish in from South America. Of course, I had met Muhammad Ali, at the time. So I just looked up to what they were doing. I thought it was a good model. In fact, I still think it is a good model."

Born in Alabama, Adams is from a family that had always stressed education. "My mother was born in 1906; her parents pushed all their children to education, and they pushed all their children to education. I thought that education could move you to any level you wanted to move to. Then I went into business, from the influence of just being around Muslims. It sort of felt like they had the same kind of upbringing that I had. I couldn't distinguish between the two. I just thought it was a good model. Especially for empowering the Black people. This was a way out. I don't know exactly what has happened since then. I'm very troubled by it. But I try to tell people, I try to keep planting trees and somebody hopefully one of these days will live under the shade of that tree. But I don't think we're planting trees fast enough."

Ironically, Adams, like myself and most 'Blacks' of that era, was profoundly impacted by the murder of Emmett Till. "1955, August" Adams noted. "I remember the day it happened. I remember like it was yesterday." But he has not let the terror of that event paralyze his obligation and commitment to work today and every day toward uplifting African Americans. "Coming out of West Africa in slave ships, the whole triangle of trade… all those people were, regardless of circumstances and the humiliation they went through, they were always pushing the next generation. It was the next generation. And it seems somewhere around the 60s, 65 or 70s, somebody said, 'I'm not going to push anymore.' And it's like a malaise has come over us and in that process we've lost 4 or 5 generations I think."

Somehow we must try to regain that spirit. It is a necessity in our soul. And it has to involve an allegiance and adherence to those of this shared experience first. We cannot integrate and contribute to the broader human society until we have become thoroughly comfortable in our own skin. Until then there will always be a sense of dependency and inferiority.

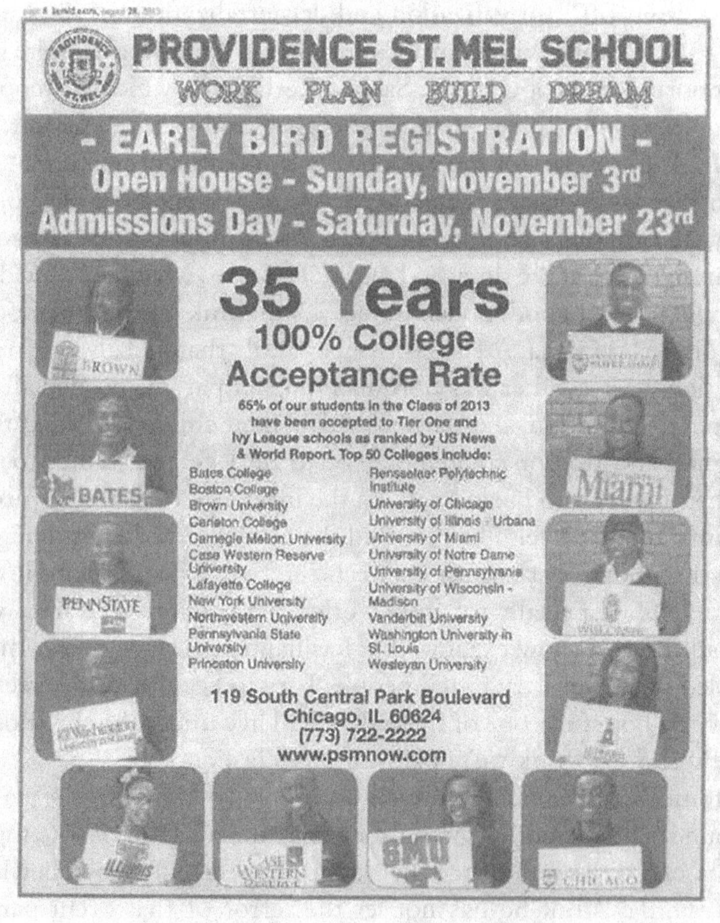

Providence St. Mel graduates of 2013; Abd-eljaami Madina in upper right hand corner with his full ride ticket to University of Notre Dame. Reprinted from Herald Extra, August 28, 2013.

12:69 Now when they came into Joseph's presence, he received his (full) brother to stay with him. He said (to him): "Behold! I am thy (own) brother; so grieve not at aught of their doings."

Chapter 69

We Have to Love Ourselves First

Blood Adhering

Even the primitive man understood the concept of blood adhering. Imam Mohammed (RAA) wisely gave a better translation and meaning to the term "clot" in Qur'an's very well-known ayat in which Allah says: *"Then We made the sperm into a clot of congealed blood; then of that clot We made a (foetus) lump; then we made out of that lump bones and clothed the bones with flesh; then we developed out of it another creature. So blessed be Allah, the best to create!" 23:14.* A clot, he pointed out does not imply a good thing. No one wants a clot. The Arabic word "alaq" should better be described as "blood adhering." I found many beautiful definitions of the word *adhere – conform to or follow rules exactly; to be attached, to be constant, to be faithful, loyal, true, stand by and support; to stick fast by or as if by suction or glue; or remain devoted to or be in support of something*--all beautiful meanings. The primitive man, even before he was introduced to any science and any revelation, understood that when his mate did not expel blood during her menstruation period in a given cycle, it was good news. It was a blessing because he could expect a child. And when she did expel blood, it meant that blood was not adhering and he could expect no production from tilling the field of his mate.

G-d did not have to send a messenger for us to understand this forming of the physical human being. It is the social origins that we need to understand. So we see this blood adhering as the beginning of man's social and community development. It still means the same thing. Allah says it is He who created you in tribes and nations, that you should know each other. So as we evolve from these simple structures, from sperm and from blood adhering, we don't lose these properties. We don't lose our essence. We are still blood. But we gain structure, bones, and flesh and as we do so, we are able to do more and activate or actualize more potential. In addition to this biological bond of racial identification, we were also subjected to the same shared experience.

We, African Americans, are brothers of the same mother. It is understandable therefore that we would come together and organize as racial brothers under the Nation of Islam before we came into the full universal brotherhood of Islam.[1] Joseph (PBUH) and his brother Benjamin were the children of Jacob's (PBUH) union with Rachel. He had loved Rachel from the beginning but was tricked by her father, Laban, into marrying her older sister Leah. The other 10 brothers from that union could not help having problems of jealousy with Joseph (PBUH) and Benjamin.

For generations leaders have struggled with the concept of how to organize African Americans as a community. We have all entered the "gates" of the "city" through some access point or another. Efforts to organize solely on the basis of shared economic interests have met limited success. Efforts focusing solely on political interests have similarly been limited—our circumstances warrant a broader range of solutions that politics cannot address. Even the moral imperatives of the church have failed to impact the race as a whole. I believe we have come to a point where only a recognition of ourselves as a G-d inspired group, with a Destiny and universal mission, will unite us and truly free us. That is a position that is warranted by G-d's justice. Joseph (PBUH) tells his brother, Benjamin, "grieve not at aught of their doings." That is a call for us to relieve our hearts of the burden of our past mistreatment and accept the fact that today we have become favored by G-d.

12:70 At length when he had furnished them forth with provisions (suitable) for them, he put the drinking cup into his brother's saddle-bag. Then shouted out a crier: "O ye (in) the caravan! behold! ye are thieves, without doubt!"

Chapter 70

What Goes Around Comes Around

Allah commands us to "give measure and weight with (full) justice."[1] Joseph (PBUH) could not in good conscience put his innocent brother Benjamin through what he had gone through. He had to reveal himself. We should all gauge our actions by how we would feel if what we are about to do would be done to us. Just as he meted out fairly the justice to Benjamin, he's now about to mete out justice to his other brothers; all according to what they deserve.

Some men have always been in a position to distribute resources to other men. Ancient man distributed the material of the earth by simply cupping his hands and scooping it up. Just as time was measured by periods of the sun, moon, and other heavenly bodies, early units of measure came from parts of the body and people's surroundings. Measures of length came from the forearm, hand or finger, and the foot. Seeds, grains, and stones were also used as weights and measures. As civilizations evolved, it became necessary to adopt standard weights and measures that were uniform and could be used in commerce. Everybody had to speak the same language commercially. Thus, the cup became a unit of measurement for volume. The cup evolved in mythology into a "horn of plenty or abundance"-cornucopia, a horn overflowing with the produce of the earth. The symbol of abundance finds its way into the Bible in Psalm 23:5, where it says, "Thou preparest a table before me in the presence of mine enemies: thou anointest my head with oil; my cup runneth over." It means 'I have more than enough for my needs.' That's quite a different picture than most of us find ourselves in where we are constantly short of our needs. Seeing the cup in a context of abundance gives us a key to relieving our social oppression and a key to our material success that might be buried deep in the baggage of our past hurts and rancor. But we've got to have faith in G-d's perfect justice.

The brothers are now experiencing what some might call Karma or the concept of 'what goes around comes around.'[2] They accused Joseph (PBUH) falsely and are now being falsely accused themselves. They are accused of stealing the cup that was hidden in the bag of Joseph's (PBUH) brother. In its context as a cup of abundance, if we look at the history of the commercial society in America, we will see that there is an element that is hidden within our own commerce and within our own commercial potential, that we do not even know is there. The rulers of modern Egypt know it is there. They sell their products and their popular culture through the African American. There is an image that is engrained in the icon of the African American that is powerful and subconscious that symbolizes wholesomeness and trustworthiness. They have been able to sell products based on that image. Today, Hip Hop, which originated in the urban communities, is a predominant music genre throughout the world and it has become a metaphor for authenticity in the culture. The sports world is propelled into international prominence by the presence of African American superstar athletes.

In the early history of commercial retail, many of your dominant brands that have evolved into multinational corporations such as Nestle, Quaker, etc., were established behind the image of the African American – Uncle Ben, the image of the loyal butler; Aunt Jemima, the image of the Mammy who nourished the master's children. As a child, I remember posters promoting Carnation Evaporated milk and it was propelled by the image of four African American children, the Signer Quadruplets, and Pet Evaporated Milk, by the Fultz Quadruplets. When the Fultz girls were born in 1946, everyone wanted a piece of the babies. "What better way to reel in African American business than with four beautiful, black baby girls. Borden and Carnation threw their hat in the ring but in the end, it was Pet Milk that Klenner (Fred Klenner, the doctor who delivered the children), chose to let represent the girls. Klenner was awarded a contract with Pet Milk and made the girls guinea pigs for his "Vitamin C Therapy." In exchange for using the girls for promotional purposes, the Fultz's were given a nurse and medical care, food and a farm by Pet."[3]

How often do we find ourselves part of someone else's plan, not even realizing it? Today the same strategy is used even beyond the commercial context. When they want to push the envelope of social issues in this experimental democracy, they use the African American. On January 28th, 2015 First Lady Michelle Obama appeared with the President in Saudi Arabia at a gathering commemorating the death of King Abdullah. Their presence there and any meaning that might have been attached to it was completely overshadowed by the fact that she appeared without a headscarf. We know that all of these protocols and decisions, regardless of how minute, are analyzed by social and political scientists. They advise the President and his staff and associates as to the effective consequences of all their public actions. It could not have been an accident, it could only have been an intention of this country to push the limits of the Saudi's acceptance of other cultures and traditions within their tightly religious orthodoxy. Even more sinister is the popular media in which they use programs and African American stars such as Viola Davis, an African American actress, in *How to Get Away with Murder*, to advance an agenda. In their very first episode they included a gratuitous scene of two men having sex in bed. In the popular program *Scandal* starring African American Kerry Washington, we regularly see homosexual scenes and dialogue.

All of the movements for fair and equal treatment of diverse attitudes and lifestyles use the Civil Rights Movement of African Americans as an example. A distinction needs to be made between civil rights and human rights. Civil Rights are rights afforded based on a person's citizenry, and all citizens should be treated fairly and equal. These rights should be based on human principles but they can vary from place to place and can be given and taken away. Human rights are inherent rights given by G-d to every creature. If you look closely at it, it is those who have deprived others of their rights that are most paranoid today. Something in their souls tells them that every deed must be accounted for – what goes around comes around. The brothers are now experiencing what it feels like to be rejected, lied on, and powerless to defend themselves or prove their worth.

12:71 They said, turning towards them: "What is it that ye miss?"

Chapter 71

They Can Only Grasp the Obvious

Since this is the king's cup and he is a symbol of the whole society, it points to the broader concept of the measurement of justice and fair dealing-social justice. Just as the test of America's commitment to social justice was tested by her dealing with her former slaves, the test of our Muslim brother's sense of social justice will be their dealing with us. Here again, we find that this measurement of justice and equity is hidden in the baggage of the brother's commerce and they don't even know it's there.

Most immigrant Muslims have engaged the African American community primarily on a commercial basis. They recognize the advantage of commerce in our communities. This has been a sore point in communities across the country-the exploitation of ignorant masses by selling death producing products such as narcotic paraphernalia, cigarettes, alcohol, etc.

We have to have discernment, along with the ability to do justice and have fair dealings with all people. As a virtue, a discerning individual is considered to possess wisdom and be of good judgment; especially with regard to subject matters often overlooked by others.[1]

There are broad human concerns and interests that touch all people in the society and Dr. Fard touched that common chord with his promise of money, good homes, and friendships in all walks of life. Malcolm X was asked once by an interviewer, "What do you want?" *(as in 'you people are complaining and whining and protesting; what is that you' all really want?')* Malcolm responded, "The same thing that your people want." The common complaint of President Obama is that he has not done enough for Black people. I think what those critics fail to see is the broad efforts he has made to advance the country in general, fairness and justice in general, and it is our failure, African Americans, to see our place and our benefit within that context. I have to claim my place in the country just like everyone else. I have to earn and demand my piece of the American dream.

Of course, there are going to be specific concerns too. The dominant culture is not going to be sensitive to the needs of its underclass. I've had conversations with whites about terrorism. I am as concerned about the security of my country as anyone. However, I do not live with the constant fear of a terrorist attack. My concern is that my grown African American sons, get home safely every day through violent streets and rogue police. In that regard we have failed to use economic and other levers that are within our control. Stop buying Nike's until they side with us in police reform. Close down liquor stores that have single-handedly decimated entire African American communities.

But within the justice that we seek, there is also benefit to the whole society. The success of the African American's human rights struggle represented a fulfillment of the founding father's dream that had before been only hypocritical rhetoric.

The dominant culture, therefore, doesn't realize what it is lacking and we don't realize we have the key within our own control. What they've got in their bags is perishable corn, but the true abundance is the wisdom and the virtue of good judgment. The drinking cup is hidden and immediately discovered in contrast to the stock in trade that he causes not to be discovered until the brothers return home.

When we are exercising this discernment, we have our head on right; we have our cup where it needs to be. There is a relationship between the word "cup" and the word "cap" and the "cap" is our head. One idiom has cup meaning head, i.e. in one's cup, meaning intoxicated or drunk. Another idiom is the vulgar Jewish advice of not 'putting your schmuck in your cup.' In either event, it refers to a condition where the person is not using good judgment or is letting the immediate/pressing concerns of the appetite or the obvious color their decisions. In any event, we have to be vigilant in seeking the hidden meanings and agendas that are always present when you don't control the flow of information.

12:72 They said, "We miss the great beaker of the king; for him who produces it, is (the reward of) a camel load; I will be bound by it."

Chapter 72

Discernment Requires Looking Past the Obvious

Referring back to the cup's origin as a unit of measurement, note that it is the king's cup, not Joseph's (PBUH). In Genesis 44, Joseph tells his servants to hide the cup in his brothers' bag and then find it and say, "Is this not my lord's drinking cup that he uses for telling about the future?"[1] Joseph (PBUH) doesn't need a cup to divine. Divination is an intuitive process that seeks to gain insight into the natural world, to know the nature of events, and when and where they will happen. Divination by way of cups was practiced in Egypt as well as in other parts of the ancient East. In fact, the first ones that Pharaoh consulted when confronted by Moses (PBUH) were his magicians. Joseph (PBUH) has proven his ability to predict events but he clearly states that is by G-d's grace that he is able to do this. In 12:37 he says, "I will surely reveal to you the truth and meaning of this ere it befall you: that is part of the (duty) which **my Lord hath taught me**." Later in 12:101, in his very beautiful prayer, he says, "My Lord! **Thou** hast indeed bestowed upon me some power and taught me something of the interpretation of dreams and events."

The whole mission of Joseph (PBUH), as it is with all servants to G-d, was to establish Truth and Reality and to eliminate superstition, magic, and mysticism from the worship of G-d. We find the same strategy by Joseph (PBUH) in 12:39 where he attacks the logic of the Trinitarianism that would later dominate Christianity. "O my two companions of the prison. (I ask you) are many lords differing among themselves better, or the One Allah, Supreme, and Irresistible?"

If the cup represents discernment and also a sign of the abundance that G-d intends for us, shouldn't we be trying to find some meaning, some salvation in our modern culture for our struggling brothers in the wilderness here? Discernment requires looking past the obvious. Perhaps the keys to abundance are mixed right in with their baggage, without them even being aware of it. In the summer of 2014, an 18-year-old unarmed African American, Michael Brown, was shot by a police officer in Ferguson, Missouri. His killing ignited protests throughout the country and brought attention to a number of other shootings of unarmed African American men.

In Cleveland in November 2014, 12-year-old Tamir Rice, who had an air pistol in his hand was shot and killed by police officers outside a Cleveland recreation center. After the shootings, the officers refused to call for medical help for the boy and tackled his sister when she tried to approach and help her brother. On July 17, 2014, in Staten Island, New York, an unarmed African American, Eric Garner, was being taken into police custody by way of a choke hold, which had been outlawed in many jurisdictions because of its deadly potential. Garner died and in the video of the incident, he is heard consistently appealing that "I can't breathe." This too sparked protest throughout the country and coincided with the Grand Jury decision in Ferguson not to indict the police officer that killed Michael Brown. These protests, sometimes violent, prompted the slogans that "Black Lives Matter" and "I Can't Breathe." The protests also pointed out an apparent lack of leadership and direction as to the African American community's response to this epidemic of killing young Black men. Oprah Winfrey was criticized for pointing this out and comparing it to the well-organized, coherent, and effective leadership of the Civil Rights Movement depicted in the movie *Selma* released during the same period. I decried the same lack of leadership based on the fact that an emotional response or a spasmodic flailing of the African American community was not going to be effective.

By March of 2015, the Civil Rights division of the United States Department of Justice issued a scathing report on the investigation of the Ferguson Police Department, in which it confirmed systemic racism in the Department and the city's municipal court system. FBI Director James B. Comey publicly acknowledged racial bias among law enforcement officers and a "disconnect" between the police and communities of color. This report could have been written about any hundreds of communities across the country. In April 2015, Robert Bates, a 73-year-old insurance company executive serving as a Tulsa, Oklahoma reserve deputy, claimed to have mistaken his gun for a Taser and fatally shot 44-year-old Eric Harris. In the same month, another unarmed African American man was killed by a white police officer in North Charleston, South Carolina. The video of the man running away and officer Michael Slager, firing eight shots at him, hitting him twice, went viral and Slager was charged with murder. Without that video, it would have been another "justifiable use of deadly force." In Baltimore, 25-year-old Freddie Gray died after being in police custody and the medical examiner's results showed he had a severed spine. The police have no explanation as to how he sustained his injuries or why they failed to get him medical help despite his repeated pleas.

In April, 2016 in a report echoing that Ferguson report, a Task Force set up by Chicago Mayor, Rahm Emmanuel found systemic racism within that city's police department. "The community's lack of trust in C.P.D. (Chicago Police Department) is justified," according to the report, "There is substantial evidence that people of color — particularly African-Americans — have had disproportionately negative experiences with the police over an extended period of time." The report documented what African American residents of Chicago have known for decades—that they are stopped without justification, verbally and physically abused, and in some instances arrested, and then detained without counsel. The task force was formed in response to protests after the release of a dashboard camera video of African American teenager, Laquan McDonald, 17, being shot 16 times by a Chicago police officer on Oct. 20, 2014.

As the events culminated toward the end of 2014, I would have liked to see a response to the police brutality where it hurts. As we have discussed, the system does not respond to anything but economic loss. As the debate ensued as to what should be an appropriate response and an effective long-term solution and as the community body continued to flail, I felt that a *Black Christmas* should have been promoted.

Ideally, it should have been a Black *anything but Christmas*. We don't even hear anymore the spirit of "Peace on Earth and goodwill toward men," in the dialogue and it has become embarrassing to promote the concept of a little white baby Jesus as an image of divinity. They don't even pretend anymore that it's anything but a commercial opportunity. What we hear and see now is a mad rush from Thanksgiving, which is almost an annoyance, to Black Friday, where they balance their books. Now they are trying to move the shopping frenzy of a Black Friday up to pre-Thanksgiving 'Purple' Tuesday or 'Blue' Wednesday to extend the holiday shopping season. The supposed birth of Prophet Jesus (PBUH) is lost in the dialogue altogether. Since it's lost already, let's be real and call a spade a spade. Let's call it exactly what it is-the biggest commercial holiday of the year. If we are going to hit the system where it hurts or where it's going to be effective in bringing about a change, we should keep our money in our pockets. We should sacrifice and deny ourselves for true freedom. We should sit down with our children and tell them, "Son, you know it is shameful for a people to attribute divinity to any human being, white or black. You know there is no Santa Claus. You know there is no fat Caucasian man in a red suit that brings you gifts. You know that I am the one that gives you gifts on this day. I will give you whatever you need just as I do all year round. But I will not shop on this day or before this day until I know that your future is secure and you aren't vulnerable to being shot down in the street because you look suspicious or are a young African American portrayed in an intimidating image. I will not let you lose your life to the forces in this system. I must ask you to share this responsibility toward your future during this season of family togetherness. Let us come together and get to know each other better and love each other more. This is how we will celebrate. We will keep our money in our pockets until I know that you are safe and secure in the streets."

That would have been my response. I believe if this had been done on a mass scale, not only would the police come to respect the lives of young black men more, but they are so serious about their economic 'god' that the police would begin to fulfill their real mission to serve and protect. They'd help young African American men across the street and make sure they didn't accidentally fall in the streets and hurt themselves to protect their economic system.

Allah did not condemn the accumulation of wealth. Instead, he reminded us that the poor had rights in a portion of what we acquired.[2] It is the inordinate love of wealth that he condemned.[3] This is also not saying that a *Dajjal* has come to dominate the life of America only. In the small nation of Brunei, the Sultan there just built the biggest palace in the world at $1.5 billion dollars-much bigger than even the Vatican palace. He has bought over $789 million worth of high-performance cars as part of his 7,000-car collection. At the same time, people in Africa are forced to walk miles a day just for a cup of water and people in Asia are forced to subsist on a few grains of rice a day. These are just signs of how pervasive and overpowering the forces of materialism can become.

12:73 (The brothers) said, "By Allah! well ye know that we came not to make mischief in the land, and we are no thieves!"

Chapter 73

The Guilty Are the Loudest in Proclaiming Their Innocence

The first thing the brothers say when the issue of fair dealing and justice is brought to them is, "We are no thieves." That is technically true. You buy a product and sell it to a ready market when you live in the free enterprise, market-driven system of America. But can you say that it really is fair to sell those things that you yourself would not even partake of? Doesn't your religion teach you that everybody in the chain of commerce of *khamr* (intoxicants) is guilty? How are they not thieves? Didn't they steal their fathers' favor by getting rid of Joseph (PBUH)? He was the rightful heir to the inheritance of innocence and righteousness passed down from their fathers, Jacob (PBUH), Isaac (PBUH), and Ibrahim (PBUH). Didn't they steal that too? Joseph (PBUH) told his fellow inmates in 12:38 that he followed the ways of his monotheistic fathers, although most people do not. But isn't it the case that usually the guilty are the loudest in proclaiming their innocence? And aren't most thieves motivated by greed?

So now the brothers are accused of being thieves. The concept of freedom that African Americans have today does not belong to them. It is a perverted concept of freedom; an attitude that "If I am truly free, I can do whatever I have the capacity to do, irrespective of whether it's intelligent or decent or proper." That attitude is inconsistent with the nature and nurture of the African American. It doesn't belong to him. But it's hidden in our subconscious baggage and we don't even know it. Rami Nashashibi, Executive Director of the Inner-City Muslim Action Network (IMAN), himself a Jordanian, has implemented a program called Muslim Run-a campaign for health, wellness, and healing designed to improve relations between African American residents in Chicago and the Muslim families who run liquor stores and other businesses in African American neighborhoods. He explained, "We want to challenge Muslim store owners to implement the higher principles and ideals of their faith in their businesses." Since the 1970s and '80s, these stores have proliferated throughout predominantly Black major cities such as Chicago. A popular song in Hip Hop culture, *Bigger than the Liquor Store,* by Mikkey Halsted and Rhymefest, a sequel to Mikkey's powerful and provocative original song, *Liquor Store* from 2008, grows in part, from their involvement in IMAN's program.

Is it enough for us to say that we comply with the laws of America? Or, if we believe in higher standards, aren't we obligated to follow that? How often do you see African Americans, when confronted with something they know their grandparents would never condone, say, "Well, the white man did it?" This is why Allah clearly states in the Qur'an that this will not be an acceptable excuse for us on the Day of Judgment-that I was just following my fathers or following my leaders or the people ahead of me. It is not going to be acceptable for our brothers to say the African Americans were slaves and they were used to being oppressed and oppressing themselves, so I think I should inherit them from the white man and give them the same treatment. Imam Mohammed (RAA) put it even more blunt in addressing the white society's justification for our mistreatment and our Muslim brothers neglect in addressing it.[1]

12:74 (The Egyptians) said, "What then shall be the penalty of this, if ye are (proved) to have lied?"

Chapter 74

Choose Your Own Punishment

How do we get from being considered inherited property to become inheritors? How do we go from a commodity or a currency[1] to a just distributor of the resources? How do we know that Allah is with the rise of this new people here in America in prominence and power; not just to serve the elder brothers from this position of authority but as the leader, just as Joseph (PBUH) envisioned in his dream. First, we know, as Allah tells us, that there was never a time and place when He was not present – the All-Seeing, the All-Knowing, the Ever-Present and Always Existing. We also know that there is no scheme that is not encompassed in His plan. Therefore, He saw what was being done to us and has promised that when the innocent are oppressed, He will come to their aid. Whatever we endure for His sake, the reward is incumbent on Him.

It is in Allah's authority to punish the wrongdoer, but here, the Egyptians tell the brothers in essence to 'choose your own punishment.' They ask, "What then shall be the penalty?" The word used is from the root meaning to *reward, to satisfy a debt, recompense or give an equivalent.* It's talking about the penalty for the brothers' theft but it points up a dichotomy between man-made or temporal justice and the perfect justice of Allah. Everything has a recompense that must be satisfied and in some cases that compensation is incumbent upon Allah Himself because of His own promise.

The brothers themselves were thieves, but then there was also the lie. Look at our circumstances here in America. To claim that a people enslaved deserve their plight, knowing they have done nothing wrong, is a lie. To interpret G-d's word in the Bible to say they are cursed by G-d for the sin of an ancient ancestor is a lie. And to say that they are a separate species, less than human, and not a descendant of our common parent, Adam (PBUH), is an even bigger lie. It's reminiscent of the lie the brothers told on Joseph, (PBUH) when they first sold him into slavery-that they were racing and not paying attention and the wolf ate him up. They stained his shirt with false blood. Joseph (PBUH) was rescued and prospered because he never let his bad circumstance warp his righteous character and he never got impatient when the rescue took a long time.

We too have to demonstrate the same traits. We cannot let our history of mistreatment make us bitter and cruel toward any other human being. We cannot let the lack of material benefits of society turn us into thieves. We cannot let short-term and superficial advantages turn us into liars. It's normal for an oppressed people to wonder when G-d's relief will come.[2] It also happens that the reward does not come when we think it should. It takes too long and we lose those who lose faith in the promise.[3] What it requires, to be worthy of the reward, is patience and an unwavering belief in Allah's promise and His perfect justice, such that even if we don't see it on our narrow temporal schedule, we know it's coming under Allah's Plan.[4] Don't you know that our ancestors knew that complete freedom would not come in their lifetime? They suffered, fought and died for those who would come after them. And we need to do the same thing. That patience is what describes Joseph (PBUH) best and it is the virtue that enabled him to eventually become inheritor/trustee of all the material benefits of the land.[5]

12:75 They said, "The penalty should be that he in whose saddle-bag it is found, should be held (as bondman) to atone for the (crime). Thus it is we punish the wrong-doers!"

Chapter 75

A Level Playing Field

The king's cup is Joseph's (PBUH) tool for bringing the brothers to the reality of their fraudulent acts. The record of their act is in *Sijjin.* **Sijjeen** (Arabic:نیجس)means a *'register'*wherein the deeds of all Mankind are recorded. The word is based on sijn which means:*'prison, hard, anything hard, a terrible place in the bottom of Hell'*-the place where the records of the Wicked are held, and it is a proper name for the fire of*Hell.*[1]

Joseph (PBUH) became a master of his prison and ultimately his freedom. There is no way to escape the record of our deeds or the justice for them. Despite all of Joseph's (PBUH) magnanimity, the price must still be paid. We know there will be a complete and perfect accounting. The *Day of Judgment* can just as accurately be rendered, *Day of Accounting* or period when our debts are paid in full. But there will be a measure of justice in this life that we will be able to see. That same verse above, on Sijjin also tells us what will come before this hard justice. It comes when the earth is flattened, the mountains and valleys (the great and powerful and the poor and lowly) we'll all be on the same plain (plane) – "a level playing field."[2] And when things are cast forth and become empty, there'll be no secrets, nothing hidden, and no knowledge that man will be able to lord over his fellow human beings.

As rational creatures, we naturally seek justification for circumstances. We want balance—an innate sense of fairness. We are creatures of intellect and our main hunger is for knowledge and understanding. To exist as human beings, we have to develop our mind, raise our knowledge, and clear up our understanding. In our true human form, we are not satisfied just going through gestures, making motions, feeling something and not seeing it or understanding it. It is knowledge that illuminates the mind, that satisfies the hunger and that heals whatever burdens our minds. This is what was lost by the People of the Book in favor of empty rituals.

Today they still keep their secret knowledge safe among the select few and use it to control the masses. They do not share with the poor who have been deprived of the knowledge of how to cultivate their minds and control their human appetites.[3] This knowledge is symbolized in the ancient Egyptian mythology of Isis. Isis represents the pure, original scripture without any corruption. In the mythology, Isis says, "No one has ever removed my veil," meaning that no one had removed the secret language, the symbolism so that they could see the real message. Ancient Egypt used the same tools on the masses to keep them as mental and spiritual slaves. Today, Western civilization identifies its current crop of extremists as ISIS, implying that the establishment of Islamic life and the freeing of the mind of the masses from symbolism are pre-eminent threats to its civilization.

Another ritual that represents our life force, our regenerative power coming out from the covering is circumcision. This represents the removal of the veil or the symbolism from the code language. When you take the symbolic meaning and the ritualism off of the knowledge then you have circumcised yourself. To complete your circumcision, you then have to sacrifice bad manners and bad appetites. Those who formulated the Christian religious teachings of today learned to maintain the veil of secrecy over the true essence of religious knowledge. The doctrines were corrupted by false teachings and appeals to the animal nature of the people. America has the most advanced and destructive weaponry in the history of mankind. But it takes a human being, directed by the mind, to push the buttons, so control of the mind is the real control of the human being. America cannot boast of their material or intellectual superiority as long as they follow a scriptural language that has been corrupted.[4]

Controlling the Human Being

No one wants to acknowledge that they are being controlled by someone else, but we have to acknowledge truth and reality. The masses did not organize the religion or the religious language that was given to them. They do not control the social influences that feed their human appetites. Someone is pushing the buttons and holding the key and in Egyptian mythology, Isis is seen with a key. This means that she has the formula for regulating the extremes in society. She has the science of man's life (dog/symbol of the social life) and how to control his life. She controls the seasons, fall, winter, spring, and summer. She can turn him on or off to spiritual orientation. She has the key to heaven & hell in the ancient mythology.[5] The threat to the current world order is not the irrational and ineffective thrashing about of violent extremists, but rather the masses freeing their minds and coming out from under the control of those hiding secret knowledge.

12:76 So he began (the search) with their baggage, before (he came to) the baggage of his brother: at length he brought it out of his brother's baggage. Thus did we plan for Joseph. He could not take his brother by the law of the king except that Allah willed it (so). We raise to degrees (of wisdom) whom We please: but over all endued with knowledge is one, the All-Knowing.

Chapter 76

A Free Black Mind is a Concealed Weapon

Looking closely, we see a divine plan to get Jacob (PBUH) and his sons into Egypt[1] and later the raising of Moses (PBUH) and the Exodus of them out of Egypt. This Exodus parallels the extraction by the Greeks of natural science and religious science knowledge from Egypt. Most honest scholars acknowledge that the loftiest pursuits of the Greeks would not have been possible if not for the ancient Kemet civilization in Egypt. In Kemet, Hippocrates, the father of medicine, learned of disease from the previous explorations of Imhotep, who established diagnostic medicine 2,500 years earlier. Pythagoras, the father of mathematics, learned calculus and geometry from the Kemetic priests based on a millennia-old papyrus. Plato's work was based upon a wide array of human knowledge encompassing math, writing, physical science, religion, and the supernatural-all the time integrating religion and science. "This idea that the universe is rational and that the "truth" of the universe is the underlying rationality and order of the universe rather than its diverse phenomena, passed from the Egyptians to the Greeks,"[2] writes historian Richard Hooker. The Greeks' name for this concept was logos. In his Republic, Plato describes a dichotomy between a higher and lower self. The higher self (reason) pursues knowledge, reason, and discipline. The lower self (the more prominent of the two) is concerned with more crude aspects like sex, addiction, and other self-serving pursuits. Reason must ultimately win over emotion for a life to be worthwhile. Thus, the emphasis on reason over all else was born and the concepts of spirituality and reason began to diverge. The emphasis on reason ultimately led to the Age of Enlightenment, from which we draw our worldview today.

We find these contributions written out of history: "During the 19th century, many European writers, limited by ethnocentrism and racism, decided that blacks in Africa could have had nothing to do with Europe's rise to greatness,"[3] wrote Josh Davis quoting Gloria Dickenson, professor of African American Studies at The College of New Jersey. At a time when Western society was building itself on the labor of African slaves, white Europeans could not logically credit their slaves' ancestors with providing the foundation of that very same society.

Martin Gardiner Bernal is credited with much of the scholarly research documenting Greek philosophy rooted in Egyptian thought and what Greeks owed to earlier and evolved civilizations. Bernal, an emeritus professor of government and near eastern studies at Cornell University, is best known for his work *Black Athena*, which has generated much controversy. *Black Athena: The Afroasiatic Roots of Classical Civilization* deals with several aspects of this obscured and often denied history. Other works include *The Fabrication of Ancient Greece, The Archaeological and Documentary Evidence,* and *The Linguistic Evidence.* Bernal wrote that African history, as opposed to African prehistory, began with the Egyptian records after the upper Egyptian unification of Egypt around 3400 B.C. (Bernal, 1991. pp.207-211). Two hundred years before then, however, there is evidence of a sophisticated state in Nubia; between the second and first cataracts of the Nile. Royal tombs found along the riverbank, now under Lake Nasser, indicated the existence of a rich stratified society and the fact that symbols of royalty such as the hawk on a *serech* or palace facade, and the white crown later used by Egyptian pharaohs were already in use there. Dr. Bruce B. Williams of the University of Chicago, author of five volumes in a continuing series on Nubian excavations notes that local pottery showed that the culture was Nubian not Egyptian, and pots and other objects found in the tombs indicate a pattern of trade stretching from the Kordofan Mountains in what is now south central Sudan, to the Levant, now Syria and Palestine/Israel. Nubia is the homeland of Africa's earliest black culture with a history that can be traced from 3100 B.C. onward through Nubian monuments and artifacts, as well as written records from Egypt and Rome. The Nubian wealth appears to have come from cultivation along the river banks and herding and hunting in the Acacia desert scrub that existed then, where there is now desert. It is also possible that Nubians were already trading in gold, which was abundant in the region.

For the Romans and Greeks, there were three types of blacks. There were those who lived within the empire, who were generally, though not always, in the lower classes. Then there were the admired civilized and philosophical *Ethiopians* who were generally located in the Nubian state of Meroë. The name *Ethiopia* has maintained this high status into the modern period. The third type, the fierce nomadic Ethiopians of the desert from Egypt to the Atlantic, resisted Roman attacks and raided cities within the empire. From these and black forces in the Roman legions, Africans gained a reputation for soldierly qualities. In Christian times, the patron saint of soldiers became St Maurice, a soldier from Upper Egypt of the 3rd century CE, who was always portrayed as black. Ptolemy the mathematician and astronomer of the second century CE, was also an upper Egyptian and known to Arab writers as black, (Bernal, 1992, p.606). Christian writers did not refer to his appearance. Thus, despite the widespread fear and suspicion of blacks among western Europeans of the Middle Ages, the dominant figures or authorities in their theology, warfare, and science – St. Augustine, St Maurice,[4] and the learned Ptolemy – were Africans and the last two were sometimes or more often seen as blacks. The ancient Greeks acknowledged the Egyptian influence on their society and Bernal notes that this view held up until the 1820s and 1830s when outside forces like the revival of Christianity, Romanticism, and persistent racism forced the narrative to change. Around that time, the *Aryan model* currently used today was introduced. As could be expected, the academic community, thoroughly immersed in that model, launched intense criticism of *Black Athena* and its succeeding two volumes. Mary Lefkowitz, a professor at Wellesley College, published a response to Bernal's book entitled *Not Out of Africa*, which was nearly as controversial as the original. Later on, *Black Athena Revisited*, edited by Lefkowitz and Guy MacLean Rogers, a collection of responses to *Black Athena*, was published.

Why all of this effort to hide history and to hide the blessing of knowledge upon which society is built? Is it because this civilization is built on an artificial foundation and that foundation and the structures that sit upon it would crumble if the truth were known? It is Allah (G-d) who raises people in knowledge as He sees fit, and as long as a people can suppress that knowledge they can rule. But what happens when that rulership is based on a false premise?

Fareed Zakaria pointed out in a recent article entitled, "Middle America is killing itself," the study that shows that white Americans are dying in increasing numbers. The main causes of death are suicide, alcoholism, and overdoses of prescription and illegal drugs. These circumstances are caused by stress, depression and despair, and I have no doubt that the destruction of the false construct of white supremacy is what is driving these middle-aged whites to depression and self-medication. It's hard to see Blacks in the negative stereotype you've been indoctrinated in all your life when you look at Washington and see the Leader of the Free World looking like that stereotype. I can understand the kind of dissonance that could create in the mind.

There is something intimidating about an African American that sees himself outside of the stereotype imposed on him by a racist society. There's also something pathetic about an African American who is willing to exchange a white slave master for an Arab or any other master. Sam Greenlee, noted novelist and author of the book *The Spook Who Sat by the Door*, shared with me before his passing what he described as his shortest poem: "A free black mind is a concealed weapon."

12:77 They said, "If he steals, there was a brother of his who did steal before (him)." But these things did Joseph keep locked in his heart, revealing not the secrets to them. He (simply) said (to himself): "Ye are the worse situated; and Allah knoweth best the truth of what ye assert!"

Chapter 77

It Runs in the Family

When confronted with a false charge against their brother Benjamin, whom they know is righteous, do they defend him? Do they confess their own wrong or do they repent? No, they compound their theft and their previous lie with another lie. They have gone so far in their wrong doing that Allah caused them to prove their guilt in front of the very one they had wronged. Oh, what a tangled web we weave when first we practice to deceive.[1] The wisdom of this adage is evident. The act of lying is called fabrication because we *sew* together pieces into the story we want. When those falsehoods have no basis in truth at all, we say the tale is made "out of whole cloth." As a predator, the spider weaves a web to trap its prey. We cannot escape the trap of our own falsehoods. The very nature of the lie itself and the nature of the universe itself, created for just ends, dictate that falsehood cannot stand.[2] True or not, there is no excuse for backbiting or slandering our brother.[3] They show no remorse for the wrongdoing and their unworthiness is now proven. Some people just don't have repentance in them until they are the very end of their road and there is no other alternative.[4] They share no blame themselves but throw the false claim onto the brother of another mother. "They wronged Benjamin, too." Instead of saying, "He is a righteous young man, as was his brother, Joseph (PBUH), and would never steal," they lie again. Their jealousy remains and as with many people, they don't repent until they are totally over a barrel and have absolutely no other way out.

Just as they stained Joseph's (PBUH) shirt with animal blood and projected their own blood lust onto him, they now accuse him of having been a thief. It is bad enough to commit a wrong yourself, but it is an even graver sin to project your sin onto another.[5] When we do something wrong the best course is to admit it and not blame someone else.

Projection

In the brothers' case, their projection of their own faults onto Joseph (PBUH) and his brother is a conscious sin. Many people have a psychological dysfunction that causes them to project. It is a defense mechanism where a person unconsciously denies his own attributes, thoughts, and emotions, which are then ascribed to other people. Projection reduces anxiety by allowing the expression of the unwanted unconscious impulses or desires without letting the conscious mind recognize them. An example of this behavior might be blaming another for our own failure. The mind may avoid the discomfort of consciously admitting personal faults by keeping those feelings unconscious and by projecting those same faults onto another person. It's particularly easy for us to demonize others that don't look like us or those who speak a different language.

We blame all of the wrong in the world on others, never acknowledging our own wrong doing and never realizing that we may have created the desperation that caused the extreme behavior. President Obama was criticized when he addressed the scourge of extremism around the world in a speech where he said, "Humanity has been grappling with these questions throughout human history and lest we get on our high horse and think this is unique to some other place, remember that during the Crusades and the Inquisition, people committed terrible deeds in the name of Christ. In our home country, slavery and Jim Crow all too often was justified in the name of Christ." There was criticism and even outrage that he would acknowledge such an unvarnished truth. But that's the nature of wrongdoers. They forget all of their past wrongs and convince themselves of their own innocence. They project Islam as the religion that was spread by violence, but that is again projecting their own sins onto others. Thomas Carlayle, the Scottish philosopher, satirical writer, essayist, historian and teacher and considered one of the most important social commentators of his time said: "Accusing [the Prophet] of relying on the sword for people to respond to his preaching is incomprehensible nonsense!" Sometimes we have to do the same thing Joseph (PBUH) did and lock these secrets in our heart. In today's environment, if you state the true facts about the Western world's own wrong, you could conceivably be seen as supporting extremism.

In France, just days after the attacks that killed 12 people at the offices of the satirical newspaper *Charlie Hebdo*, on January 7, 2015, provocative French comedian Dieudonné M'bala M'bala wrote on his Facebook page that he felt like "Charlie Coulibaly." (the last name of one of the attackers). M'bala was convicted under a new law enacted in November meant to rein in speech supporting terrorism. While Charlie Hebdo was praised for its irreverent exercise of freedom of speech, the same country convicted M'bala for his free speech and has another law that criminalizes even factual or truthful statements that play down or whitewash the Holocaust. What hypocrisy!

After the terrorist attack on Charlie Hebdo and killings of a police officer and innocent people at a Jewish bakery, they wanted everybody in France to say "I am Charlie," and many people around the world expressed that sentiment. I was as saddened and horrified by the attacks as anybody but it didn't motivate me to give up my identity. I am not Charlie. "I am Nuri. And I am Mohammed."

We would have never killed those journalists in France. But we also would never have done what Charlie did. We would never have disrespected G-d, His Prophets, (PBUT) Jesus (PBUH) or Mohammed (PBUH). We would have done what the Qur'an commanded of us and that is stay away from those in their ignorance when they satirize (revile) the Prophet. Allah has already promised them punishment for that, but again sometimes we have to wait for justice. And sometimes we have to hold our peace and keep the secrets inside us as Joseph (PBUH) did as part of a broader plan.

12:78 They said, "O exalted one! Behold! he has a father, aged and venerable, (who will grieve for him); so take one of us in his place; for we see that thou art (gracious) in doing good."

Chapter 78

How the Mighty Have Fallen

When we have exhausted all of the disciplines and skills that we thought would bring us peace and satisfaction, we'll find that we must come to a humility-to an innocence. We see people every day that have acquired the good things of this life-power, money, recognition, knowledge-and many of them still feel a lack and a dissatisfaction. If you question them, many of them will tell you, I'd give up any one of these accomplishments to have peace in my soul.

O, how are the mighty fallen.[1] You can't even frighten the world's people today with your military might. How men's fortunes are reversed. Joseph (PBUH) has come up in the world. In 12:31, he is the servant of the Aziz and falsely accused by the wife of the Aziz. Now he is the mighty one himself. The brothers still don't recognize him as their brother, but they, at least, recognize him as having beautiful character and one who does good. The father Jacob (PBUH) is now a venerable *Shaikh*, a title denoting honor and respect. They express their concern about his welfare when they have to return to him without his son, Benjamin. Where was that concern when they sold Joseph (PBUH) into slavery? Where was that respect when they lied to their father to cover their own wicked deeds? If we can see Joseph (PBUH) as an inherent faculty of the individual mind, governing imagination and intuition, we can also see his brothers as other faculties. His estrangement from these brothers then could be seen as jealousy of the superiority of imagination and intuition. The rational faculty and other mental disciplines are prone to accept only the seen, the known, the logical, and the scientific and scorn the unseen, vision and faith. Often we hear the media reporting on something that our common sense tells us is right or correct, but they always add, "We don't have scientific studies to confirm this."

We all start out as dreamers; imagining a beautiful future for ourselves. We sleep for months in the wombs of our mothers and then sleep for most of the day when we are delivered. As we grow older, the world forces us to scale down our expectations of ourselves. So our potential engineers and scientists somewhere along the way convince themselves that their destiny is working at Walmart.

But we must never lose our imagination. We must never give up on its power to visualize ourselves outside of present circumstances. If we preserve that there is hope for everything else. The brothers are on their way to respect for the good and the valuable, but sometimes our awakening is a gradual process, and that is the message: that we have to be patient with each other and with ourselves.

12:79 He said, "Allah forbid that we take other than him with whom we found our property, indeed (if we did so), we should be acting wrongfully."

Chapter 79

You Can't Do to Them What They Did to You

The United States is rapidly becoming a nation of younger minorities and older whites. 50.4% of children born in 2011 were minority – Hispanics, Blacks, Asians, and other minorities and by 2042, the U.S. Census estimates that minorities will outnumber non-Hispanic whites. This growing diversity has implications for politics, business, and education. It is understandable that these institutions would now work to ensure that their power continues.

I think one fear that the current non-minority population has is feeling that they will be called to justice when new groups come into power, especially groups that they have historically enslaved and persecuted. There is no need to fear that.

I remember the day in April 1968, that Dr. Martin Luther King was assassinated in Memphis Tennessee like it was yesterday. I was in my grandparents' house and they had an old radio on top of the refrigerator in the kitchen when I heard the news announced. I had been studying the Nation of Islam teaching and visiting Temple #2 at 5335 S. Greenwood in Chicago. I was also studying other movements. But news of that event made my decision for me. I reasoned that if they would kill a man of peace that promoted non-violence, there was no chance of survival unless I chose the strongest, most militant group out there. To say that the "white man was the devil," that "Allah was going to destroy him for his wickedness," and "we have to separate," and "we want some of this land for ourselves" was as radical as you could get. I saw that as the only antidote to the venom and terror of white's toward African Americans. I didn't waver after that and I began writing my letter to be accepted in the Nation of Islam. Others responded differently.

The day after Dr. King's assassination, Jane Elliot, a third-grade teacher in Riceville, Iowa, whom I would honor as one of the greatest educators in history, conducted an experiment to teach her students the effects of racism. She separated her students in the classroom according to eye color and lectured on fictional superiorities of brown-eyed people over blue-eyed people, citing melanin content to scientifically support the claim that brown-eyed people were smarter and blue-eyed people were lazy and shiftless. The brown-eyed kids immediately became confident, outgoing, and aggressive, while the blue-eyed ones became withdrawn, defensive, and demonstrated inferiority. At lunchtime, she described her experiment to the other teachers in the break room and while most were supportive, one remarked, "It's about time someone shot that son-of-a-bitch (referring to Dr. King)." The next day she reversed the roles, with the blue-eyed children as the superiors and the brown-eyed ones as inferior. The expectation was that the blue-eyed children that had been oppressed the previous day, would come back when they were in power and take it out on the brown-eyed children. To the contrary, she discovered that the blue-eyed children did the exact opposite. Having been oppressed themselves, they were able to empathize with the brown-eyed children who had imposed tyranny on them the previous day. Years later, almost every child would acknowledge how the experiment changed their lives and strengthened their character. How did the parents respond? In addition to the expected hateful comments and treatment, each year 20% of the parents requested that their child not be assigned to her class. Some thought it cruel that their child should be exposed to a day of discrimination and hatred. Elliott replied, "Why are we so worried about the fragile egos of white children who experience a couple of hours of made-up racism one day when blacks experience real racism every day of their lives?"

Her logic is the same as that of Imam Mohammed (RAA) when he encouraged formation of CRAID (Committee to Remove All Images of the Divine) committees across the country, and their singular *Message of Concern*[1] advocating for the elimination of racial images of divine in religion. He asked the question, "What would happen if people would sit in churches throughout the world for centuries with the image of an African American man as savior of the world before them?" Elliott provided an idea of what would happen with her experiment of one day. The higher morality demands that we forgive. You can't do to them what they did to you; even if they have hated you and even if they have persecuted you.[2] We were reminded of this principle in the Nation of Islam, when we were taught that it was our job to wake up the Lost-Found Nation in North America and to build a Nation. Allah (G-d) would take care of the 'devil.' Vengeance is a poison that can't help but warp our good intentions.

Joseph (PBUH) reminds the brothers that he is not willing to do an injustice to anyone. He acknowledges the higher justice of Allah and demonstrates no tendency to act based on his own emotions. He has already schemed against the brothers by hiding the cup in their baggage but there is support that his actions were motivated by a greater good. His secret plan, in concert with his Egyptian servants, was part of a deed of charity; it was moving toward establishing justice and it was a plan to bring about reconciliation between him and his brothers.[3] Even so, there are limits as to strategies that are acceptable to bring about a greater good. When Solomon (PBUH) wanted the throne of the Queen of Saba (Sheba), a jinn said he could bring it to Solomon (PBUH) before he could stand up. But one who had knowledge of the book was able to do it even quicker.[4]

We have to trust the righteous methods and not fall prey to the temptation to take a shortcut to accomplish our objective easier and faster with questionable tactics. Imam Mohammed (RAA) addressed this issue in explaining the work of W. D. Fard. He noted that he felt he could have brought the *Lost Found* nation to Islam just as quick by using the pure language of the Qur'an. Fard felt the need to present Islam in a language that resonated with our history of oppression under the white man. Instead of *La Illaha Ilallah*, (There is no god but Allah), he used language that implied our own divinity. The question was asked in his Lessons, and answered: ("Who is the Original Man? The Original Man is the Asiatic Black Man, the Maker, the Owner, the Cream of the Planet Earth-God of the Universe.") I don't doubt that Fard had good intentions, but you also have to look at its effect today. Many African Americans today that are blinded in the total darkness of Blackness. It is a religion to them and it is hard for them to put moral, spiritual or intellectual concerns above Blackness.

I understand the fear and paranoia of some of white America. Perhaps they think that if the African American comes into power, we will enslave them. Maybe they think we will work them from "can't to can't" for no pay and beat and mutilate them. Maybe they think we will lynch them for sport or maybe they think we will tear their families apart and sell off their children or spouses. That's not in us and it would not have been in them either had not the white image of racial divinity been instilled in them. They should not worry. You can't do to them what they did to you. Joseph (PBUH) was clear that in spite of whatever had been done to him, he could not act vengefully toward anyone.

12:80 Now when they saw no hope of his (yielding), they held a conference in private. The leader among them said, "Know ye not that your father did take an oath from you in Allah's name, and how, before this, ye did fail in your duty with Joseph? Therefore will I not leave this land until my father permits me, or Allah commands me; and He is the best to command."

Chapter 80

If You Keep Doing What You're Doing, You'll Keep Getting What You're Getting

Now the conscience of the brothers is coming alive. The leader realizes that if you keep doing what you're doing, you'll keep getting what you're getting. He reminds his other brothers of the oath they made in Allah's name. He reminds them of their injustice toward Joseph (PBUH). All of us have a voice within us that will remind us of our duty and of our failures in that regard. This leader of the brothers agrees to fulfill his word and he finally realizes that Allah is in charge. Yet Allah Himself requires that we change the condition of our hearts. Don't underestimate the power of a "change of heart." On the authority of Abu Saeed al-Khudri (may Allah be pleased with him) who said, "I heard the Messenger of Allah say whoever of you sees an evil must then change it with his hand. If he is not able to do so, then [he must change it] with his tongue. And if he is not able to do so, then [he must change it] with his heart. And that is the slightest [effect of] faith." (Recorded in Muslim). However weak the change of heart might be, on the scale of faith, it's a start, and it's a start that will lead to bigger changes in actions and deeds. We all have to desire to do better.

It is said that desire is the mother all things and it is also said that Eve is the mother of all people. Although Adam's (PBUH) wife is mentioned throughout the Qur'an, the name Eve is not mentioned, so we come to this characterization through tradition. In Classical Hebrew, she is called *Ḥawwāh*, and Hawwa in Arabic. There is the Arabic word, *hawa*, from which the meaning 'desire' is derived. But a more direct meaning of the word is to fall prey to or be overturned or pulled down.[1] This might be why there is so much sexism in the world and misinterpretation of the woman, as Eve, being susceptible to evil.

Many times we don't have the means to physically change a situation. In our history, we find people such as Nat Turner who tried as best they could. Then there were those such as Dr. Martin Luther King, who recognized that we were no match for America's army. There were also others such as the Deacons for Defense and Justice, an African-American civil rights organization in the Southern states during the 1960s that believed in armed self-defense. There were many, many others, white and black, who detested the oppression and ill-treatment in their heart but were not able to march or speak out in the cause. Nevertheless, they let their feelings be known and eventually forced the government to support a change. The message is that we all have the power to bring about change, but it begins within ourselves. We must want something different. It is so strange to hear people every day complain about the circumstances in their lives but see no connection at all with how they're living and what they're doing. It was the wise man Albert Einstein who defined insanity as doing the same thing over and over again and expecting different results.

The brothers' injustice and deceit have caught up with them and something within them just as in all of us, tells them, "I have not done right and if I want G-d's blessing I have to do something different." It is the *leader* among them that comes to this understanding and the word used for leader is from the root word *Khabara* meaning among other things, *to know* or *understand.* It is distinguishable from *Alim*, also translated as knowledge, in that Alim implies a knowledge, even before the happening of an event, while Khabara implies a knowledge learned by experience.[2] In any event, we see the brothers finally beginning to see the light. They remember the oath they made to their father and commit to fulfilling it. In the Nation of Islam, we were taught the importance of the word and asked the question, "Have you heard that the Muslim's word is bond?" The answer was yes, "The Muslim word is bond and bond is life and I will give my life before my word shall fail." Here we see all of the faculties finally coming around and supporting the vision of the excellent human model and the brothers were coming around to the upright life of their prophet father (PBUH) and their prophet brother, Joseph (PBUH).

12:81 "Turn ye back to your father, and say, 'O our father! behold! thy son committed theft! we bear witness only to what we know, and we could not well guard against the unseen!"

Chapter 81

We Should Consider the Unseen Forces That Got Us Here

What the brothers think they know is on the surface. They didn't know what Joseph's (PBUH) plan was nor what G-d's Plan was. Consider those claiming knowledge and truth who have only touched the surface. Sometimes it takes bad circumstances to show us that we are not in control. Allah challenges those who think they are in control to forestall death when He has called the life from the body.[1] We were not in control when we were ill and our condition was cured. We did all we could do. The doctors did all they could. The rest was up to Allah and unseen forces.[2]

The brothers are realizing that there is a higher plan in place above their own schemes. They knew that they would eventually have to return to right. They justified their acts toward Joseph (PBUH) saying, "There will be time for us to be righteous later." They see that 'later' is upon them and that Allah protects the innocent. He protects his righteous servants; he protects the new life in the womb. He commands the unseen forces within which the universe operates and which operate within our own beings.

Neil DeGrasse Tyson, an African American and one of the world's foremost astrophysicists, loves talking about the universe. He acknowledges what we have heard from even ancient philosophers, that everything we see in the material world is also in every individual.[3]

Allah confirms this and that both the origin of the universe and our own creation point to Him.[4] Tyson said, "The most astonishing fact is that the molecules that comprise our body are traceable to the crucibles of the centers of stars, that manufactured these elements from lighter versions of themselves and then exploded; scattering this enrichment across the galaxy into gas clouds that would later collapse to form next generation star systems. One of those star systems was ours. These atoms and molecules are in us because, in fact, the universe is in us." And yet we take all of this for granted because it is unseen.

We have been protected and under Allah's Divine plan, even before we were put on the slave ships during the Trans-Atlantic slave trade. Those innocent ones who died on the voyage over are under His care. Throughout our sojourn, in the womb of darkness (ignorance) and the oppression (pressure) of development and birth, He was there. Now that we are free and live in the *Day of Religion* (Accounting & Judgment), we should consider the unseen forces that operated to get us here. Now the brothers acknowledge the unseen. Only Allah has perfect knowledge and has knowledge of the unseen, but He blesses his servants as He pleases with keys to the unseen.[5] Those who possess those keys are indeed invested with knowledge and as we see in Joseph's (PBUH) life, knowledge is power.

12:82 "Ask at the town where we have been and the caravan in which we returned, and (you will find) we are indeed telling the truth."

Chapter 82

Can I Get a Witness?

When I was a child growing up on Chicago's Southside, my grandfather, Walter McCann, a former Garveyite, would sit us down in the living room and tell us the stories of Aesop and Uncle Remus. As we discussed, Brer Rabbit always tricked Brer Fox and outsmarted the other animals. I learned from the story of the tortoise and the hare that if you keep moving forward in the race, no matter how slow, you'll reach the finish line ahead of the competitor who stops, starts, and takes frolics and detours. I remember hearing often the story of the little boy who cried wolf and learned that once you get a reputation for lying, you'll get to the point where no one will believe anything you say. When a person's language is deceitful, we are justified in disregarding whatever they say.

Sometimes you get so known for telling lies that you can't get a witness even when you're telling the truth.

These were just some of the ways in which we passed down the best traditions of the people. We sometimes deviate from the good path laid out by our parents, but once it is in you, you can't stay astray for long; it begins to register on your conscience. That is why it is so sad to see African American parents waiting for someone to come into their communities and save their youth. This wisdom imparted by Uncle Remus has been turned on its head in this society. We don't demonstrate the inherent native sense of his animals. Too many of our youth spend their whole lives living the stereotype. The late Poet

Laureate Gwendolyn Brook's poem *We Real Cool*, about young men's short lives on Chicago's Southside has always resonated within me. The Pool Players. Seven at the Golden Shovel:

We real cool. We Left school.
We Lurk late.
We Strike straight.
We Sing sin.
We Thin gin.
We Jazz June. We Die soon.

The brothers now find themselves with no credibility. They know they have lied to their father. They acknowledged early on at 12:17 that they knew their father would never believe them.[1] Now they are telling the truth, as they see it, and in order to get their father to accept their story, they invoke all the witnesses they can, "Ask the people in the town, ask the people in the caravan." Can I Get a Witness? But no one is going to bear witness on their behalf because we are cautioned not to just pick up things from dishonest or deceitful people and just go on repeating them as fact.[2] We have an obligation to investigate and determine the truth of what we are putting out. We can readily see how lies in religion have been accepted and repeated for generations and the harm they have caused.

12:83 Jacob said, "Nay, but ye have yourselves contrived a story (good enough) for you. So patience is most fitting (for me). Maybe Allah will bring them (back) all to me (in the end). For He is indeed full of knowledge and wisdom."

Chapter 83

They Are Made from What They Know

Jacob (PBUH) says, "Patience is most fitting [for me]." In Yusuf's (PBUH) life, in the true test of patience, he constantly found himself in circumstances he did not create and had no control over. In each situation, however, we find him faithful and patient. Here again is the proof that Joseph (PBUH) was abundantly blessed by G-d, despite his difficult circumstances.[1] It is a lack of patience and the lack of control that produces the stress that most of us experience. Research shows that jobs in which employees have the least control tend to be the most stressful. Everybody wants instant results and instant solutions and unfortunately, life doesn't work like that. It proceeds through stages and we have to practice managing the stress that each level of circumstances produces.

Stress is the individual's response to internal and external forces and is built into the natural makeup of the human being. Internal factors may include nutrition, overall health and fitness, emotional well-being, and the amount of sleep and rest we get. These internal factors also influence our body's ability to deal with external stress-inducing factors. External factors include the physical environment, our job, our relationships with others, our home, and the many other challenges we face on a daily basis. Most of us are stressed out by even the least of difficulties – traffic, inconvenience, losing our keys and small things that don't go our way. Because of the hectic pace and super stimulation in our modern lives, we usually think of stress as a negative experience, but from a biological point of view, stress can be positive, negative, or neutral.

The secretion of adrenaline by the adrenal medulla upon stimulation by the central nervous system in response to conditions such as anger or fear is an important function that has served man well since his primitive days. It stimulated his reaction to danger-fight or flight. He was then energized for running from a -predatory beast or fighting a less mighty animal that might feed his family that day. That response was responsible for his survival and that of other species. We don't often face those dangers today. Nevertheless, that same hormone still acts to increase heart rate, blood pressure, cardiac output, and carbohydrate metabolism. Our heart rate still races out of control and our blood pressure still elevates wildly, but now it's in response to mundane things. We carry these upsets around with us all day. They affect our relationships with our families and fellow human beings. They inhibit us from having the relaxation of peaceful sleep at night.

Physical Reactions

Stress not only takes its toll on our body but on our emotions too. When we have those feelings that are repressed instead of expressed, the body, particularly that part that is associated with giving expressions to those feelings, clenches. This release of the stress hormone also causes us to crave pleasure. Then we engage in many types of unhealthy habits such as drugs, alcohol, and nicotine. The positive thinking that typically comes with optimism is a key part of effective stress management. Positive thinking means that we approach the unpleasantness in a more positive and productive way. You think the best is going to happen, not the worst. Positive thinking often starts with self-talk. Self-talk is the endless stream of unspoken thoughts that run through our head every day. These automatic thoughts can be positive or negative. Some of our self-talk comes from logic and reason. Other self-talk may arise from misconceptions that we create due to lack of information.

Researchers continue to explore the effects of positive thinking and optimism on health. Potential benefits of positive thinking include better coping skills during hardships and times of stress, increased life span, lower rates of depression, lower levels of distress, greater resistance to the common cold, better psychological and physical well-being, and reduced risk of death from cardiovascular disease.

Our impulsiveness accounts for a lot of our stress. We can't tolerate not being in control and we can't wait for time and conditions to work the situation out. We can't wait for the resources we need to work with, and we can't acknowledge that G-d is bigger than us and everything.

Allah says man is *zalum* (hasty) and *Jalul* (ignorant/foolish).[2] When Allah offered the rule of Earth to the mountains they refused, but when he offered it to man he rushed to take it on. He is talking about the man that has an exaggerated view of his own importance. But there is another, broader social dimension to this desire to have dominion. The word *zalum* implies tyranny and oppression. In societies of oppressed people this is men wanting to dominate the lives of others. Jacob (PBUH) notes that even though their stories may not be true, the stories may satisfy the brothers. How is this? It is because we are formed by what we bring into our being.[3] You are what you eat. Those who subsist on a diet of lies and deceit become formed by those things; they become liars. Christians who are emotionally constituted are very satisfied with an excited, happy feeling on Sundays. It doesn't matter much if that translates into intelligent life and behavior throughout the rest of week. When you talk to them, they don't seem to even have an appetite for the knowledge or deeper meaning behind the scripture they study. They are happy with the happy feeling. The brothers are satisfied with what they know, even if it disparages their brother, Benjamin, but Jacob (PBUH) follows the same patience as his son Joseph (PBUH) and keeps hope that any temporary trials will be a part of Allah's bigger and greater Plan.

12:84 And he turned away from them, and said, "How great is my grief for Joseph!" And his eyes became white with sorrow, and he fell into silent melancholy.

Chapter 84

Your Resurrection is as That of One Man

Can One Person Make a Difference?

It may have been hard for the brothers to understand Jacob's (PBUH) enduring sorrow for the loss of his beloved Joseph (PBUH), but history is full of stories where one person made all the difference in the world. There are stories where individuals demonstrated the best in their human nature and stood up to the establishment, speaking truth to power. Both scripture and history record people who made significant changes in human society-socially, morally, militarily, and politically. Of course, they had their nations, tribes, and communities that followed them and implemented their ideas. Scripture likewise records the best aspirations and the highest social and human development of communities, although the story may be told in the context of one prophet or seer's work.[1] The genetic and environmental influences, along with the experiences of the whole community, are focused in that one person.[2]

Anthropologist, Margaret Mead, who went outside her own cultural constraints to better understand broader human influences by studying the Samoan people of the South Pacific Islands, noted: "Never doubt that a small group of thoughtful, committed citizens can change the world; indeed, it's the only thing that ever does." Many more or less famous people have demonstrated this inherent nobility.[3]

Hugh Thompson was also such a person. Thompson was the U.S. Army helicopter pilot who stopped the slaughter of civilians at the village of My Lai during the Vietnam War in 1968. 504 civilians were killed by American soldiers in the massacre. He and his crew are credited with directly saving the lives of nine unarmed civilians who were about to be killed by fellow U.S. soldiers. They also rescued a five-year-old girl from an irrigation ditch filled with the bodies of some 170 dead or dying Vietnamese women, children and old men. His story is recounted in the book *The Forgotten Hero of My Lai: The Hugh Thompson Story* by Trent Angers and published by Acadian House Publishing of Lafayette, La. Thompson and Larry Colburn, the gunner on his aircraft, were finally decorated for heroism by the U.S. Army in March of 1998, some 30 years after the massacre. They received the Soldier's Medal at the Vietnam Wall in Washington in a ceremony that was publicized internationally. We also will never forget the great inspiration of our champion, Muhammad Ali to an entire generation of young people including myself, who protested an unjust war. One person can be a symbol that represents the best of the whole race or humanity, so we can understand Jacob's (PBUH) continued sadness over the loss of Joseph (PBUH).

Jacob (PBUH) knew Who his reward was from and from Whom his relief would come, so his melancholy was silent. On the authority of Abu Hurayrah (may Allah be pleased with him), the Messenger of Allah (peace and blessings of Allah be upon him) said, "Allah (mighty and sublime be he) says 'My faithful servant's reward from me, if I have taken to me his best friend from amongst the inhabitants of the world and he has then borne it patiently for my sake, shall be nothing less than Paradise.' [Bukhari] Jacob (PBUH) did not get angry, lash out or show hatred. Similar Hadith states, "He who represses the anger, Allah rewards him. He who perseveres in a misfortune, Allah indemnities him. He who has patience, Allah gives him double." Ironically, Joseph's (PBUH) name symbolizes a "double portion of blessing."

12:85 They said, "By Allah! (never) wilt thou cease to remember Joseph until thou reach the last extremity of illness, or until thou die!"

Chapter 85

The Soul Remembers What the Mind Forgot

When Emmett Till was lynched in 1955 his mother Mamie Till Mobley demanded that his casket be open for the world to see the racism and cruelty that we lived through in America at that time. "I think everybody needed to know what had happened to Emmett Till," she said. My mother was pregnant with my youngest brother and she was discouraged from going to see the body because her mother, my grandmother, feared it would mark her unborn child. My mother and my grandmother did not sit me down to explain to me what had happened. I picked that up from the news and from the environment. They did not sit me down and tell me how to feel about it. I felt their pain and their fear. I felt the pain of all those around me. I felt the terror that 14-year-old Till must have experienced.

Allah created us from one human soul and all things that were once one, will at some point be reunited. But even as they are separate there is still a commonness; a collective consciousness if you will. This is why they say that if any part of the body hurts, the whole body hurts.[1] Similarly, we should see that the member of the body that is healed or uplifted edifies the whole body.[2] Thus, it is said that as long as any man is not free, I am not free.[3] This points to a lifetime struggle and commitment to all of humanity. This tells us that there is a part of us that survives separation. Allah says that He created us in tribes and nations and we might look at this as a separation. But He says he did it so we would know or recognize each other. Once we recognize that common soul, we then come together as a stronger whole. I feel the pain of all oppressed people today, but also the pain, the hopes, and the dreams of people past. I feel Frederick Douglass and his desire to be recognized as the equal of any man. I feel Dr. King and his dream to one day be judged, even if through his children, by the content of his character. The tragedy today is that too few of us feel these things.[4] But the soul remembers what the mind forgets.

Many of us have the former slave masters' blood in us, and many of us are mixing our blood with theirs today. But in that infant child, there is nothing but love on both sides of its family. G-d has His way of bringing us all together and the distinctions of race and skin color are becoming less and less relevant. I had to caution myself from saying white blood because that blood is another common stream that runs through all of our veins. So we not only have the bad memories in our genes; we have the triumphs, the great victories. We have the best aspirations of any of the people as part of own collective consciousness. Do you think we have forgotten the dream of America's founding fathers or their ambition of a Manifest Destiny supported by G-d? We are not foreigners to this land or this destiny and the soul remembers what the mind forgets. For those with a deep appreciation of the jazz tradition, I reference the lyrics sung by the great Sarah Vaughn in the song, *I Remember You*, addressing the memory of the individual soul:

> When my life is through,
> And the angels ask me to recall
> The thrill of them all
> Then I shall tell them I remember you.

Jacob (PBUH) must have known that his destiny was not to end with the loss of his two beloved sons. He also knew of G-d's promise to his grandfather, Abraham (PBUH), that his righteous offspring would be as numerous as the stars in the heavens (symbols of leadership and guidance) and that the nations would be blessed through him. Now the brothers recognize that Jacob (PBUH) has never accepted their plan. What they still don't understand is that his plan will survive his physical life. No matter what they do, that desire will live through his posterity until it is fulfilled. When our ancestors prayed to G-d for relief, they realized it would not come in their lifetime. Many times they had to be satisfied with just small relief from their oppression. Riding on the bus and eating at the counter with the white man was not the destination. Dr. King acknowledged that some of us would die to realize freedom. He also knew that he would probably be one of the first martyrs in that cause. In our soul, we know that this is not the end. We know that there will be a fair and a perfect accounting one day. We know that no good deeds or sacrifice will go unrewarded. We know that G-d will remove any pain that his innocent servants suffer.

12:86 He said, "I only complain of my distraction and anguish to Allah, and I know from Allah that which ye know not."

Chapter 86

We Don't Share Our Misery

In his hit single recording, *The Puzzle*, Hip-Hop artist Brother Ali reminds us to, "Never let your chest and your chin touch in public; those that stand against us would love this." Our body is a loyal servant of our mind. It conforms to our dominant way of thinking. Most of us will agree that the person who walks around with their head down all the time is a person burdened by life circumstances; a person who has nothing positive to look up to. Pick up a heavy object and hoist it onto your shoulders and see if it won't bend you down. Now imagine choosing a career that does this to you. It will break you down. Stress is a known contributor to poor posture, so it is clear that our state of mind ultimately translates into a condition of the body. This is not the person who is relaxed, confident, and positive about life. Confidence is from the same root word as *faith*, so the faithful person is not the one who is constantly depressed.

We will all experience pain, frustration or disappointment. As the saying goes 'into each life some rain must fall.' The point is how we deal with these adversities. Even the Prophets of G-d (PBUT) went through trials with no end in sight[1] and Prophet Muhammad (PBUH), in acknowledging that he had no knowledge of the unseen, noted that if he had, he would have done the same thing most of us would do – have all good things for ourselves and avoid all the bad.[2] The key is accepting that it is all from Allah. And that which is anguishing, we will appeal only to Allah – the only One with the power to relieve it.

The Messenger of Allah (PBUH), said, "How amazing is the case of the believer; there is good for him in everything and this is only so for the believer. If he experiences something pleasant, he is thankful, and that is good for him; and if he comes across adversity, he is patient, and that is good for him." [Muslim] It is counterproductive to complain to someone else about something that only Allah controls. It demonstrates weakness on our part and an unwillingness to patiently endure our trials.

Jacob (PBUH) teaches us another important principle. Sometimes in our search for sympathy and our desire to share our misery, we broadcast our misfortunes and our injuries to anybody that will listen. When we do that, we magnify it. Words are creative and every time we complain and repeat the negative things in our life, we re-create them; giving them new energy and new life. Soon we have magnified them so large that we've charged our entire personality with the negative; and eventually our entire environment. How can we ever get over an injury if every time it begins to scab we scratch if off and never let it heal? We all have talked to people who will readily tell us their problems. We see the pain in their face. We recognize the pain in their body language. We can feel their emotional hurt as though they'd just had this experience yesterday. You question them and find out this is something that happened to them 40 years ago. But in their mind, in their heart, it's happening as they speak. We've all heard that misery loves company, but that's a sick side of us that want's someone else to feel the same grief and tribulation that we're going through. We don't share our misery. We bear it with patience and know that G- d is a loving and merciful G-d that allows us pain and suffering to strengthen us in faith.

Another Hadith is related by Al-Bukhari on the authority of two of the Prophet's (PBUH) companions, Abu Saeed Al-Khudri and Abu Hurairah who quote the Prophet as saying, "Whatever befalls a Muslim of exhaustion, illness, worry, grief, nuisance or trouble, even though it may be no more than a prick of a thorn, earns him forgiveness by Allah of some of his sins." Not only is Jacob (PBUH) more aware of the great Plan of Allah for His people, but he's also aware that there is blessing and forgiveness in what he has gone through at their expense. They do not yet understand.

12:87 "O my sons! go ye and enquire about Joseph and his brother, and never give up hope of Allah's Soothing Mercy: truly no one despairs of Allah's Soothing Mercy, except those who have no faith."

Chapter 87

Is Shame You Fall Down Nobody Push You

Prophet Muhammad (PBUH) said, "When we are faced with misfortune, we are to say, *Al-hamdullillah-All Praise is due to Allah*." The question was asked why do we thank Allah for misfortune. He stated three reasons:[1]. It did not cause us to lose our faith;[2]. It could have been worse; [3] and whatever we endure for G-d's sake is a reward due. Life itself presents enough obstacles for us to overcome; we don't need to add to them by our own negative attitude. One of Allah's attributes is *the believer*-- Al-Mu'min.[1] He believes in us and we know this from the story of our creation. It was Satan who thought G-d had made a mistake and that man would not be up to the task of managing creation. We too are believers. We believe in Allah; we believe in His angels; we believe in His Books; we believe in His Messengers; we believe in a divinely ordained destiny; and we believe in the Hereafter. We believe in ourselves and each other. This is necessary to avoid self-defeating behavior.

We've all heard the saying of someone being their own worst enemy. This point is eloquently addressed in Amy Tan's best-selling novel, *The Joy Luck Club*. The book focused on four Chinese-American, immigrant families in San Francisco, California. Four mothers, four daughters, four families, and the clash between their traditional Chinese culture and American culture. The advice one mother gives to her daughter is:

"Is shame you fall down nobody push you."[2] We've got to believe in ourselves and in a friendly universe that's there for our service. Allah says here in 12:87, speaking through His Prophet Jacob (PBUH), "No one despairs except those with no faith." The word used for despair is *'yay-asu'* from *Ya' isa* meaning to despair or to give up hope. Despair is also synonymous with discouragement and one of Satan's attribute is *discourager.* It is also related to the word desperate. It is this desperation that drives many to extremism.

America's legal system recognizes mental illness as a defense to many crimes as well as the justification of temporary insanity. They acknowledge that circumstances can drive a person to do heinous things. But this recognition extends only to its citizens. They can't see it in reference to others. Allah says do justice whether it goes against you or your kin. They can't see the desperation, indeed insanity, that they may have driven others to through their actions.

Desperation and Extremism

Pharaoh's threat to the people he dominated in Egypt, described in the Qur'an, was to drive the believer to extremism.[3] The hands and feet are **extremities**, and they provide balance for us when we walk. One hand moves forward when we walk and on the opposite side of the foot moves forward. If those hands and feet are cut off from opposite sides, we have no balance when we move. We can't make progress like that. Extremism destroys both our vertical and horizontal balance. We become either overly spiritual in our otherworldliness or extremely worldly devoid of spirituality. Pharaoh's plan was: "Once I oppress you until you lose your mental balance and drive you crazy and you become desperate, let's see how faithful you'll be to your G-d then." For the Muslim, this means not progressing on the *Sirat al-Mustaqim*, vertical progress or uprightness. As we climb into the higher and higher altitudes, the air, just as our spirit, gets purer and purer. At the same time, it gets rarer and rarer and pretty soon, we are forced back down into the earth to breathe the same air that the rest of the people breath. Nor can we progress on the *Sabeel-Allah* horizontal path of our progress in the material earth. Our upright posture and vertical striving to overcome the gravity of that material attraction, and the horizontal striving for progress in the earth, illustrate the two members of a cross and its balance.[4]

The media does not even consider what may have driven extremists to their actions, but at some point, any man will choose death over continued persecution. Everyone must overcome their fear of death in order to be free and any people who want to be free have to be willing to pay the ultimate price. America's own patriot, Patrick Henry said, "Give me liberty or give me death." This is not a foreign concept; it is common to all human beings. Allah says that oppression, or so the expression goes "death by a thousand cuts" is worse than outright slaughter.[5] I listened to radio broadcasts on September 11, 2011, the 10th anniversary of the 9/11 attacks on the World Trade Center, the Pentagon, and Pennsylvania. They interviewed different participants in the tragedy: victims, families, first responders, officials. It was apparent that the impact of the events was deep and lasting that even children who were very young or not even born at the time recounted the effect the attack had on them. What I did not hear was any attempt to analyze what might have driven the attackers to such desperate extremes. I also have a concern that we not become traumatized in our pain and elevate it to an object of worship such as the Holocaust. I prayed for the 3,000 lives lost on that day and their families and a thought occurred to me. Many more African Americans were tortured and murdered in slavery and during the slave trade. Many more than 3,000 African Americans were lynched in the decades up to the 1960's. Can our fellow Americans share and empathize with that grief?

Zionism and Apartheid

In this modern world, in the time of instant everything, extreme lifestyles, whacked out sports, ultimate fighting, and maxed out overwhelmed lives, we should take a sober look at ourselves and the world around us. We all want the blessings of G-d and it says in the Bible that "blessed are the peacemakers." The making of peace has been defined by our political leaders as "us against them (the extremists)." The question that should be asked therefore is who are the extremists and who are the peacemakers?[6]

The Bible's directive to annihilate the Amalek men, women, children, and even cattle is the extremists' interpretation. It is the Zionist, the Netanyahu call for *ethnic cleansing* and genocide. Not all Jewish people support this viewpoint and while we must respect Judaism as a monotheistic religion, it has been the extremist Zionist philosophy and viewpoint that has dominated Israeli politics since its creation. Zionism is based on the concept of ethnic superiority, occupation, terrorism, colonization, and racism. We have to admit and empathize with the persecution of the Jews prior to and during World War II, however, we also have to recognize the tendency of abused children and people to become abusers themselves. Friedrich Nietzsche wrote, "He who fights against monsters should see to it that he does not become a monster in the process. And when you stare persistently into an abyss, the abyss also stares into you."[7] Don't we all become what we fixate on?

The United Nations, in its Resolution 3379 in 1975, determined that "Zionism is a form of racism and racial discrimination." That resolution referred back to the 1973 resolution condemning "the unholy alliance between South African racism and Zionism," and to the 1963 resolution which determined that "any doctrine of racial differentiation or superiority is scientifically false, morally condemnable, socially unjust, and dangerous." Under intense political pressure, the General Assembly, on December 16, 1991, revoked the previous resolution by Resolution 46/86. In the history of the UN, this is the only resolution that has ever been revoked. Former U.S. president Jimmy Carter published his book, *Palestine: Peace Not Apartheid*, in 2006, which he said was meant to spark U.S. discussion of Israeli policies. "The hope is that my book will at least stimulate a debate, which has not existed in this country. There's never been any debate on this issue, of any significance." Needless to say, the book was roundly criticized from most American quarters. Recent polls have identified him as the worst U.S. President ever. But you have yet to have anyone challenge the truths exposed in the book. He points out that Israeli policy in the West Bank represented instances of apartheid worse than those that once held sway in South Africa. "When Israel does occupy this territory deep within the West Bank, and connects the 200 or so settlements with each other, with a road, and then prohibits the Palestinians from using that road, or in many cases even crossing the road, this perpetrates even worse instances of apartness or apartheid, than we witnessed even in South Africa." It's ironic that the same pollsters are pointing to President Obama as the next to the worst President in history.

It's also ironic that both Carter and Obama have received the Nobel Prize for Peace. Carter has dedicated his life to peace in Palestine but has given an honest assessment that there will never be peace there until Israel withdraws from the occupied territory. That truth is probably the source of the attacks on him by the establishment media. It's completely understandable that Obama and Carter would be seen as the worst by those whose power and institutions are built on false notions of superiority and false religious doctrines.

Anyone who suggests a rational viewpoint of the religious faiths or a rational relationship with other human beings of different faiths must expect that type of criticism. Christian Evangelist Rick Warren addressed the Islamic Society of North America convention in 2009. Warren, the founder of Saddleback Community Church in Orange County, Calif., is the author of "The Purpose Driven Life," which has sold more than 30 million copies worldwide. He told that gathering: "the two largest faiths on the planet" (Islam and Christianity) must work together to combat stereotypes and solve global problems, (just as we are commanded to do by G-d). He came under immediate and intense criticism from fellow conservatives who denounced his appearance at the convention as cozying up to extremists. Warren said Muslims and Christians should be partners in working to end what he calls "the five global giants" of war, poverty, corruption, disease, and illiteracy. America though has been unwilling to accept its own extremism and the oppression that it has produced in the world.

The Hate that Hate Produced

In 1959 Mike Wallace and TV commentator/journalist Louis Lomax documented the rise of what Wallace described as the racist and extremist teachings of the Nation of Islam and other Black Nationalist groups. What he titled the documentary was an honest perspective of the conditions that actually produced these sentiments among Black people in America, *The Hate That Hate Produced.* Four hundred years of slavery, lynching, Jim Crow laws, discrimination, and segregation could not help but have an effect. We need to look today at world conditions in Palestine and elsewhere and consider *The Terrorism that Terror Produced.*"

12:88 Then, when they came (back) into (Joseph's) presence they said, "O exalted one! distress has seized us and our family: we have (now) brought but scanty capital: so pay us full measure, (we pray thee), and treat it as charity to us: for Allah doth reward the charitable."

Chapter 88

Allah Rotates the Power

The brothers have shown no compassion or charity before, even to their own brother, Joseph (PBUH), but now want full measure but they have 'short money' (*scanty capital).* They want equal justice and mercy when they are the ones in distress. But Allah raises new generations of leaders[1] and Allah rotates the power[2] and everybody gets the chance to see how they behave with both the upper and the lower hand.

In October 2014, the International Monetary Fund (IMF) announced that China had overtaken the U.S. as the world's largest economy. China will produce $17.6 trillion in terms of goods and services; compared with $17.4 trillion for the U.S. By another measure, *purchasing power parity* or PPP – the rate at which the currency of one country would have to be converted into that of another country to buy the same amount of goods and services in each country, China now accounts for 16.5% of the global economy when measured in real PPP terms, compared with 16.3% for the U.S. The U. S. has held this position since 1872, when it overtook the United Kingdom, and we now know that the United Kingdom is just a shadow of its former self in terms of economy, power, and influence. We are reminded of their boast of the 19th century that the "sun never sets on the British Empire." Indeed, the extent of their colonization had daylight on the opposite end of the globe when it might have been night in England. Before them, history points to the Spanish as a pre-eminent world power. Even now almost an entire continent, South America, across an entire ocean, speaks Spanish and islands as far away as the Philippines find their language, culture, and religion largely influenced by the Spanish. The Spanish rise in power coincided with the decline of Islamic rule in Spain after 700 years. It was the Muslim defeat at Cordoba that freed up the treasury of Queen Isabella and King Ferdinand of Spain to finance Columbus' trip to the Americas of the New World.

Before that, the Persian Empire extended through Asia and up to North Africa and Europe. We've discussed much of the Rule of Egypt and the Greeks that borrowed from the Persians and the Romans who built the modern Euro-centric society from the Greek. What is less obvious though is not the military superiority or economic dominance that characterized these civilizations, but the ideology and the language. If we look at dominance from that standpoint, we have to refer to Scripture to get a true picture of who holds true power and how it is rotated.

We have discussed the scope of language as the human ability to acquire and use complex systems of communication[3] and whether we choose to accept it or not, it is language that has dominated human society for over a thousand years and we see its power being rotated now. That language is the message in the Bible that translates to "god is incarnate in this white image. This is your mandate to go out and conquer and bring the whole world under your sway." That is exactly what has happened, but it is the originators of that language who are the ones actually controlling the power.

In the Bible (Isaiah 54:3) it says, addressing the Jews, "For you will spread abroad to the right and to the left. And your descendants will possess nations and will resettle the desolate cities." That is a New American Standard Bible translation, but an older King James translation, one which the church has been following for centuries says that "For thou shalt break forth on the right hand and on the left; and thy seed shall inherit the Gentiles and make the desolate cities to be inhabited." This is the Bible telling a certain mindset among the Jews that they will actually "inherit" the Gentiles. What kind of god is talking here that is promising one group of his servants that he will let them come under the complete ownership and domination of another people? But this was the scheme and the plan that was followed.

The First Council of Nicaea convened in AD 325 by the Roman Emperor Constantine I, among other things, legislated the concept of the divinity of Christ, although this was never accepted by Eastern Orthodox or Oriental Orthodox churches. There was no imagery of Christ by the early church and it is no coincidence that during this period, Jews in Arabia and the Orthodox Church lived side-by-side, in peace. Constantine also introduced the image of the cross, supposedly based on a vision he had to make Christianity dominant in the world. He put this image of the divine Christ on the cross and used this to strike terror into the ignorant masses with already pagan backgrounds. The Bible prophecy has been fulfilled that Christianity, under the rule of the Gentiles, has spread across the world and today, they and all of their material wealth are owned by those who control this philosophy. Don't think that there are not people here today who live by this scheme and are open about it. Jonah Mandel of the *Jerusalem Post* reported to the Jewish News on October 19, 2010 "The sole purpose of non-Jews is to serve Jews," according to Rabbi Ovadia Yosef, the head of Shas's Council of Torah Sages and a senior Sephardi adjudicator, "Goyim were born only to serve us. Without that, they have no place in the world – only to serve the People of Israel." He said this in his weekly Saturday night sermon on the laws regarding the actions non-Jews are permitted to perform on Shabbat. According to Yosef, the lives of non-Jews in Israel are safeguarded by divinity to prevent losses to Jews. "In Israel, death has no dominion over them. With gentiles, it will be like any person – they need to die, but [God] will give them longevity. Why? Imagine that one's donkey would die, they'd lose their money. This is his servant. That's why he gets a long life, to work well for this Jew," Yosef said, "Why are gentiles needed? They will work, they will plow, they will reap. We will sit like an effendi and eat. That is why Gentiles were created,"[4] he added.

There are evangelical Christians and some Muslims who have ingested the same poison. They are today waiting for the return of a physical Jesus Christ, a human white man, to emerge out of Israel as the savior of the world. If Allah is going to rotate the power, it has to involve more than just rotating the tool or machine that is implementing the power. He must rotate the mind and the language that is directing the power. That is why we should not look to Saudi Arabia as the new power in this new order. They have the material wealth and a superior grasp of the Arabic language, but their understanding of Qur'an and its spirit is lacking. They too seek domination. They too profess a superiority that is not based on human conduct. With all that they have, we don't see a sincere embrace of a higher understanding and meaning of the Qur'an's truth, nor a higher practice of the charity demanded by an evolved human sensitivity.

The translator of Qur'an, says Allah doth reward the "charitable ones-*mutaasaddiqina*." The trilateral root of *mutaasaddiqina* are the letters *Sad Dal Qaf*. Meanings of this root imply truthfulness, sincerity, trustworthiness, and excellence in a variety of contexts. This same word is used in 12:51, when the wife of the Aziz acknowledges that Joseph, "Is indeed of those who are (ever) true (and virtuous)." When we say that Islam will become the dominant religion, I see this coming about. Islam is a philosophy of life demanding complete submission to a One Creator of the Heavens and Earth, with no partners or associates. It means submission to Him as the author of truth and the author of peace-fulfilling the demands for freedom, justice, and equality for all people. These things are coming to be recognized as the superior human language. This language is now being spoken and accepted throughout the world. The new currency of today is information, the new 'oil' of today is wisdom and correct knowledge,[5] and it is all available now to anybody who would seek it.

12:89 He said, "Know ye how ye dealt with Joseph and his brother, not knowing (what ye were doing)?"

Chapter 89

Do You Acknowledge What You Did?

It is sad that some of us have to be at the very limit of our ability before we recognize the need for help but that is just the nature of man.[1] It is also hard for us to admit the creation of our own condition. The fifth step in the well-recognized Alcoholic Anonymous' 12-Step Program for alcohol and substance abuse recovery is that we have admitted the exact nature of our wrongs to G-d, to ourselves, and to another human being. One reason why I have been impressed by the success of the program and why it has been applied successfully to other addictions and dysfunctional behaviors is that it embraces universal principles of healing and forgiveness. Previous steps include the admission that we are powerless over our addiction; that our lives have become unmanageable and we believe only a power greater than us can restore us to sanity. That we have made the decision to surrender our lives over to the care of G-d. Aren't these the same things that we as Muslims acknowledge and seek G-d's help for every day? We accept that the world has been changed from its original creation and that those changes have brought challenges to man. We acknowledge that the world is too big for us to manage without His Help. So we are advised by Allah to recognize our own limited power in relation to the big creation. Without G-d's Help, the pressures of this big complicated world can drive you to drink.

We, therefore, submit ourselves to G-d in our prayers five times a day and submit all the activities in our lives to the care of G-d. We ask constantly for His guidance towards the right path. Joseph's (PBUH) question to them, therefore, is a required step toward their healing and necessary for their forgiveness. For me to feel that you are sincere about wanting me to forgive the wrong you've done to me, I have to ask you if you acknowledge what you did. It's like the halfhearted apology we give sometimes. "If I have wronged you, I sorry." I'm telling you you've wronged me. If you hadn't, we wouldn't be having this conversation. But instead of you saying, "I'm sorry for the particular wrong I did to you," you preface it with "If I did…" You hedged your apology like the *No Contest* plea in court where you accept the punishment without acknowledging any guilt. But Joseph (PBUH) still in his truthfulness and compassion notes that they did not know what they were doing. They knew only of their plan to put Joseph (PBUH) away and get their father's favor for themselves. They did not know that G-d's Plan was to use the brothers' plan to put Joseph (PBUH) in power.

12:90 They said, "Art thou indeed Joseph?" He said, "I am Joseph, and this is my brother: Allah has indeed been gracious to us (all): behold, he that is righteous and patient,- never will Allah suffer the reward to be lost, of those who do right."

Chapter 90

Yes, I am Your Brother

The concept of Muslim Brotherhood goes well beyond the political movement in Egypt that has been persecuted for decades and now, after arriving at the seat of power, find themselves again persecuted. Allah reminds us in the Qur'an that believers are a single Brotherhood.[1] The Qur'an commentator, Yusuf Ali, emphasizes this relationship among all Muslims, as it was emphasized by the Prophet (PBUH):[2] "The enforcement of the Muslim Brotherhood is the greatest social ideal of Islam. On it is based the Prophet's Sermon at his last pilgrimage, and Islam cannot be completely realized until this ideal is achieved." It's an ideal that could benefit all humanity. Most decent people acknowledge the common origin of all people.

During the ritual pilgrimage Hajj, in the later part of the ninth day of Dhul-Hijjah, the month of the pilgrimage, pilgrims halt at the valley of Arafat, about nine miles east of the Ka'bah. There at the mountain, they meet each other and leaders from around the world. They recognize the merits in each other and respect each other as brothers. Isn't this how we should be toward all humanity? Our Prophet (PBUH) said that this meeting on Mount Arafat is the most important time of the Hajj and if you miss the prayers at the meeting on Arafat, you have missed your whole Hajj. That is the importance of our recognition of each other. The word *Arafat* itself comes from the verb

Arafa, which means to know. G-d says, "We created you from a single (pair) of a male and a female, and made you into nations and tribes, that ye may know each other, not that ye may despise (each other)." Holy Qur'an 49:13.[3] We use the terms *know* and *recognize* interchangeably. How do you not recognize your own brother? How do we lose sight of the common origin of humanity to the extent that we have to re-introduce ourselves to the family? What has happened such that African Americans have to go through a whole Civil Rights Movement in order to say to our fellow citizens, "Yes, I am Your Brother?" What has happened such that African American Muslims have to re-introduce themselves to the worldwide community and remind them that, "Yes, I am Your Brother?" And sadly, what has happened such that black-on-black crime and murder has become such an epidemic that there is no recognition that, "Yes, I am Your Brother?" And these are the brothers with whom we have shared blood, space, experiences, and history.

Acceptance

Shortly after I was accepted into the Nation of Islam, I was assigned as a secretary on the staff at Temple No.2. Each brother's attendance was recorded for each meeting; his donations were recorded as well as his purchase of *Muhammad Speaks* newspapers. The first step in being accepted in the temple was submitting a letter to 'Saviour' W. D. Fard. The letter had to be written by hand with all spelling and punctuation correct exactly as the draft that was provided. If it wasn't perfect, it was rejected and you had to rewrite it and submit it again until it was accepted. I was blessed to write mine, submit it, and have it accepted the first time. I know many brothers who had to rewrite theirs and submit it several times. This process refined my understanding that only a perfect presentation is acceptable in some things. I had already been taught from childhood by my grandfather, "If a task is once begun, never leave it 'til it's done; be it labor great or small, do it well or not at all." I later found no difference in this and Prophet's (PBUH) Hadith, "Whatever the Muslim undertakes, he seeks to perfect it." There was always a lot of mystery in my mind surrounding that letter. A curious thing about the letter was that it was directed to W. D. Fard, but we were taught that he had disappeared in the 1930s. Who transmitted the letters to Fard? Did he personally approve them? Was the Honorable Elijah Muhammad still in contact with Fard? Brother Henry and

Brother James were my supervisors and brother Osie Muhammad was also on the staff. At the Annual Muslim Convention in 2011, brother Osie, who had come in the Temple in 1951, mentioned in his remarks at a Pioneers event that he had been responsible for reviewing the letters and making sure they were correct. I talked to him later and he agreed that the object was to instill that requirement of perfect performance in us and he also noted that many brothers and sisters had to re-write their letter up to 12 times before it was accepted. I also shared with him my experience that I had never met any brother or sister who wanted to enter the Nation of Islam who have given up or did not keep writing their letter until it was accepted.

Rejection/Ostracization

In most of the later years of the Nation of Islam, Raymond Sharrieff, who became Minister of Justice under Imam W. Deen Mohammed (RAA), was the Supreme Captain. If a member was found guilty of violating the laws of the Nation of Islam, he or she was given "time out of the Temple." Class C was for relatively minor violations and was similar to restricted activity in which a member could return upon proven good behavior. But as mentioned earlier, Class F was a determinate amount of time "out of the Temple" from 1 to 5 years and "F" represented the "Fire." The ultimate punishment was that G-d would bring the fire of destruction on America before one's time was up while you were out of the Temple. But the real punishment was the social ostracization, meaning "to exclude from a group or banish." Many members were already isolated from their Christian families and friends who still practiced old habits, so the Nation was our social connection. While in Class F, you were not allowed to visit any Temple or any Temple businesses and you could not associate with any members in good standing. Imam Mohammed (RAA) has spoken on many occasions of his time out of the Temple and how he was not even able to have contact with his mother, Sister Clara Muhammad.

Captain Sharrieff was the one who passed the sentence for most members, but at Temple #2, he was also most remembered for being the one who greeted new members at the first Fruit of Islam meeting. Many of us will remember his firm handshake and remarks welcoming us to the Brotherhood: "You are taking hold of something that won't break off from you unless you break off from it."[4] In our attempts to follow the best behavior (*m'aroof*), we were in most cases following the Qur'an and Sunnah.

M'aroof

The word *m'aroof* refers back to our discussion of the root word *Arafa*. It describes a known or recognized thing which is universally accepted as good. "Whoever submits his whole self to Allah and **is a doer of good**, has grasped indeed the most trustworthy hand-hold: and with Allah rests the end and decision of (all) affairs." Holy Qur'an, 31:22. For example, "Do unto others as you would have them do unto you," is accepted as good and decent in most civilized cultures and could be seen as m'aroof. It is the highest and the best principles that are represented by the best of human conduct, by the best of human society, and by the best in relationships between human beings. The importance of the meeting of Arafat and indeed the entire Hajj is the struggle to overcome the social difficulty. While Ramadan focuses on overcoming the personal and spiritual difficulty, the community, the social body is the bigger challenge – how we get along with our fellow human beings. How do we respect them and look out for their needs? How do we educate them and encourage their development? These are the big issues in society. So Allah tells us despite the differences, the diversity, that He created within us, we all came from the one soul and his purpose in creating this diversity is *lita 'arafu*, that "we know each other," recognize each other, and do good to each other.[5]

In this context, m'aroof implies a high conduct passed down from "the learning of the people." The word *Folklore* – the learning of the people – was coined in 1846 by the late Mr. W. J. Thomas, to replace the earlier expression *popular antiquities*.[6] It means the traditions or habits that over time, have been proven to be based on knowledge (science and logic) as opposed to superstition.

Primitive Is Not Always Backward

We make a mistake when we assume that just because a people or a custom was primitive, that they were not intelligent. There is a social logic that extends over time and space. For example, "Among nomadic peoples, individual ownership is naturally limited to a man's personal belongings, and there is no private property in land."[7] This is consistent with the highest logic and understanding given to us in the Qur'an that the earth belongs to Allah.

Rites connected with birth, death, and marriage are important parts of our present day culture, although in many cases we have lost the underlying logic of them in favor of empty rituals. We know that the institution of marriage, not the particular ritual, is maroof.[8] "Initiation ceremonies continue to this day and where secret societies flourish, initiation into them replaces initiation into adult tribal life. Shorn of their savage features, initiatory rites are still retained by Freemasonry, and similar societies."[9] Despite primitiveness in some areas, there were advanced scientific views, even where they were manifested in primitive practices and understanding. Modern science tells us that the complete blueprint of the physical human being is contained in a person's DNA. In the late 19th century, the Voodoo conjurer, King Alexander, stated to Miss Owen as recorded in Trans. FL. Congr. 1891, p. 235, "I could save you or ruin you if I could get hold of so much as one eye-winker or the peeling of one freckle"..."Hence, the care universally taken of stray hairs or nail-parings. For things that have once formed parts of a whole are held to continue in sympathy though separated."[10] Isn't this also a recognition of the unity of creation. Everything G-d created is recorded and even the primitive man saw that such a record, an entire DNA, may well be recorded in that eyelash or freckle.

12:91 They said, "By Allah! indeed has Allah preferred thee above us, and we certainly have been guilty of sin!"

Chapter 91

The Best of You Is the One Who is Best in Conduct

We find people throughout history and scripture who claimed to have been *chosen people*. It is no sin to say that 'G-d has preferred me above you' or 'he has chosen me above you,' because G-d has always expressed a preference for those people who were obedient to him and serving the needs of his creatures. But, we also find those same people being rejected and punished when they lose sight of the basis for their superiority. G-d's promise has always been to choose and reward you for your obedience and substitute another people when you deviated.[1]

Rationality as well as faith has to be the bedrock of all religious expression and humanity has come a long way in understanding that, yet there are still remnants of backwardness. Any person of any faith should be able to agree with Prophet Muhammad's (PBUH) words that "the best of you is the one who is best in conduct." It's hard to even picture a rational person today, standing upon a belief such as "I am better than you because of my skin color." The concept of blackness as a religion promises the same moral and intellectual bankruptcy of white supremacy, apartheid, and Zionism. To be a chosen people without regard to merit imputes favoritism on G-d's part and injustice towards other people. In time, this belief may give us a temporary advantage but ultimately creates an even bigger internal prison of ignorance, false belief, and will alienate us from all other people in the world. This conflict of ideas has never been eliminated from the Jewish consciousness, but it was addressed in the consciousness of African Americans when Imam Mohammed (RAA) became the leader of the Nation of Islam.

Remaking of Man-Remake the World

That first bold initiative of Imam W. Deen Mohammed (RAA), *Remake the World*, was accompanied by the insight that 'words make people.' It would, therefore, be words that would remake the man first. A new language of moral and rational words, was introduced, and the remaking began. But really there was not that drastic a change in the mission. We had been taught that our mission was to save the entire Lost Found Nation in America (Blacks). Now we see that mission as expanded to the Universal Mission of Prophet Muhammad (PBUH) to all humanity. "Primitive communities certainly remade man; but once they had found their special mold, common to the whole, they sought to forfend or circumscribe further changes. In the city, on the contrary, the making and remaking of selves is one of its principal functions. In any generation, each urban period provides a multitude of new roles and an equal diversity of new potentialities. These bring about corresponding changes in laws, manners, moral evaluations, costume, and architecture, and finally, they transform the city as a living whole." The City in History, Lewis Mumford, p116. We can compare this transformation of the city as a living whole to the transformation of the Nation of Islam.

We were taught that the white man was the cave man. Allah references the youth that were sleeping in the cave and we now know that this refers to the Jinn people – Gentiles who were sleep to the social development that would raise them above animal passions. Similarly, we were told in the Nation of Islam that we were a baby nation; young in knowledge, not developed, not mature, not advanced in knowledge or experience. It should have been understandable then that there was something that we needed to become mature. With the Truth of Qur'an and with the model of Prophet Muhammad (PBUH) we are now grown.

The Muslim world has had the Qur'an now for over 1400 years but today that world is seen as the poster child for backwardness. We forget the great glory of Prophet Muhammad's (PBUH) time; the 700-year Muslim rule in Spain and the Renaissance in knowledge that it inspired. The Christian West is in the same condition now, with the masses suffering from lack of knowledge. Someone must bring a new vision to those that claim prophecy and to the world of modernity. There is nothing prideful in us saying that we are a special people. The thing that the statement requires is a commitment to accept the best of what G- d has revealed to his creatures; to commit to obedience and to following the best example of human conduct that has evolved over man's history—this is enlightenment.

The alternative to this enlightenment is darkness. Darkness in the material creation is simply a metaphor for ignorance in the human and social development. Thus, the period in Europe after the decline of the Roman Empire, characterized by mental and cultural deterioration is known as the Dark Ages. And similarly, the period in the pre-Islamic, Arabian Peninsula in which savagery reigned, is called the Jahilliyyah, or Age or Period of Ignorance from the word, Jahila, which means: To be ignorant, unlearned, foolish, unaware of a thing, unacquainted, lack knowledge; or not to realize. Darkness, by its nature, is oppressive of the physical sense of sight, just as ignorance oppresses insight.

Allah says He created us "in the wombs of our mothers, in stages, one after another, in three veils of darkness."[3] These wombs can also be seen as social constructs or confined spaces where we are nourished until we are formed and delivered to the next level. Humanly and socially, it is knowledge that forms us in these wombs. And it is ignorance that causes us to not evolve and not be born again. The Qur'an, according to Râghib, describes three kinds of ignorance: 1.) Having no knowledge. 2.) Being unacquainted with the reality. 3.) Ignoring to act upon the real knowledge.[4]

There are some who call themselves Muslims simply because they don't want to identify with typical African Americans. Some are stuck in triple wombs of Blackness-*worship of black skin, on top of ignorance, on top of not even wanting to know better.* And some come to Islam with the same identity crisis as our African American brothers except, whereas the African American brother might want to be white, they now want to be Arab or Pakistani. The bottom line is that they both want to be anybody other than themselves.

Allah description of man hasty,[5] also implies injustice, tyranny, and oppression by the man that thinks he can manage creation. Our condition, our identity crisis made us receptive to being oppressed. Note that the Brothers now confess their sin. The ignorant are not the only victims of racism. Consider the oppressor that has presided under centuries of tyranny over the ignorant masses based on a false sense of superiority, that now has to face his own infirmities and the equality or superiority of others. There is a basis upon which G-d considers superiority, but it's something you have to qualify for and not be born into.[6]

12:92 He said, "This day let no reproach be (cast) on you: Allah will forgive you, and He is the Most Merciful of those who show mercy!"

Chapter 92

The Wrongdoer Has Admitted His Wrong; G-d Has Blessed You. What Else Is There?

The first thing Joseph (PBUH) does when the brothers admit their guilt is to forgive them. And with that, he releases them and frees himself. How many of us make ourselves lifelong prisoners to our past oppression by refusing to let it go? Despite the oppressive history of some of mankind against its brothers, we still all have to learn to love our brothers and to forgive them.

Islam addresses two aspects of forgiveness: Allah's forgiveness and human forgiveness. There are three accepted requirements for forgiveness from G-d: 1. Recognizing the offense and admitting it before G-d; 2. making a commitment not to repeat the offense, and 3. asking for forgiveness from G-d. If these conditions are met in sincerity, forgiveness from G-d is assured. Our sincerity protects us from repeating the same offense again. In addition, G-d will change his punishment for the offense into a reward. If the offense was committed against another human being or society, a fourth condition is added and the order is changed: 1. recognizing the offense before those against whom offense was committed and before G-d; 2. committing oneself not to repeat the offense; 3. doing whatever needs to be done to rectify the offense (within reason) and asking pardon of the offended party; and finally, 4. asking G-d for forgiveness. This added requirement helps to heal the wounds of society. It is society as a whole that suffers from the wrongs we vent upon each other. This is why serving time in prison was once referred to as "paying your debt to society," while now it is becoming a lifelong sentence of poverty and exclusion.

"In the Babemba tribe of South Africa, when a person acts irresponsibly or unjustly, he is placed in the center of the village, alone and unfettered. All work ceases and every man, woman, and child in the village gathers in a large circle around the accused individual. Each person in the tribe speaks to the accused, one at a time, recalling the good things the person in the center of the circle has done in his lifetime. Every incident, every experience that can be recalled with any detail and accuracy, is recounted. All his positive attributes, good deeds, strengths, and kindnesses are recited carefully and at length. This tribal ceremony often lasts for several days. At the end, the tribal circle is broken, a joyous celebration takes place, and the person is symbolically and literally welcomed back into the tribe."[1]

When Prophet Muhammad (PBUH) entered the city of Makkah on Friday, Ramadan, 8 A.H. (January 530 A.D.) after his victory, the Prophet had in front of him some of his staunchest enemies; those who had fought him for many years, persecuted his followers, and killed many of them. He had full power to do whatever he wanted to punish them for their crimes. It is reported that the Prophet asked them, "What do you think I shall do to you now?" They pleaded for mercy. The Prophet said, "I say to you what Joseph (PBUH) said to his brothers "*no reproach is upon you today; may Allah forgive you and he is the most compassionate of the compassionates.* Go away; you are free." Soon they all came and accepted Islam at his hands. He forgave even Hind who had caused the murder of his uncle Hamza. After killing him she had his body mutilated and chewed his liver. When she accepted Islam, the Prophet (PBUH) even forgave her.

"No alienation, antagonism or hostility could find any permanent abode in his heart. His heart was absolutely free of injustice, of malice, of tyranny or false pride. In the most decisive moment, G-d gave him power over his enemy. But Muhammad chose to forgive, thereby giving to mankind and all the generations the most perfect example of goodness, truthfulness, of nobility and magnanimity."[2]

Forgiveness means to "give-for" or "give" one thing in exchange "for" another. We give up our anger in return for tranquility and peace. We give up our lurking sense of injury for healing. We give up our desire for vengeance in return for Allah's perfect justice. He says that whatever we endure in his name, our reward is then due from Him.[3] Everything of this life has its counterpart in the hereafter, but in complete and perfect measure.[4] We are to always choose the best of available alternatives, so we must always choose Allah's just accounting, instead of trying to weigh and exact justice here. Equally important is our need to forgive ourselves.[5] We cannot function and succeed carrying a burden of guilt through our lives.

And we will not be able to see clearly until we have released our burdens.

12:93 "Go with this my shirt, and cast it over the face of my father: he will come to see (clearly). Then come ye (here) to me together with all your family."

Chapter 93

I Can See Clearly Now

Sometimes after generations have past, we become so absorbed in our rituals that we forget their meanings. When that happens, we can lose the true message of Revelation and the true meaning of righteousness.[1] Joseph (PBUH) qualified himself to bring about the transformation from material or base state to an enlightened and ethical society. In addition to maintaining his original innocence, his belief, and following the maroof, he also remained "firm and patient, in pain (or suffering) and adversity and throughout all periods of panic."[2] His life story also involved a remaking of Egypt. What did this remaking involve and what was it about Egypt that made this remaking possible?

The concept of "city", as a center and focus point, brings together within a limited area many functions that had previously been scattered and unorganized. The components of the community were enclosed within city walls. However, in Egypt, the functions of the city-enclosure, assembly, and intermixture–were performed by the land itself. Desert and mountain constituted the 'walls.' "The city proved not merely a means of expressing in concrete terms the magnification of sacred and secular power, but, in a manner that went far beyond any conscious intention, it also enlarged all the dimensions of life. Beginning as a representation of the cosmos, a means of bringing heaven down to earth, the city became a symbol of the possible. Utopia was an integral part of its original constitution, and precisely because it first took form as an ideal projection, it brought into existence realities that might have remained latent for an indefinite time in more soberly governed small communities, pitched to lower expectations and unwilling to make exertions that transcended both their workaday habits and their mundane hopes." The City in History, Lewis Mumford, p 31. In this sense, the city itself was very much a container or vehicle for remaking the man. Allah alludes to Egypt representing this symbol when he tells the disgruntled and complaining children of Israel, to go to any city, to get what they want. What He says is go to any Egypt.

In the city, "an implosion of forces took place. (A) magnification of centralized power and release of communal energies. A new will-to-power, hitherto exercised only in the rituals of magic, expressed itself in exorbitant fantasies and practical achievement. Whatever a god might do in mythical deeds in one generation, a hero or king would undertake in the next. Under these conditions, the unconscious itself now released explosive powers." The City in History, Lewis Mumford, p59. We can compare this same process to a centralization that is not based on geography. There is a great power in coming into unity and concentrating our human potentialities toward one goal. I believe the city, or even a cultural construct, are metaphors for this process and the Honorable Elijah Muhammad demonstrated the success of this model.

The Muslim Parade showcased the businesses established by Honorable Elijah Muhammad and demonstrated the power of unity and discipline. Notice the lower right photo of the newlyweds and particularly the rear of the float in which the United States flag and Nation of Islam flag are displayed side by side. Photos by John Fleming, Courtesy of Nuri Madina. Honorable Elijah Muhammad set the stage for the transition that would be brought about by his son, W. Deen Mohammed (RAA), who raised the U. S. flag in July 1977, encouraged us to respect it, and instituted Patriotism Day Parades, photo below. Reprinted from Muslim Journal, August 17, 2012

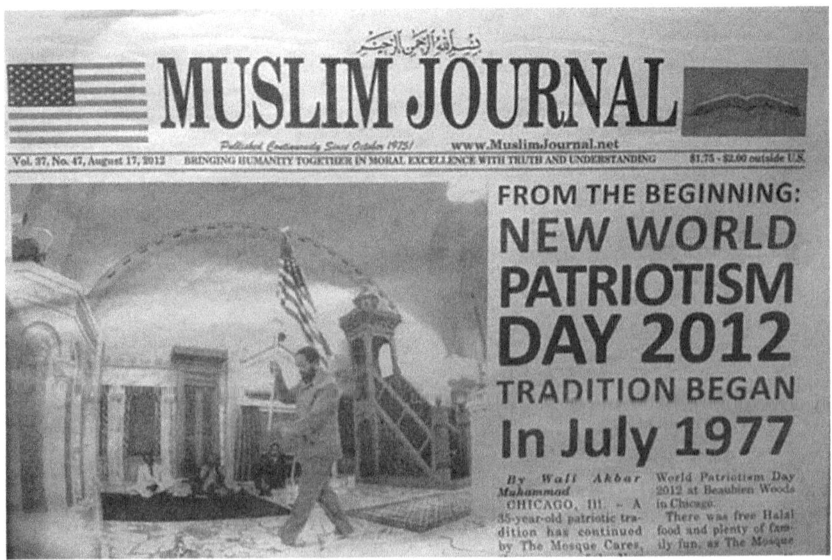

بِسْمِ اللَّهِ الرَّحْمَٰنِ الرَّحِيمِ

MUSLIM JOURNAL

Published Continuously Since October 1975! www.MuslimJournal.net

Vol. 37, No. 47, August 17, 2012 — BRINGING HUMANITY TOGETHER IN MORAL EXCELLENCE WITH TRUTH AND UNDERSTANDING — $1.75 - $2.00 outside U.S.

FROM THE BEGINNING: NEW WORLD PATRIOTISM DAY 2012 TRADITION BEGAN In July 1977

By Wali Akbar Muhammad

CHICAGO, Ill. - A 35-year-old patriotic tradition has continued by The Mosque Cares, World Patriotism Day 2012 at Beaubien Woods in Chicago.

There was free Halal food and plenty of family fun, as The Mosque

Adam (PBUH) was placed in the garden, which is another symbol of the concentration of resources and potentialities. It was a place of natural development and a place of agricultural activity, but Adam's (PBUH) destiny was industry and he had to evolve from an agriculturalist to an industrialist. History confirms this process in the social evolution of man. Imam Mohammed's (RAA) early description of the evolution of Adam (PBUH) was described as "dust to industry." The garden could also be seen as an environment of the consciousness whose ultimate cultivation is the full illumination of the mind. Prophets and seers who understand this destiny are sent as human examples and reminders. "The human soul, never really satisfied in its material prison of finite limitations, is always aspiring after the good and true; always hoping for a messenger out of other spheres, and, therefore, expectant of receiving such help."[3]

The major Prophets (PBUT) after Adam (PBUH), except Mohammed (PBUH), went to Egypt. He did not have to visit Egypt because he had already manifested in his own human nature the highest evolution of natural potentialities. The Prophets (PBUT) fulfilled their missions by implementing a social evolution utilizing science and knowledge. You can't accomplish this in a desert or wilderness. We can see this fulfillment today in the establishment of global community. From a historical perspective, we know that the church leadership did not have a complete concept of the religion they were trying to put together and Egypt provided a blueprint. The Divine mission required a base in material creation and knowledge extracted from that creation. Egypt was the prototypical source of both the material abundance and that knowledge. Without this base in material reality, we are much like the uninitiated, following empty ritual with no understanding. When Jesus (PBUH) returned to the Jews from Egypt, his principal antagonists were the Pharisees, who believed only in the rituals and the dead letter of the law.

Jesus (PBUH)

It is reported in the Bible, in reference to Jesus (PBUH): "And when they were departed, behold the angel of the Lord appeareth to Joseph in a dream, saying, 'arise and take the young child and his mother and flee into Egypt and be though there until I bring thee word; for Herod will seek the young child to destroy him.' And when he arose, he took the young child and his mother by night, and departed into Egypt and was there until the death of Herod; that it might be fulfilled, which was spoken of the Lord by the prophet, saying, 'Out of Egypt have I called my son"[4] The prophecy is that the light of knowledge would be called out of Egypt.

A curious connection can be seen in the fact that the Joseph (PBUH) in the hierarchy of seven levels of social and community development is one step higher (the leader) than Jesus (PBUH) in that progression, just as Joseph (PBUH) is said to be one level higher, the father, of Jesus (PBUH) in the Bible narrative. Joseph (PBUH) could have 'known his way around Egypt' when he took the child there.

Joseph (PBUH)

This story of Joseph (PBUH) in Qur'an gives a more detailed account of than any of the other Prophets' (PBUT) relation to Egypt. Even Moses,' (PBUH) narrative, who was raised by the Egyptian elite, begins with him as an infant and jumps to his adulthood. So, Joseph's (PBUH) story begins 12:21: The man in Egypt who bought him said to his wife, "Make his stay (among us) honorable. Maybe he will bring us much good, or we shall adopt him as a son." Thus did we establish Joseph in the land, that we might teach him the interpretation of stories (and events). And Allah hath full power and control over his affairs, but most among mankind know it not. And his story ends with the beginning of the children of Israel's history in Egypt:

12:99: Then when they entered the presence of Joseph, he provided a home for his parents with himself and said, "Enter ye Egypt (all) in safety if it please Allah."

Idris (PBUH)

Enoch (PBUH) was born and raised in Babylon, following the teachings and religion of Prophet Adam(PBUH) and his son Seth (PBUH). Enoch was the fifth generation of the Prophet Adam (PBUH). He called the people back to his forefathers' religion, but only a few listened to him; while the majority turned away. Prophet Enoch (PBUH) and his followers left Babylon for Egypt. There he carried on his mission, calling people to what is just and fair, teaching them certain prayers, and instructing them to fast on certain days while giving a portion of their wealth to the poor. Scripture says that Enoch, went to heaven, without dying, but I think this can best be seen as him being established in this constellation of permanent levels of heavenly evolution.

And Cain knew his wife; and she conceived, and bare Enoch: and he builded a city, and called the name of the city, after the name of his son, Enoch. Gen 4:17 (KJV)

Aaron (PBUH)

Aaron (PBUH), is depicted throughout Scripture as a helper to his brothers, Moses (PBUH), and a leader of the people in Moses' (PBUH) absence. At times, his leadership failed but he nevertheless is described on an honorable level of development.

10:87: We inspired Moses and his brother with this Message, "Provide dwellings for your people in Egypt, make your dwellings into places of worship, and establish regular prayers: and give glad tidings to those who believe!"

Moses (PBUH)

Moses (PBUH) story recounts the Children of Israel's devolution into oppression in Egypt, and his liberation of the people from a society that had become oppressive itself. It is a textbook survival manual for a people living under a dominant culture and the message is simply, have faith in G-d and let Pharaoh's culture go.

28:7: So we sent this inspiration to the mother of Moses, "Suckle (thy child), but when thou hast fears about him, cast him into the river, but fear not nor grieve: for We shall restore him to thee, and We shall make him one of Our messengers."

28:8: Then the people of Pharaoh picked him up (from the river). (It was intended) that (Moses) should be to them an adversary and a cause of sorrow for Pharaoh and Haman and (all) their hosts were men of sin.

"And Moses was learned in all the wisdom of the Egyptians; and he was mighty in his words and deeds." ---Acts 7:22

Mohammed the Prophet (PBUH) did not need to travel to Egypt. He was born in the area, where secret sciences had originated, but the people had lost original knowledge and fell into ignorance (Jahilliyyah). He was taught by Allah and it demonstrated that he did not need any of the world's knowledge and that which Allah gave him would outshine it all.

Joseph (PBUH) was unselfish with love and compassion for his family and his fellow human beings. After everything his brothers had done to him, he invites them to come into Egypt, along with all their families. He recognized an obligation in the blessings he had received. He recognized an obligation to help his fellow inmates; an obligation to help his fellow countrymen in Egypt; an obligation to share his wealth, his knowledge, his power.

We know he shared because later, Joseph's (PBUH) descendants had become so numerous and so powerful and wealthy in the land that they became an annoyance to the native Egyptians. Thus began the story of Moses (PBUH) and the oppression of the Children of Israel, as it says, there came along a Pharaoh who did not know Joseph (PBUH).

This is a time when we have evolved through all the necessary developments and are able to see past all of the schemes, all of the falsehoods, and when truth stands out clearly. We are able to look past all of the rituals and understand their meanings. In the first (Nation of Islam) experience, we used to refer to the *Day of Judgment* as the Day of the Manifestation of all defects and Allah describes a time when we will see with "certain sight."[5] Joseph's (PBUH) shirt cured his father's blindness and reminds us of the popular song written and recorded by Johnny Nash in 1972, *I Can See Clearly Now.* Joseph's (PBUH) presence and survival in this new and advanced environment have been confirmed and the Prophet Jacob (PBUH) now sees that the destiny of human development is in good hands.

12:94 When the caravan left (Egypt), their father said, "I do indeed scent the presence of Joseph: Nay, think me not a dotard."

Chapter 94

Are You Senile If You Don't Know How You Know What You Know?

A dotard is a person who is weak-minded, especially through senility. This world portrays religious people as from a different era. They acknowledge that maybe G-d did create the world, but "He's retired now and we're in charge. The world has evolved into something He doesn't know anything about—the technology, the social norms, the lifestyle choices. We can do whatever we want now." They present religion as fundamental, primitive even, but not really relevant in the modern world. They discount intuition because it can't be proven or scientifically quantified. Of course, they can't see atoms either but they acknowledge their existence because they can measure their influence or their effects.

They also discount faith in general, although their own scientific disciplines are based on the same principles. Scientists operate on theories. The scientific method is a body of techniques for investigating phenomena, acquiring new knowledge or correcting and integrating previous knowledge.[1] The process begins with a hypothesis and ends with a conclusion or final statement, which is sometimes called a theory. In religion, we call the same process belief. We acknowledge that we don't know all of what we're talking about. We are students. We are seekers trying to understand what we believe. So our process and our establishment is no weaker than that of the scientists. In fact, it is stronger because even as we advance our own knowledge, we are acknowledging that a complete knowledge exists with the Creator of the system of knowledge. It is similar to the seven levels of evolution of knowledge represented by the Prophets, in that each level represents a higher level of knowledge and more certainty. In Islam, we have what is called *'ilm-ul yaqin, certainty by reasoning or inference*, or *'ain-ul-yaqin, certainty by personal inspection*. Both are referenced in Surah At-Takathur.[2]

Religion and Science

It is hard to imagine that an intellectual of this day who has studied and mastered the deep mysteries of life and the material creation, still cannot see the 'Hand' of G-d at work. Some scientists of this world have boasted of their discoveries as if they themselves created them. World-renowned physicist Stephen Hawking promotes the idea that there is no G-d responsible for this magnificent universe. In a statement that angered Christians and Muslims alike, he said, "I regard the brain as a computer which will stop working when its components fail. There is no heaven or afterlife for broken down computers; that is a fairy story for people afraid of the dark."[3] He went further to say that it was "not necessary to invoke God to get the universe going."

Noted atheist, author, and biologist Richard Dawkins believes faith has no place in science. In his 2006 bestseller, *The God Delusion*, he contends that a supernatural creator almost certainly does not exist and that such beliefs are based on faith rather than on evidence and qualify as delusions. He contends that only "evidence" can lay the groundwork for science, not "superstition, authority, holy books or revelation."

Perhaps they don't see the consistent logic behind those universal laws that they study and that all creation must obey. Or they don't see that both religion and science are part of one universal truth that must come together.[4] The truly great thinkers followed this logic and came to the idea of G-d because they believed that all effects have causes. While these universal thinkers may not have given the same name to that cause – G-d, Jehovah or Allah, they all acknowledged that the universe did not create itself and there must have been a First Cause. Allah says in Qur'an that, "He is Eternal," eternal coming from the word *Samad.* Various translators render the word, *absolute, eternal, self-sufficient, and independent of all while all are dependent on him.* The translation I prefer in this context is the "*Uncaused Cause.*"[5] Even business follows similar laws and principles. We have to first believe in what we are going into.

We then move on that faith until we complete each stage successfully. When we develop our business plans, we are not recording that which is a present reality. We are making a projection, a prediction of what we believe we can make happen given a certain set of circumstances and a certain set of actions and behaviors on our part. We are making our projection also based on a certain set of circumstances we *believe* will exist in the outer environment over which we have no control—the market. And based on all of these things that we believe in, we invest our money.

If we were able to put G-d under a microscope and analyze His Nature and Origins like we do everything else of the material creation, we then would be the masters and he would just be another of our subjects. Adam (PBUH) was given the power to "tell them their names," or analyze a thing and identify its value. But the purity of Islam is that the G-d is supreme above any imperfection, any limitation or any infirmity.

That inordinate reverence, even worship of science and its method of reliance only on observable physical phenomena, results in the dismissal of intuition. Yet Joseph's (PBUH) story and Jacob's (PBUH) unwavering faith in Joseph's (PBUH) survival, point to a sixth sense, a psychic awareness of things beyond the manifest. That intuition is a mysterious part of the mind but it is the very thing that brought Joseph (PBUH) to power in Egypt. So Jacob (PBUH) senses things and the people accuse him of the same thing they accused Prophets (PBUT) of in the past, and the same thing the brothers accused him of early in the story at 12:8[6]--"wandering in the mind."[7]

12:95 They said, "By Allah! truly thou art in thine old wandering mind."

Chapter 95

And Even Your Religion Has Become Just Rituals

Modern culture is always maintaining that the fundamentals of religion are obsolete; that they must be adjusted to fit modern times. The leaders of the popular culture accuse those who hold on to best traditions of being senile, out of tune or wandering in the mind.

Janusian thinking

How do you reconcile the need to advance while holding on to those important things that are essential to our progress? There is a concept in psychology called *Janusian Thinking*. It involves, "Bringing two opposites together in your mind, holding them there at the same time, considering their relationships, similarities, pros and cons, and interplay, then creating something new and useful." It is derived from the concept of *paradox*. The concept takes its name from Janus, the Greek 'god' of doors, gates, beginnings, and endings and was most often depicted as a man with two heads, each facing in opposite directions. The underlying power and obvious benefit of such a dual perspective is that it provides the ability to consider multiple perspectives simultaneously.

In an April 8, 2013, interview by WBEZ reporter Natalie Moore, Ezekiel Emanuel, eldest brother of Chicago Mayor Rahm Emanuel, discussed his new book, Brothers Emanuel: A Memoir of an American Family. He tells of his mother, who had been involved in the Civil

Rights Movement. His father was a doctor, who was uniquely sensitive to his individual patients, understanding that behind everything there was an individual life or person. They emphasized how to live as a community, a neighborhood, and people of Jewish faith with responsibility to others. Mayor Emanuel noted, "Our parents raised us with two and I think it's unique to hold two contradictory values at the same time – incredible respect for authority and the incredible responsibility to challenge it." It reminds us of the relationship of Imam Mohammed (RAA) with his father, the Honorable Elijah Muhammad, in which Imam Mohammed (RAA) had to maintain his insistence of seeing G-d correctly while accommodating, with respect, his father's perspective.

Prophet Muhammad (PBUH) said, "Live life as if you are going to live forever; and live life as if today is your last." We can see the extremes in society today of those who can only live in one of the two poles. But seldom are we faced with decisions that are mutually exclusive of each other. In most cases there are subtle variations and shades of benefits or detriments that we have to discern.

Our modern existence requires us to weigh complex, competing phenomena concurrently and make decisions we can stick by, despite having incomplete information. Studying paradoxes is important to the development of a creative mind. Paradoxes allow the mind to reach beyond what appears to be obvious which is the essence of creativity. Failure to do this results in decision- making paralysis, depression or wasted effort and false goals. In our history under Imam Mohammed (RAA), we may remember when he said the Fruit of Islam (FOI) no longer had to sell a quota of *Muhammad Speaks Newspapers*. We should have seen that as merely saying that no one outside ourselves could obligate us to do it, but we should. The paper was our economic engine and was responsible for most of the material progress of the community at that time. He removed the military hierarchal structure of the Fruit of Islam and told us, "We don't need captains over the men anymore. We need doctors of psychology." That should have been seen as a transition from someone having to direct us to us directing ourselves under self-government. It meant that we would no longer persuade men toward nation/community building based on some external rank, but rather as a doctor of psychology. We would persuade them by converting them to a higher thinking and a higher functioning. But to many it meant "can't nobody tell me what to do now." Many of us will remember an address in St. Louis, Missouri in later years in which Imam Mohammed (RAA) said he wished that he had an FOI then.

Imam Mohammed (RAA) relieved himself of administrative responsibilities of the American-Muslim community. He would not govern any individual masjid or Imam. Instead of the leadership recognizing that freedom as an opportunity for greater responsibility for the establishment of Mutual Consultation (Shura) as required by the Qur'an, many of them merely saw it as an opportunity to not support any central efforts and in effect any efforts of Imam Mohammed (RAA).

We were encouraged to join our worldwide community of Muslims and also join any people of faith who were doing good works. His value, and consequently our value as a community, was recognized throughout the world, from the Pope to the Grand Muftis. Yes, the Muslim world recognized his role yet most of them rejected the message of transformation and revival that he brought. It was hard for them to accept from him that even your religion has become just rituals. Yet today, Islam is viewed with respect by all except the most backward and uninformed while at the same time, the Muslim world is viewed as in total disarray. And because many of us still struggled with feelings of inferiority and weak faith, we went to the extreme of avoiding any mention of our distinctive community history or race. The consequence of all this was that we did not support him as we should have, just as Moses' (PBUH) followers failed to support him.[1]

12:96 Then when the bearer of the good news came, he cast (the shirt) over his face, and he forthwith regained clear sight. He said, "Did I not say to you I know from Allah that which ye know not?"

Chapter 96

The Good News is for Everybody

Even those blessed with the message can lose sight of G-d's Plan over time. Jacob (PBUH) and his family were still in the wilderness while the modern world of Egypt was moving forward with great commerce, industry, and science. If the mission is not broadened to its universal dimensions and applied to modern times, what good is it? Look at the Muslim world today as it struggles to reconcile the revelation of the Qur'an and the traditions of our prophet with modernity. Most see only a conflict in the societies. Today the world is one universal family and any interpretation of Islam or any religion that does not recognize the inherent worth of every human being (not just those of our locale or of our race), is going to fail.

We know that the brothers were convinced not to slay Joseph (PBUH) but just to put him in bad circumstances to give themselves the temporary favor of the religious community (Jacob) (PBUH). Later in Egypt when the Joseph's (PBUH) descendants had risen in wealth and power, Pharaoh again sought to curtail their development. His solution was to kill the male children.[1] Killing the leadership among the people effectively reduces them to a commercial commodity. That is what Pharaoh wants, someone who feeds into his system and does not use independent thinking.[2] The first casualty of this state is the subservient culture's cultural and community life.

Social Death

When community life dies, the death of the individual members follows behind. Orlando Patterson wrote what has been described as the first full- scale, comparative study of the nature of slavery. He examines the tribal, ancient, premodern, and modern world's slavery in 66 societies over time, including Greece and Rome, medieval Europe, China, Korea, the Islamic kingdoms, Africa, the Caribbean islands, and the American South. In America, slavery was described as a "peculiar institution," primarily because of the aspect that actively disconnected the slave from country, language, culture, and history and actually denied the human origin and human nature of the slave. "Slavery is shown to be a parasitic relationship between master and slave, invariably entailing the violent domination of a natally alienated or socially dead, person."[3] This is perhaps a most overlooked paradigm of the Black Lives Matter movement, and that is that we have to accept to establish an independent community life before we can even be respected in the context of 'All Lives Mattering."

In scripture, the death that is referred to is not the physical death so much, because that death is a natural process of life and not necessarily tragic. The real death is the spiritual and the social death. [4]

Social Autopsy

The lack of social cohesion and the disintegration of social structures has a direct relationship to physical death in communities. What helped bring this into focus for me was Eric Klineberg's book *Climactic Events in the Social Context: Heat Wave- a Social Autopsy of Disaster in Chicago.* It was the account of how between July 14 and July 20, 1995, an estimated 739 Chicagoans died in a massive heat wave, the worst heat-related disaster in Chicago history. It was the term *social autopsy* that intrigued me. Autopsy means *see for yourself.* It is a surgical operation performed by specially-trained physicians on a dead body. Its purpose is to learn the truth about the person's health during life and conclude how the person died. "The principal cause of the July 1995 heat wave was a slow-moving, hot, and humid air mass produced by the chance occurrence at the same time of an unusually strong upper-level ridge of high pressure and unusually moist ground conditions." National Weather Service, 1995. A report by the Cook County Medical Examiner's Office City Agencies and Scientific Research Centers revealed a social order in crisis. "This study establishes that the heat wave deaths represent what Paul Farmer calls "biological reflections of social fault lines for which we and not nature are responsible."[5] While this confluence of natural circumstances all represent acts of G-d, the catastrophic number of deaths were a result of social circumstances. By comparison, this was double the number of casualties that resulted from the Great Chicago Fire of 1871. Over a thousand people in excess of the July norm were admitted to inpatient units in local hospitals because of heatstroke, dehydration, heat exhaustion, renal failure, and electrolytic imbalances. "Heat waves receive little public attention not only because they fail to generate the massive property damage and fantastic images produced by other weather-related disasters, but also because their victims are primarily social outcasts – the elderly, the poor, and the isolated – from whom we customarily turn away."[6] Klinenberg points out these facts: African Americans had the highest proportional death rates of any age group in the city. Heat wave deaths were concentrated in the low-income, elderly, African American, and violent regions of the city. It struck the old, the alone, the impoverished, and those who are seldom visited. And society's support systems, which were designed to protect the most vulnerable, failed. If we look at other mass deaths, we will find similarities in drought-stricken and other areas where we have stopped being our brother's keeper. It's hard to see a Divine plan in these type of catastrophic events but what else will point out to us that we have been robbed of community life? Even now that we have supposed freedom, we have failed to establish community life. Jacob (PBUH) saw past the brothers lies from the beginning and as a righteous servant of G-d, he knew that Allah was the best planner and could truly say, "I know from Allah that which ye know not."

Coat of Many Colors

The shirt or coat of many colors that the brothers were so jealous of appears again here as a sign to Joseph's (PBUH) father Jacob (PBUH). Known as *the coat of many colors*, it has been portrayed in popular culture in the play, *Joseph and His Amazing Technicolor Dreamcoat*, which was the first musical to be performed publicly by Andrew Lloyd Webber who was considered "the most commercially successful composer in history,"[7] and lyricist Tim Rice. But we have to see an importance beyond a display of pretty colors. The coat represents the accommodation of the many cultures/color of the world into one beautiful garment of humanness. The one who is sensitive to the masses of the people of the world, the poor, rejected, and denied people, who retains his innocent human nature, is the one who is qualified to wear that coat and be the leader.[8] If we are going to be the bearers of good news to the whole world, we have to accept that the good news is for everybody. We can't let past hurts and injustice keep us from establishing the universality of the message.

In spite of his language that praised blackness, the Honorable Elijah Muhammad reminded African Americans that G-d had allowed the different shades of the world's people to develop in us – black, brown, red, yellow, and even *pass* for white. Despite these differences, African Americans never had a color problem until America's peculiar institution of slavery that was justified by demonizing black skin. They introduced an image of Divine (Jesus) in white flesh. It was only then that we too began to glorify lighter (fair) skin and scorned nappy (bad) hair. If we keep our faces oriented toward the thing that really makes us special, obedience to G-d, instead of skin color, we too will regain clear sight.[9] When Joseph's (PBUH) shirt is cast over Jacob's (PBUH) face, he regains clear sight. The word implies one who sees clearly or has understanding. Clear sight is 20/20 vision and if we add the 20 and 20 we get 40 which points to that same universal dimension. We can rise and be the community that G-d wants us to be – loving self, as G-d created us, respecting our unique experiences and recognizing that the human color is the best and highest identification we can have.

12:97 They said, "O our father! ask for us forgiveness for our sins, for we were truly at fault."

Chapter 97

We All Will Have to Testify

They say that confession is good for the soul but that confession should not be to one that we consider an intercessor between us and our Lord. The confession must be direct and recognizing as Allah has said that He is as close to us as our jugular vein.[1] The brothers are still not acknowledging that closeness to Allah, and aren't feeling worthy of approaching Him themselves for forgiveness. But at least they recognize their father, as one whom G-d has blessed and whose prayers are heard. Once this is done, the burden is lifted from our souls. Allah says in Qur'an, 7:*172*: *When thy Lord drew forth from the Children of Adam – from their loins - their descendants, and made them testify concerning themselves, (saying), "Am I not your Lord (who cherishes and sustains you)?" They said, "Yea! We do testify!" (This), lest ye should say on the Day of Judgment: Of this we were never mindful.*" He says about that Day of Judgment, and about the People of the Book, that they will have to believe in Jesus (PBUH) before their death, and that he Jesus, (PBUH) will be a witness against them. And He says that Muhammad (PBUH) will be a witness against us, as Muslims.[2]

In all of our prayers, we ask Allah, Al-Ghafoor, *(The Forgiving)*, for forgiveness but we often forget the need to be forgiving of others and to forgive ourselves.[3] Forgiveness does not involve praying to G-d to exact vengeance on our enemy. G-d says vengeance is Mine and that is a recognition that we will destroy ourselves from within when we harbor these strong negative emotions toward others. We create our own prison, our own misery, and our own accommodating environment for a host of other negative influences. Dr. Catherine Ponder wrote, "When you hold resentment toward another, you are bound to that person or condition by an emotional link that is stronger than steel. Forgiveness is the only way to dissolve that link and get free." Many times we are faced with a choice to forgive or to take recompense or retribution that is due.[4] When we accept the higher choice of forgiveness, we then allow Allah to bless us with His reward or Recompense.

Some of us who harbor a lot of anger are really mad at G-d. We can't understand why He would allow us to be made slaves and endure the treatment that we did. The person of faith knows that whatever injustice a soul endures for G-d's sake, his reward is with his Lord. But as long as we continue to look at the white man or white America as the source of our problem or as the solution to our problem, we will remain bound by emotional chains to him or it and our Lord should leave us to depend on whoever we are serving beside Him.

Justice

Allah says that on the Day of Judgment each of us will be paid according to our deeds and that that accounting will be full and perfect. If we also are to live our life as if today is going to be our last and also as if we are going to live forever, we have to be thinking of making that fair and just accounting every day and in every transaction. We all come up short in this because we all are human, and when we do come up short, the right thing to do is to ask for forgiveness. The brothers still have not come to the understanding that they too must face their Lord—personally and alone; they request their father, Jacob (PBUH), to ask for forgiveness for them, but they are getting there.

12:98 He said, "Soon will I ask my Lord for forgiveness for you: for he is indeed Oft-Forgiving, Most Merciful."

Chapter 98

We Cannot Stay Amid the Ruins

African Americans have to believe that one day they will be given something better in exchange for the pain and torture endured by their ancestors. To say that we may have neglected responsibilities on our part is not to blame the victim. Haven't we, at times, followed the same attitude of the children of Israel when they were delivered by G-d from the oppression of Egypt. Weren't there leaders then who tried to convince the people how good things were under Pharaoh and why would we even want to be on our own? Weren't there leaders then and now who had attained some success, even some wealth under Pharaoh? And weren't there some who were oppressive to their own people? Remember the character, Dathan, in the movie, Ten Commandments, how he rode in his ornate chariot while the poor, elderly woman, struggled along the bumpy road?

Then they arrived in the wilderness and G-d destroyed their enemies who were pursuing them. But they were never satisfied. They complained constantly to Moses (PBUH). After all the decades of wanting freedom, when they finally did get it, all they could do was complain about some condiments.[1] Haven't we, to a great extent, betrayed the sacrifices and the legacy of our ancestors. Look how obsessed we have become with trivia: Jordan shoes, false status, conspicuous consumption, and neglect and disrespect of important things, like family and community. Look at how we have neglected the establishment of community life-and then complain about the foreigners that come in our neighborhoods and provide our basic needs. Look at how dependent, addicted even, to the dominant culture's commercial interests, with no thought at all about establishing anything of our own. Look how we marginalize and ignore independent thinkers who aren't approved by white America.

It's so much easier to hold onto and mourn pain. It is so much easier to blame our past oppression. It is so much harder to accept our own faults and our own shortcomings. It's so much easier to live with the subconscious fear and doubt than it is to have faith. And yet it is G-d who has brought us this far and had us in 'His Hands' all along.

Belief is the key and sometimes those who believe in that have to ask G-d for forgiveness for the rest who don't know of his boundless forgiveness and mercy. We have to leave this comfort zone of oppression here in America. Man loves certainty or as they say, *'better the devil you know, than the devil you don't,'* so even fear, doubt, and abuse can get comfortable. This society and many of our individual psyches is a house that is in shambles and we have to leave it in order to enter the mansions we desire. As Emerson points out, "We cannot stay amid the ruins."

Releasing the Past

He wrote: "We cannot part with our friends. We cannot let our angels go. We do not see that they only go out so that archangels may come in. We are idolaters of the old. We do not believe in the riches of the soul; in its proper eternity and omnipresence. We do not believe there is any force in today to rival or recreate that beautiful yesterday. We linger in the ruins of the old tent, where once we had bread and shelter and organs, nor believe that the spirit can feed, cover, and nerve us again. We cannot find aught so dear, so sweet, so graceful. But we sit and weep in vain. The voice of the Almighty saith, 'Up and onward for ever more.' We cannot stay amid the ruins. Neither will we rely on the new; and so we walk ever with reverted eyes, like those monsters who look backwards."

How many of us have painful childhood experiences that still haunt us today? We think we are living in the moment, but the slightest perceived offense or any conversation or encounter which involves a lie, disagreement or disrespect brings back painful and powerful childhood memories. And they are just as vivid as if they had happened yesterday. That pain remains the 800-pound gorilla in the room, sucking up all of the air and keeping fear in the heart of the occupant. Consider how often we hear people blaming their father or mother for their circumstances. I believe that whatever hatred and resentment we harbor against our parents is mirrored and magnified within ourselves. We are a product of these parents. We are their genes. So any negative feeling toward them is going to manifest in us as low self-esteem, self-hatred, and self-destruction. Everything has its price. We have to give something up, be it anger, hatred or resentment for, something else. It is true that no one can know the pain of another person and some scars heal faster than others, but it is equally true that G-d's promise to us is life and life abundant. We must choose life. Every decision, every choice, is one of life or death. So let us not judge our parents, our fellow man or even ourselves so harshly.

Several years ago I attended a lecture by Sister Helen Prejean. Sister Helen has been active for many years in ministering to inmates on death row and advocating for abolition of the death penalty. Her work was popularized in the movie *Dead Man Walking* starring Sean Penn and Susan Sarandon. The question comes up frequently as to how she can befriend and empathize with people that committed heinous crimes. She made a point which resonated with me. "Which one of us would want our whole life characterized by the worst thing that we have ever done?"[2]

12:99 Then when they entered the presence of Joseph, he provided a home for his parents with himself, and said, "Enter ye Egypt (all) in safety if it please Allah."

Chapter 99

From Egypt-Breadbasket of the Ancient World-to the American Dream

Ancient Egypt was the epitome of agricultural advancement and was called at that time the bread basket of the world. The success of ancient Egyptian civilization came partly from its ability to adapt to the conditions of the Nile River Valley. The Nile's waters increase in the summer due to the heavy rainfall that occurs in the tropical Ethiopian highlands. In April, flooding begins in southern Sudan. It is July before the floods reach Aswan, Egypt. The Egyptians started their year at the summer solstice when the constellation Orion rose with the sun to mark the beginning of the flooding there. The river continues to rise until it peaks in mid-September. In Cairo, the floods are delayed until October. After the river has peaked, the levels fall quickly during November and December. The Nile is at its lowest levels between March and May. The predictable flooding and controlled irrigation of the fertile valley produced surplus crops, which fueled social development and culture. The Nile and its tributaries flow through nine countries. The White Nile flows through Uganda, Sudan, and Egypt. The Blue Nile starts in Ethiopia. Zaire, Kenya, Tanzanian, Rwanda, and Burundi all have tributaries, which flow into the Nile or into Lake Victoria Nyanes. The annually recurring flooding is now controlled by means of the Aswan Dam. With resources to spare, the rulers extracted minerals from the valley and surrounding desert regions. Culturally, they developed an independent writing system. They organized collective construction and agricultural projects and engaged in trade with surrounding regions. They developed a military intended to defeat foreign enemies and assert Egyptian dominance. Motivating and organizing these activities was a bureaucracy of elite scribes, religious leaders, and administrators under the control of a Pharaoh who ensured the cooperation and unity of the Egyptian people in the context of an elaborate system of religious beliefs.

Religious Science

Under this system, a secure political order with few wars and little force, Egypt flourished. The sacred (secret) power and knowledge was held by the ruling classes, the many-privileged nobles, and priests. Although many today may view the ancient Egyptian religion as only mythology and symbolism, in actuality the religion had its basis in the universal order found in the material creation. The problem is that it was shrouded in secrecy and symbolism just like ours is today. Long before men began to build cities, wandering herdsmen, no doubt descendants of Abel, *(Abel was a keeper of sheep, but Cain was a tiller of the ground. Gen 4:1-2 – Cain was the first born or born first. Man is firstly materially oriented and engaged, (with) his curiosity, but later he becomes a shepherd.)*, observed the movement of the heavenly bodies at night. They observed them just as we would watch late night TV or the more pious might observe his night prayers. At any rate, they would have noticed the almost imperceptible changes over time from season to season. As a tradition, they preserved the knowledge of the names and movements of the principal luminaries. The scientists Albert Einstein said, "Two things inspire me to awe-the starry heavens above and the moral universe within." Prophet Abraham (PBUH) observed and studied the heavenly bodies from an analytical standpoint and this perfected his belief in the one G-d, the First Cause of all effects. 41:37 "Among his signs are the night and the day, and the sun and the moon. Adore not the sun and the moon, but adore Allah who created them, if it is him ye wish to serve." Joseph (PBUH) was from this family of herdsmen when he had his vision but he was established in Egypt and in its knowledge before it was fulfilled.

Prophet Muhammad (PBUH) also was a herdsman. Muhammad Husayn Haykal, in his excellent history of the Prophet Muhammad

(PBUH), wrote that Muhammad's (PBUH) occupation as herdsman during the years of his youth provided him with plenty of leisure to ponder and contemplate. Later, he used to recall these early days with joy and say proudly that "God sent no prophet who was not a herdsman. Moses was a herdsman; David was a herdsman; I, too, was commissioned to prophethood while I grazed my family's cattle at Ajyad."

The ancients saw that the heavenly drama of the sun, moon, and stars was so enduring and of such magnitude that it mirrored forces that play out in the lives of the individual man. They organized their system of worship on the perfect planetary order, but this was provisional and was to give way to one more perfect. The thinkers of the ancient Egyptians knew that the primary search of man was for his own soul and that every deed, word, and thought that made up the sum total of his human experience was engraved upon his subconscious — that this inner self or subconscious keeps an unerring record of all things that will one day be presented as a judgment of the human life and conduct. The consistency of this heavenly drama had a likeness in the immutable record of man's life and history.[1]

This heavenly order inspires in man the quest in his very nature to aspire to a similar order and perfection. "The essence or spirit of genuine religion was always, and still is understood by men who are not bereft of the highest human capacity for devotional feelings, as the establishment by man of his relation to the infinite being or beings whose power he feels above himself, for his personal benefit and advancement toward a greater and higher life."[2] Any form of government, beginning with the first formation of a society among men to the present time, which did not incorporate religion or spiritual concepts into its statutes, has ever been short lived.[3] From Egypt-breadbasket of the ancient world to the American Dream, America has been blessed because she has acknowledged in her Constitution, certain inalienable rights of human beings-life, liberty and the pursuit of happiness. Inalienable means they cannot be taken away; that they are a G-d given, inherent human property. G-d has blessed America because she has acknowledged Him as the source of her blessings and because the true American Dream is consistent with G-d's vision for the destiny of man. But she has to acknowledge that it was our struggle in this country for these human rights that gave life and reality to the words on paper.

12:100 And he raised his parents high on the throne (of dignity) and they fell down in prostration, (all) before him. he said, "O my father! this is the fulfillment of my vision of old! Allah hath made it come true! He was indeed good to me when he took me out of prison and brought you (all here) out of the desert, (even) after Satan had sown enmity between me and my brothers. Verily my Lord understandeth best the mysteries of all that he planneth to do, for verily he is full of knowledge and wisdom."

Chapter 100

Imagine-A Brotherhood of Man… Sharing All the World

Joseph's (PBUH) vision of his destiny is fulfilled. He elevated the sun – knowledge of our material human existence – and the moon – knowledge or interpretation of scripture – (rational religion-intelligent behavior) to its proper status in society. Even his brothers, leadership of the vital influences in society, submitted to his leadership.

The sun, which rules the 12-hour day while the moon and stars govern the 12-hour night, do so by their passage through the 12 signs of the Zodiac, which completes the great circle of the heavens of 360 (12 x 30) degrees or division and thus govern the year.[1] We should look beyond the elementary picture of brothers making sajdah to Joseph (PBUH). G-d wants us to see these heavenly bodies as the embodiment of knowledge and science (and Joseph (PBUH) said, "O my father! This is the Ta'wil of my dream aforetime!") We translate *Ta'wil* as *interpretation* and Ta'wil has two meanings in the Qur'an: the true reality of things and what they will turn out to be. Everything, even the sun, moon, and stars know their mode of worship and that mode is obedience to G-d's laws. We will find all of creation governed by systems, each a world of knowledge unto itself, yet all governed by a universal system of laws. Imam Mohammed (RAA) taught us to see and translate *Rabbil Al-amin*, as "Lord of all Systems of Knowledge,"[2] and that is more edifying than just seeing the heavenly bodies as beautiful objects in the sky.

This logic is bigger than our judgment. Allah says, "Think not that your creation is bigger than the universe!" Allah made the stars, the moon, and the sun, along with man and many worlds out there. He made man above the angels, meaning that human beings can rise above the forces of creation. We shouldn't think though that we are greater than that creation. It is not us who reduced these things to our service, it is G-d. And we don't get the full utility of these creations unless we willingly submit ourselves to His service.

From man's beginning, when Allah ordered the angels to submit to him, man inherently understood his ability, his obligation, to control his environment, his circumstances, and his events. Christian teaching holds that man was created a little below the angels and this belief may come from primitive man's attribution of power, spiritual or magical, to these forces of nature. "The widespread belief in inherent magical virtue has been already noted. There is hardly anything in the universe, be it man or beast or bird, rock or tree or falling water, to which some amount of this mysterious property is not somewhere attributed. Every human being is tacitly credited with the possession of enough of it for the purpose of ordinary blessing and cursing, though some may have more than others. That the power of spirits or demons surpasses that of mankind goes without saying. Sounds, words, gestures, actions, processes, places, times, numbers, figures, colours, odours, all may have a certain amount of magical power." Handbook of Folk-Lore, Charlotte Sophia Burne, Senate, 1995. What she describes as a magical power, is nothing more than some part of G-d's spirit that He put into everything. Here, even the scholarly author cites a superior power in created matter. This is a corruption of Allah's original command to everything in nature to submit, and yield its utility to man. But it is only the evolved man such as Joseph (PBUH) who is able to command obeisance of these forces.

Joseph (PBUH) was warned earlier not to describe his dream to his brothers. This spiritual vision and leadership is rejected and scorned by business, political, social, and intellectual influences when they have become materialized and remain unawakened. Look at how the society mocks moral or spiritual concerns, particularly in the educational system. But when that spiritual development that remained obedient to G-d comes into power, they all have to submit to that.[3] One definition of *sujjudan*, translated here as "fell down in prostration" and that fits this context here, is *make obeisance*. Obeisance means compliance and other synonyms include acquiescence, capitulation, and submission. Joseph (PBUH) did not come into this power easily and the brothers did not come into submission willingly.

John Lennon of the Beatles popularized the song *Imagine*, which became an anthem of the peace movement. He wrote, "Imagine no heaven, no hell nothing to kill or die for, and no religion too/no possessions, no greed or hunger and a brotherhood of man/sharing all the world." While some might view these goals as unreal and idealistic and others may view them as irreverent, what he is identifying is all the things that people have fought for and are still fighting wars about. He acknowledges that these are the goals of the dreamer, but he also realizes that these types of dreams have and will come true. "You may say I'm a dreamer, but I'm not the only one, I hope someday you'll join us and the world will live as one." They all should submit to the one who has the disposition to make this happen.

The brothers are united again, and it has been the work of the dreamer, Joseph (PBUH). Within our own psyches, it is the faculty of imagination that enables this unity, this cognitive consonance.[4] Our intuitive sense informs us how we must bring each of our important disciplines under our control. Two fundamental principles operate in the human being. One inspires him to improve his ability to cultivate the material world and the other inspires him to improve his ability to cultivate human spirituality. Joseph (PBUH) finally gains freedom to exercise both of those abilities. His moral and spiritual sacrifice has been rewarded.[5] Joseph (PBUH) recognizes that he has been liberated from limiting circumstances (he took me out of prison) and that his brothers have been brought from circumstances devoid of cultivation, true spiritual life (brought you (all here) out of the desert). Muslim scholars are selfishly holding their people back. Their learned ones and *shaikhs* require you to worship them before sharing the knowledge; claiming some unique or distinct knowledge or claiming to possess more of this power than the ordinary man. The Christian leadership does exactly the same thing with only the religious establishment having an insight into the scripture and the masses thirsting in the dry desert. That idea is the influence of Satan, but G-d is complete in knowledge and wisdom and His Plan is for the whole of humanity.

12:101 "O my Lord! Thou hast indeed bestowed on me some power, and taught me something of the interpretation of dreams and events, O Thou Creator of the heavens and the earth! Thou art my Protector in this world and in the Hereafter. Take Thou my soul (at death) as one submitting to Thy will (as a Muslim), and unite me with the righteous."

Chapter 101

See No Evil, Hear No Evil, Speak No Evil

Even in his confinement, G-d's favor was still on Joseph (PBUH). Because he was patient and grateful, G-d granted him power. It is said that "the fear of the LORD *is* the beginning of wisdom: and the knowledge of the holy *is* understanding."[1] I would describe this more so as a regard or reverence as opposed to "fear" but the message is the same. It is through recognition of G-d's Favor that we are able to overcome obstacles and survive and prosper.

I remember my grandmother telling me about her early life- her trials and difficulties in her youth in Mississippi and even later in Chicago, after arriving during the Great Migration of Blacks from the South. What I remember most is her attitude of gratitude and blessing; she never ended her stories without the acknowledgment, "But I've had a good life." That positive energy showed her recognition of G-d's favor in spite of any circumstances.

Energy has many manifestations but it is always related to power. While energy can be defined in the narrow context of physical vitality, it can also be viewed in its broader sense as a component or essential ingredient of all living things.[2] Islam urges Muslims to gain mastery over nature because, according to the Qur'an, all resources in the heavens and the earth have been created for the service of mankind[3] and when we have this energy, which can also be seen as spirit, we can rise above any limitation. The Prophet also said there is no malady for which G-d has not created a cure.[4,5] We need only to access this power to overcome adverse circumstances.

Energy

Energy is defined in terms of physics as the capacity for doing work. The energy of a moving object is called kinetic energy. Stored energy is called potential energy. Space and Time also have a relationship to energy. Time is an essential component of the equation that determines an amount of work performed. In the earlier industrial age, time studies were done to determine exactly how much work a worker should be able to produce in a given time frame.

Work is the transfer of energy through the application of a force over a distance. Lifting a weight from the ground and putting it on a shelf is a good example of work and thus, we see the relationship between space and energy. Power is the measure of the amount of work done in a certain amount of time and thus, we see the relationship between work and time. Some relationships between various energy forms are common in the language, "Knowledge is power;" or "Time is money." When we proclaimed "Black Power" in the 60s, it was recognition of our capacity to bring about some change. The concept, however, was short-circuited into an emotional charge-a discharge really-loose electrons that created sparks and flashes but was unable to accomplish much work.

The classical mechanics sub-field of physics, described by Isaac Newton, took a material perspective in which the Universe was composed of solid and discrete building blocks. The pre-Newtonian era was characterized by the search for constancy in nature associated with material things such as the earth, the sun, the stars, and the heavens in general. "These were pictured in Christian theology as having been created by God to be unchanging and eternal." The Story of Physics, Lloyd Motz and Jefferson Hanes Weaver, p89. "The post-Newtonian physicists, accepting the idea of constant change in material things, were looking for constancy in the principles that govern the behavior of the Universe." Ibid p90. The law of conservation of mass provided a measure of constancy. It established that matter cannot be created or destroyed, although it may be rearranged in space and changed into different types of particles. Curiously, Newton later became very interested in theology. He studied Hebrew scholars and ancient and modern theologians at great length. He became convinced that Christianity had departed from the original teachings of Christ.

It took Albert Einstein years later in 1905 to explain the relationship between energy and matter with his formula $E=mc^2$. Mass is a manifestation of energy such that, energy and matter are interchangeable; proposing therefore that, in reality, everything is energy, fluid energy.

The quantum mechanics theory, which some recognize as a science, replaced the Newtonian laws of motion and teaches that nothing is fixed, that everything is fluid – ever-changing, vibrating energy in various states of potential. It describes the behavior of matter at the subatomic level where basic units are neither particles nor waves but act like both. The law of conservation of energy is likewise a fundamental concept of physics and it states that the amount of energy remains constant and is neither created nor destroyed, but can be converted from one form to another. As creators, we shape, form, and mold the energy of the Universe through our thoughts. In Genesis, it is said, "In the beginning was the word" and it also says that "the word was made flesh and dwelt among us." This tells us that material manifestations began as ideas and concepts. The law of attraction teaches us that we attract into our lives whatever we focus on. By applying both of these concepts into our lives, we can have faith that our creative powers can change anything in our lives.

The Energy of Emotions

According to scientists, relationships involve both emotions and energy. How many times have we seen a person enter the room and change the whole atmosphere; negatively or positively? It is accepted that people can charge their space or place, even an entire city, with their prevailing state of mind. We are obligated to use our talents and I will extend that logic to say we are obligated to use our blessings. If our innocence, our patience, and our righteousness are rewarded, we are granted power but it must be for a purpose. Power is transformative, thus, we should accept a responsibility to change ourselves and the community condition.

Dr. Caroline Myss wrote, "Experiences that carry emotional energy in our energy systems include past and present relationships, both personal and professional; profound or traumatic experiences and memories; and belief patterns and attitudes, including all spiritual and superstitious beliefs. The emotions from these experiences become encoded in our biological systems and contribute to the formation of our cell tissue, which then generates a quality of energy that reflects those emotions."[6]

Neurobiologist Dr. Candace Pert has proven that neuropeptides – the chemicals triggered by emotions – are thoughts converted into matter. In an interview with Bill Moyers, she said, "Our emotions reside physically in our bodies and interact with our cells and tissues. Your mind is in every cell of your body." Moyers asked, "You're saying that my emotions are stored in my body?" Pert's response, absolutely. "Just as radio stations operate according to specific energy wavelengths, each organ and system in the body is calibrated to absorb and process specific emotional and psychological energies." *Anatomy of the Spirit, Dr. Caroline Myss.* Is this a new concept that your mind is in every cell of your body? No. Allah points out in the Qur'an that parts of the body will testify against us on judgment day. Testifying implies some consciousness. Dr. Abdel J. Nurriddin, wrote in a column in the Muslim Journal, entitled *Health is Predicated in Energy*: "Choices determine our life, and choices can carry with them at the extremes death." He noted how the vibrational effects of thought affect vital metabolic processes at the cellular level. "We talk to our bodies every second of the day and the body through vibration accepts your information and molds itself to it."

"The substance that your body's essence is made up of is energy and information. You, as a physical body, are energy and information as a human body. Quantum physics tells us at the ground state of the energy and information, all matter formed is consciousness. This consciousness is a field of all possibilities in terms of substance taking form."

"Most people think they tell themselves what to think. However, this is not true. Most people think based upon what the outer world tells them to think. The outer world consists of all stimuli, from books to media to professors, etc. Most people are not directed from the internal world or the "Kingdom of Heaven." Most people have not found it.

"The Bible says, 'First seek ye the kingdom,' which means you must first find it before the other things can be added unto you, which we believe to be health, wealth, and happiness." Muslim Journal, September 3, 2010.

The Flow of Energy

We must learn to manage this flow of energy through ourselves and we do this by controlling perceptions. What we see, hear and get through our other senses are those perceptions and our voice then gives us expression when we speak. If we continually try seeing the blessing in circumstances, we can remain positive and express positive energy. Thus, the saying, *see no evil, hear no evil, speak no evil.* That positive energy is what gives increase. Man does not live by bread alone. No amount of money can bring us harmony and spiritual well-being, but if we have those things we can transform the substance around us into wealth in time. There is no life in money itself but it represents life's energy that has been put into something. Money is only one of many tokens or symbolic expressions of wealth. In fact, wealth can sometimes buy things money cannot. If we look at the physical thing itself (the token), seeing only dust (the dry material thing) and not respecting the life that has produced it, that is a curse. It puts us further and further away from the real substance and human obligations of the money, which is a form of human energy. Those people whose diet consists only of earth are eating dust (something without life). They then become lifeless themselves because they do not have feelings for people, nor regard life anymore.[7]

So what is true wealth? "We can roughly define wealth as any possession, shared or not, that has what economists call *utility*; it provides us with some form of well-being or can be traded for some other form of wealth that does. New wealth systems don't come often, and they don't travel alone. Each carries with it a new way of life, a civilization."[8] Witness the dot.com boom that created a whole new wealthy class and the Industrial Age which created a new class of industrialists. The Prophet Muhammad (peace be upon him) said, "Wealth consists of various kinds of treasures, and those treasures (all) have keys. Blessed is the man whom G-d has made a key for good and a lock for evil." Al- Tirmidhi, Hadith 1366. The wealth of the future will be based on correct knowledge and we, like Joseph (PBUH), have been blessed with that key.

12:102 Such is one of the stories of what happened unseen, which We reveal by inspiration unto thee; nor wast thou (present) with them then when they concerted their plans together in the process of weaving their plots.

Chapter 102

There is Nothing Covered That Will Not Be Revealed, Nor Hidden That Will Not Be Made Known and Come into the Open

There are limits as to what is discoverable through the rational process alone. Einstein noted that "The intuitive mind is a sacred gift and the rational mind is a faithful servant. We have created a society that honors the servant and has forgotten the gift." G-d can reveal to us the schemes of Satan and uncover for us the secret knowledge that has been used to control man. "There is nothing covered that will not be revealed, neither hidden that will not be made known and come into the open."[1]

City as Container and Control Mechanism

To understand the establishment of the religious science, it is necessary to understand some aspects of the evolution and development of the city, as the prototypical container of the social structures and activities of the people. In the city, "all the essential elements brought into operation by civilization were present from the beginning but they were at first held together, perhaps, not by separately established urban walls, but by the common natural walls about the whole country, as they were polarized, not only by the many local deities and shrines, but by the single presence of the Divine Pharaoh, in a kind of political monotheism that preceded any theological creed of the same nature. In short, the magnet was more important than the container, because the religious assumption was more persuasive, in contrast to the secular pressures and coercions of Sumer and Akkad." The City in History, Lewis Mumford, p83,4

Secret Knowledge

Egypt required the combined intelligence and means of the people to organize a complete system of stellar symbolism. The heavens soon began to be considered the abode of the gods and it became the business of those appointed as priests of their religious services and ceremonies to locate them in their appropriate houses. These men who were so set apart by the people became their teachers and leaders and their religious form naturally came to be viewed in an astronomical context. The priests soon became the sole conservators of the mysteries and, as a result, they naturally were given authority over the people.[2] The great truths were for the few and became known as the lesser and greater mysteries. The Bible despite its messages of inspiration and transformation, also contains the language outlining the scheme to rule over the people. It could well have been said to these few in Egypt just as it was said to the few in the Bible: "To you is given to know the mysteries of the Kingdom of God (or Heaven), to others it is not so given." Matthew 13:11.

If anything proves that the city was primarily a control center, long before it became a center of communication, the persistent restrictions exercised over the extension and communication of knowledge would support this interpretation. As in the United States and Soviet Russia today, the great business of the citadel is to *keep the official secrets.* "These secrets created a gap between the rulers and the ruled that almost turned them into different biological species; and it was not until the achievements of civilization themselves were called into question by popular revolt, that any part of these secrets was shared." Ancient Egyptian Initiation, p105

There is a bitter lament from Egypt's first great popular uprising that reveals the indignation of the upper classes, because the lower orders had broken into their precincts, and not merely turned their wives into prostitutes, but what seemed equally bad, captured knowledge that had been withheld from them. "The writings of the august enclosure [the temple] are read. The place of secrets is [now] laid bare. Magic is exposed." (Admonitions of Ipu-wer: 2300-2050 B.C.?) The City in History, Lewis Mumford, p99, 100. This idea that the ignorant masses were a separate species continues to the present. The Greek word *gnosis* (knowledge) is a standard translation of the Hebrew word knowledge (תעד da`ath) in the Septuagint. Gnosis was first and foremost a matter of self-knowledge, which was considered the path leading to the goal of enlightenment of hidden knowledge of the various pre-Judeo-Christian pagan mystery-religions, including Egypt's. The Gnostics among the Jews of Jesus (PBUH) time were those who possessed the highest knowledge and considered the masses to not have souls because they did not have that knowledge or have insight into their secrets.

This idea was easily adopted by the slave masters to justify their enslavement and mistreatment of African Americans. We were meticulously robbed of any knowledge of self, of language, of culture and religion, and were similarly considered a separate species and lacking souls. Not until 1978, when their leader had a vision, were African Americans allowed into the priesthood of the Church of Latter Day Saints (Mormons), because of their belief that African Americans did not have souls. And yet many of our people felt comfortable following the sect and believing that it was godly. Allah points out that it was not our efforts that revealed, unfolded, and unraveled the plot against his human creature.[3] It was He that was Master of the Unseen and He that brought about circumstances in our favor.

12:103 Yet no faith will the greater part of mankind have, however ardently thou dost desire it.

Chapter 103

The Majority of People Will Not Believe

Pharisees

Most people, despite their profession of faith or their adherence to organized religion, do not have an articulated and uncorrupted belief in One G-d, Creator of the Heaven and Earth, and Creator of all people from one human soul. They may have a doctrine that they were raised in. They may have a way of life that works for them. But seeking the highest and best relationship between themselves and G-d and between themselves and their fellow man generally does not characterize their belief. Each age and group expressed the revelation of their prophet in their own way but most of them went astray. The Jews, for example, were divided into four classes: "The Pharisees, the Sadducees, the Essenes, and the common people. The Pharisees, following the Persian captivity, had adopted the Persian fire-worship in form, knowing little or nothing of its spirit. The name Pharisee, Parsee, and Persia are derived from the *Pur* of the Greeks, meaning fire." Ancient Egyptian Initiation, p133. Today the language spoken by Persians is Farsi, and I believe the word Pharisee has aptly been passed down to describe those who worship the great knowledge that they have.

The Pharisees are the people who believe in sticking strictly to the letter of the Scripture. They are seen in the Bible as the sanctimonious, self-righteous or hypocritical person. Jesus PBUH) told them, "Woe unto you, scribes and Pharisees, hypocrites! For ye make clean the outside of the cup and of the platter, but within they are full of extortion and excess. Thou blind Pharisee, cleanse first that which is within the cup and platter, that the outside of them may be clean also." Matt 23:25-26 (KJV). They were meticulous about the rituals and the traditions but had lost human compassion.

The Jews are not the only ones with their Pharisees. In our own community of Al-Islam, many criticize this indigenous African American community, its origins, and its leaders. Even today many undermine our work and seek to supplant an immigrant mind into an indigenous soul. Why? Because we might not speak the flowing Arabic or the know correct Islamic term. But G-d says matters in Islam are judged on intent and that religion is sincerity. To those who think so much of their great knowledge but have gone to sleep on the real human compassion that the revelation is supposed to inculcate, you've concerned yourself with pots and containers, but you've lost the value of actual contents of the container or rituals.

Sadducees

The Sadducees took their name from *Sadoc*, a teacher of the law in a divinity school in Jerusalem. They are those who don't believe in a resurrection or any life after death.[1] They believe in materialism; that everything in the human life comes from something physical.[2] Jesus (PBUH) pointed the finger at both the Pharisees and Sadducees, saying, "Take heed and beware of the leaven of the Pharisees and the Sadducees."[3] The leaven is true doctrine, bread, once it is blown up with lies, false teachings, and false spirit. Although history claims the Sadducees have since been destroyed, in the modern world, these are your materialists and communists.[4] We may look at the fall of the Communist Soviet Union and think that this philosophy is gone but look at how many people today will tell you they believe only in the here and now or who live their lives like there is no accountability in the hereafter. The Essenes taught and practiced the highest morality and it was their spirit that influenced the early teachers and thinkers of Christianity.

Today finding the true message of the Prophets (PBUT) is difficult. The descendants of these varying philosophies and those who have formed their own belief based on whatever appeals to them dominate the religious landscape today. And as Allah says often in Qur'an, most of them don't believe, and most of them don't understand.

12:104 And no reward dost thou ask of them for this, it is no less than a message for all creatures.

Chapter 104

The Purpose of Sense is Perception

Allah reminds us many times in the Qur'an, 'tell the people, no reward do I ask of you; this message is for your benefit and my reward is with my Lord.'[1] We are to expect our reward from Allah.[2] When we ask for anything, we are to ask of Allah, even though we recognize that we ask for things and seek help through other people.[3] Then there is never any failure or disappointment in the bargain. Our relationship with others can become corrupted by selfish motives. We all have influences of vanity, that can sometimes corrupt the message and our motive. Allah says that Satan even tried to inject this into the message of the prophets.[4] Vanity was the sin of Satan who had an exaggerated view of his own importance and a desire to have all the attention. It is akin to selfishness and it has caused even religious communities to color and corrupt their original message until it favored their race or their group. Even in our charity, our expectation should be the favor and reward from Allah alone and not from he to whom the charity is given.

W. Clement Stone, an American insurance magnate, and philanthropist, also called Mr. Positive Mental Attitude, turned $100 into millions with a strong desire to succeed and by putting into practice the principles in the book *Think and Grow Rich* by Napoleon Hill. Stone seemed to repel negativity and even the Great Depression couldn't diminish his spirit. Stone believed in giving with no expectation of return. Advice from Stone originally published in *Success Unlimited* sums up his philanthropic beliefs: "Be generous! Give to those you love; give to those who love you; give to the fortunate; give to the unfortunate; yes, give especially to those to whom you don't want to give. Your most precious, valued possessions and your greatest powers are invisible and intangible. No one can take them. You and you alone can give them. You will receive abundance for your giving. The more you give, the more you will have." When he died several months after his 100th birthday in 2002, W. Clement Stone had given an estimated $275 million away to charity.

That spirit of charity must extend to all people and that's why Joseph's (PBUH) coat was so beautiful. It contained all the colors in its social fabric. It inspired the jealousy of his brothers because their perspective was so narrow. When we say Islam is the universal religion, we are saying what the Prophet Muhammad (PBUH) said, that there is no superiority of a black over a white or a white over a black, except by virtue of their conduct. The blessings of the religion extend to all. The obedience required is incumbent on all. Allah gives us the logic for coming to a common understanding with all people. Regardless to wherein our beliefs differ, He tells us that we should agree on this one basis. He says, "O People of the Book! come to common terms as between us and you, that we worship none but Allah; that we associate no partners with him; that we erect not, from among ourselves, Lords, and patrons other than Allah." If then they turn back, say ye, "Bear witness that we (at least) are Muslims (bowing to Allah's Will)." Holy Qur'an, 3:64. If they can just accept that truth about us, we could get along much better.

It is a misunderstanding that we are trying to convert the religious people of the world to Islam. What we want is the highest and best human life for all people and we have been blessed to identify what has denied the common people this life – corrupt scripture, false knowledge, selfishness, and jealousy. It is Allah Himself who has condemned the things that people have worshiped besides G-d.[5] He challenged them by appealing to their own logic and intelligence.[6] He uses the term *Uffin* to connote disrespect to them and the things they were worshipping. He asks them: "Have you no sense?" indicating that your own intelligence that I bestowed on you would have given you a correct insight.

That mysterious property that the ancients attributed to every created thing can be seen as that thing's ability to present a message to man's mind through his perception. Allah says that every created thing knows its own mode of worship[7] and its obedience to Divine Law and its message to man's mind can be seen as its worship. Everything that we perceive and know comes to us through our senses. So when G-d asks "Do you have no sense?" He is telling us that the whole purpose of the senses is perception. And once we perceive something, it becomes knowledge to us and should translate into good sense. The knowledge to advance our life and our civilization comes from the messages in the material creation. He is telling us that we are not even using our five senses. The five senses are the common property of all human beings so whatever message and insight that we derive from science or from the Word of G-d is for all creatures.

12:105 And how many Signs in the heavens and the earth do they pass by? Yet they turn (their faces) away from them!

Chapter 105

Creation is Readable, Teachable Information

Our Religion, indeed everything that exists that G-d made, is there to give us knowledge or science and mercy.[1] And all these created things are alive and pulsate with energy containing this information. Quantum physicists acknowledge the existence of an electromagnetic field generated by the body's biological processes. Living tissue generates energy and is surrounded by an energy field. Many people, some called intuitives, can perceive this energy and read this information and messages. A feature of this energy field that surrounds us is that it carries with us the emotional energy created by our internal and external experiences, both positive and negative. Allah says he created everything in pairs. This tells us that with everything we encounter in life, we form a relationship, a pair, and it is that pair or pairing that produces offspring, a result-experiences, memories, perceptions, attitudes, and beliefs. A traumatic experience in our early childhood may elicit the same response years, even decades later, in response to totally unrelated circumstances. Based on quantum mechanics some physicists have concluded that reality itself must be defined as a relation between our minds and the things we observe. We also form relationships with time, space, energy, and money, creativity. "This emotional force influences the physical tissue within our bodies. In this way your biography, that is the experiences that make up your life, becomes your biology." Anatomy of the Spirit, Dr. Caroline Myss.

Imam Mohammed (RAA) has pointed out that both the Qur'an and the natural creation provide us with a "creation supported social logic." G-d did not leave man alone with no guidance before the Qur'an was revealed. He gave him the ayats in creation and the ayats in himself. The language was in creation before oral language and before written language. Creation gives us the picture and the object and it is much later that we learn or develop words to describe the object. Our original transmission of these words come from oral transmission-word of mouth. Words transmitted by written language and on paper is a much later phenomenon. Printed words in books came even later than that. A good definition of words will also define them as pictures, ideas, and concepts.

We have to learn to see things in their reality. We think we see things; we see the physical objects in creation but a scientist sees those same objects differently. He sees them through scientific eyes, through their structure, their properties, their potentialities. Allah says in Qur'an, "This whole world, as we see it, is only *Guruur* meaning deception, illusion."[2] All of these objects are not as we see them, touch them, or feel them. We will be lost if we don't believe and rely on a higher sense or perception to understand the reality of these things.

Allah says he created the universe out of smoky chaos.[3] The Christian tradition identifies this origin from Cosmos from Greek Cosmogony. They both point to the fact that we have to structure our lives and society in the same way. Bring order, discipline, and law into our life in order to make progress and create.

Once writing was established it also produced a change in man's thinking. It enabled abstract thought-logic, analysis, and synthesis-the ability to see or experience one situation and then apply it to another. This level of analysis and synthesis is represented by the higher levels of development of the prophets (PBUT). Some primitive cultures today still do not have a written language and they are not able to think in abstract terms. "The uncultured native is not accustomed to deal with things in the abstract and his mind does not readily grasp them. He cannot generalize from details." The Handbook of Folklore – Traditional Beliefs, Practices, Customs, Stories and Sayings, by Charlotte Sophia Burne, 1914. p.166

One problem with this limited thinking ability is that we might see the creation of Adam (PBUH) narrowly as that of a physical man-a flesh creation. That enables a perception of flesh as sinful because we are told that the first man fell and had to be redeemed. It also causes us to see that first man in flesh color only and that is planting the seeds of racism, which will blossom generations later in our religious and other languages.

The better language carries a message of structuring our social life so we can create and maintain a healthy environment. G-d created all of these things to keep man in the best shape and then bring him back after he slips. Every day new human beings are born and each child born is born pure and upright. And every day the sun rises and lights the earth anew, bringing it life and a new chance. Yet we don't see the meaning in all of it. Allah says in the Qur'an that "Most of them don't understand. Most of them don't acknowledge." It is no wonder that He asks here, "What sign after this can I send them? What is after this that they will believe in?"

12:106 And most of them believe not in Allah without associating (other as partners) with Him!

Chapter 106

The Idea That There is More than One G-d is the Worst Form of Oppression

When we look at the concept of confinement we will see limitations that are imposed on the human mind and spirit that are much stronger than just chains and bars. And because what is restricted is unseen potential many inmates don't even realize they are confined. What is society's most powerful method of enslavement? It is the idea that there is more than One G-d. Allah says that false worship is the highest wrong we can commit[1] and also He forbids sins against truth and reason and assigning partners to Him.[2] False worship is the worst form of oppression because it oppresses the best of man. G-d tells us that the best thing He created in the whole universe is the human intellect. We should be able to see then the oppression in the violation of our rational faculties. Look at the many ways in which the intellect is oppressed by associating partners with G-d. The concept of the Holy Prophet Jesus (PBUH) being the son or the offspring of the Creator of the Heavens and Earth is an underlying cause of racism. Racism itself is irrational; if Jesus (PBUH) is seen in white flesh, what does that do to me in my black flesh? To say that G-d could have a son is a monumental assault on reason. It implies an infirmity in G-d-that He needs to have a relationship with the thing He created to have an offspring. This is the same G-d that created Adam (PBUH) from dust, from mud, and from clay. And He clearly states how He creates. He says "Be, and it is"[3] and everything in creation comes to Him as a servant.[4]

Some see Jesus (PBUH) as a divine figure and that too defies logic;[5] G-d should not need food, sleep, experience sickness and death. It's against man's own nature to worship something that is equal or inferior to himself. Jesus' (PBUH) own assertions dispute this. He prayed to G-d and acknowledged his own submission to G-d as a servant. Before he chose his 12 disciples, he prayed all night to G-d.[6] And when they asked him to teach them to pray, he taught them the Lord's Prayer, which begins, "Our Father, who art in heaven."[7] When he was tortured, he prayed to the Father to forgive his tormentors.[8] At his most vulnerable moment, when his death was imminent, he did not invoke his own power; he prayed to the only One with power to save him.[9] And with his apparent dying breath, he acknowledged a Master over Himself and over All.[10] This concept of Jesus' (PBUH) divinity and the Trinity was imposed upon Christians by political and military power.

Then there are the more subtle things we associate with G-d in His worship. There are those of us who have fallen prey to personality worship, where, in our heart we view our Shaikh, our Rabbi, or our Bishop as an intercessor. There are those who follow their own instincts and desires until those things leave them in a bind and then they call on G-d. And there is a whole pantheon of saints and angels that people pray to hoping for intercession with G-d. Joseph (PBUH) did not worship on the verge: "I'm gonna take this as far as I can by myself and then when I get in a bind, I'll call on you." He acknowledged Allah in 12:38 when he was captive and also in 12:108 when he was elevated.

Allah asks us, "Who is more unjust than one who invents a lie against Allah or rejects his signs? For such, their portion appointed must reach them from the Book (of decrees) until, when our messengers (of death) arrive and take their souls, they say "Where are the things that ye used to invoke besides Allah?" They will reply, "They have left us in the lurch," And they will bear witness against themselves; that they had rejected Allah. Holy Qur'an, 7:37

12:107 Do they then feel secure from the coming against them of the covering veil of the wrath of Allah, or of the coming against them of the (final) Hour all of a sudden while they perceive not?

Chapter 107

Whatsoever a Man Soweth, That Shall He Also Reap

Joseph's (PBUH) life is a perfect portrait of G-d's Justice. What is described here is an overwhelming, all-encompassing punishment, from which there is no escape. We can also see a Time when we will invariably reap what we sow. Who can successfully live their life without awareness of consequences? How many are fooled because they don't see the immediate results of their actions and are fooled into thinking they have avoided those consequences? Bible verses emphasize that we "sow to Spirit" or, as Allah says in the Qur'an, who invests in his soul and look to what we have put away for the future and the Hereafter.[1] We have to invest in our soul for the benefit of both our present life and the life to come. This basic law operates as effectively and powerfully in our minds as they do in our gardens. We eventually become what we think about. Conversely, the person that has no goal, who doesn't know where he's going and whose thoughts are thoughts of confusion, anxiety, and worry, will eventually see a life full of frustration, fear, anxiety, and worry. Words of truth have life in them so they will produce life in us. The human mind is a fertile field that brings forth, in due course, everything that is planted in it. Scientists tell us that everything that we perceive through our senses is recorded in our subconscious minds. Some even suggest that we have outside our individual consciousness, memories from a super-conscious-things we may not have even experienced personally.

The nature of the reaping can also be deceptive. Once we plant the seed, we have to depend on unseen forces for its maturation. It will produce according to the nature of the seed. But if we don't have patience, we may lose sight that it will eventually blossom. The consequences can be so far down the line that we are disconnected from the act that produced it and we think we have escaped justice.[2,3] That belief in the justice of a Final Accounting is necessary.

We know that neither our wealth nor status will shield us at that time. But G-d, in His Mercy, even prepares us for that. As we get older, we lose the vitality of our youth. Vitality comes from the Latin root which means *life*. Sometimes we lose our wealth and sometimes we must depend on our children and strangers to care for us. This should show us that we are approaching ever closer a time when nothing will avail us but that which we've put forward for our souls and G-d's Mercy.

Then there are catastrophic events that overwhelm us and in the twinkling of an eye, we are made humble and helpless. We are warned of the ultimate overwhelming event by signs in the earth where we see mighty mountains crumbled by eruptions and landslides and vast expanses of earth torn apart by quakes.[4] In this Time of Judgment, we should be looking for all of the events and all of the people that had been prophesized. Today, we should be looking for the Joseph (PBUH) type-that patient, righteous long suffering people that endured oppression, remained obedient to G-d and eventually come into power.

12:108 Say thou, "This is my way: I do invite unto Allah,- on evidence clear as the seeing with one's eyes, I and whoever follows me. Glory to Allah! and never will I join gods with Allah!"

Chapter 108

Each to His Own

When we establish what we are standing on and the way we are following, we eliminate much confusion and confrontation. The proselytizers will avoid you because they recognize the firmness of your position and the precariousness of their own. So our path must be made clear. By the same token, we are not to compel another human being with free will to follow our way.[1] The Christian theologian Saint Augustine said, "He who created us without our help will not save us without our consent." Allah did not even compel Satan to submit to His Will. He gave him respite. We too have to have confidence in the power of truth and its ultimate triumph over falsehood and the patience to wait on this. This is not to say we are not to try to actively bring the message of Al-Islam to the world. We are to present this message clearly and openly.[2] We are to debate with them, but in a good spirit and with good sentiments and intentions. This style of presentation is made in both word and deed and history has shown the power of this approach to convert. This is also an important key to world peace – living the life we claim, being the best human being we can be, and trusting that example will influence those we come in contact with.

Islam was brought into Indonesia, the world's most populous Muslim country, by traders from Gujarat, India during the thirteenth century and it was spread primarily by traders and nine well-respected missionaries. They did not come with guns and racial supremacy philosophies. They came with the truth, sincerity, fair dealing, and exemplary moral conduct. Similarly, Joseph (PBUH) invited people to truth with clear proof, Alā baṣīratin, "with insight" (on evidence clear as the seeing with one's eyes) and he clearly separated himself from those who corrupted their worship and made it clear that there was nothing that would take him off that path.[3]

Today religion has been corrupted, in most cases, through the subconscious. The formulators of Christianity studied ancient Egypt and other theologies of that time and took ideas from them all. The ancient Egyptians worshiped many gods but most of their gods were creatures of nature – dogs, snakes, cats, and other animals and insects. They worshiped *Anubis*, a dog, as one of their gods. Imam Mohammed (RAA) noted, "I know where it comes from, the using a word for G-d in English that can be read backwards or reversed, and it says dog."[4]

Even the worship of man is not new and is not unique. Father Divine (Reverend Major Jealous Divine, a spiritual leader from around 1907 until his death who was also known as "the Messenger"), promoted economic independence and racial equality and as his name implies, he told his mainly African American followers to look to him to see God. He taught during the same period as Noble Drew Ali and it is known that W. D. Fard borrowed from his language, along with many other African American leaders of that time. But now we have the pure language of the Qur'an and we should put Fard in a historical context and his language in the mythology and satirical context where it belongs. The legitimacy of the languages themselves is what should impress the rational mind – clarity and truth vs. symbolism and hyperbole. We may all have the same goals. We all want to save our families and our loved ones as Allah has commanded,[5] but we have to remember that He makes believers. At the end of the day, we have to be willing to say, 'to each his own.'

12:109 Nor did We send before thee (as messengers) any but men, whom we did inspire, (men) living in human habitations. Do they not travel through the earth, and see what was the end of those before them? But the home of the hereafter is best, for those who do right. Will ye not then understand?

Chapter 109

We Are the Champions of the World

Allah says in the Qur'an that He gave us our shape, our hue, and created us in tribes and nations. From this we can conclude that he made us, African Americans, as a people and that the conditions we were formed under are a part of what gives us the shape He wants us to have.

Imam Mohammed (RAA) pointed out what G-d says, "You are the best in the history of the development and rise of community life."[1] He adds, however, that "He does not give us this message to generate arrogance in us. For man to be prepared for [global excellence] he has to be universal in his heart, universal in his thinking, and universal in his aspirations. He has to include everybody in his dreams, not only in his works, but also in his dreams. Allah (SWT) included everybody in the dream (future) for Muslims." Time and circumstance has united the world into one global community. Transportation and communication has also moved the world into universal dimension. It is now time for the social sensitivities of the world to catch up with the technology. G-d calls for this special group to rise and he promises this group success.[2] Nowhere in His language does He refer to or confine this mandate to a particular race, ethnic group or nationality. He's speaking to G-d fearing, righteous people.

We have the choice to be a part of that group or not and it is that choice and the obligations that go along with it, that enables us to boldly say we are the champions of the world. We will have defeated all the challengers against man. We will have made our own jinn a Muslim. We will have stood up for right and decent behavior. We will have condemned wrongdoing, immorality, and indecency. And we will have humbled ourselves by acknowledging that we could not have done this without G-d's Help.

Acknowledging this type of mission and G-d's help in attaining it has historically proven to be successful. We recognize America as the social and industrial giant of the world but we don't often appreciate our own role in arriving there. Sven Beckert writes in his book, *Empire of Cotton: A Global History*, that slave plantations were America's first big business. He explained in his essay, "How the West got rich and modern capitalism was born," published in *Making Sen$e,* how slavery was at the heart of modern, global capitalism.

"By 1830, one million Americans, most of them enslaved, grew cotton. Raw cotton was the most important export of the United States at the center of America's financial flows and emerging modern business practices and at the core of its first modern manufacturing industry. Just as cotton, and with it slavery, became key to the U.S. economy, it also moved to the center of the world economy and its most consequential transformations: the creation of a globally interconnected economy, the Industrial Revolution, the rapid spread of capitalist social relations in many parts of the world. To understand capitalism's relationship to slavery, we need to see the control of cultivators in Africa over their land and labor, as well as the transformations of the Indian countryside, the institutional structures of capitalism in Britain, and the state structures of Egypt." We can thus see the comparison between modern America and ancient Egypt and why that ancient kingdom can be seen as merely a metaphor for today's human advancement. Just as Egypt fed upon and evolved based on the energy and resources of the surrounding countryside, the modern colonizers were masters at exploiting every ounce of material resource and human capital. Beckert writes further, "A global perspective allows us to comprehend in new ways how slavery became central to the Industrial Revolution. Europe's ability to industrialize rested at first entirely on the control of expropriated lands and enslaved labor in the Americas."

This industry driven motivation to expand and dominate was inherited by the new Americans and influenced their own concept of Manifest Destiny. This concept, prevalent during the 19th century period of American expansion, held that the United States not only could, but was destined to stretch from coast to coast. This attitude helped fuel western settlement, Native American removal, and war with Mexico. *www.history.com/topics/manifest-destiny.* These early settlers saw a divine obligation to exhaust the full geography and potential of the new land and the new experimental democracy. Why is it so hard for African Americans to see themselves with a similar divine obligation-a similar destiny to advance the cause of humanity here in America?

"A spirit of nationalism that swept the nation in the next two decades, after the War of 1812, demanded more territory. The 'every man is equal' mentality of the Jacksonian Era fueled this optimism." *http://www.ushistory.org/us/29.asp* Why shouldn't our struggle for true, every-man equality, fuel a similar optimism for social and ethical advancement of the nation? Despite their ulterior economic motives and their essential belief in American cultural and racial superiority, early Americans still advanced. How much more could we advance with pure motives and a sincere belief in G-d and divine mission?

12:110 (Respite will be granted) until, when the messengers give up hope (of their people) and (come to) think that they were treated as liars, there reaches them Our help, and those whom We will are delivered into safety. But never will be warded off our punishment from those who are in sin.

Chapter 110

Go Your Way but Don't Deny or Belie the Right Way

America has a vested interest in supporting justice for her former slaves, but I also know that African Americans must overcome the pain, the fear, the doubts, and insecurities of our past experience. I believe that we are chosen for justice and favor in this country. I occasionally talk to Caucasians who ask, "Why don't you all let all of that go. That was 150 years ago; times have changed and we've made progress." I tell my brothers and sisters the same thing when I see them making excuses for their own shortcomings. But to those Caucasians, I say this, "I can forget it when you stop doing it."

Every time a young African-American is killed by the police, I am reminded of the times when killing black men was a Saturday afternoon picnic event. Every time I see images of distressed African Americans, I am reminded of plantation life. Every time I see images of a white Jesus (PBUH) on the cross and see poor dejected African Americans docile and accepting their condition and bowing their heads, it reminds me of the systemic racism that still exists. What Joseph (PBUH) represents is the spirit to rise above whatever circumstances we find ourselves in so there is no excuse for us. There is something inherent in our souls that tell us that justice must be done; that justice will be done. We have seen progress toward social justice, but much work has to be done toward economic justice.

In 2004, the median net worth of white households was $134,280, compared with $13,450 for black households, according to an analysis of Federal Reserve data by the Economic Policy Institute. In 2009, 39.9% of African American households had zero or negative net worth. The median net worth for white households had fallen 24% to $97,860, 44.5 times that of black households; the median black net worth had fallen 83% to $2,200; the lowest ever recorded.[1] Algernon Austin, director of the EPI's Program on Race, Ethnicity, and the Economy, described the wealth gap this way, "In 2009, for every dollar of wealth the average white household had, black households only had two cents." At the end of the recession, the overall unemployment rate had fallen from 9.4 to 9.1%, while the black unemployment rate had risen from 14.7 to 16.2%, according to the Department of Labor.

"History is going to say that the black middle class was decimated over the past few years," says Maya Wiley, director of the Center for Social Inclusion. In August 2011, the black homeownership rate was 45%, compared with 74% for whites. Nearly 8% of African Americans who bought homes from 2005-2008 have lost them to foreclosure, compared with 4.5% of whites, according to an estimate by the Center for Responsible Lending. Despite all of this African Americans, more than any other group, have kept faith. We have believed in the American dream. We have believed that we would be delivered into safety. We have remained optimistic despite the fear mongering, complaining, pessimism and mean spirit of many other Americans.

Of course, conditions have improved considerably since those numbers chronicled this country's Greatest Recession since the Great Depression. And many are unwilling to give credit to President Obama and his policies for this turnaround, but here are the numbers compared to the same indicators in 2009:

As of March 17, 2016, the DOW was 17,481 compared to 6,626. The S&P 500 (Standard & Poor's) was 2,040 compared to 683. Unemployment was 4.9% compared to 10%. Uninsured Adults were 11.8% compared to 18%. The number of American Cars Sold was 15.5 million compared to 10.4 million. The Deficit, as a percentage of GDP (Gross Domestic Product), was 2.8% compared to 9.8%. Consumer Confidence was at 92.2 compared to 37.7. It's clear to me that President Obama, in many areas, has performed in the same role for America as Joseph (PBUH) did for Egypt. He is the leader of a new generation of leaders. I think that is one reason why the so-called conservatives who have tried to undermine his leadership for over 7 years, have kept the belief alive that the President is a Muslim. One poll in November 2015 showed that 43 percent of Republicans think Obama is Muslim, compared with 15 percent of Democrats and 29 percent of independents. What they are playing on is that he is different. We know he is Christian, but he is also different from many extreme fundamentalist Christians. And he is different from many African Americans. He is a model of a new independent thinking.

Imam W. Deen Mohammed, pictured seated front left, next to friend, Khalil El-Khalil, U.S. Senator Alan Dixon, U.S. Senator Orrin Hatch, (head turned, talking to World Champion, Muhammad Ali, standing. Left of Ali is veteran community member Imam Ilyas Muhammad of Nashville, Tennessee, and seated behind Imam Mohammed is Imam Yahya Abdullah of Dallas, Texas. The occasion is the 1992 visit to Washington, D.C. when Imam Mohammed delivered the fist invocation by a Muslim on the floor of the U.S. Senate.

Rep. Keith Ellison is another leader of this new generation and he is a Muslim. He believes as I do that "America's best days are ahead." To Donald Trump's slogan, "Make America Great Again," I say America is greater than it has ever been. In a blog in the Politics section of the Huffington Post, Rep. Keith Ellison, in a November, 2011 blog entry entitled, "America's Best Days Are Ahead," wrote that yes, "Times are tough. Most Americans are experiencing the greatest financial crisis of their lifetimes and many are still struggling to find work. In times like these, it is easy to despair. Instead of supporting legislation to solve the jobs crisis, right-wing pundits and politicians are encouraging this gloom by claiming America is in decline. These critics are cynical and wrong. Great crises have historically forged great leaders, and this one is no exception. We have hope. America remains the greatest country in the world and we inspire millions struggling for freedom around the world in times of crisis, we step up."

What we need now more than anything else is the freedom of independent thinking. That will enable us to choose our life, choose our religion, give good guidance to our families, and take responsibility for our communities.

12:111 There is, in their stories, instruction for men endued with understanding. It is not a tale invented, but a confirmation of what went before it, a detailed exposition of all things, and a guide and a mercy to any such as believe.

Chapter 111

There is a History in All Men's Lives

"There is a history in all men's lives." William Shakespeare, 1564–1616 (Henry IV). This story of Joseph (PBUH) mirrors the many stories of the prophets and messengers and the lessons that can be gained if we are blessed with understanding. These stories are in scripture because they are the stories of nations and the stories of men lives.

Imam Mohammed (RAA) described the mystical teachings and lessons of W. D. Fard as satire. Satire is a literary mode that blends criticism with wit and humor in an effort to improve society. It seeks to expose the folly of its subjects, which may be individuals, institutions or states. The satirist challenges accepted social ideas or conventions by making them seem ridiculous; not simply to mock or degrade the subject but instead, to show the reader (or audience) that subject's hypocrisy or vice. This exposure is meant to encourage change, to improve society morally or restore a moral order that society has abandoned. Didn't W. D. Fard's teachings accomplish exactly those goals? We found ourselves in the 1930s living in the Jim Crow successor to chattel slavery. Lynching reached genocidal proportions and the segregated Jewish ghettos of Europe paled in comparison to our conditions here. And yet, this nation claimed the mantle throughout the world as enlightened and as the examples of humanity. What hypocrisy!

Until only recently, the most common image that was presented and seen in idols, images, and statues of the Divine was the blond-haired, blue-eyed Jesus. The story of the slave, Julia, was told over 100 years ago in a book called *The People Who Walk In Darkness Have Seen A Great Light*, a title borrowed from scripture, Isaiah 9:2 and Matthew 4:16, by a German writer. She indicted the white slave masters of the Christian church with her statement, "You look like God in the face, but act like the devil in your hearts." Frederick Douglass also said, "You claim the religion of Christ, to be Christ like, and you claim to be the teachers of Democracy for the whole world, but your behavior is such that would shame a nation of savages." Fard, likewise, pointed out the evils of this view of racial superiority and challenged the inordinate love of an oppressor and inherent hatred of black self. Perhaps our modern day psychologists may have a kinder description of that dysfunction, but in lay terms you would have to say, how ridiculous! Fard's work included all the characteristics of typical satire: Ridicule and anger, irony, exaggeration, comedy, and wit. It should embarrass us today to still take these exaggerations literally.

Conclusion

Yes, everyone has a story and I am urging my readers not just to value their own story but also the story of their brothers. Of course doing that requires a certain level of consciousness. It requires a human sensibility and a human sensitivity that we all start out with as infants. Jesus (PBUH) said we have to become as little children to enter Heaven and I see this to mean we have to go back to that innocence and common sense that we are all born with as the babies. We have to have a conscience and live consciously.

Consciousness is the 5th level or plane of expression for the human being. When the child is born, the doctor strikes it into consciousness, and the mother examines its 'five'-fingers and toes. She waits anxiously to see it respond with its five senses. The doctor will tell her that it will take some time for the baby to develop its vision. After all, it has been in the dark environment of the womb for nine months. Communities evolve the same way. Ten represents a higher expression of the five senses, the ability to record our expressions, so the child begins to remember its mother's teaching and respond. We have all labored under the burden of corrupt scripture and doctrine and this has deprived us of the expression of our senses. We all yearn for the security of our mothers' womb as the mournful spirituals of our ancestors refrained, (*'sometimes I feel like a motherless child'*). But we must evolve beyond the confining wombs of skin color, of dependency, and of ignorance. Even mother Africa is now too narrow and restrictive for us. A higher plane, so to speak, is needed or in the language of the Nation of Islam, a *mother plane.* All it takes is a slight adjustment in our perception of 'mother plane' from a mother airplane to a mother plane of expression or plane of social consciousness. That plane represents a transition from one rule to another. We know the expression of how hard it is to turn a battleship around in the other direction. The lessons of W. D. Fard taught that the mother plane moved in any direction instantaneously and could turn on a dime. Some followers would not make the transition but all some of us did to make the transition was to pivot.

The members of the Nation of Islam were promised that the Mahdi would come, the "long-awaited Messiah." *Masih* or messiah means one anointed with wisdom and it is merely a man that has been educated by the Qur'an and inspired by G-d. Imam Mohammed (RAA) did not like the term messiah applied to himself[1] and he avoided any accouterments that might result in personality worship. The return of a messiah like David (PBUH) merely means the return of an unshakeable truth that can withstand any powers of the existing order. His role in this day is to reconcile the separation of Prophet Jesus (PBUH) from Prophet Mohammed (PBUH), as Prophet Muhammad (PBUH) saw that in this Last Day, the people would see him and the Prophet Jesus (PBUH) together. That is the return of Islam in its pure state and this community of indigenous African American Muslims has been blessed to receive the seed of that revival in Imam Mohammed (RAA).[2]

Imam Mohammed (RAA) did acknowledge himself as a Mujeddid (Reviver) and we should not be afraid of acknowledging him as such. The Prophet Muhammed (PBUH) told us that at the beginning of every 100 years, conditions would produce someone to revive the religion. Imam Mohammed also described himself as the Mahdi. The *Mahdi* is a person that is established upon the *huda* or guidance from the Qur'an and when it is received by him he is capable of giving it to the people. There is no mystery that this person should emerge from the community of African Americans.

Jesus (PBUH) and his mother are both signs of this community of indigenous African American Muslims. The picture of Jesus (PBUH) in the cradle is the picture of every child that is born with the original nature that guides us when we do not have revelation from Allah. As Prophet Abraham (PBUH) told the Pharaoh, "The one who created me will guide me." That nature grows in moral and intellectual knowledge. And Jesus' (PBUH) mother, Mary, was a community that remained pure and untouched, not influenced by man's understanding until it produced one in whom that morality and intellect would be 'crystallized.' For centuries, we as a community, similarly, did not know anything and no one tried to teach us anything. Because of its obedience, G-d blessed it with the word that was personified as Jesus (PBUH), as the Qur'an says Jesus (PBUH) was a sign and a spirit.

Instead of this enlightened understanding of the Prophet Jesus (PBUH), the ruling order has presented to the world the image of a savior in white flesh and other well-intentioned leaders have tried to solve that problem by changing the representation to black flesh. The true sign of Jesus (PBUH) is that of a crucified and then resurrected community. Though they may try to get the Christian church leadership and government to see Israel in a divine image,[3] there will be no European or other individual that will emerge from the state of Israel or anywhere else as a savior.

Some people cannot understand why G-d would allow African Americans to have been separated from their families, their continent, their culture, their language, and their religion and work under forced labor for 400 years, building America's institutions and economy. Then we see the condition of our communities today, and the cries for social and economic equality and ask, "Where's the justice?" G-d is obligated and that is where we have to look for the solution. G-d has conditioned this people over generations, from ancient times until now and strengthened us to carry a Divine mission. Part of that mission is respecting leadership in our lives, first of all in ourselves, obeying the best self within us and best traditions, which our ancestors tried to pass down to us. It means respecting the leadership of our aspirations-those who advanced those G-d inspired goals for us.[4]

I have referenced the Qur'an extensively in this book because it is a Book of guidance to mankind as long as he exists on the earth. I have also referenced Imam W. Deen Mohammed (RAA) extensively and have tried to faithfully represent his language and his interpretation of scripture. He would never allow himself to be seen as a savior or divine figure and, in fact, his mission was to eliminate personality worship. He wanted more so for us to respect the body of knowledge that he represents. But we must respect him as the recipient of this weighty message to mankind. The dreams, hopes and aspirations of any community can be manifested in one man.[5] We must be respected as a community if we are to carry the message from G-d that will solve the problems of the world. What the world needs is religion in its purity and that is what we have been blessed with. Islam began with the poor, the common people and it shall return to the poor.[6] I pray that the reader will see all of us in that light and in the light of this most beautiful story of the Prophet Joseph (PBUH). We all face limiting circumstances in our lives but none of them can contain us except those which we impose on ourselves. That is the promise of G-d and that is our message to the world.

Endnotes

Chapter 1

1 Imam Salim Mu'min, another student of Imam Mohammed (RAA) and founder of Muslim American Logic Institute, (M.A.L.I.), a Qur'anic study and research group recalled similar advice from Imam Mohammed (RAA). In encouraging Mu'min to learn Arabic and to stop reading the Qur'an translations, he told him: "Look at what others say; look at what I say. Then say what you have to say."

2 *On the earth are signs for those of assured Faith, As also in your own selves: Will ye not then see? Holy Qur'an, 51:20-21*

Chapter 2

1 Hazrat Murza Ghulam Ahmed, *Arabic-the Mother of all Languages.* https://www.alislam.org/topics/arabic/ . Accessed May 5, 2016

2 *We have made it a Qur'an in Arabic, that ye may be able to understand (and learn wisdom). Holy Qur'an, 43:3*

3 *In the perspicuous Arabic tongue. Holy Qur'an, 26:195*

4 *Had We revealed it to any of the non-Arabs, Holy Qur'an,26:198*

5 *We have not instructed the (Prophet) in Poetry, nor is it meet for him: this is no less than a Message and a Qur'an making things clear: Holy Qur'an, 36:69*

6 *"O our Lord! I have made some of my offspring to dwell in a valley without cultivation, by Thy Sacred House; in order, O our Lord, that they may establish regular Prayer: so fill the hearts of some among men with love towards them, and feed them with fruits: so that they may give thanks. Holy Qur'an, 14:37*

7 *Or do they say, "He has forged it"? Nay, it is the Truth from thy Lord, that thou mayest admonish a people to whom no warner has come before thee: in order that they may receive guidance. Holy Qur'an, 32:3*

8 "Howbeit when he, the Spirit of truth, is come, he will guide you into all truth: for he shall not speak of himself; but whatsoever he shall hear, that shall he

speak: and he will show you things to come." Bible, John 16:1, King James Version

9 "I have also seen children successfully surmounting the effects of an evil inheritance. That is due to purity being an inherent attribute of the soul." Gandhi, Mahatma

10 *Had We sent this as a Qur'an (in the language) other than Arabic, they would have said: "Why are not its verses explained in detail? What! (a Book) not in Arabic and (a Messenger) an Arab?" Say: "It is a Guide and a Healing to those who believe; and for those who believe not, there is a deafness in their ears, and it is blindness in their (eyes): They are (as it were) being called from a place far distant! "Holy Qur'an, 41:44*

11 Ayesha (RAA) said, the Prophet was the Qur'an living. Hadith

Chapter 3

1 *He it is Who has sent down to thee the Book: In it are verses basic or fundamental (of established meaning); they are the foundation of the Book: others are allegorical. But those in whose hearts is perversity follow the part thereof that is allegorical, seeking discord, and searching for its hidden meanings, but no one knows its hidden meanings except Allah. And those who are firmly grounded in knowledge say: "We believe in the Book; the whole of it is from our Lord:" and none will grasp the Message except men of understanding. Holy Qur'an 3:7*

Chapter 4

1 She named him Joseph, and said, "May the LORD add to me another son." Genesis 30:24, New International Version 1984

2 6583. Abu Salama heard Abu Qatada say that the Prophet, may Allah bless him and grant him peace, said, "The true dream is from Allah and the bad dream (*hulm*) is from Shaytan." *Al-Bukhari*

3 6589. Sa'id ibn al-Musayyab related that Abu Hurayra said, "I heard the Messenger of Allah, may Allah bless him and grant him peace, say, 'Only good signs remains of prophethood.' They asked, 'What are good signs?' He answered, 'The true dream.'" *Al-Bukhari*

4 "This beautiful piece of art work is also an effect, not a cause with no cause preceding it, but it itself is an effect, because it is conforming to something. What is it conforming to scientifically speaking? It is conforming to the nature of its own existence." W. Deen Mohammed (RAA).

5 *6:75 So also did We show Abraham the power and the laws of the heavens and the earth, that he might (with understanding) have certitude.*

6:76 When the night covered him over, He PBUH a star: He said: "This is my Lord." But when it set, He said: "I love not those that set."

6:77 When he PBUH the moon rising in splendour, he said: "This is my Lord." But when the moon set, He said: "unless my Lord guide me, I shall surely be among those who go astray."

6:78 When he PBUH the sun rising in splendour, he said: "This is my Lord; this is the greatest (of all)." But when the sun set, he said: "O my people! I am indeed free from your (guilt) of giving partners to Allah.

6:79 "For me, I have set my face, firmly and truly, towards Him Who created the heavens and the earth, and never shall I give partners to Allah."

6 *41:37 Among His Signs are the Night and the Day, and the Sun and the Moon. Prostrate not to the sun and the moon, but prostrate to Allah, Who created them, if it is Him ye wish to serve.*

7 *23:13 Then We placed him as (a drop of) sperm in a place of rest, firmly fixed;*

23:14 Then We made the sperm into a clot of congealed blood; then of that clot We made a (foetus) lump; then we made out of that lump bones and clothed the bones with flesh; then we developed out of it another creature. So blessed be Allah, the best to create!

8 "And G'd teach us through Mohammed that for us there is a like number in us, in other words, whatever is in this ascension is also in your potential, it is also a human possession, it's also in you. That you have in your creation also the potential to arise or ascend to these levels of human excellence. So this light is not the light of Revelation this is the light of human nature, not the light of Revelation. So these men in their bodies agreeing with the nature G'd created, became light. So Mohammed in his Uswa he's a light in his Uswa before he was called to be a messenger of G'd, and the seal of the Prophet, he was already a light in his Uswaa in his balanced life Uswaa. In his balanced life that G'd intended for him, he was a walking light, a star a brilliant star in the world of humanity then G'd gave him the Qur'an, the guidance for that light that was so perfect in the world. He never worshiped idols, he never did wrong by people, he was a perfect man, never you read in the Qur'an and we're going to purify you, cleanse you of your sins he had no sins, G'd only say we're going to take the burden off your back and we're gonna teach you so you will know. G'd doesn't say we're gonna clean you up, he needed no cleaning up just like Abraham, these men were perfect in their lives. So they are light of the creation that G'd made Himself; His is light, and when you are in the created form G'd made you, your own matter is the light, it's a brilliant star, we can get guidance just from your light, we have light on our feet." Imam W. D. Mohammed (RAA) 1999

9 *So He completed them as seven firmaments in two Days, and He assigned to each heaven its duty and command. And We adorned the lower heaven with lights, and (provided it) with*

guard. Such is the Decree of (Him) the Exalted in Might, Full of Knowledge. Holy Qur'an, 41:12

10 The ascension for the potential in man's creation for his life is Adam, the natural body, with the potential to express the whole scheme of matter. Jesus and John, the spirit from matter, one positive and the other negative, equal in their nature. but one proceeding the other. Joseph, the human psychic, mysteries of the mind, why Joseph was loved in Egypt -the natural properties of human creation. Idris, the knowledge for the human society, the great potential, universal culture of mankind, culture in its innocence......Aaron, the need to take charge of five, your five senses or you could be subject to error/a bad trip, a bad errand. Also logical connection, bones......Moses--the teacher of logic for the intellect, but for a particular situation......Abraham, representing the focus for keeping the whole knowledge, preserving the knowledge for the whole world, man's mind impregnating matter universally. Now Prophet Mohammed (PBUH), upon that knowledge-on 8 -body lead all the others in prayer. With that 7 elevations, 7 planes. The power in us to rise up to our excellence. With those 7, the Prophet being the eighth, Allah swt saying that 8 has to be established down on earth, and the Prophet did that, in the City of light, Medina a model, a prototype for all times. Imam W. D. Mohammed (RAA) 1999 Ramadan Session

11 The Night Journey- Al-Mi'raaj Volume 5, Book 58, Number 227 Sahih Bukhari, Sahih Muslim, Ibn Majah, Abu Dawud, and At-Tirmidhi

12 Genesis 2

1 Thus the heavens and the earth were completed in all their vast array.

2 By the seventh day God had finished the work he had been doing; so on the seventh day he rested from all his work. Bible

13 "These seven represent the individual. But there are also seven tracts above you. And who is above the individual? It is society. The seven tracts above represent society. This means that the evolution of society is above or more important than the evolution of the individual. Yet we need the evolution of the individual to bring about the evolution of society. But once society evolves, the individual should live in society, not in his own little private world. Society is above the individual. The individual's head is his heaven or leadership. In society, heaven is the leadership. In scripture, heaven means leadership. The Bible says, "G-d shall bring in a new heaven" meaning that He shall replace the "Old world leadership." It says that He shall bring in a new heaven and a new earth. Earth represents the ignorant people, the people who have not evolved. New leadership will bring a new earth. It will nourish and cultivate the good life of the people who are on the bottom so that they will become productive

and grow food for civilization. The first development is Adam, The second is Christ Jesus and John. The third is Joseph, fourth is Idris (Enoch), five is Harun (Aaron), six is Musa, (Moses) and seven is Abraham. We are not talking about persons, we are talking about concepts personified." W. Deen Mohammed, (RAA) 2-5-1978

14 *And He taught Adam the names of all things; then He placed them before the angels, and said: "Tell me the names of these if ye are right." Holy Qur'an, 2:31*

15 *Man We did create from a quintessence (of clay). Holy Qur'an, 23:12*

16 *95:1 By the Fig and the Olive,*

95:2 And the Mount of Sinai,

95:3 And this City of security,-

95:4 ***We have indeed created man in the best of moulds,***

95:5 Then do We abase him (to be) the lowest of the low,-

95:6 Except such as believe and do righteous deeds: For they shall have a reward unfailing.

95:7 Then what can, after this, contradict thee, as to the judgment (to come)?

95:8 Is not Allah the wisest of judges?

17 The Qur'an is saying that the freedom to think is an excellent mold in which Allah has created you. (That is saying) that the Bible is wrong. Not 'cursed be the **fig** tree, that it wither up and bear no more fruit'?" The Qur'an is saying, no — that's not right. The Qur'an is saying...Allah has created that as an excellent mold for human progress. It is a necessary step in the progression of the intellect, to take the mind from **figment** of imagination to truth and reality. Imam W. Deen Mohammed (RAA)

18 *http://www.officeport.com/edu/blooms.htm*

19 *Holy Qur'an, Sura 84, Inshiqaq, or the Rending Asunder*

6. O thou man! Verily thou art ever toiling on towards the Lord—painfully toiling— but though shalt meet Him

16. So I do call to witness the ruddy glow of sunset;

17. The Night and its homing

18. And the moon in her fullness;

19. Ye shall surely travel from stage to stage

Chapter 5

1 Genesis Chapter 4:*4* : And Abel, he also brought of the firstlings of his flock and of the fat thereof. And the LORD had respect unto Abel and to his offering:*5:* But unto Cain and to his offering he had not respect. And Cain was very wroth, and his countenance fell.*6:* And the LORD said unto Cain, Why art thou wroth? and why is thy countenance fallen?*7:* If thou doest well, shalt thou not be accepted? and if thou doest not well, sin lieth at the door. And unto thee shall be his desire, and thou shalt rule over him.*8:* And Cain talked with Abel his brother: and it came to pass, when they were in the field, that Cain rose up against Abel his brother, and slew him.

2 *"Behold, thy Lord said to the angels: "I will create a vicegerent on earth." They said: "Wilt Thou place therein one who will make mischief therein and shed blood?- whilst we do celebrate Thy praises and glorify Thy holy (name)?" He said: "I know what ye know not." Holy Qur'an 2:30*

3 Genesis 3:1...the serpent was more subtle than any beast of the field which the LORD God had made. Bible

4 *O ye Children of Adam! Let not Satan seduce you, in the same manner as He got your parents out of the Garden, stripping them of their raiment, to expose their shame: for he and his tribe watch you from a position where ye cannot see them: We made the evil ones friends (only) to those without faith. Holy Qur'an 7:27*

5 *The Evil one threatens you with poverty and bids you to conduct unseemly. Allah promiseth you His forgiveness and bounties. And Allah careth for all and He knoweth all things. Holy Qur'an, 2:268*

6 *Holy Qur'an 53:39 That man can have nothing but what he strives for;*

53:40 That (the fruit of) his striving will soon come in sight:

7 6584. 'Abdullah ibn Khabbab related that Abu Sa'id al-Khudri heard the Prophet, may Allah bless him and grant him peace, say, "When one of you sees a dream that he likes, it is from Allah and so he should praise Allah and talk about it. When he sees other, that which he dislikes, it is from Shaytan and he should seek refuge from its evil and not mention it to anyone. It will not harm him." Al-Bukhari

8 *Holy Qur'an*

5:22 They said: "O Moses! In this land are a people of exceeding strength: Never shall we enter it until they leave it: if (once) they leave, then shall we enter."

5:23 (But) among (their) Allah-fearing men were two on whom Allah had bestowed His grace: They said: "Assault them at the (proper) Gate: when once ye are in, victory will be yours; But on Allah put your trust if ye have faith."

Chapter 6

1 *The same religion has He established for you as that which He enjoined on Noah - the which We have sent by inspiration to thee - and that which We enjoined on Abraham, Moses, and Jesus: Namely, that ye should remain steadfast in religion, and make no divisions therein: to those who worship other things than Allah, hard is the (way) to which thou callest them. Allah chooses to Himself those whom He pleases, and guides to Himself those who turn (to Him). Holy Qur'an, 42:13.*

For God said to Moses, "I will show mercy to anyone I choose, and I will show compassion to anyone I choose." Romans 9:15, New Living Translation (©2007)

2 *And Pharaoh proclaimed among his people, saying: "O my people! Does not the dominion of Egypt belong to me, (witness) these streams flowing underneath my (palace)? What! see ye not then? Holy Qur'an, 43:51*

3 From *Nahara:* to cause stream to flow; flow abundantly, *Dictionary of the Holy Qur'an*, Abdul Mannan Omar

Cairo is from Qahara, meaning to overwhelm their senses. They have to keep their knowledge up and it goes back to ancient Egypt, in their myth they have their secret knowledge, their secret sciences. And in the myth of Egypt, Qahara is a word that means to overwhelm the senses, to subdue the senses, and make the senses helpless to perceive or deal with Qahara. And Qahar is the name of the capital of Egypt. W. Deen Mohammed (RAA)

4 *Pharaoh said: "O Chiefs! no god do I know for you but myself: therefore, O Haman! light me a (kiln to bake bricks) out of clay, and build me a lofty palace, that I may mount up to the god of Moses: but as far as I am concerned, I think (Moses) is a liar!" Holy Qur'an, 28:38*

5 And Isaac digged again the wells of water, which they had digged in the days of Abraham his father; for the Philistines had stopped them after the death of Abraham: and he called their names after the names by which his father had called them. Genesis 26:18, King James Version

6 10 When Jacob saw Rachel daughter of his uncle Laban, and Laban's sheep, he went over and rolled the stone away from the mouth of the well and watered his uncle's sheep. 11 Then Jacob kissed Rachel and began to weep aloud. 12 He had told Rachel that he was a relative of her father and a son of Rebekah. So she ran and told her father. 13 As soon as Laban heard the news about Jacob, his sister's son, he hurried to meet him. He embraced him and kissed him and brought him to his home, and there Jacob told him all these things. Genesis 29:10-13, King James Version

7 *So he began (the search) with their baggage, before (he came to) the baggage of his brother: at length he brought it out of his brother's baggage. Thus did We plan for Joseph. He could not*

take his brother by the law of the king except that Allah willed it (so). We raise to degrees (of wisdom) whom We please: but ***over all endued with knowledge is one, the All-Knowing.*** *Holy Qur'an, 12:76*

8 *He said: "Shall I seek for you a god other than the (true) Allah, when it is Allah Who hath endowed you with gifts above the nations?" Holy Qur'an, 7:14*

Chapter 7

1 Gen 2:10 And a river went out of Eden to water the garden; and from thence it was parted, and became into four heads; 11 The name of the first is Pison: that is it which compasseth the whole land of Havilah, where there is gold; 12 And the gold of that land is good: there is bdellium and the onyx stone. 13 And the name of the second river is Gihon: the same is it that compasseth the whole land of Ethiopia. 14 And the name of the third river is Hiddekel: that is it which goeth toward the east of Assyria. And the fourth river is Euphrates. Gen 2:10-14 (KJV).

He set on the (earth) Mountains standing firm high above it and bestowed blessings on the earth and measured therein all things to give them nourishment in due proportion ***in four Days*** *in accordance with (the needs of) those who seek (sustenance)". Holy Qur'an, 41:10*

2 *When Abraham said: "Show me, Lord, how You will raise the dead," He replied: "Have you no faith?" He said "Yes, but just to reassure my heart." Allah said, "Take four birds, draw them to you, and cut their bodies to pieces. Scatter them over the mountain-tops, then call them back. They will come swiftly to you. Know that Allah is Mighty, Wise." Holy Qur'an 2:260*

3 Four sacred months represent 4 sacred concerns: spiritual, industrial, dialectical and political. Imam W. Deen Mohammed (RAA).

4 "This is our right. We have right to life, we have right to property, we have rights to engage the material world and get the benefits, we have the right to have our aspirations express themselves, we have the right to pursue our appetites or our passions, we have the inherent right to do that. And we have the right to speak from our sensitivity to say what is morally correct and what is morally incorrect. These are the essential features of life, these and the necessary features of life, from these four follow all the other developments. -Imam W. Deen Mohammed (RAA).

5 *(Here is) a Parable of the Garden which the righteous are promised: in it are rivers of water incorruptible; rivers of milk of which the taste never changes; rivers of wine, a joy to those who drink; and rivers of honey pure and clear. In it there are for them all kinds of fruits; and Grace from their Lord. (Can those in such Bliss) be compared to such as shall dwell forever in*

the Fire, and be given, to drink, boiling water, so that it cuts up their bowels (to pieces)? Holy Qur'an 47:15.

6 *The number of months in the sight of Allah is twelve (in a year)- so ordained by Him the day He created the heavens and the earth; of them four are sacred: that is the straight usage. So wrong not yourselves therein, and fight the Pagans all together as they fight you all together. But know that Allah is with those who restrain themselves. Holy Qur'an, 9:36*

7 28 All these are the twelve tribes of Israel, and this is what their father said to them when he blessed them, giving each the blessing appropriate to him. Genesis 48:1-28

8 *(But) among (their) Allah-fearing men were two on whom Allah had bestowed His grace: They said: "Assault them at the (proper) Gate: when once ye are in, victory will be yours; But on Allah put your trust if ye have faith." Holy Qur'an. 5:23*

9 And Reuben said unto them, Shed no blood, *but* cast him into this pit that *is* in the wilderness, and lay no hand upon him; that he might rid him out of their hands, to deliver him to his father again. Genesis 37:22, King James Version

10 *On that account: We ordained for the Children of Israel that if any one slew a person - unless it be for murder or for spreading mischief in the land - it would be as if he slew the whole people: and if any one saved a life, it would be as if he saved the life of the whole people. Then although there came to them Our messengers with clear signs, yet, even after that, many of them continued to commit excesses in the land. Holy Qur'an, 5:32*

11 *We divided them into twelve tribes or nations. We directed Moses by inspiration, when his (thirsty) people asked him for water: "Strike the rock with thy staff": out of it there gushed forth twelve springs: Each group knew its own place for water. We gave them the shade of clouds, and sent down to them manna and quails, (saying): "Eat of the good things We have provided for you": (but they rebelled); to Us they did no harm, but they harmed their own souls. Holy Qur'an 7:160*

12 *Thenceforth were your hearts hardened: They became like a rock and even worse in hardness. For among rocks there are some from which rivers gush forth; others there are which when split asunder send forth water; and others which sink for fear of Allah. And Allah is not unmindful of what ye do. Holy Qur'an 2:74*

13 *But give glad tidings to those who believe and work righteousness, that their portion is Gardens, beneath which rivers flow. Every time they are fed with fruits therefrom, they say: "Why, this is what we were fed with before," for they are given things in similitude; and they have therein companions pure (and holy); and they abide therein (for ever). Holy Qur'an 2:25*

14 *Allah has revealed (from time to time) the most beautiful Message in the form of a Book, consistent with itself, (yet) repeating (its teaching in various aspects): the skins of those who fear their Lord tremble thereat; then their skins and* ***their hearts do soften*** *to the celebration of Allah's praises. Such is the guidance of Allah: He guides therewith whom He pleases, but such as Allah leaves to stray, can have none to guide. Holy Qur'an 39:23*

15 *He set on the (earth), mountains standing firm, high above it, and bestowed blessings on the earth, and measure therein all things to give them nourishment in due proportion, in four Days, in accordance with (the needs of) those who s eek (Sustenance). Holy Qur'an 41:10*

16 *Verily in the heavens and the earth, are Signs for* ***those who believe.*** *45:4 And in the creation of yourselves and the fact that animals are scattered (through the earth), are Signs for* ***those of assured Faith.*** *45:5 And in the alternation of Night and Day, and the fact that Allah sends down Sustenance from the sky, and revives therewith the earth after its death, and in the change of the winds,- are Signs for* ***those that are wise.*** *Holy Qur'an: 45:3*

Chapter 8

1 *Holy Qur'an*

7:11 It is We Who created you and gave you shape; then We bade the angels prostrate to Adam, and they prostrate; not so Iblis; He refused to be of those who prostrate.

7:12 (Allah) said: "What prevented thee from prostrating when I commanded thee?" He said: ***"I am better than he:*** *Thou didst create me from fire, and him from clay."*

2 "We want to make it very clear to you what this mission is all about. We are here to Remake the World, not just the world of mosques, but the World of America and the World outside of America." Imam W. Deen Mohammed (RAA), 1975.

3 As late as 1943, while the Jews of Europe were supposedly being exterminated in the millions, the U.S. Congress proposed to set up a commission to "study" the problem. Rabbi Stephen Wise, who was the principal American spokesperson for Zionism, came to Washington to testify against the rescue bill because it would divert attention from the colonization of Palestine. This is the same Rabbi Wise who, in 1938, in his capacity as leader of the American Jewish Congress, wrote a letter in which he opposed any change in U.S. immigration laws which would enable Jews to find refuge. He stated: "It may interest you to know that some weeks ago the representatives of all the leading Jewish organizations met in conference ... It was decided that no Jewish organization would, at this time, sponsor a bill which would in any way alter the immigration laws."

The Hidden History of Zionism, Ralph Schoenman citing Brenner, Zionism. http://www.marxists.de/middleast/schoenman/ch06.htm

4 "Now go, attack the Amalekites and totally destroy all that belongs to them. Do not spare them; put to death men and women, children and infants, cattle and sheep, camels and donkeys." Samuel 15:3, New International Version.

Chapter 9

1 *Said one who had knowledge of the Book: "I will bring it to thee within the twinkling of an eye!" Then when (Solomon) saw it placed firmly before him, he said: "This is by the Grace of my Lord!- to test me whether I am grateful or ungrateful! and if any is grateful, truly his gratitude is (a gain) for his own soul; but if any is ungrateful, truly my Lord is Free of all Needs, Supreme in Honour !" Holy Qur'an, 27:40*

2 *113:1 Say: I seek refuge with the Lord of the Dawn*

113:2 From the mischief of created things;

113:3 From the mischief of Darkness as it overspreads

113:4 From the mischief of those who practise secret arts;

113:5 And from the mischief of the envious one as he practises envy.

3 *O mankind! We created you from a single (pair) of a male and a female, and made you into nations and tribes, that ye may know each other (not that ye may despise (each other). Verily the most honoured of you in the sight of Allah is (he who is) the most righteous of you. And Allah has full knowledge and is well acquainted (with all things). Holy Qur'an 49:13*

4 *Thus, have We made of you an Ummat justly balanced, that ye might be witnesses over the nations, and the Messenger a witness over yourselves; and We appointed the* ***Qibla*** *to which thou wast used, only to test those who followed the Messenger from those who would turn on their heels (From the Faith). Indeed it was (A change) momentous, except to those guided by Allah. And* ***never would Allah Make your faith of no effect.*** *For Allah is to all people Most surely full of kindness, Most Merciful. Holy Qur'an 2:143*

5 He then added, "I tell you the truth, you shall see heaven open, and the angels of God ascending and descending on the Son of Man." John 1:51 New International Version 1984

6 *"But whosoever turns away from My Message, verily for him is* ***a life narrowed down,*** *and We shall raise him up blind on the Day of Judgment." Holy Qur'an, 20:124*

Chapter 10

1 *On that account: We ordained for the Children of Israel that if any one slew a person - unless it be for murder or for spreading mischief in the land - it would be as if he slew the whole people: and if any one saved a life, it would be as if he saved the life of the whole people. Then although there came to them Our messengers with clear signs, yet, even after that, many of them continued to commit excesses in the land. Holy Qur'an 5:32*

2 *And slay them wherever ye catch them, and turn them out from where they have Turned you out; for tumult and oppression are worse than slaughter; but fight them not at the Sacred Mosque, unless they (first) fight you there; but if they fight you, slay them. Such is the reward of those who suppress faith. Holy Qur'an 2:191*

3 "But his bow abode in strength, and the arms of his hands were made strong by the hands of the mighty God of Jacob; (from thence is the shepherd, the stone of Israel:)" Genesis 49:24, King James Version.

Chapter 11

1 *The son replied: "I will betake myself to some mountain: it will save me from the water." Noah said: "This day nothing can save, from the command of Allah, any but those on whom He hath mercy! "And the waves came between them, and the son was among those overwhelmed in the Flood. Holy Qur'an, 11:43*

2 *We said: "O Adam! dwell thou and thy wife in the Garden; and eat of the bountiful things therein as (where and when) ye will; but approach not this tree, or ye run into harm and transgression." Holy Qur'an, 2:035*

3 *"But if they strive to make thee join in worship with Me things of which thou hast no knowledge obey them not; Yet bear them company in this life with justice (and consideration) and follow the way of those who turn to Me (in love): in the End the return of you all is to Me and I will tell you the truth (and meaning) of all that ye did." Holy Qur'an 31:15*

4 *O ye that believe! betray not the trust of Allah and the Messenger, nor misappropriate knowingly things entrusted to you. Holy Qur'an, 8:27*

Chapter 12

1 *Why should ye not eat of (meats) on which Allah's name hath been pronounced, when He hath explained to you in detail what is forbidden to you - except under compulsion of necessity? But many do mislead (men) by their appetites unchecked by knowledge. Thy Lord knoweth best those who transgress. Holy Qur'an, 6:119*

Allah did curse him, but he said: "I will take of Thy servants a portion Marked off;

"I will mislead them, and I will create in them false desires; I will order them to slit the ears of cattle, and to deface the (fair) nature created by Allah." Whoever, forsaking Allah, takes satan for a friend, hath of a surety suffered a loss that is manifest. Holy Qur'an, 4:118-119

"And his tail swept away a third of the stars of heaven, and threw them to the earth. And the dragon stood before the woman who was about to give birth, so that when she gave birth he might devour her child." Revelation 12:4, New American Standard Bible

Chapter 13

1 Really their situation is even worse than that. They're not only limited to the growth of their scholars of the past. Their disposition will keep them smaller than their scholars of the past, because they put more importance on their

scholars products than they do on the Qur'an, and the sunnah of the Prophet himself. So they are going to stay smaller than their idols and that's their spirit. Their spirit is to make sajda before their idols. Allah didn't say follow them like that. It says follow them upon their excellence. And that's history. That is what makes man evolve." Imam W. D. Mohammed (RAA), Ramadan 1995.

2 And he supplants or comes from underneath our human aspirations. He goes to the root of the aspirations and finds out where it's germinating, then he supplants it. He turns the top in the ground and sticks the roots in the sky so that it will not grow, but die in a false spiritualism...Peter was hung upside down on the cross. Who is Peter? Catholicism. And where did Protestantism come from? Out of Peter. Are you free? No! You are still turned upside down! Imam W. Deen Mohammed (RAA)

Chapter 14

1 "I have read in the Bible where it says the world would come to a deathly state where there is no hope. People in time were trying to trace the problem and they located it in the sanctuary, itself. Pollution had come into the sanctuary, and for that reason the whole society was messed up. That is the sanctuary of your own good self-interest. When that interest becomes polluted, twisted, corrupt, the whole life is eventually lost. We have to keep our own self-interest healthy and in good condition, honest, upright, and respectful of things that should be respected. This applies especially to the value of the human soul that Allah has created. It seems that everything comes into life through the door of self-concern." Imam W. Deen Mohammed (RAA).

2 "Allah blesses human innocence to rise and expand with mind and thought and interest, to feed on the heavens and the earth, to feed on sky and earth. If he feeds on sky and earth with his mind, he is being increased in knowledge, in sensitivities, in human body and what that body can do. He is growing as a person, as though he is now in the womb of mother again. But his womb of mother is the universe, the womb of the cosmos. He is born a cosmos child… This is true by scientific learning and inquiry, but it is also true spiritually. The material principle and spiritual principle always go together. Everything that G-d made materially speaks to what He made for us spiritually, our soul and its nature and how it performs". Imam W. Deen Mohammed (RAA), Washington, D.C. 1-14-2007

Chapter 15

1 "My soul is just crying, I have Elijah's hopes & fire in me, & I have whatever was before him & I have my soul, it's just crying for us to be Adam again & have

faith in your own creation, not just faith in G-d, have faith in your own creation. Don't you know faith in Mohammed (saw) means faith in your own creation, because G-d shows that before he spoke to Mohammed, Mohammed was already good enough for G-d as a human being." Imam W. Deen Mohammed (RAA)

2 "We are free to take our minds out of the small confines of our created nature into the nature of energy and matter and just delve into everything that our minds can reach. We can study it, get information from it and have our own lives influenced by what we find." W. D. Mohammed (RAA), 1-14-2007, D.C.

3 "A simple change in language without your recognition that language is changing can cut off the growth of your freedom struggle- stop it dead. Kill it. And allow the wild forces of the enemy to take it over." W. Deen Mohammed (RAA)

4 *Behold! a woman of 'Imran said: "O my Lord! I do dedicate unto Thee what is in my womb for Thy special service: So accept this of me: For Thou hearest and knowest all things." Holy Qur'an, 3:35*

When she was delivered, she said: "O my Lord! Behold! I am delivered of a female child!"- and Allah knew best what she brought forth- "And no wise is the male Like the female. I have named her Mary, and I commend her and her offspring to Thy protection from the Evil One, the Rejected." Holy Qur'an, 3:35

5 "So you are going to follow these sheiks, mufti's, & so called Imam's from around the world, that lock you in a little piss hole & you think you got the real religion, & you won't listen to me. We're not going to worship Imam W. Deen Mohammed, not while I'm around. I won't let you worship me. But you are worshiping those gurus that call themselves sheiks & Imam's that don't know anything, but make slaves. You become their slaves & you think you're in heaven eating halal & brushing your teeth with a stick. Islam wants progress for us, we have to make improvements on that stick..." Imam W. Deen Mohammed (RAA)

6 *O ye who believe! there are indeed many among the priests and anchorites, who in Falsehood devour the substance of men and hinder (them) from the way of Allah. And there are those who bury gold and silver and spend it not in the way of Allah: announce unto them a most grievous penalty- Holy Qur'an, 9:34*

7 http://www.colostate.edu/Orgs/MSA/find_more/iia.html

8 Fatimah Abdul-Tawwab Fanusie, *Fard Muhammad in Historical Context: An Islamic Thread in the American Religious and Cultural Quilt*, Howard University, May 2008.

9 "I was sitting over there with the big boys of Saudi Arabia, in a meeting of the top scholars, and I told them, "There is no way that you all could get me to become a Muslim, if I had not experienced what I experienced in America

under the Hon. Elijah Muhammad. There would be no appeal." Imam W. Deen Mohammed (RAA)

10 "When G'd formed me outside of their vision, outside of their sight and established me in my position before they knew me. Now they know me and respect me should I say "now you led me", I would be the worst fool on this earth; and any of you that would do that knowing me you make yourself the worst fool on earth. You have always had to go to other races to get information, and now Allah has blessed you with someone from your own family, someone from your own lot, your circumstances, He has blessed you with someone from your own lot to have the knowledge so you don't have to stoop or bow or play favorites to anybody." Imam W. Deen Mohammed (RAA), 12/28/1980, 4th Sunday Hookup - Chicago, Ill

11 *There is no moving creature on earth but its sustenance dependeth on Allah: He knoweth the time and place of its definite abode and its temporary deposit: All is in a clear Record. Holy Qur'an 11:6*

Chapter 16

1 *By the Night as it conceals (the light);Holy Qur'an 92:1*

2 *Said an 'Ifrit, of the Jinns: "I will bring it to thee before thou rise from thy council: indeed I have full strength for the purpose, and may be trusted." Holy Qur'an, 27:39*

3 *Even so, in the eyes of most of the pagans, their "partners" made alluring the slaughter of their children, in order to lead them to their own destruction, and cause confusion in their religion. If Allah had willed, they would not have done so: But leave alone them and their inventions. Holy Qur'an 6:137*

When news is brought to one of them, of (the birth of) a female (child), his face darkens, and he is filled with inward grief!

With shame does he hide himself from his people, because of the bad news he has had! Shall he retain it on (sufferance and) contempt, or bury it in the dust? Ah! what an evil (choice) they decide on? Holy Qur'an, 16:58, 16:59

4 *Holy Qur'an*

30:2 The Roman Empire has been defeated-

30:3 In a land close by; but they, (even) after (this) defeat of theirs, will soon be victorious-

5 "Didn't they try to come out with this so-called shroud to prove that Jesus is a Semitic, is a Jew? Yes. They want to tell you that Jesus is a Jew. And for satan, he is a sign of what happened to the Jewish society. They killed the Jewish society They destroyed the Jewish people as a nation. "But we are not dead. We are resurrected. You are worshipping the death, we have the life." That's what they

are telling the Gentile people and you too that believe in them. Say "We have given you our signs, the sign of the fallen Jerusalem. Of the defeated Jerusalem. You worship our death and you wait for us to come back from our death to save you. We (are) already back from our death and we are laughing at you. We are going to save you alright. Salvation that we got planned for you is more fire. We are going to fire your passions up `til you become a drooling beast." That's satan's plan for you all. Yes. So You're waiting for Christ to come back and the Christ that's been given is Anti-Christ. And the one that they have planned to give you as the returned Christ is satan himself." Imam W. Deen Mohammed (RAA)

6 *http://en.wikipedia.org/wiki/Br%27er_Rabbit*

Chapter 17

1 "This is a play on ancient Egypt, (Ham) and the highly developed sciences they had, and how to make the offspring of this once great civilization "Shine" for them...Noah's naked means his culture was gone, his mind was not as skillful as it once was, and he had lost his balance. So the curse on Ham, because of this lost balance, he would be the carriers of water, and wood for his brothers. Meaning they would be used to fire off lust, extreme love in the society, as wood makes a fire. So this was an attempt to rob us of our natural life. To channel all our energies into fun, dancing, singing, etc for their benefit and profit. We, a whole race of people would be used as a scapegoat." Imam W. Deen Mohammed (RAA)

2 *To every people is a term appointed: when their term is reached, not an hour can they cause delay, nor (an hour) can they advance (it in anticipation). Holy Qur'an, 7:34*

3 *"If not Him, ye worship nothing but names which ye have named,- ye and your fathers,- for which Allah hath sent down no authority: the command is for none but Allah: He hath commanded that ye worship none but Him: that is the right religion, but most men understand not...Holy Qur'an, 12:40*

4 "...when the saints go marching in." Title and lyrics of an American gospel song, originated as a Christian hymn, but often performed in other music genres. This song was famously recorded on May 13, 1938 by Louis Armstrong and his Orchestra.

Chapter 18

1 "The frog is a Creature that must be metamorphized. The frog is born as a little fish-looking thing in the water with gills. He developed gills — something that enables him to live in a world he's not destined for. As Jesus said, "It is expedient that I go away. For if I do not go away the Comforter will not come unto you."

Meaning you will not be metamorphized. "I have taught you how to come out of the water and lose the gills of that small world, but now I have to go. I was only fishing you out." Someone has to come now, behind me, and give you the new generation so that you will develop the lungs and nostrils of a man. That takes a little doing, in fact, that's a Divine work." W. Deen Mohammed (RAA)

2 When the soldiers crucified Jesus, they took his clothes, dividing them into four shares, one for each of them, with the undergarment remaining. This garment was seamless, woven in one piece from top to bottom. John 19:23, New International Version (©1984)

3 The Mysteries of Osiris, Ancient Egyptian Initiation by Dr. R. Swinburne Clymer (1951), p217

4 Charles Larson, *Heroic Ethnocentrism: The Idea of Universality in Literature,* The American Scholar 42(3)(Summer), 1973.

Chapter 19

1 22 And the keeper of the prison committed to Joseph's hand all the prisoners that were in the prison; and whatsoever they did there, he was the doer of it. 23 The keeper of the prison looked not to any thing that was under his hand; because the LORD was with him, and that which he did, the LORD made it to prosper. Gen 39:22-23 (KJV)

2 Thou shalt be over my house, and according unto thy word shall all my people be ruled: only in the throne will I be greater than thou. Gen 41:40 (KJV)

3 Now the next creation it would not just be "Lahma" because "Lahma" does not say skin, skin says sensitivity, "Lahma" does not say skin or sensitivity. So He says, "Thumma ansha'naa khalqan akhar." Meaning the next progression will create the "Bashar" the one who is alive to the needs of his fellow man, alive to the life of his fellow man as he is alive to his own life. And really he becomes more live to his own life when he becomes more humanly sensitive. So this is the "Sayydenaa Bashar" The humanly sensitive person. Imam W. Deen Mohammed (RAA), 11-23-02 Ramadan Session, Fajr Prayer

4 *Those who reject our Signs, We shall soon cast into the Fire: as often as their skins are roasted through, We shall change them for fresh skins, that they may taste the penalty: for Allah is Exalted in Power, Wise. Holy Qur'an 4:56*

5 *Those who sustain the Throne (of Allah) and those around it Sing Glory and Praise to their Lord; believe in Him; and implore Forgiveness for those who believe: "Our Lord! Thy Reach is over all things, in Mercy and Knowledge. Forgive, then, those who turn in Repentance, and follow Thy Path; and preserve them from the Penalty of the Blazing Fire! Holy Qur'an 40:7*

6 "Wasia kul la shayen rahmatan wa ilman." Translated, He has caused everything to communicate, to extend both science and mercy. Imam W. Deen Mohammed (RAA)

Chapter 20

1 Frederick Douglass, September 25, 1883

2 Moliere-French actor and playwright considered the greatest of all writers of French comedy, 1622-1673

3 Thomas Wentworth Higginson, *Army Life in a Black Regiment* (1870).

During the early part of the Civil War, Higginson was a captain in the 51st Massachusetts Infantry. He later became colonel of the First South Carolina Volunteers, the first authorized regiment recruited from freedmen for Union military service, since Secretary of War Edwin M. Stanton required that black regiments be commanded by white officers.

4 What did they say of Bilal; "A worthless person." Do you know that the word Bilal is in the Bible? But it's not pronounced Bilal in the Bible; it's pronounced "Bi-li-al," and the Bible calls it a worthless thing. Look up the name in the dictionary for Bilial; it says a worthless thing. Now, let us look again. Doesn't the society's leadership and their attitude towards us, the common people, say to us we are worthless things? Why do they regard us as worthless things? Because we don't have science; we have it just as a habit; we have it as a training. We don't know how to master or how to chase the epistemological origin of the knowledge we use. We don't have any epistemological conception of the knowledge we use. In other words, we don't have the root of the knowledge we use. And since we don't know the roots of the knowledge we use, those who know the roots laugh at our ignorance and say we should trust them with the affairs of the world. Imam W. Deen Mohammad

5 Psychology came from ancient Egypt to the western world through the Greeks and others. Even today, in their symbolic religion or symbolic wisdom, we find most advanced concepts of the human nature, human soul, human intellect, human passion. They were well informed or well learned on the subject of psychology, the mind, the nature of the mind, the nature of the soul and the spirit. W. Deen Mohammed (RAA), Circumcision of the Mind

6 *The first House (of worship) appointed for men was that at Bakka: Full of blessing and of guidance for all kinds of beings: Holy Qur'an, 3:96*

7 When they deciphered it, they saw that Pharaoh was using Satan's rule for managing the world, monopolizing the human and material resources. And instead of obeying the Makkah disciplines, they took up Egypt's disciplines and

oppressed the world. And when the Jews say that they came out of Egypt, they are telling you that they came out of what the Western man was put into...and that they used Pharaoh's style of rule from satan, for managing & controlling the world. Imam W. Deen Mohammed (RAA)

Chapter 21

1 Sayyid Abul Ala Maududi - *Tafhim al-Qur'an - The Meaning of the Qur'an*

2 *Holy Qur'an*

16:68 And thy Lord taught the Bee to build its cells in hills, on trees, and in (men's) habitations;

16:69 Then to eat of all the produce (of the earth), and find with skill the spacious paths of its Lord: there issues from within their bodies a drink of varying colours, wherein is healing for men: verily in this is a Sign for those who give thought.

3 Lewis Mumford, The City in History, p6.

4 *And remember ye said: "O Moses! we cannot endure one kind of food (always); so beseech thy Lord for us to produce for us of what the earth groweth, -its pot-herbs, and cucumbers, Its garlic, lentils, and onions." He said: "Will ye exchange the better for the worse? Go ye down to any town, and ye shall find what ye want!" They were covered with humiliation and misery; they drew on themselves the wrath of Allah. This because they went on rejecting the Signs of Allah and slaying His Messengers without just cause. This because they rebelled and went on transgressing. Holy Qur'an, 2:61*

5 Ralph Waldo Emerson (1803-1882), U.S. essayist, poet, philosopher. "Manners," Essays, Second Series (1844).

6 Dr. R. Swinburne Clymer, The Mysteries of Osiris, Ancient Egyptian Initiation, (1951), p167

7 *And your creation or your resurrection is in no wise but as an individual soul: for Allah is He Who hears and sees (all things). Holy Qur'an 31:28*

8 "I have been blessed with the wisdom of the ages, because my people deserved it...Don't let others talk you out of your glory, the great blessing Allah(swt) gave to us via the leadership of Imam WD Mohammed." W. Deen Mohammed (RAA)

9 *Waq[a]lati imraatu firAAawna qurratu AAaynin lee walaka l[a] taqtuloohu AAas[a] an yanfaAAan[a] aw nattakhi[th]ahu waladan wahum l[a] yashAAuroon(a)*

The wife of Pharaoh said: "(Here is) joy of the eye, for me and for thee: slay him not. It may be that he will be use to us, or we may adopt him as a son." And they perceived not (what they were doing)! Holy Qur'an 28:9

10 Note 3264, of Sura 34, Saba, Holy Qur'an, Yusuf Ali translation.

11 Abu Muhammad 'Abd al-Malik bin Hisham or Ibn Hisham who edited an earliest the biography of Prophet Muhammad written by Ibn Ishaq.

Chapter 22

1 *We appointed for Moses thirty nights, and completed (the period) with ten (more): thus was completed the term (of communion) with his Lord, forty nights. Holy Qur'an, 7:142*

2 Matthew 25:29, King James Version.

3 Malcolm Gladwell, Outliers

4 So Joshua did as Moses had said to him, and fought with Amalek: and Moses, Aaron, and Hur went up to the top of the hill. 11 And it came to pass, when Moses held up his hand, that Israel prevailed: and when he let down his hand, Amalek prevailed. 12 But Moses' hands were heavy; and they took a stone, and put it under him, and he sat thereon; and Aaron and Hur stayed up his hands, the one on the one side, and the other on the other side; and his hands were steady until the going down of the sun. King James Version.

5 *Holy Qur'an,*

28:34 "And my brother Aaron - He is more eloquent in speech than I: so send him with me as a helper, to confirm (and strengthen) me: for I fear that they may accuse me of falsehood."

28:35 He said: "We will certainly strengthen thy arm through thy brother, and invest you both with authority, so they shall not be able to touch you: with Our Sign shall ye triumph,- you two as well as those who follow you."

6 Dr. Catherine Ponder, The Millionaire Moses: His Prosperity Secrets for You!, 1977

7 *When Moses came back to his people, angry and grieved, he said: "Evil it is that ye have done in my place in my absence: did ye make haste to bring on the judgment of your Lord?" He put down the tablets, seized his brother by (the hair of) his head, and dragged him to him. Aaron said: "Son of my mother! the people did indeed reckon me as naught, and went near to slaying me! Make not the enemies rejoice over my misfortune, nor count thou me amongst the people of sin." Holy Qur'an 7:150*

8 *In whatever business thou mayest be, and whatever portion thou mayest be reciting from the Qur'an,- and whatever deed ye (mankind) may be doing,- We are witnesses thereof when ye are deeply engrossed therein. Nor is hidden from thy Lord (so much as) the weight of an atom on the earth or in heaven. And not the least and not the greatest of these things but are recorded in a clear record. Holy Qur'an, 10:61*

9 Holy Qur'an,

102:1 The mutual rivalry for piling up (the good things of this world) diverts you (from the more serious things),

102:2 Until ye visit the graves. Holy Qur'an

10 *Behold, Moses said to his attendant, "I will not give up until I reach the junction of the two seas or (until) I spend years and years in travel." Holy Qur'an, 18:60*

11 So the sun stood still, and the moon stopped, till the nation avenged itself on its enemies, as it is written in the Book of Jashar. The sun stopped in the middle of the sky and delayed going down about a full day. Joshua 10:13, New International Version (©1984)

Chapter 23

Imam W. Deen Mohammed (RAA)

Chapter 24

1 *Nor come nigh to adultery: for it is a shameful (deed) and an evil, opening the road (to other evils). Holy Qur'an, 17:32*

2 "Though I speak with the tongues of men and of angels, and have not charity, I am become as sounding brass, or a tinkling cymbal." 1 Corinthians 13:1, Webster's Bible Translation

Brass is a metal that can't take a lot of heat. Too much heat destroys the quality of the brass. It becomes I think what they call tinkling brass-dead brass. It becomes dead. Brass rings when it's healthy, when it has its quality. It rings. But if you put too much heat to brass, it will get dark and burnish, and when you strike it, it won't ring. G-d says in the Qur'an that He made man from clay. G-d says to Prophet Muhammad (PBUH) also, 'sounding clay.' One with a ring. Means He made man not only obedient, but He made him expressive... You can tell him something and he can repeat it; give it back to you. You touch him he responds. When the brass becomes dead, it loses it ability to express itself. So Moses was teaching his people: "If you become hot headed, if you stay hot headed and want to get all fired up and argue with me, remember nut, you're brass. Your brain ain't gold, your brain is brass. And the hotter headed you get, the less sense you got. Pretty soon you can't express yourself intelligently, you sound, thump, thump, thump, thump. Don't have the fine quality of expression. You lose your eloquence, you come down to tinkling brass. That's what he was teaching them, and that's what I am teaching you right now. Stop letting your passions burn out the quality of your intelligence." Imam W. Deen Mohammed (RAA)

3 See also where Allah urges the People of the Book to believe before He *"turn them hindwards, or curse them as We cursed the Sabbath-breakers." Holy Qur'an, 4:47*

4 *Holy Qur'an,*

95:4 We have indeed created man in the best of moulds,

95:4 Then do We abase him (to be) the lowest of the low

5 *If it had been Our will, We should have elevated him with Our signs; but he inclined to the earth, and followed his own vain desires. His similitude is that of a dog: if you attack him, he lolls out his tongue, or if you leave him alone, he (still) lolls out his tongue. That is the similitude of those who reject Our signs; So relate the story; perchance they may reflect. Holy Qur'an, 7:176*

6 James Allen, *As A Man Thinketh.* Borders Press/Grange Books. p21.

7 Muslim ibn al-Hajjaj al-Naysaburi, *Sahih Muslim*

Chapter 25

1 "Let us go down and confound their language so they babble and speak no more." Genesis 11:7

2 **Flee** also youthful lusts: but follow righteousness, faith, charity, peace, with them that call on the Lord out of a pure heart. 2 Timothy 2:22 (King James Version)

3 *O ye Children of* ***Adam****! Let not Satan seduce you, in the same manner as He got your parents out of the Garden, stripping them of their raiment, to expose their shame: for he and his tribe watch you from a position where ye cannot see them: We made the evil ones friends (only) to those without faith. Holy Qur'an 7-27*

Chapter 26

1 *And mention in the Book Idris. Verily! He was a man of truth, (and) a prophet. And We raised him to a high station. Holy Qur'an 19: 56-57*

2 Narrated Aisha: The commencement of (the Divine Inspirations to) Allah's Apostle was in the form of true dreams. The Angel came to him and said, "Read! In the Name of your Lord Who has created all (that) exists, has created man from a clot. Read! And your Lord is Most Generous, Who has taught (the writing) by the pen (the first person to write was Prophet Idris. (96.1-4) [From Bukhari]] 6.480:

3 James Gleick, Pantheon/Random House, p31

4 Ibid.

5 James Gleick, Smithsonian Magazine, May 2011, http://www.smithsonianmag.com/arts-culture/what-defines-a-meme-1904778/?no-ist

6 James Gleick, *The Information: A History, a Theory, a Flood*, Pantheon/Random House

7 In the beginning was the Word, and the Word was with God, and the Word was God, John 1:1; Bible, New International Version, 1984.

8 The Word became flesh and made his dwelling among us, John 1:14; Bible, New International Version, 1984.

Chapter 28

1 "In the body of your mother is where you start to get form from something that is no more than milky looking water. And then you start to have form so likewise for your thoughts, your mental interest, your intellectual curiosity, you can't have them up here in heaven...You have to qualify down there in order to be to up here. You are starting up here and you don't have any form yet, you're nothing but watery fluid, praise be to Allah" Imam W. Deen Mohammed (RAA)

2 *And remember, We delivered you from the people of Pharaoh: They set you hard tasks and punishments, slaughtered your sons and let your women-folk live; therein was a tremendous trial from your Lord. Holy Qur'an 2:49*

Chapter 29

1 *And We shall remove from their hearts any lurking sense of injury;- beneath them will be rivers flowing;- and they shall say: "Praise be to Allah, who hath guided us to this (felicity): never could we have found guidance, had it not been for the guidance of Allah: indeed it was the truth, that the messengers of our Lord brought unto us." And they shall hear the cry: "Behold! the garden before you! Ye have been made its inheritors, for your deeds (of righteousness)." Holy Qur'an 7:43*

And We shall remove from their hearts any lurking sense of injury: (they will be) brothers (joyfully) facing each other on thrones (of dignity). Holy Qur'an 15:47

2 17 year old Trayvon Martin was shot and killed by a wanna be police officer and community watch volunteer, George Zimmerman, who chased down Martin and then claimed he feared for his life. He was acquited under Florida's "stand your ground" law. Young Jordan Davis was killed under similar circumstances. Yet in the same state, an African American, Marissa Alexander was sentenced to 20 years in prison for firing a warning shot in self-defense to stop her abusive husband. Her sentenced was appealed but Florida's "killingest Prosecutor", Angela Corey, gears up to retry her. Current statistics show that fifty-four percent of people murdered with a firearm between 2000-2010 were black, even though African Americans make up just thirteen percent of the population in the United States.

Chapter 30

1 Henry The Sixth, Part 2 Act 4, scene 2, 71–78, *William Shakespeare*

2 So every member in your body has been dignified because of the high development of yourself internally. Every creature in creation, every molecule of water, every atom of matter has been dignified by the high development of any single part of creation. If any single part of creation reaches a high peak in worth, in value, or in dignity— all the creation is dignified and all the creation is lifted in value. 04/22/1977 Bilalian News, Imam W. D. Muhammad

3 We have had our original focus taken away from us by the attractions of the world and we don't focus on human life like we used to in the South when we were fearing G-d. We don't focus on family life like we did when we were in the South fearing Allah, fearing G-d. We called him Jesus or whatever you called him. He was the superior, it was the Supernatural. Imam W. Deen Mohammed (RAA), Ramadan Sessions, 2006

Chapter 31

1 On the authority of Abu Dharr Jundub ibn Junadah, and Abu 'Abd-ir-Rahman Mu'adh bin Jabal (may Allah be pleased with them) that the Messenger of Allah (peace and blessing of Allah be upon him) said: "Be conscious of Allah wherever you are. Follow the bad deed with a good one to erase it, and engage others with beautiful character." Related by Tirmidhi

2 *If a suggestion from Satan assail thy (mind), seek refuge with Allah; for He heareth and knoweth (all things). Holy Qur'an, 7:200*

3 "Your beliefs become your thoughts, Your thoughts become your words, Your words become your actions, Your actions become your habits, Your habits become your values, Your values become your destiny." — Mahatma Gandhi

4 But I, when I am lifted up from the earth, will draw all men to myself." John 12:32, New International Version (©1984)

5 *He created the heavens without any pillars that ye can see; He set on the earth mountains standing firm, lest it should shake with you; and He scattered through it beasts of all kinds. We send down rain from the sky, and produce on the earth every kind of noble creature, in pairs. Holy Qur'an, 31:10*

6 *"When I have fashioned him (in due proportion) and breathed into him of My spirit, fall ye down in obeisance unto him." Holy Qur'an, 15:29*

7 *The Jews say: "The Christians have naught (to stand) upon; and the Christians say: "The Jews have naught (To stand) upon." Yet they (Profess to) study the (same) Book. Like unto their word is what those say who know not; but Allah will judge between them in their quarrel on the Day of Judgment, Holy Qur'an, 2:113*

8 ...he poured water into a basin and began to wash his disciples' feet, John 13:5

12 When he had finished washing their feet, he put on his clothes and returned to his place. "Do you understand what I have done for you?" he asked them. 13 "You call me 'Teacher' and 'Lord,' and rightly so, for that is what I am. 14 Now that I, your Lord and Teacher, have washed your feet, you also should wash one another's feet. 15 I have set you an example that you should do as I have done for you. 16 Very truly I tell you, no servant is greater than his master, nor is a messenger greater than the one who sent him. 17 Now that you know these things, you will be blessed if you do them. John 13:12-17

Chapter 32

1 When Pilate saw that he was getting nowhere, but that instead an uproar was starting, he took water and washed his hands in front of the crowd. "I am innocent of this man's blood," he said. "It is your responsibility!" Matthew 27:24, New International Version

2 The Price of Prisons | Illinois, WHAT INCARCERATION COSTS TAXPAYERS, FACT SHEET, JANUARY 2012

3 The poor economic condition of the African American race is a moral problem. If we were morally strong, we could do more with our dollars. We wouldn't be on welfare in the numbers that we are, or confined in prisons in such large numbers. You may say, "I don't want to hear any religious talk." Well you need religion more than you need an economist. And I'm not talking about a Jesus to come and work some miracles. You need some good common sense talk to enable you to see that moral life is the base of other life. Humanity is a moral body, and no matter what we are involved in, it depends upon our moral strength. Imam W. Deen Mohammed (RAA)

I went to see Mike Tyson. I had heard he was interested in Islam. The first thing I said to the group of Muslim inmates was, "I greet you brothers, As-Salaam-Alaikum. But I don't feel comfortable greeting you in this situation. Muslims should not be in this situation, and that's what I'd like to say to all Muslims in prison. Muslims are not supposed to go to prison. Muslims are supposed to obey God, respect the law of the land and stay out of prison, and that's not a good place for them. W. Deen Mohammed (RAA), Muslim Journal, Question, and Answer session on June 9, 1993, in Forsyth, Georgia.

Chapter 33

1 W. Deen Mohammed (RAA), Muslim Journal, Question, and Answer session on June 9, 1993, in Forsyth, Georgia.

2 *But whosoever turns away from My Message, verily for him is a life narrowed down, and We shall raise him up blind on the Day of Judgment. Holy Qur'an 20:124*

3 *O ye who believe! when ye prepare for prayer, wash your faces, and your hands (and arms) to the elbows; Rub your heads (with water); and (wash) your feet to the ankles. If ye are in a state of ceremonial impurity, bathe your whole body. But if ye are ill, or on a journey, or one of you cometh from offices of nature, or ye have been in contact with women, and ye find no water, then take for yourselves clean sand or earth, and rub therewith your faces and hands,* ***Allah doth not wish to place you in a difficulty, but to make you clean,*** *and to complete his favour to you, that ye may be grateful. Holy Qur'an, 5:6*

4 "I want to say to you brothers, you have been conditioned by trouble & mistreatment & bad things in the world to lose your original life history as a people & that means as individuals too. G'd has allowed that to happen so that He will make a new people from the beginning. So don't look back at your trouble anymore & see it as a bad thing that happened only, see bad people, but see G'd using bad people to work His plan, because he wants a to create a new people." Imam W. D. Mohammed (RAA) 4/ 2003.

5 **2**The Lord was with Joseph so that he prospered, and he lived in the house of his Egyptian master. **3**When his master saw that the Lord was with him and that the Lord gave him success in everything he did, Genesis 39:2-3, New International Version

Chapter 34

1 The "Nafsal lawwaamah" is self-accusing, critical of oneself, self critical, putting the blame on self. The verb of that word really means to cast blame. So really you're blaming yourself more than you blame something outside of you. You're blaming yourself all the time. These are characteristics of the soul that are true for everybody.

"Nafsal La ammaru." is the tendency to be in command, to be in charge, the tendency to come from your own self and insisting upon something. It is insisting, it is demanding, taking charge. From the very root of this word, you can get the word amir and amir means one who is in charge, or prince. But, literally, or the real meaning is one in charge, one giving commands, the one who is giving commands, orders. The word or verb, "to order" is "Amara". It means to give an order. To this "La ammarah" is the insisting spirit in the soul and this gets us in trouble. "La", when it is used this way...is an intensifier. It says that this is very strong, in the soul. So Allah (swt) says, ..."this tendency in the soul leads to sin except, the soul that receives G-d's mercy". If it were not for G-d's mercy, we all would be sinners, lost in sin, because we have that tendency to take charge, act independently, insist upon our own way, assert authority, make demands.

These characteristics are with us when we're born and the mothers can tell you more about this than I can. But I have observed little babies, infants, and the mother, too, attending their infants. The little infants come here and they have serenity written all across their face, just as peaceful and tranquil. That is "Mutma'innah." Ramadan sessions 2002 Ramadan in Homewood hotel, Lecturer Imam W. Deen Mohammed (RAA)

2 *"Be ye foremost (in seeking) forgiveness from your Lord and a Garden (of Bliss) the width whereof is as the width of heaven and earth prepared for those who believe in Allah and His apostles: that is the Grace of Allah which He bestows on whom He pleases: and Allah is the Lord of Grace abounding." Holy Qur'an, 57.21*

3 Holy Qur'an,

89:27 (To the righteous soul will be said:) "O (thou) soul, in (complete) rest and satisfaction!

89:28 "Come back thou to thy Lord,- well pleased (thyself), and well-pleasing unto Him!

89:29 "Enter thou, then, among My devotees!

89:30 "Yea, enter thou My Heaven!

Chapter 35

1 Christian Parenti, "Lockdown America: Police and Prisons in the Age of Crisis, Verso, 2000.

2 The Top 10 Most Startling Facts About People of Color and Criminal Justice in the United States, A Look at the Racial Disparities Inherent in Our Nation's Criminal-Justice System, Center for American Progress, https://www.americanprogress.org/issues/race/news/2012/03/13/11351/the-top-10-most-startling-facts-about-people-of-color-and-criminal-justice-in-the-united-states/

3 Chicago Sun-Times, September 22, 2010

4 Donna St. George, Washington Post Staff Writer, Thursday, August 26, 2010.

5 Prophet Muhammed said to one who was asking him how to share himself with this mother and father, both of whom had become old and needed his help: "Help your mother." The man was still waiting for more from the Prophet. The Prophet again said, "Help your mother." And then finally he said, "And help your father." So the emphasis is on the mother, and the mother is symbolic of the collective group, the family, the community, the congregation. Bukhari and Muslim.

Chapter 36

1 *And Allah has produced you from the earth growing (gradually), Holy Qur'an, 71:17*

2 1 All the commandments which I command thee this day shall ye observe to do, that ye may live, and multiply, and go in and possess the land which the LORD sware unto your fathers. 2 And thou shalt remember all the way which the LORD thy God led thee these forty years in the wilderness, to humble thee, and to prove thee, to know what was in thine heart, whether thou wouldest keep his commandments, or no. 3 And he humbled thee, and suffered thee to hunger, and fed thee with manna, which thou knewest not, neither did thy fathers know; that he might make thee know that man doth not live by bread only, but by every word that proceedeth out of the mouth of the LORD doth man live. Old King James Version of the Bible: Deuteronomy 8:1-3

3 Old King James Version of the Bible: Luke 4:1-13 1 And Jesus being full of the Holy Ghost returned from Jordan, and was led by the Spirit into the wilderness, 2 Being forty days tempted of the devil. And in those days he did eat nothing: and when they were ended, he afterward hungered. 3 And the devil said unto him, If thou be the Son of God, command this stone that it be made bread. 4 And Jesus answered him, saying, It is written, That man shall not live by bread alone, but by every word of God. "Therefore let us keep the feast...with the unleavened bread of sincerity and truth." I Corinthians 5:8

4 *Who originates creation, then repeats it, and who gives you sustenance from heaven and earth? (Can there be another) god besides Allah? Say, "Bring forth your argument, if ye are telling the truth!" Holy Qur'an 27:64*

5 *We have indeed created man in the best of moulds, Holy Qur an, 95:4*

6 *But the chiefs of the Unbelievers among his people said: "We see (in) thee nothing but a man like ourselves: Nor do we see that any follow thee but the meanest among us, in judgment immature: Nor do we see in you (all) any merit above us: in fact we think ye are liars!" Holy Qur'an, 11:27*

7 Abdul Mannan Omar, *Dictionary of the Holy Qur'an*, NOOR Foundation International, Inc.

8 For the thing which I greatly feared is come upon me, and that which I was afraid of is come unto me. Job 3:25, King James Bible

9 The vine is thinking outward. The vine wants to go out, and for going out it gets a heavier proportion of products than the tree that stands in its place. Imam W Deen Mohammed (RAA)

Chapter 37

1 Prophet Muhammad (PBUH) said: "Take benefit of five before five:"

Your **youth** before your **old age**,

Your **health** before your **sickness**,

Your **wealth** before your **poverty**,

Your **free-time** before your **occupation**, and

Your **life** before your **death**."

2 Recorded in the two Sahihs

3 *That it is He Who giveth wealth and satisfaction; Holy Qur'an, 53:48*

4 Deirdre Barrett "Supernormal Stimuli: How Primal Urges Overran Their Evolutionary Purpose," W. W. Norton & Company, February 21, 2010

5 *"I will mislead them, and I will create in them false desires; I will order them to slit the ears of cattle, and to deface the (fair) nature created by Allah." Whoever, forsaking Allah, takes satan for a friend, hath of a surety suffered a loss that is manifest. Holy Qur'an 4:119*

Chapter 38

1 *Allah is He, than Whom there is no other god;- the Sovereign, the Holy One, the Source of Peace (and Perfection), the Guardian of Faith, the Preserver of Safety, the Exalted in Might, the Irresistible, the Supreme: Glory to Allah! (High is He) above the partners they attribute to Him. Holy Qur'an, 59:23*

2 *Lo! Abraham said to his father Azar: "Takest thou idols for gods? For I see thee and thy people in manifest error." Holy Qur'an, 6:74*

3 *And this was the legacy that Abraham left to his sons, and so did Jacob; "Oh my sons! Allah hath chosen the Faith for you; then die not except in the Faith of Islam." Holy Qur'an, 2:132*

4 *Remember Abraham said: "O my Lord! make this city one of peace and security: and preserve me and my sons from worshipping idols. Holy Qur'an, 14:35*

And remember that Abraham was tried by his Lord with certain commands, which he fulfilled: He said: "I will make thee an Imam to the Nations." He pleaded: "And also (Imams) from my offspring!" He answered: "But My Promise is not within the reach of evil-doers." Holy Qur'an, 2:124

5 *(Abraham) said, "Do ye then worship, besides Allah, things that can neither be of any good to you nor do you harm? "Fie upon you, and upon the things that ye worship besides Allah!* ***Have ye no sense?"*** *Holy Qur'an 21:66, 67*

6 *And they set up (idols) as equal to Allah, to mislead (men) from the Path! Say: "Enjoy (your brief power)! But verily ye are making straightway for Hell!" Holy Qur'an, 14:30*

Chapter 39

1 *The Way of Allah, to Whom belongs whatever is in the heavens and whatever is on earth. Behold (how) all affairs tend towards Allah! Holy Qur'an, 42:53*

2 Source: Black Elk (1863-1950)

3 *Holy Qur'an*

96:6 Nay, but man doth transgress all bounds,

96:7 In that he looketh upon himself as self-sufficient.

96:8 Verily, to thy Lord is the return (of all).

4 "The fig comes before the olive in our development; the many brings us to recognize the one. This is really logic that you'll find in colleges and universities; you go from generalities to specifics. Even in logic, you go from generalities the many things considered looking for the logic, and you come to the specifics one logic that ties all things together." Imam W. Deen Mohammed (RAA)

Chapter 40

1 *Holy Qur'an*

40:73 Then shall it be said to them: "Where are the (deities) to which ye gave part- worship-

40:74 "In derogation of Allah?" They will reply: "They have left us in the lurch: Nay, we invoked not, of old, anything (that had real existence)." Thus does Allah leave the Unbelievers to stray.

2 *We have enjoined on man kindness to parents: but if they (either of them) strive (to force) thee to join with Me (in worship) anything of which thou hast no knowledge, obey them not. Ye have (all) to return to me, and I will tell you (the truth) of all that ye did. Holy Qur'an, 29:8*

3 syn·cre·tism, noun: the amalgamation or attempted amalgamation of different religions, cultures, or schools of thought.

https://www.google.com/?gws_rd=ssl#q=syncretism+definition

4 *And remember, We delivered you from the people of Pharaoh: They set you hard tasks and punishments, slaughtered your sons and let your women-folk live; therein was a tremendous trial from your Lord. Holy Qur'an 2:49*

5 Animism (from Latin *anima* "soul, life")[1] refers to a set of beliefs that revolve around the existence of non-human spiritual beings" or similar kinds of embodied principles.[2] The core beliefs of animism are held in common by a diverse group of people, primarily the world's remaining "primitive" tribal peoples and many of the living descendants of tribal peoples previously colonized. *http://en.wikipedia.org/wiki/Animism*

6 Indeed, one might say that every significant idea or claim put forward by Afrocentrists today was earlier expressed by him (though as we have seen, many of them also have a much older, more diffuse ancestry). The only real exceptions to this are the wilder, more mystical and more racially exclusivist

assertions made by extreme Afrocentrists. These Diop did not anticipate; for although his work involves many unsustainable claims, his was primarily a career of rational intellectual inquiry. Not only did his writings precede those of the currently high-profile US Afrocentrists, they are in almost every respect superior. Afrocentrism: Mythical Pasts and Imagined Homes, Stephen Howe, p163

7 *Allah is the Light of the heavens and the earth. The Parable of His Light is as if there were a Niche and within it a Lamp: the Lamp enclosed in Glass: the glass as it were a brilliant star: Lit from a blessed Tree, an Olive, neither of the east nor of the west,* ***whose oil is well-nigh luminous, though fire scarce touched it:*** *Light upon Light! Allah doth guide whom He will to His Light: Allah doth set forth Parables for men: and Allah doth know all things. Holy Qur'an, 24:35*

8 Dr. Chancellor Williams, *The Destruction of Black Civilization,* Third World Press. Chicago, 1987

9 **A Message of Concern**--What would happen if people would sit in churches throughout the world for centuries with the image of an African American man as savior of the world before them? What would this do to the mind of the world's children? What would happen to the world's children put under a figure of a particular race presented, pitiable, and in pain "the Savior of all men"?

Qur'an, Surah 3, verse 64: *"Say, Oh people of the Book! Come to common terms as between us and you: that we worship none but G-d, that we associate no partner with Him, that we erect not from among ourselves lords and patrons other than G-d. If then they turn back, say ye 'bear witness that we (at least) are Muslims (bowing to G-d's Will)."* Civilized nations should want that their religions be also civilized. False worship is the worst form of oppression. We are no gods. We are only men, "mortals from the mortals, He (Allah) created." (Qur'an) Imam W. Deen Mohammed (RAA)

10 It is peculiar that coming from an Islamic experience. they would play up primitive experiences in our African past. I'm talking about the so-called educators. They make a point of trying to play up the primitive experience in the African man's past. What would the Germans do if we would search out their past. They were some of the most superstitious and savage people on the earth, but they found the torch of enlightenment and they grew out of their superstition and they began the history of civilization for the German man. Suppose somebody had the power to impose an idea on the Germans and make them think that the best that they have done in the past was done during the time of their wild-man, backwoods, dark region of superstition. That would be awfully cruel. African American students on the college university or high school campuses have been duped. You are being fooled. You are being told

that your past in Africa is primitive religion. Ancestral spirit worship, animism. etcetera. They don't want to tell you that you have had centuries of a history as scientists, even before Prophet Muhammad. But it didn't last too long. It was only a small quarter of the African continent. And then Prophet Muhammad came with the religion and brought about a renaissance, a revival, a renewal of the interest in science. He didn't only awaken and quicken the intellect of the West, Europe, but he also touched the black man's mind in Africa, and brought him back to his scientific pursuits. And the results was Mali, Timbuctoo, Ghana, etcetera, thus the glorious past of us here, Islam, Africa. Who can challenge that? Ain't nobody on earth that can challenge that. And you know it. I am talking to the learned ones here today. So join me and stop fooling our people. Imam W. Deen Muhammad, April13, 1986, Jacob Javits Convention Center, New York, New York.

11 Sherman A. Jackson, *Islam And The Blackamerican: Looking Toward the Third Resurrection,*

Chapter 41

1 New International Version, Luke 23:46

2 *"That they said (in boast), "We killed Christ Jesus the son of Mary, the Messenger of Allah";- but they killed him not, nor crucified him, but so it was made to appear to them, and those who differ therein are full of doubts, with no (certain) knowledge, but only conjecture to follow, for of a surety they killed him not:-" Holy Qur'an, 4:157*

3 "We are members in the Body of Christ." Imam W. Deen Mohammed (RAA)

4 The Book is telling us that his followers would be crucified, and they would be crucified because they will be taken off course by the Jahcubite (ungodly Jews); not crucified physically so much, but crucified mentally and given to superstition without any sense...If you want to know what happened to the Christian world, look at what happened to Jesus, because he is a sign of what happened to the Christian world and not to him. Ridiculed and mocked, whipped. Is not that what the Gentiles did to him at first? Then they put him up on a cross, right? The cross has four points. It means nail him to, or put him helplessly under the mercy of his instinctive drives. Make him a helpless servant of material appetite, of his academic search appetite, of his political appetite. Make him helpless under his natural drives, nail him to it. He has no freedom of hand, no freedom of legs. Imam W. Deen Mohammed (RAA)

5 If they fall away, to be brought back to repentance, because to their loss they are crucifying the Son of God all over again and subjecting him to public disgrace. Hebrews 6:6, New International Version 1984)

Christ asks, "Why do you crucify me continually?" That means he was saying I was here on this earth before and you crucified me, not in my body or in my name or in my person, but the same life that G-d gave to save you from sin before, you now crucify that same life today in my body and in my name you are crucifying that same life. So what is that same life? He is the second Adam he's called, it is the life in its original state, in its innocent, pure and upright nature being crucified over and over again. Imam W. Deen Mohammed (RAA)

6 *Holy Qur'an*

16:79 Do they not look at the birds, held poised in the midst of (the air and) the sky? Nothing holds them up but (the power of) Allah. Verily in this are signs for those who believe.

67:19 Do they not observe the birds above them, spreading their wings and folding them in? None can uphold them except (Allah) Most Gracious: Truly (Allah) Most Gracious: Truly it is He that watches over all things.

7 *we bestowed (in the past) Wisdom on Luqman: "Show (thy) gratitude to Allah." Any who is (so) grateful does so to the profit of his own soul: but if any is ungrateful, verily Allah is free of all wants, Worthy of all praise. Holy Qur'an 31:12*

8 *For We assuredly sent amongst every People a messenger, (with the Command), "Serve Allah, and eschew Evil": of the People were some whom Allah guided, and some on whom error became inevitably (established). So travel through the earth, and see what was the end of those who denied (the Truth). Holy Qur'an, 16:36*

And before thee also the messengers We sent were but men, to whom We granted inspiration: if ye realise this not, ask of those who possess the Message. Holy Qur'an, 16:43

9 http://www.phrases.org.uk/meanings/chickens-come-home-to-roost.html

Chapter 42

1 Now, here Joseph has helped one of the inmates. And he told one of the inmates after he had helped him—he said, "When you get to your lord, mention me. Let your lord know the situation that I am in". Showing how cold the world can become, even the best people fail you. These people recognized the goodness in Joseph and they were trying to find a way out of the bad life. And Joseph helped them and when he told him, "now when you get in a good situation, "mention me to your lord". He got in a good situation and forgot to mention to his chief, the boss—that there is a good man down there in prison. Your ladies have put him away for good. He was a good man. Why didn't he put in a word for Joseph? He was so much occupied by his own interest that he couldn't remember the man that helped him, relieved him when he was in this bad situation too. Now, think of ourselves as a people. Don't you know many

of your grand parents, your grand mothers and fathers and relatives-many of them told us to remember them. Say, "Now look! Freedom is going to come one day. Now when you are freed, remember us". But freedom came and we became so much overcome by our own desires to please our own selves right now, immediately, right here—that we forgot them. We should be remembering them to our Lord, to G-d— "O G-d, have mercy on the souls of our ancestors. They were in the dark. They were oppressed. And they wanted to see the day of light. O G-d, forgive them for whatever sins they did and admit them into Your paradise". But instead of remembering them to our Lord, we indulged into foolishness and self destruction—just for a quick thrill. So, that is what we are doing, aren't we?-Pouring wine or crucifying. Imam W. Deen Mohammed (RAA)

2 *"Whoever fears Allah, Allah will find a way out for him (from every difficulty) and He will provide for him from sources that he could never have imagined." Holy Qur'an 65:2-3*

3 "Beware that, when fighting monsters, you yourself do not become a monster... for when you gaze long into the abyss. The abyss gazes also into you." — Friedrich Nietzsche

4 10He saved them from the hand of the foe;

from the hand of the enemy he redeemed them.

11The waters covered their adversaries;

not one of them survived.

12Then they believed his promises and sang his praise.

13But they soon forgot what he had done

and did not wait for his counsel.

14In the desert they gave in to their craving;

in the wasteland they put God to the test.

15So he gave them what they asked for,

but sent a wasting disease upon them

Psalms 106:10-15

Chapter 43

1 *The parable of those who spend their substance in the way of Allah is that of a grain of corn: it groweth seven ears, and each ear Hath a hundred grains. Allah giveth manifold increase to whom He pleaseth: And Allah careth for all and He knoweth all things. Holy Qur'an 2:261*

2 *Those who spend their substance in the cause of Allah, and follow not up their gifts with reminders of their generosity or with injury,-for them their reward is with their Lord: on them shall be no fear, nor shall they grieve. Holy Qur'an 2:262*

3 The popcorn, explains what they have done to the soul of this world. The soul is given the term white. Meaning that the original nature of the soul is innocent. The human soul is born innocent. It's white. The soul is the inmost part, so says their own description of the human soul, the inmost part of the being is his soul. They take the corn, and they pop it under heat and they put animal fat with it. And they feed the heat to it, get it real hot. And put it, lock it up so it can't get out. That right? The popcorn has in its kernel, even though it's dry, a bit of moisture. And that bit of moisture under extreme heat, has to pop out. It has to come out. So you find steam, even though you pop popcorn dry, you wonder where the water came from. Is that right? You pop the corn, it's dry corn. But water comes out too. Because it holds it, it seals the moisture in, the corn kernel. You pop it and there it comes, it pops out. When the popcorn pops out, what color is it? White on the outside. Soul on the outside. Where the knowledge went? Where the color went? Look at the popcorn, the color is on the inside. So they turn you wrong side out, they reverse you, they make you soul people. You're just all soul, and no sense. The soul that G-d put inside to be brought out, is now on the outside with no knowledge. And the knowledge, that's supposed to be outside protecting the soul, is now on the inside and the soul is exposed. That's your popcorn. Imam W. Deen Mohammed (RAA)

Chapter 45

1 Dr. Carolyn Myss, *Anatomy of the Spirit*, p. 135

2 Ibid, p. 67

3 *And pursue not that of which thou hast no knowledge; for every act of hearing, or of seeing or of (feeling in) the heart will be enquired into (on the Day of Reckoning). Holy Qur'an, 17:36*

4 "There is not any one of you except that he has been assigned his companion from among the Jinn and his companion from among the Angels." They the Companions said, "Even you, O Messenger of Allah," He replied "Even me, except that Allah has helped me against the Jinn, so that I am unharmed, and so he orders me to do nothing but good." Prophet Muhammad (PBUH) Hadith - Sahih Muslim Vol. 7, Book 39, Hadith 6757, Narrated Abdullah ibn Mas'ud, similar narration 6759 by 'Aisha, (RAA)

5 Sacks, Oliver (December 1985). *The Man Who Mistook His Wife for a Hat, and Other Clinical Tales.* Summit Books

6 *"In whatever business thou mayest be and whatever portion thou mayest be reciting from the Qur'an and whatever deed ye (mankind) may be doing, We are Witnesses thereof when ye are deeply engrossed therein." Holy Qur'an, 10:61.*

7 *Recite what is sent of the Book by inspiration to thee, and establish regular Prayer: for Prayer restrains from shameful and unjust deeds; and* ***remembrance of Allah is the greatest (thing in life)*** *without doubt. And Allah knows the (deeds) that ye do. Holy Qur'an, 29:45*

Chapter 46

1 1Thus the heavens and the earth were finished, and all the host of them. 2And on the seventh day God ended his work which he had made; and he rested on the seventh day from all his work which he had made. 3And God blessed the seventh day, and sanctified it: because that in it he had rested from all his work which God created and made. Genesis 1-3, King James Bible

2 *And We have bestowed upon thee the Seven Oft-repeated (verses) and the Grand Qur'an. Holy Qur'an, 15:87*

3 http://dictionary.reference.com/browse/kine

4 "The Trinitarian doctrine is a doctrine that takes you out of this world, out of the material world, out of rational understanding up into a false spiritualism, a sky religion. Blue, deceptive. The sky is not blue. The higher you go up there, the more the blue gets black. You can never find the blue. The blue is a deception. It's created by rays of light and it's a deception, and you never find it. So, a sky religion is a religion that ignores community development and concentrates only on spiritual development. They teach you that the spiritual life is all. Say, "I can lose the whole world, but give me Jesus." You remember that song. You can have the whole world, but give me Jesus. This is the sky religion. And you want to go, what, up in the sky. Ohhhh, over yonder "We have it bad now, but when we get over yonder," Where? Up in the sky somewhere. That is where you are going to get all of your blessings, fulfillment of life. Is that right? That ain't nothing new. That is how the ancient wicked pharaoh controlled the masses, and the ***Jahcubite*** discovered it and used it on the world." Imam W. Deen Mohammed (RAA)

5 "So-called Jewish people were in Egypt, and the Book says that they floated Moses down the river to Egypt to pharaoh's palace and his wife took up Moses out of a basket; a basket of small wood; pieces of the burning bush. The burning bush was a frail thing. The basket is made of the burning bush, but no light is in it now. And they float Moses down the river to Egypt for what? This is not the real Moses; this is Moses, the thief. He is going to Egypt to steal their knowledge. What is the proof? They also put pitch on this basket so that no water would come into the basket. Here is a little simple ark, going in to Egypt

and they are going to do to the Egyptians what they did to the society of Noah. In time they are going to reduce Egypt like they reduced Noah, but first they've got to get in. And Moses worked in the palace of pharaoh. He became one of the leaders in his palace. And they drove him out. Why? Because G-d called him." Imam W. Deen Mohammed (RAA)

6 And what does the scripture says? They were ordered to slay, say slaughter, the cow, the sacred cow, and they didn't want to do it, but they did it anyway because they were ordered to do it. Is that right? (It) Says that they did it, but didn't have a mind to do it. This is in the Qur'an. They were ordered to slay the sacred cow. They did it, but they didn't have the mind to do it." 2:71 "Then they offered her in sacrifice, but not with good-will." Meaning that the Jews accepted Moses' command to them that they stop believing in this Trinitarian doctrine that came out of ancient Egypt. They gave it up, but they didn't want to do it and as soon as Moses went away for a while and came back, they were building the golden calf. *(2:92-93)* Is that right? Said, "Well if he don't want us to have Trinitarian doctrine, we see that now that that's weak, but what about the golden one." Imam W. Deen Mohammed (RAA)

7 *Then woe to those who write the Book with their own hands, and then say: "This is from Allah," to traffic with it for miserable price!- Woe to them for what their hands do write, and for the gain they make thereby. Holy Qur'an, 2:79*

Ye People of the Book! Why do ye clothe Truth with falsehood, and conceal the Truth, while ye have knowledge? Holy Qur'an, 3:71

There is among them a section who distort the Book with their tongues: (As they read) you would think it is a part of the Book, but it is no part of the Book; and they say, "That is from Allah," but it is not from Allah: It is they who tell a lie against Allah, and (well) they know it! Holy Qur'an, 3:78

8 Imam W. Deen Muhammad (RAA), A.M. Journal, Muhammad Speaks, March 16, 1984

Chapter 47

1 *Holy Qur'an,*

67:1 Blessed be He in Whose hands is Dominion; and He over all things hath Power;-

67:2 He Who created Death and Life, that He may try which of you is best in deed: and He is the Exalted in Might, Oft- Forgiving;-

67:3 He Who created the seven heavens one above another: No want of proportion wilt thou see in the Creation of (Allah) Most Gracious. So turn thy vision again: seest thou any flaw?

67:4 Again turn thy vision a second time: (thy) vision will come back to thee dull and discomfited, in a state worn out.

2 And ye shall hear of wars and rumours of wars: see that ye be not troubled: for all these things must come to pass, but the end is not yet. King James Bible, Matthew 24:6

3 For ye have the poor with you always, and whensoever ye will ye may do them good: but me ye have not always. King James Bible, Mark 14:7

4 *O ye who believe! Fear Allah, and let every soul look to what (provision) He has sent forth for the morrow. Yea, fearAllah: for Allah is well-acquainted with (all) that ye do. Holy Qur'an, 59:18*

5 *Holy Qur'an,*

18:32 Set forth to them the parable of two men: for one of them We provided two gardens of grape-vines and surrounded them with date palms; in between the two We placed corn-fields.

18:33 Each of those gardens brought forth its produce, and failed not in the least therein: in the midst of them We caused a river to flow.

18:34 (Abundant) was the produce this man had : he said to his companion, in the course of a mutual argument: "more wealth have I than you, and more honour and power in (my following of) men."

18:35 He went into his garden in a state (of mind) unjust to his soul: He said, "I deem not that this will ever perish,

18:36 "Nor do I deem that the Hour (of Judgment) will (ever) come: Even if I am brought back to my Lord, I shall surely find (there) something better in exchange."

18:37 His companion said to him, in the course of the argument with him: "Dost thou deny Him Who created thee out of dust, then out of a sperm-drop, then fashioned thee into a man?

18:38 "But (I think) for my part that He is Allah, My Lord, and none shall I associate with my Lord.

18:39 "Why didst thou not, as thou wentest into thy garden, say: 'Allah's will (be done)! There is no power but with Allah!' If thou dost see me less than thee in wealth and sons,

18:40 "It may be that my Lord will give me something better than thy garden, and that He will send on thy garden thunderbolts (by way of reckoning) from heaven, making it (but) slippery sand!-

18:41 "Or the water of the garden will run off underground so that thou wilt never be able to find it."

18:42 So his fruits (and enjoyment) were encompassed (with ruin), and he remained twisting and turning his hands over what he had spent on his property, which had (now) tumbled to pieces to its very foundations, and he could only say, "Woe is me! Would I had never ascribed partners to my Lord and Cherisher!"

Chapter 48

1 "Can a blind man lead a blind man? Will they not both fall into a pit? A student is not above his teacher, but everyone who is fully trained will be like his teacher."— Luke 6:39-40, New International Version

2 *...And his (Jacob) eyes became white with sorrow, Holy Qur'an, 12:84*

3 "And he (the master) hath committed all that he hath to my hand Genesis 39.8.

There is none greater in this house than I." Genesis 39.9

4 *Praise be to Allah, Who created (out of nothing) the heavens and the earth, Who made the angels, messengers with wings,- two, or three, or four (pairs): He adds to Creation as He pleases: for Allah has power over all things. Holy Qur'an, 35:1*

5 *They ask thee concerning the New Moons. Say: They are but signs to mark fixed periods of time in (the affairs of) men, and for Pilgrimage. It is no virtue if ye enter your houses from the back: It is virtue if ye fear Allah. Enter houses through the proper doors: And fear Allah: That ye may prosper. Holy Qur'an 2:189*

6 Gleich, Information, p148

7 *www.thefreedictionary.com/**devour*** 3. to take in greedily with the senses or intellect: to **devour** a book. 4. to absorb or engross wholly: a mind **devoured** by hatred.

Chapter 49

1 *Holy Qur'an*

94:1 Have We not expanded thee thy breast?-

94:2 And removed from thee thy burden

94:3 The which did gall thy back?-

94:4 And raised high the esteem (in which) thou (art held)?

94:5 So, verily, with every difficulty, there is relief:

94:6 Verily, with every difficulty there is relief.

*94:7 Therefore, **when thou art free (from thine immediate task), still labour hard,***

*94:8 **And to thy Lord turn (all) thy attention.***

2 Faithful religious people discovered that water was a good symbol for the moral and spiritual elements in the human being. They found that water was really composed of the same elements that are found in the air — hydrogen and oxygen. God doesn't want us to remain oxygen in water form always. He wants it to become aggressive, and if you bring those elements into a gas, it becomes aggressive. The wind will move from one side of the world to another. The wind can take the water and carry it to the land that needs it. Imam W. Deen Mohammed (RAA), Radisson Muehlebach Hotel in Kansas City, Mo., June 23, 1979

3 Prophet Muhammad said "No child is born except upon Fitra (as a Muslim). It is his parents who make him a Jew or a Christian or a Polytheist." (Sahih Muslim)

4 *O mankind! reverence your Guardian-Lord, who created you from a single person, created, of like nature, His mate, and from them twain scattered (like seeds) countless men and women;- reverence Allah, through whom ye demand your mutual (rights), and (reverence) the wombs (That bore you): for Allah ever watches over you. Holy Qur'an 4:1*

5 Genesis 39:21 But the Lord was with Joseph, and shewed him mercy, and gave him favour in the sight of the keeper of the prison.

39:22 And the keeper of the prison committed to Joseph's hand all the prisoners that were in the prison; and whatsoever they did there, he was the doer of it.

39:23 The keeper of the prison looked not to any thing that was under his hand; because the Lord was with him, and that which he did, the Lord made it to prosper. King James Bible

6 James Gleick, *The Information: A History, a Theory, a Flood*, p121.

7 With Him are the keys of the unseen, the treasures that none knoweth but He. He knoweth whatever there is on the earth and in the sea. Not a leaf doth fall but with His knowledge: there is not a grain in the darkness (or depths) of the earth, nor anything fresh or dry (green or withered), but is (inscribed) in a record clear (to those who can read). Holy Qur'an, 6:59

8 James Gleick, *The Information: A History, a Theory, a Flood*

9 James Gleick, *The Information: A History, a Theory, a Flood*

10 James Gleick, *The Information: A History, a Theory, a Flood*, p126, quoting Scientific American, 1880

11 James Allen, *As A Man Thinketh*. Borders Press/Grange Books. p24.

Chapter 50

1 "And he spake also a parable unto them; No man putteth a piece of a new garment upon an old; if otherwise, then both the new maketh a rent, and the piece that was taken out of the new agreeth not with the old. And no man

putteth new wine into old bottles; else the new wine will burst the bottles, and be spilled, and the bottles shall perish. But new wine must be put into new bottles; and both are preserved. No man also having drunk old wine straightway desireth new: for he saith, The old is better."—Luke 5:36-39, KJV

Chapter 51

1 *Wert thou to follow the common run of those on earth, they will lead thee away from the way of Allah. They follow nothing but conjecture: they do nothing but lie. Surah Al-Anaam, Verse 116:*

Chapter 52

1 *O ye who believe! save yourselves and your families from a Fire whose fuel is Men and Stones, over which are (appointed) angels stern (and) severe, who flinch not (from executing) the Commands they receive from Allah, but do (precisely) what they are commanded. Holy Qur'an 66:6*

2 *Eschew all sin, open or secret: those who earn sin will get due recompense for their "earnings." Holy Qur'an 6:120*

Chapter 53

1 *Whatever misfortune happens to you, is because of the things your hands have wrought, and for many (of them) He grants forgiveness. Holy Qur'an,42:30*

2 *Every man's fate We have fastened on his own neck: On the Day of Judgment We shall bring out for him a scroll, which he will see spread open. Holy Qur'an, 17:13*

3 *And pursue not that of which thou hast no knowledge; for every act of hearing, or of seeing or of (feeling in) the heart will be enquired into (on the Day of Reckoning). Holy Qur'an, 17:36*

4 Translation of Sahih Bukhari, Book 89: Volume 9, Book 89, Number 252:

Chapter 54

1 *Holy Qur'an,*

7:113 So there came the sorcerers to Pharaoh: They said, "of course we shall have a (suitable) reward if we win!"

7:114 He said: "Yea, (and more),- for ye shall in that case be (raised to posts) nearest (to my person)."

2 We have to be our own selves. Being your own self means more than conforming to your own nature; it means preserving yourself; saving yourself from slavery to other people or to other ideas. The Muslim cannot be a slave to any people or to any other ideas. We are the slaves of Allah. We can't be a slave to any ideology, to the Labor Party doctrine, to communism, to Shiite-ism or any other of the

isms, Wahhabiism, or Sunniism. Once a Muslim becomes a "Sunni" rather than a Muslim first, he has taken on Sunni-ism. And Sunni-ism leads to the worship of Prophet Mohammed (PBUH), over the obedience to G-d or slavery to G-d. Imam W. Deen Mohammed (RAA)

3 *Then set your face upright for religion in the right state—the nature made by Allah in which He has made men; there is no altering of Allah's creation; that is the right religion; but most people do not know--Holy Qur'an 30:30*

4 *He said: "Our Lord is He Who gave to each (created) thing its form and nature, and further, gave (it) guidance." Holy Qur'an 20:50*

Chapter 55

1 *It was We Who taught him the making of coats of mail for your benefit, to guard you from each other's violence: will ye then be grateful? Holy Qur'an, 21:80*

2 *He said: "Our Lord is He Who gave to each (created) thing its form and nature, and further, gave (it) guidance." Holy Qur'an, 20:50*

3 James Allen, *As A Man Thinketh.* Borders Press/Grange Books

Chapter 56

1 *Say: "O Allah! Lord of Power (And Rule), Thou givest power to whom Thou pleasest, and Thou strippest off power from whom Thou pleases: Thou enduest with honour whom Thou pleasest, and Thou bringest low whom Thou pleasest: In Thy hand is all good. Verily, over all things Thou hast power." Holy Qur'an 3:26*

2 The Bible says, "a beast came up with ten horns." A beast came up off the earth, a mighty beast with ten horns. Prophet Muhammad (PBUH) says, "take charge of five before five defeats you." What does that mean? It means that you have to use your five senses, feelings included (which gives the circle to it and makes it visible), to keep your life on an intelligent course. If you do not use your five senses to keep your life on an intelligent course, the influences of the world, the adverse spirit of the cultural world, or corrupt culture, is going to influence your sensitivity and bring the intelligent use of your five senses under the power of the adverse influences of the world. Imam W. Deen Mohammed (RAA)

3 Remember this! G-d says that **"That is how he established Joseph in the land"**. Now if we find in our circumstances as an enslaved people, kept subdued people in this part of the world. If we find in our circumstances events similar to those that were in the life of Joseph, and if we believe in the word of G -d, the Qur'an—then we should take hints from that story and strengthen our life. Look! We do not have economic power. We don't have political power. We are not favored in this country. Now, you can make yourself believe whatever you want to believe. You can just drift out there in the world of make believe. That

is up to you. But, I am talking reality. We are not favored in this country. We are the disfavored in this country. Our circumstances are still bad-- G-d, O Lord. Our circumstances are still bad. Then take the hints from that story. Say now G-d will establish us if we keep our moral tenacity. G-d will establish us if we be morally consistent; if we would want right by everybody. If we would want good for everybody—not just for Blacks—but for everybody. Here a people in slavery and a people freed, so called liberated. And for all the time they were trying to get equal opportunity or get into the mainstream of these United States or the life of America—they were claiming that they had a belief in a G-d. And that they had a belief in moral justice, Divine justice. They were claiming to be good people. Wasn't that our claim? As a race, our politicians and our religious people, our church people was speaking in the name of all of us—and they were claiming before the world that we are a G-d fearing people that believe in the moral justice of G-d. And as soon as we get the freedom that we want –to play and have some ice cream cone, and some hot dogs, and chili. As soon as we get that freedom to play and have some common food, we forget what it was all about. We forget the moral message that we sent out. And betray it right in our own life so soon. You see how come we are not getting anywhere now? Imam W. Deen Mohammed (RAA)

4 There is a time for everything, and a season for every activity under heaven: Ecclesiastes 3:1, New, International Version 1984

Chapter 57

1 *And verily the Hereafter will be better for thee than the present Holy Qur'an, 93:4*

"The end of a matter is better than its beginning, and patience is better than pride." Ecclesiastes 7:8, New International Version (©1984)

2 *Holy Qur'an, 93:4 And verily the Hereafter will be better for thee than the present,* Yusuf Ali. Commentary 6179 To the truly devout man, each succeeding moment is better than the one preceding it. In this sense the "hereafter" refers not only to the Future Life after death, but also to "the soul of goodness in things" in this very life. For even though some outward trappings of this shadow world may be wanting, his soul is filled with more and more satisfaction as he goes on.

3 "The latter glory of this house will be greater than the former,' says the LORD of hosts, 'and in this place I will give peace,' declares the LORD of hosts." Haggai 2:9, New American Standard Bible

4 James Allen, *As A Man Thinketh.* Borders Press/Grange Books, p24.

Chapter 58

1 Imam Mohammed (RAA) speaking of other races who would come here and try to lead African American Muslims to inherit us from the white man as their slaves: "G'd formed me outside of their vision, outside of their sight and established me in my position before they knew me."

2 [8] Will a man rob God? Yet ye have robbed me. But ye say, Wherein have we robbed thee? In tithes and offerings.

[9] Ye are cursed with a curse: for ye have robbed me, even this whole nation. Malachi 3:8-9, King James Version (KJV)

Chapter 59

1 *To Him is due the primal origin of the heavens and the earth: When He decreeth a matter, He saith to it: "Be," and it is. Holy Qur'an, 2:117*

2 *Those men,-Allah knows what is in their hearts; so keep clear of them, but admonish them, and speak to them a word to reach their very souls. Holy Qur'an, 4:63*

3 *To the Madyan people We sent Shu'aib, one of their own brethren: he said: "O my people! worship Allah; Ye have no other god but Him. Now hath come unto you a clear (Sign) from your Lord! Give just measure and weight, nor withhold from the people the things that are their due; and do no mischief on the earth after it has been set in order: that will be best for you, if ye have Faith. Holy Qur'an, 7:85*

4 *Holy Qur'an,*

83:1 Woe to those that deal in fraud,

83:2 Those who, when they have to receive by measure from men, exact full measure,

83:3 But when they have to give by measure or weight to men, give less than due.

Chapter 61

1 *Holy Qur'an,*

86:15 As for them, they are but plotting a scheme,

86:16 And I am planning a scheme.

And (the unbelievers) plotted and planned, and Allah too planned, and the best of planners is Allah. Holy Qur'an, 3:54

2 *Remember how the Unbelievers plotted against thee, to keep thee in bonds, or slay thee, or get thee out (of thy home). They plot and plan, and Allah too plans; but the best of planners is Allah. Holy Qur'an, 8:30*

3 *What! have they settled some plan (among themselves)? But it is We Who settle things. Holy Qur'an, 43:79*

Chapter 62

1 *Say: If it be that your fathers, your sons, your brothers, your mates, or your kindred; the wealth that ye have gained; the commerce in which ye fear a decline: or the dwellings in which ye delight - are dearer to you than Allah, or His Messenger, or the striving in His cause;- then wait until Allah brings about His decision: and Allah guides not the rebellious. Holy Qur'an, 9:24*

Chapter 64

1 *They ask thee concerning the New Moons. Say: They are but signs to mark fixed periods of time in (the affairs of) men, and fo r Pilgrimage. It is no virtue if ye enter your houses from the back: It is virtue if ye fear Allah. Enter houses through the proper doors: And fear Allah: That ye may prosper. Holy Qur'an,* 2:189

Chapter 65

1 verb: **worm**; treat (an animal) with a preparation designed to expel parasitic worms. https://www.google.com/?gws_rd=ssl#q=worm

2 noun: **worms;** any of a number of creeping or burrowing invertebrate animals with long, slender, soft bodies and no limbs. https://www.google.com/?gws_rd=ssl#q=worm

Chapter 66

1 Fatimah Abdul-Tawwab Fanusie, *W. D. Fard Muhammad in Historical Context: An Islamic Thread in the American Religious and Cultural Quilt*, p 478.

2 Dale Gieringer, Ph.D. *Economics of Cannabis Legalization (1994) Detailed Analysis of the Benefits of Ending Cannabis Prohibition,* June 1994,.

Chapter 67

1 *"I am a worker, work you in your places…" Holy Qur'an 39:39*

2 Booker T. Washington, Atlanta Compromise Speech, Cotton States and International Exposition, September 18, 1895

3 "Food deserts are communities, particularly low-income areas, in which residents do not live in close proximity to affordable and healthy food retailers. Healthy food options in these communities are hard to find or are unaffordable." http://www.acf.hhs.gov/programs/ocs/ocs_food.html

Chapter 68

1 *Remember how the Unbelievers plotted against thee, to keep thee in bonds, or slay thee, or get thee out (of thy home). They plot and plan, and Allah too plans; but the best of planners is Allah. Holy Qur'an 8:30*

Chapter 69

1 We share an experience, and it is an experience that has left strong imprints on our very souls. So in this soul life or spiritual life, we have strong ties to one another. It is because we have experienced over the generations, over a long period of time, things that left hurt and things that left joy and pleasure. That is what makes us kin-folk. That is what really makes us soul brothers and sisters. It is the experience that we shared that others did not share with us. So we don't have that spiritual bond with them, that depth of soul with them that we have with one another. Imam W. Deen Mohammed (RAA), First Sunday Address, Homewood Hotel, Homewood, III., Nov. 5, 2006

Chapter 70

1 *And come not nigh to the orphan's property, except to improve it, until he attain the age of full strength; give measure and weight with (full) justice;- no burden do We place on any soul, but that which it can bear;- whenever ye speak, speak justly, even if a near relative is concerned; and fulfil the covenant of Allah: thus doth He command you, that ye may remember. Holy Qur'an, 6:152*

2 "For the day of the LORD *is* near upon all the heathen: as thou hast done, it shall be done unto thee: thy reward shall return upon thine own head." King James Bible, Obadiah 1:15

3 http://mid-centurypink.blogspot.com/2013/07/growing-up-strong-on-pet-milk-fultz.html

Chapter 71

1 http://en.wikipedia.org/wiki/Discernment

Chapter 72

1 And Joseph said unto them, What deed is this that ye have done? wot ye not that such a man as I can certainly divine? Genesis 44:15, King James Version (KJV)

2 *Holy Qur'an*

70:22 Not so those devoted to Prayer;-

70:23 Those who remain steadfast to their prayer;

70:24 And those in whose wealth is a recognised right.

70:25 For the (needy) who asks and him who is prevented (for some reason from asking);

3 *And ye love wealth with inordinate love! Holy Qur'an, 89:20*

Chapter 73

1 Why didn't they speak from the Holy Quran and say, "our Book tells that you have an incorrect reading of your Book, you are not getting the beauty of your own Book, you're not getting the help that G-d put for you in your own Book, your rule is wicked? Why didn't they come out and speak if they didn't have the power to pick up arms or the means the wherewithal to deal with the man materially? How come they did not use the second form of Jihad to speak out against it? Why? Because they were the elder brothers of Joseph…and they had sold Joseph in slavery and hoping that Joseph would one day be rescued by G-d, not them.

And that G-d would be obligated to rescue Joseph because they were putting Joseph in a situation where G-d would have to come to his aid. And when Joseph is rescued and when he rises up in the government of the Pharaoh or the ruler, he will be there to serve his elder brothers. Elder brother go to hell.

They have been planning for these centuries while we have been suffering and they have passed their hopes on to their children, those who died passed their hopes on to their children secretly… coming in our neighborhood opening the grocery stores, investing materially in our community thinking that, "These are still Niggers, they are still Negroes, they are waiting on the white man to run the neighborhoods, provide for them their needs. Why don't we go in, they are ours.

They claim us, "They are ours, why don't we go in their neighborhood, why don't we be the material life, business life of their neighborhood? And make money but also to decide their fate and their future."

Never, it won't happen. Imam W. Deen Mohammed (RAA), Ramadan Sessions 2002

Chapter 74

1 Thomas Wentworth Higginson, quoting Corporal Price Lambkin, of the First Black Regiment in the Civil War: "Our mas'rs dey hab lib under de flag, dey got dere wealth under it, and ebryting beautiful for dere chilen. Under it dey hab grind us up, and put us in dere pocket for money." *Army Life in a Black Regiment.* Penguin Books, 2002

2 *They ask: When will this promise be (fulfilled)? - If ye are telling the truth. Holy Qur'an, 67:25*

3 *So Moses returned to his people in a state of indignation and sorrow. He said: "O my people! did not your Lord make a handsome promise to you? Did then the promise seem to you long*

(in coming)? Or did ye desire that Wrath should descend from your Lord on you, and so ye broke your promise to me?" Holy Qur'an, 20:86

4 *So persevere in patience; for the Promise of Allah is true: and whether We show thee (in this life) some part of what We promise them,- or We take thy soul (to Our Mercy) (before that),-(in any case) it is to Us that they shall (all) return. Holy Qur'an, 40:77*

5 *They will say: "Praise be to Allah, Who has truly fulfilled His Promise to us, and has given us (this) land in heritage: We can dwell in the Garden as we will: how excellent a reward for those who work (righteousness)!" Holy Qur'an, 39:74*

Chapter 75

1 *Holy Qur'an,*

83:7 Nay! Surely the record of the wicked is (preserved) in Sijjin.

83:8 And what will explain to thee what Sijjin is?

83:9 (There is) a Register (fully) inscribed.

2 *Holy Qur'an,*

84:3 And when the earth is flattened out,

84:4 And casts forth what is within it and becomes (clean) empty,

3 *Holy Qur'an 2"104, "Oh you who have accepted trust, do not say 'ra'inaa' (as to twist its meaning), but say, 'wait for us,' then listen. For the disregardful is a severe punishment."*

Translation and analysis by Imam Salim Mu'min: "Among the religious establishments during the time of Muhammed the Prophet or any period of a great reformer in religion, the leading religious leaders presupposes that the reformer does not have adequate knowledge of truth and the universal realities seemingly that he wasn't their pupil. Not only does he have the wisdom or logic, which the former religious leaders feel that is only privy to them, he excels them in light years as to the thinking and interpretation of religious scriptural ideas.

Due to these circumstances, their hearts desire that the reformer slow down so their minds can catch up to what he is teaching. In addition, they want the reformer to delay his teachings because they think he should not give such knowledge to the common ignorant masses that have been under their influence for many years.

Thus, they twist the word that means to slow down for a cuss word. They are cussing him while at the same time trying to demonstrate to his followers that they too respect and follow him.

Thereby, Allah informs the trustworthy that they should not be of such character and use a plain word to ask that the teacher slow down so they may comprehend. Then Allah instructs them to listen intently to what the teacher is presenting. Do not confuse it with your previous teachings or the logic of his predecessors and thus find yourselves lagging. For those who do not accept the reformer will endure a severe punishment in the reformation period."

4 If the religious language of today had been interpreted from the original religious language and composed in the likeness of the original religious language, we would have an intelligent religious world instead of the confused, false religious philosophies of a Tower of Babel. In an intelligent religious world, there is religious life, light, human success, and prosperity. We would have these benefits not only in the physical world, but in the moral world and in the intellectual world also...The growth of natural religious life is producing an intelligent religious community in the West. The great truth of Divine Mind has given us a light and a life from Almighty God which removes us from the confused, grafted "baby talk" of this world's modern Tower of Babel. Imam W. Deen Mohammed (RAA)

5 Right now they're turning it northward with conservative values. They're turning it northward with the religious community supporting the secular society. They're turning the key, orientating the American peoples' spirit & life northward & pretty soon we're going to see the influence of the north assuage the misery of this hellish south that we've come to. And it's going to be beautiful for a while. But the society again will go to extremes & they'll have to turn the key back & orientate it southward to take the cold winter chill off of human life. But Allah tells us don't worship that science that enabled their social order to control the affect of winter & summer on them, or the seasons in their lives. *Faal ya'budu rabba haadhaal bait.* "Therefore worship the Lord of this house. The G-d that created the science, that created the form & the knowledge in the form." *Faal ya' budu rabba haadhal bait.*" *Alladhee at' amahum min juu'in.* "The one who fed you in time of hunger." *Wa aamanahum min khaaf.* "And secured you against fear." Imam WD Mohammed (RAA)

Holy Qur'an

106:1 For the covenants (of security and safeguard enjoyed) by the Quraish,

106:2 Their covenants (covering) journeys by winter and summer,-

106:3 Let them adore the Lord of this House,

106:4 Who provides them with food against hunger, and with security against fear (of danger).

Aa an example of how cold and unfeeling it can get, during one of the Republican party Presidential primary debates in 2011, the two statements that received the most thunderous applause were 1. The Tea Party audience cheered Ron Paul's suggestion that freedom means letting an uninsured man die; 2. Another audience cheered the 234 executions Governor Rick Perry has presided over. Now in this season, Donald Trump has taken ignorance, insensitive, bigotry and hatred to a whole new level.

Chapter 76

1 *"Enter ye Egypt (all) in safety if it please Allah." Holy Qur'an, 12:99*

2 http://richard-hooker.com/sites/worldcultures/EGYPT/MAAT.HTM

3 Josh Clark, Did the ancient Greeks get their ideas from the Africans?, quoting Gloria Dickinson, http://history.howstuffworks.com/history-vs-myth/greek-philosophers-african-tribes3.htm, May 4, 2016

4 For hundreds of years, this revered patron and saint of Roman tradition, from Thebes, Egypt in North Africa was depicted as black. However, "Images of the saint died out in the mid-sixteenth century, undermined," Suckale-Redlefsen suggests, "by the developing African slave trade." "Once again, as in the early Middle Ages, the color black had become associated with spiritual darkness and cultural 'otherness'". Dorothy Gillerman, reviewing Suckale-Redlefsen 1988 in *Speculum* **65**.3 (July 1990:764).

Chapter 77

1 Sir Walter Scott (Marmion, 1808)

2 *Behold! how they lie against their own souls! But the (lie) which they invented will leave them in the lurch. Holy Qur'an, 6:24*

(Lurch is defined as "a vulnerable and unsupported position" and the Arabic word implies a state "weakened and diminished.")

3 *Prophet Muhammad (peace be upon him) said:" Do you know what backbiting is?" They said, "God and His Messenger know best." He then said, "It is to say something about your brother that he would dislike." Someone asked him, "But what if what I say is true?" The Messenger of God said, "If what you say about him is true, you are backbiting him, but if it is not true then you have slandered him." (Muslim)*

4 *Of no effect is the repentance of those who continue to do evil, until death faces one of them, and he says, "Now have I repented indeed;" nor of those who die rejecting Faith: for them have We prepared a punishment most grievous. Holy Qur'an, 4:18*

5 *But if any one earns a fault or a sin and throws it on to one that is innocent, He carries (on himself) (Both) a falsehood and a flagrant sin. Holy Qur'an, 4:112*

Chapter 78

1 "How are the mighty fallen, and the weapons of war perished!" 2 Samuel 27 King James Bible

Chapter 79

1 A Message of Concern by Imam W. Deen Mohammed (RAA)

What would happen if people would sit in churches throughout the world for centuries with the image of an African American man as savior of the world before them?" What would this do to the mind of the world's children?

What would happen to the world's children put under a figure of a particular race presented pitiable, and in pain

"the Savior of all Men?

Qur'an, Surah 3, verse 64: "Say, Oh People of the Book! Come top common terms as between us and you: that we worship none but God, that we associate no partner with Him, that we erect not from among ourselves lords and patrons other than God. If then they turn back, say ye "bear witness that we (at least) are Muslims (bowing to God's Will).'"

Civilized nations should want their religions be also civilized.

False worship is the worse form of oppression. We are no gods. We are only men, "mortals from the mortals, He (Allah) created." Qur'an.

2 *O ye who believe! stand out firmly for Allah, as witnesses to fair dealing, and let not the hatred of others to you make you swerve to wrong and depart from justice. Be just: that is next to piety: and fear Allah. For Allah is well-acquainted with all that ye do. Holy Qur'an, 5:8*

3 *In most of their secret talks there is no good: But if one exhorts to a deed of charity or justice or conciliation between men, (Secrecy is permissible): To him who does this, seeking the good pleasure of Allah, We shall soon give a reward of the highest (value). Holy Qur'an, 4:114*

4 *Said an 'Ifrit, of the Jinns: "I will bring it to thee before thou rise from thy council: indeed I have full strength for the purpose, and may be trusted." Holy Qur'an 27:39*

Said one who had knowledge of the Book: "I will bring it to thee within the twinkling of an eye!" Then when (Solomon) saw it placed firmly before him, he said: "This is by the Grace of my Lord!- to test me whether I am grateful or ungrateful! and if any is grateful, truly his gratitude is (a gain) for his own soul; but if any is ungrateful, truly my Lord is Free of all Needs, Supreme in Honour !" Holy Qur'an 27:40

Chapter 80

1 Dictionary of the Holy Qur'an, Abdul Mannan Omar, p 146, 7

2 Dictionary of the Holy Qur'an, Abdul Mannan Omar, p 597

Chapter 81

1 *Holy Qur'an,*

56:83Then why do ye not (intervene) when (the soul of the dying man) reaches the throat,-

56:84 And ye the while (sit) looking on,-

2 *"And when I am ill, it is He Who cures me; Holy Qur'an, 26:80*

3 *On the earth are signs for those of assured Faith, 51:21 As also in your own selves: Will ye not then see? Holy Qur'an, 51:20*

4 *Holy Qur'an,*

45:3 Verily in the heavens and the earth, are Signs for those who believe.

45:4 And in the creation of yourselves and the fact that animals are scattered (through the earth), are Signs for those of assured Faith

5 *This is part of the tidings of the things unseen, which We reveal unto thee (O Messenger!) by inspiration: Thou wast not with them when they cast lots with arrows, as to which of them should be charged with the care of Mary: Nor wast thou with them when they disputed (the point). Holy Qur'an, 3:44*

Chapter 82

1 *They said: "O our father! We went racing with one another, and left Joseph with our things; and the wolf devoured him.... But thou wilt never believe us even though we tell the truth." Holy Qur'an, 12:17*

2 *O ye who believe! If a wicked person comes to you with any news, ascertain the truth, lest ye harm people unwit tingly, and afterwards become full of repentance for what ye have done. Holy Qur'an 49:6*

Chapter 83

1 HADITH: "No one can be given a better and more abundant gift than patience." ~ Recorded by Imam Bukhari

2 *We did indeed offer the Trust to the Heavens and the Earth and the Mountains; but they refused to undertake it, being afraid thereof: but man undertook it;- He was indeed unjust and foolish;- Holy Qur'an, 33:72*

3 *By no means! For We have created them out of the (base matter) they know! Holy Qur'an, 70:39*

Chapter 84

1 We should be the head of our people & we should work out the life for our people; we should pay the price for our people. Don't expect dumb, lazy people to work out their own future. Their head is their intelligent ones, informed ones, industrious ones, energetic ones; that is the head of the people. It's up to us to lead the whole people." Imam W. Deen Mohammed (RAA)

2 *And your creation or your resurrection is in no wise but as an individual soul: for Allah is He Who hears and sees (all things). Holy Qur'an 31:28*

3 Referring to the statement 'your death & resurrection is as one people': "One standing up in the right character, having the right life, can lift the whole people up; this is Barack Obama...He is new life in the spirit of Black America." Imam W. Deen Mohammed (RAA)

Chapter 85

1 If one part of our body hurts, we hurt all over. If one part of our body is honored, the whole body will be happy. 1 Corinthians 12:26

2 Every member in your body has been dignified because of the high development of yourself internally. Every creature in creation, every molecule of water, every atom of matter has been dignified by the high development of any single part of creation. If any single part of creation reaches a high peak in worth, in value, or in dignity— all the creation is dignified and all the creation is lifted in value. 04/22/1977 Bilalian News, Imam W. D. Mohammed (RAA)

3 **If there breathe on earth a slave, Are ye truly free and brave?** If ye do not feel the chain, When it works a brother's pain, Are ye not base slaves indeed, Slaves unworthy to be freed? "Stanzas on Freedom" (1843). James Russell Lowell, American Romantic poet, critic, satirist, writer, diplomat, and abolitionist.

4 "It's a shame on us...African American people (to) let good times come and forget all about the dignity that we lost when they enslaved our fore-parents, forget all about the human freedom that we lost when they limited our life to the existence of a slave on the plantation under the white bosses, we forget about all of that. Your soul cannot forget, your mind can forget it but your soul can't forget it and you wonder how come you're miserable.

...You wonder how come the black race is miserable, it is because you are being punished for not answering the best motivations, the best aspirations, the best concerns and interest of your ancestors who wanted what you have now, freedom so they could take their own life into their own hands and make it better. Now you have your own life in your own hands but you're still sitting around like a slave waiting on a slave master to tell you to get up and go to work, come back in and go to bed. Okay you're free for Friday night, Saturday and Sunday go on and have your good time." Imam W. Deen Mohammed (RAA)

Chapter 86

1 *Or do ye think that ye shall enter the Garden (of bliss) without such (trials) as came to those who passed away before you? t hey encountered suffering and adversity, and were so shaken in spirit that even the Messenger and those of faith who were with him cried: "When (will come) the help of Allah?" Ah! Verily, the help of Allah is (always) near! Holy Qur'an, 2:214*

2 *Say: "I have no power over any good or harm to myself except as Allah willeth. If I had knowledge of the unseen, I should have multiplied all good, and no evil should have touched me: I am but a warner, and a bringer of glad tidings to those who have faith." Holy Qur'an, 7:188*

Chapter 87

1 Yusuf Ali translation, Holy Qur'an, 59:23, Note 5402. Mu-min, one who entertains Faith, who gives Faith to others, who is never false to the Faith that others place in him; hence out paraphrase "Guardian of Faith.

2 *And spend of your substance in the cause of Allah, and* ***make not your own hands contribute to (your) destruction****; but do good; for Allah loveth those who do good. Holy Qur'an, 2:195*

3 *"Be sure I will cut off your hands and your feet on apposite sides, and I will cause you all to die on the cross." Holy Qur'an, 7:124*

See also Holy Qur'an, 5:33 wherein Allah describes the punishment of those who wage war against Him and His Messenger, as the same "crucifixion, or the cutting off of hands and feet from opposite sides."

4 *"O you who believe! Fear Allah as He should be feared, and die not except in a state of Muslims, Holy Qur'an, 3:102* "It just doesn't mean die physically, it means don't give up your consciousness to something else, to another idea, to another person, don't give up your consciousness except that you be upright and in that balance." Imam W. Deen Mohammed (RAA)

5 *They ask thee concerning fighting in the Prohibited Month. Say: "Fighting therein is a grave (offence); but graver is it in the sight of Allah to prevent access to the path of Allah, to deny Him, to prevent access to the Sacred Mosque, and drive out its members."* ***Tumult and oppression are worse than slaughter.*** *Nor will they cease fighting you until they turn you back from your faith if they can. And if any of you Turn back from their faith and die in unbelief, their works will bear no fruit in this life and in the Hereafter; they will be companions of the Fire and will abide therein. Holy Qur'an, 2:217*

6 *And when it is said to them, do not make mischief in the land, they say: "We are but Peacemakers., Holy Qur'an 2:11*

7 Friedrich Nietzsche (1844-1900), German philosopher, classical scholar, critic of culture.

Chapter 88

1 *See they not how many of those before them We did destroy?- generations We had established on the earth, in strength such as We have not given to you - for whom We poured out rain from the skies in abundance, and gave (fertile) streams flowing beneath their (feet):* ***yet for their sins We destroyed them, and raised in their wake fresh generations (to succeed them).*** *Holy Qur'an, 6:6*

2 *Say: "O Allah! Lord of Power (And Rule),* ***Thou givest power to whom Thou pleasest, and Thou strippest off power from whom Thou pleasest:*** *Thou enduest with honour whom Thou pleasest, and Thou bringest low whom Thou pleasest: In Thy hand is all good. Verily, over all things Thou hast power. Holy Qur'an, 3:26*

3 http://en.wikipedia.org/wiki/Language

4 Jonah Mandel for the Jerusalem Post, Jewish News, *Rabbi Ovadia Yosef: Gentiles Exist Only to Serve Jews* http://crownheights.info/jewish-news/29404/rabbi-ovadia-yosef-gentiles-exist-only-to-serve-jews/ October 19, 2010

5 Mark Zuckerberg, founder and chief executive of Facebook, in an April 10, 2013, Washington Post opinion column wrote: "The economy of the last century was primarily based on natural resources, industrial machines and manual labor. Many of these resources were zero-sum and controlled by companies. If someone else had an oil field, then you did not. There were only so many oil fields, and only so much wealth could be created from them.

Chapter 89

1 *When We bestow favours on man, he turns away, and gets himself remote on his side (instead of coming to Us); and when evil seizes him, (he comes) full of prolonged prayer! Holy Qur'an, 41:51*

Chapter 90

1 *The Believers are but a single Brotherhood: So make peace and reconciliation between your two (contending) brothers; and fear Allah, that ye may receive Mercy. Holy Qur'an 49:10*

2 Note 4828, Yusuf Ali translation commentary, Holy Qur'an 49:10

3 Holy Qur'an 49:13

4 *"Let there be no compulsion in religion: Truth stands out clear from Error: whoever rejects evil and believes in Allah hath grasped the most trustworthy hand-hold, that never breaks. And Allah heareth and knoweth all things." 2:256*

5 *O mankind! We created you from a single (pair) of a male and a female, and made you into nations and tribes, that ye may know each other (not that ye may despise (each other). Verily the most honoured of you in the sight of Allah is (he who is) t he most righteous of you. And Allah has full knowledge and is well acquainted (with all things). Holy Qur'an, 49:13*

6 Charlotte Sophia Burne, *The Handbook of Folklore—Traditional Beliefs, Practices, Customs, Stories and Sayings*, Senate, 1914.

7 Charlotte Sophia Burne, *The Handbook of Folklore—Traditional Beliefs, Practices, Customs, Stories and Sayings*, 1914 p.171.

8 This occasion for beginning life goes back to the beginning of our father Adam and his mate. And G-d charged Adam and his mate with being responsible not only to each other to each other but being responsible to Him and being responsible for their duty in the earth, responsible for the environment...So marriage is a big thing, it a big issue, every time a couple marries that first contract is repeated and they should look at their future the same way the first people looked at their future. Here is an opportunity to start life and make it right. And to make it beautiful. Allah (swt) wants us to have life and a beautiful life and a productive life. A productive life in the sense of number one being successful as a family, as man & wife and as parents, but also a successful life in the world of opportunities. Imam W. Deen Mohammed (RAA)

9 Charlotte Sophia Burne, *The Handbook of Folklore—Traditional Beliefs, Practices, Customs, Stories and Sayings*, 1914 p 200.

10 Charlotte Sophia Burne, *The Handbook of Folklore—Traditional Beliefs, Practices, Customs, Stories and Sayings*, 1914 p 48.

Chapter 91

1 *ehold, ye are those invited to spend (of your substance) in the Way of Allah: But among you are some that are niggardly. But any who are niggardly are so at the expense of their own souls. But Allah is free of all wants, and it is ye that are needy. If ye turn back (from the Path), He will substitute in your stead another people; then they would not be like you. Holy Qur'an, 47:38*

2 Dictionary of the Holy Qur'an, Abdul Mannan Omar, Noor Foundation-International, Inc.

3 He created you (all) from a single person: then created, of like nature, his mate; and he sent down for you eight head of cattle in pairs: He makes you, in the wombs of your mothers, in stages, one after another, in three veils of darkness. such is Allah, your Lord and Cherisher: to Him belongs (all) dominion. There is no god but He: then how are ye turned away (from your true Centre)? Holy Qur'an, 39:6

4 Dictionary of the Holy Qur'an, Abdul Mannan Omar, Noor Foundation-International, Inc.

5 *We did indeed offer the Trust to the Heavens and the Earth and the Mountains; but they refused to undertake it, being afraid thereof: but man undertook it;- He was indeed unjust and foolish;- Holy Qur'an, 33:72*

6 *"O you men! surely We have created you of a male and a female, and made you tribes and families that you may know each other; surely the most honorable of you with Allah is the one among you most careful (of his duty); surely Allah is Knowing, Aware." Holy Qur'an, Al Hujuraat 49:13*

Chapter 92

1 Jack Kornfield, *The Art of Forgiveness, Lovingkindness and Peace*. Bantam Dell. New York, New York. 2002

2 Muhammad Husayn Haykal, *The Life of Muhammad*, American Trust Publications, 1993.p 408.

3 "For if you forgive men when they sin against you, your heavenly Father will also forgive you. But, if you do not forgive men their sins, your Father will not forgive your sins." Mat 6:14-15 (NIV)

4 *Be quick in the race for forgiveness from your Lord, and for a Garden whose width is that (of the whole) of the heavens and of the earth, prepared for the righteous. -Holy Qur'an, 3:133*

5 How unhappy is he who cannot forgive himself.-Publilius Syrus

Chapter 93

1 ***It is not righteousness that ye turn your faces Towards east or West;*** *but it is righteousness- to believe in Allah and the Last Day, and the Angels, and the Book, and the Messengers; to spend of your substance, out of love for Him, for your kin, for orphans, for the needy, for the wayfarer, for those who ask, and for the ransom of slaves; to be steadfast in prayer, and practice regular charity; to fulfil the contracts which ye have made;* ***and to be firm and patient, in pain (or suffering) and adversity, and throughout all periods of panic.*** *Such are the people of truth, the Allah-fearing. Holy Qur'an 2:177*

2 Ibid

3 Dr. R. Swinburne Clymer, *The Mysteries of Osiris, Ancient Egyptian Initiation*, 1951

4 Matthew 2:13-15, King James Bible

5 *Again, ye shall see it with certainty of sight! Holy Qur'an, 102:7*

Chapter 94

1 http://en.wikipedia.org/wiki/Scientific method

2 Holy Qur'an,

69:50 But truly (Revelation) is a cause of sorrow for the Unbelievers.

69:51: But verily it is Truth of assured certainty. Note 5673. All Truth is in itself certain. But as received by men, and understood with reference to men's psychology, certainty may have certain degrees. There is the ability or certainty resulting from the application of man's power of judgment and appraisement of evidence. This is 'ilm-ul-yaqin, certainty by reasoning or inference. -- there is the certainty of seeing something with our own eyes. "Seeing is believing." is 'ain-ul-yaqin, certainty by personal inspection. See cii. 5, 7. Then as here, there is --- absolute Truth, with no possibility of error or judgment or error of the eye, (which) --- for any instrument of sense perception and any ancillary aids, such as microscopes. This absolute Truth is the haqq-ul-yaqin spoken of here.

3 Allah says in Qur'an: 27:4 *"As to those who believe not in the Hereafter, we have made their deeds pleasing in their eyes; and so they wander about in distraction."*

4 *Do not the Unbelievers see that the heavens and the earth were joined together (as one unit of creation), before we clove them asunder? We made from water every living thing. Will they not then believe? Holy Qur'an, 21:30*

5 *To Him is due the primal origin of the heavens and the earth: When He decreeth a matter, He saith to it: "Be," and it is. Holy Qur'an, 2:117*

Holy Qur'an

6:101 To Him is due the ***primal origin*** *of the heavens and the earth: How can He have a son when He hath no consort? He created all things, and He hath full knowledge of all things.*

6:102 That is Allah, your Lord! there is no god but He, the Creator of all things: then worship ye Him: and He hath power to dispose of all affairs.

6:103 No vision can grasp Him, but His grasp is over all vision: He is above all comprehension, yet is acquainted with all things.

6 *They said: "Truly Joseph and his brother are loved more by our father than we: But we are a goodly body! really our father is obviously wandering (in his mind)! Holy Qur'an, 12:8*

7 *The leaders of his people said: "Ah! we see thee evidently wandering (in mind)." Holy Qur'an, 7:60*

Chapter 95

1 The so-called Hebrew people who are following Moses had betrayed him while he was up in the mountain getting direction from G-d. When he came back down, his own brother Aaron, had fallen weak to their suggestions and was helping them build a false deity-a false G-d. And they were quarrelsome people, arguing and suspicious of Moses intentions, suspicious of his ability to do what

he said G-d would bring about, or get what G-d said he would give him. They were a suspicious, thick headed, argumentative people. The Book says that they were punished by flying tongues of fire. That right? Which means that their boasting in their own knowledge was their punishment. And that is your punishment right here today. You people who won't give me the support that you should give me, who belong to this World Community of Al-Islam. Your problem is, you think I am no different than you. You say, Chief Imam and all that bull crap, but in your own mind, you're saying aw he ain't, I don't have to. I heard this before. Oh yea, he's good, but it is the same old things. I could do it myself. I got some knowledge too." So you want to show off your fiery tongue. Yes. That's your problem. Crabs in a barrel. Don't want to see one of your people go up because you think that you should go up too. "If I don't go up with him, right at the same rate of speed, then I don't think that he should go up. Bring him down." How are you going to ever have a successful society if one man doesn't rise? It says, "Lift me up and I will draw all men unto me. Naw, but you are so jealous hearted. So selfish till you lie to yourself and say, "I'm just as good as he. I got just as much sense as he got. How can you have as much sense as I got, and G-d has given it to me and not to you?" Imam W. Deen Mohammed (RAA), Circumcision of the Mind

Chapter 96

1 *Said the chiefs of Pharaoh's people: "Wilt thou leave Moses and his people, to spread mischief in the land, and to abandon thee and thy gods?" He said: "Their male children will we slay; (only) their females will we save alive; and we have over them (power) irresistible." Holy Qur'an, 7:127*

2 *(Pharaoh) said: "Did we not cherish thee as a child among us, and didst thou not stay in our midst many years of thy life? Holy Qur'an, 26:18*

3 Orlando Patterson, *Slavery and Social Death: A Comparative Study*, Harvard University Press. 1982

4 *Then We raised you up after your death: Ye had the chance to be grateful. Holy Qur'an, 2:56*

5 Eric Klineberg, *Climactic Events in the Social Context: Heat Wave- a Social Autopsy of Disaster in Chicago*, p11

6 Ibid

7 http://en.wikipedia.org/wiki/Andrew_Lloyd_Webber.

8 We are the Beautiful Coat of Joseph found in modern Egypt (America). Imam W. Deen Mohammed (RAA)

9 *(We take our) colour from Allah, and who is better at colouring. We are His worshippers. Holy Qur'an, 2:138, Pickthall translation*

Chapter 97

1 *It was We Who created man, and We know what dark suggestions his soul makes to him: for We are nearer to him than (his) jugular vein. Holy Qur'an, 50:16*

2 *Thus, have We made of you an Ummat justly balanced, that ye might be witnesses over the nations, and the Messenger a witness over yourselves; and We appointed the Qibla to which thou wast used, only to test those who followed the Messenger from those who would turn on their heels (From the Faith). Indeed it was (A change) momentous, except to those guided by Allah. And never would Allah Make your faith of no effect. For Allah is to all people Most surely full of kindness, Most Merciful. Holy Qur'an, 2:143*

3 See Holy Qur'an, 7:199: Hold to forgiveness; command what is right; But turn away from the ignorant. The Qur'an references the need for forgiving and overlooking others faults in many places: 2:109; 5:13; 42:37/43; 45:14; and 64:14

4 *The recompense for an injury is an injury equal thereto (in degree): but if a person forgives and makes reconciliation, his reward is due from Allah: for (Allah) loveth not those who do wrong. Holy Qur'an, 42:40*

Chapter 98

1 *And remember ye said: "O Moses! we cannot endure one kind of food (always); so beseech thy Lord for us to produce for us of what the earth groweth, -its pot-herbs, and cucumbers, Its garlic, lentils, and onions." He said: "Will ye exchange the better for the worse? Go ye down to any town, and ye shall find what ye want!" They were covered with humiliation and misery; they drew on themselves the wrath of Allah. This because they went on rejecting the Signs of Allah and slaying His Messengers without just cause. This because they rebelled and went on transgressing. Holy Qur'an, 2:61*

2 *So that Allah will turn off from them (even) the worst in their deeds and give them their reward according to the best of what they have done. Holy Qur'an, 39:35*

Chapter 99

1 *(It will be said to him:) "Read thine (own) record: Sufficient is thy soul this day to make out an account against thee." Holy Qur'an, 17:14*

2 Dr. R. Swinburne Clymer, *The Mysteries of Osiris, Ancient Egyptian Initiation*, 1951, p77

3 Ibid, p82.

Chapter 100

1 *He has made subject to you the Night and the Day; the sun and the moon; and the stars are in subjection by His Command: verily in this are Signs for men who are wise.16:16 And marks and sign-posts; and by the stars (men) guide themselves. Holy Qur'an, 16:12*

2 That's why it is Alameena. "He says in the Quran, "Wase-at kulla shayen rahmatan wa ilman," translated "He encompasses all things in mercy and knowledge," or He has made everything to embody and communicate knowledge or science. So when Allah swt says He is Lord of all the worlds, G-d is speaking of the worlds in a much higher and deeper meaning. He is talking about the world as objects embodying knowledge and science. 4-6-2003 Dawa Chicago, Ill Imam W. Deen Mohammed

3 *Do ye not see that Allah has subjected to your (use) all things in the heavens and on earth, and has made his bounties flow to you in exceeding measure, (both) seen and unseen? Yet there are among men those who dispute about Allah, without knowledge and without guidance, and without a Book to enlighten them! Holy Qur'an, 31:20*

4 http://www.businessdictionary.com/definition/cognitive-consonance.html

5 "Dear beloved brothers and sisters, we should recognize our blessings when the blessings come. And for what did we suffer all of these centuries praying to G'd; being better Christians than white folks; what did we make that big moral and spiritual sacrifice for? If it is not for one day to be blessed in a measure equal to our suffering, and our sacrifice; and if we are blessed in a measure equal to our sufferings and our sacrifices we're going to shoot from the bottom all the way up to the top." 12/28/1980, 4th Sunday Hookup - Chicago, Ill. Imam W. Deen Mohammed (RAA)

Chapter 101

1 Proverbs 9:10, King James Bible

2 He has given everything something of His 'Ruh' (spirit).

3 *Do ye not see that Allah has subjected to your (use) all things in the heavens and on earth, and has made his bounties flow to you in exceeding measure, (both) seen and unseen? Yet there are among men those who dispute about Allah, without knowledge and without guidance, and without a Book to enlighten them! Holy Qur'an, 31:20*

4 *And when I am ill, it is He Who cures me; Holy Qur'an, 26:80*

Bukhari, v. 7, p. 158; and Ibn Majah v. 2.p. 1138:3439

5 Objective of the Islamic Economic Order, Muhammad Umar Chapra

6 Dr. Caroline Myss, *Anatomy of the Spirit.*

7 So the LORD God said to the serpent, "Because you have done this, "Cursed are you above all livestock and all wild animals! You will crawl on your belly and you will eat dust all the days of your life. Genesis 3:14, New International Version

8 Alvin Toffler and Heidi Toffler, *Revolutionary Wealth: How it will be created and how it will change our lives*, p. 14

Chapter 102

1 Luke 8:17, New International Version, 1984

2 "Finally, be strong in the Lord, and in the strength of His might. 11 Put on the full armor of God, that you may be able to stand firm against the schemes of the devil. 12 For our struggle is not against flesh and blood, but against the rulers, against the powers, against the world forces of this darkness, against the spiritual [forces] of wickedness in the heavenly [places.]" Ephesians 6:10-12, New American Standard Bible

3 *With Him are the keys of the unseen, the treasures that none knoweth but He. He knoweth whatever there is on the earth and in the sea. Not a leaf doth fall but with His knowledge: there is not a grain in the darkness (or depths) of the earth, nor anything fresh or dry (green or withered), but is (inscribed) in a record clear (to those who can read). Holy Qur'an, 6:59*

Chapter 103

1 "Then come unto him the Sadducees, which say there is no resurrection; Mark 12:18, King James Bible

"For the Sadducees say that there is no resurrection, neither angel, nor spirit: but the Pharisees confess both." Acts 23:8, King James Bible

2 *Behold! how they lie against their own souls! But the (lie) which they invented will leave them in the lurch. Holy Qur'an, 6:24*

3 "How is it that ye do not understand that I spake it not to you concerning bread, that ye should beware of the leaven of the Pharisees and of the Sadducees? 12 Then understood them how that he bade them not beware of the leaven of bread, but of the doctrine of the Pharisees and Sadducees." Matthew 16:11, King James Bible

4 *And they (sometimes) say: "There is nothing except our life on this earth, and never shall we be raised up again." Holy Qur'an, 6:29*

Chapter 104

1 *Nor expect, in giving, any increase (for thyself)! Holy Qur'an, 74:6*

2 *Holy Qur'an*

76:8 And they feed, for the love of Allah, the indigent, the orphan, and the captive,-

76:9 (Saying), "We feed you for the sake of Allah alone: no reward do we desire from you, nor thanks.

3 "If you ask, then ask Allah; and if you seek help, seek help from Allah. And know that if the nations were to gather together in order to give you some benefit, they would not bring you any benefit, except with what Allah has written for you." Hadith

4 *Never did We send a messenger or a prophet before thee, but, when he framed a desire, Satan threw some (vanity) into his desire: but Allah will cancel anything (vain) that Satan throws in, and Allah will confirm (and establish) His Signs: for Allah is full of Knowledge and Wisdom: Holy Qur'an, 22:52*

5 *(Abraham) said, "Do ye then worship, besides Allah, things that can neither be of any good to you nor do you harm? Holy Qur'an, 21:66*

6 *"Fie upon you, and upon the things that ye worship besides Allah! Have ye no sense?" Holy Qur'an, 21:67*

7 *Seest thou not that it is Allah Whose praises all beings in the heavens and on earth do celebrate, and the birds (of the air) with wings outspread? Each one knows its own (mode of) prayer and praise. And Allah knows well all that they do. Holy Qur'an, 24:41*

Chapter 105

1 *Allah disdains not to use the similitude of things, lowest as well as highest. Those who believe know that it is truth from their Lord; but those who reject Faith say: "What means Allah by this similitude?" By it He causes many to stray, and many He leads into the right path; but He causes not to stray, except those who forsake (the path),- Holy Qur'an, 2:26*

Holy Qur'an,

45:4 And in the creation of yourselves and the fact that animals are scattered (through the earth), are Signs for those of assured Faith.

45:5 And in the alternation of Night and Day, and the fact that Allah sends down Sustenance from the sky, and revives therewith the earth after its death, and in the change of the winds,- are Signs for those that are wise.

2 *Every soul shall have a taste of death: And only on the Day of Judgment shall you be paid your full recompense. Only he who is saved far from the Fire and admitted to the Garden will have attained the object (of Life): For the life of this world is but goods and chattels of deception. Holy Qur'an, 3:185*

Know ye (all), that the life of this world is but play and amusement, pomp and mutual boasting and multiplying, (in rivalry) among yourselves, riches and children. Here is a similitude: How rain and the growth which it brings forth, delight (the hearts of) the tillers; soon it withers; thou wilt see it grow yellow; then it becomes dry and crumbles away. But in the Hereafter is a Penalty severe (for the devotees of wrong). And Forgiveness from Allah and (His) Good

Pleasure (for the devotees of Allah). And what is the life of this world, but goods and chattels of deception? Holy Qur'an, 57:20

3 *Moreover he comprehended in His design the sky, and it had been (as) smoke: he said to it and to the earth: "Come ye together, willingly or unwillingly." They said, "We do come (together), in willing obedience." Holy Qur'an, 41:11*

Chapter 106

1 *Behold, Luqman said to his son by way of instruction: "O my son! join not in worship (others) with Allah: for false worship is indeed the highest wrong-doing." Holy Qur'an, 31:13*

2 *Say: the things that my Lord hath indeed forbidden are: shameful deeds, whether open or secret; sins and trespasses against truth or reason; assigning of partners to Allah, for which He hath given no authority; and saying things about Allah of which ye have no knowledge. Holy Qur'an, 7:33.*

3 *To Him is due the primal origin of the heavens and the earth: When He decreeth a matter, He saith to it: "Be," and it is. Holy Qur'an, 2:117*

4 *Not one of the beings in the heavens and the earth but must come to (Allah) Most Gracious as a servant. Holy Qur'an, 19:93*

5 *Holy Qur'an,*

19:88 They say: "(Allah) Most Gracious has begotten a son!"

19:89 Indeed ye have put forth a thing most monstrous!

19:90 At it the skies are ready to burst, the earth to split asunder, and the mountains to fall down in utter ruin,

19:91 That they should invoke a son for (Allah) Most Gracious.

19:92 For it is not consonant with the majesty of (Allah) Most Gracious that He should beget a son.

6 And it came to pass in those days, that he went out into a mountain to pray, and continued all night in prayer to God. And when it was day, he called *unto him* his disciples: and of them he chose twelve, whom also he named apostles; Luke 6:12–13, King James Bible

7 9 After this manner therefore pray ye: Our Father which art in heaven, Hallowed be thy name.

10 Thy kingdom come, Thy will be done in earth, as it is in heaven.

11 Give us this day our daily bread.

12 And forgive us our debts, as we forgive our debtors.

13 And lead us not into temptation, but deliver us from evil: For thine is the kingdom, and the power, and the glory, forever. Amen. Matthew 6:9-13, King James Version

8 Then said Jesus, Father, forgive them; for they know not what they do. And they parted his raiment, and cast lots. Luke 23:34, King James Bible

9 And about the ninth hour Jesus cried with a loud voice, saying, Eli, Eli, lama sabachthani? that is to say, My God, my God, why hast thou forsaken me? Matthew 27:46, King James Bible

10 And when Jesus had cried with a loud voice, he said, Father, into thy hands I commend my spirit: and having said thus, he gave up the ghost. Luke 23:46, King James Bible

Chapter 107

1 *O ye who believe! Fear Allah, and let every soul look to what (provision) He has sent forth for the morrow. Yea, fear Allah: for Allah is well-acquainted with (all) that ye do. Holy Qur'an, 59:18*

2 Galatians 6-7: Be not deceived; God is not mocked: for whatsoever a man soweth, that shall he also reap.

8: For he that soweth to his flesh shall of the flesh reap corruption; but he that soweth to the Spirit shall of the Spirit reap life everlasting.

9: And let us not be weary in well doing: for in due season we shall reap, if we faint not. 7- 9, King James Bible King James Version

"She (or he!) who plants a seed beneath the sod and waits to see a plant, believes in God." Anonymous

3 *Allah the Most High says Is it such a Message that ye would hold in light esteem? And have ye made it your livelihood that ye should declare it? Then why do ye not intervene when the soul of the dying man reaches the throat and ye sit looking on but W e are nearer to him than ye and yet see not Then why do ye not if you are exempt from future account call back the soul if ye ar e true in the claim of independence? Holy Qur'an 56:81-87*

4 *Holy Qur'an*

88:1Has the story reached thee of the overwhelming (Event)?

88:2 Some faces, that Day, will be humiliated,

88:3 Labouring (hard), weary,-

88:4 The while they enter the Blazing Fire,-

88:5 The while they are given, to drink, of a boiling hot spring,

88:6 No food will there be for them but a bitter Dhari'

88:7 Which will neither nourish nor satisfy hunger.

88:8 (Other) faces that Day will be joyful,

88:9 Pleased with their striving,-

88:10 In a Garden on high,

88:11 Where they shall hear no (word) of vanity:

88:12 Therein will be a bubbling spring:

88:13 Therein will be Thrones (of dignity), raised on high,

88:14 Goblets placed (ready),

88:15 And cushions set in rows,

88:16 And rich carpets (all) spread out.

88:17 Do they not look at the Camels, how they are made?-

88:18 And at the Sky, how it is raised high?-

88:19 And at the Mountains, how they are fixed firm?-

88:20 And at the Earth, how it is spread out?

88:21 Therefore do thou give admonition, for thou art one to admonish.

88:22 Thou art not one to manage (men's) affairs.

88:23 But if any turn away and reject Allah,-

88: 24 Allah will punish him with a mighty Punishment,

88:25 For to Us will be their return;

88:26 Then it will be for Us to call them to account.

Chapter 108

1 *Let there be no compulsion in religion: Truth stands out clear from Error: whoever rejects evil and believes in Allah hath grasped the most trustworthy hand-hold, that never breaks. And Allah heareth and knoweth all things. Holy Qur'an, 2:256*

2 *And say: "I am indeed he that warneth openly and without ambiguity,"- Holy Qur'an, 15:89*

3 *Holy Qur'an,*

109.001 Say : O ye that reject Faith!

109.002 I worship not that which ye worship,

109.003 Nor will ye worship that which I worship.

109.004 And I will not worship that which ye have been wont to worship,

109:5 Nor will ye worship that which I worship.

109:6 To you be your Way, and to me mine.

4 *Of the Jews there are those who displace words from their (right) places, and say: "We hear and we disobey"; and "Hear what is not Heard"; and "Ra'ina"; with a twist of their tongues and a slander to Faith. If only they had said: "We hear and we obey"; and "Do hear"; and "Do look at us"; it would have been better for them, and more proper; but Allah hath cursed them for their Unbelief; and but few of them will believe. Holy Qur'an, 4:46*

5 *O ye who believe! save yourselves and your families from a Fire whose fuel is Men and Stones, over which are (appointed) angels stern (and) severe, who flinch not (from executing) the Commands they receive from Allah, but do (precisely) what they are commanded. Holy Qur'an, 66: 6*

Chapter 109

1 *Ye are the best of peoples, evolved for mankind, enjoining what is right, forbidding what is wrong, and believing in Allah. If only the People of the Book had faith, it were best for them: among them are some who have faith, but most of them are perverted transgressors. Holy Qur'an, 3:110*

2 *Let there arise out of you a band of people inviting to all that is good, enjoining what is right, and forbidding what is wrong: They are the ones to attain felicity. Holy Qur'an, 3:104*

Chapter 110

1 Economic Policy Institute

Chapter 111

1 *"Pagans indeed are those who say that the Messiah is Allah (God)." [Holy Qur'an (Al Maidah - The Food) 5:17]*

They do blaspheme who say: "Allah is Christ the son of Mary." But said Christ: "O Children of Israel! worship Allah, my Lord and your Lord." Whoever joins other gods with Allah, Allah will forbid him the garden, and the Fire will be his abode. There will for the wrong-doers be no one to help. Holy Qur'an, 5:72

Christ the son of Mary was no more than a messenger; many were the messengers that passed away before him. His mother was a woman of truth. They had both to eat their (daily) food.

See how Allah doth make His signs clear to them; yet see in what ways they are deluded away from the truth! Holy Qur'an, 5:75

2 We are a special people, a living cell, a seed that contains the whole life that we have to have on this planet earth. Not just for African Americans, but for everybody that wants to have the best, and we have to work to preserve the knowledge." Imam W. D. Mohammed (raa) in the second part of a Jumah Khutbah in 2006

3 "The Jacobites said, "First let us put them over everybody else. How are we going to get them over everybody else? We are going to make G'd Gentile (white) and that is going to fire them up because they are going to be white like their G'd. That is going to fire them up with a daring spirit and they are going to think that nothing can destroy them because they look like Jesus. They are going to be merciless because we are going to tell them that G'd says to have no mercy on the heathens, have no mercy on the infidels. Miserably destroy them. So, they are going to march against black, against red, and against yellow people. They are going to march against all the other colors of the earth until they bring all of them down under the white image of G'd. Then after they do it, the poison spirit of religion that we have given them is going to degenerate and deteriorate their minds and their spirits and they are going to be helpless. They are going to pray that they are ready to come to Israel." Imam W. Deen Mohammed (RAA)

4 If what I say does not compliment what Frederick Douglass had to say; Dubois had to say. What Booker T. Washington had to say, what Noble Drew Ali, Garvey and the Honorable Elijah Muhammad had to say. If what I say don't compliment the excellence of our history. Nothing will! I'm not speaking from myself. I'm speaking from the urge in the life of my people. And, what I'm asking for is for them to fulfill the aspirations of my forefathers. I'm asking for something that has divine providence on its side. It's the demand from yesterda y, mushrooming into its full perspective. And that's the only thing that will bring us the dignity that we want. Imam W. D. Mohammed (RAA), Atlanta, GA August 21, 1981

5 "I am the whole community, in my heart, and head. I'm the depositor of the seed." Savior's Day 2008- his last one. W. Deen Mohammed (RAA)

6 *And We made a people, considered weak (and of no account), inheritors of lands in both east and west, Holy Qur'an, 7:137*

Bibliography

Abu Dawud. 656. *Sunan Abu Dāwūd.* Dar-us-Salam Publications. January 1, 2008

Ahmed, Hazrat Murza Ghulam. *Arabic-the Mother of all Languages.* https://www.alislam.org/topics/arabic/. Accessed May 5, 2016

Alexander, Michelle. 2010. *The New Jim Crow: Mass Incarceration in the Age of Colorblindness.* Washington Journal interview. February, 2010

Alexander, Brian. 2011. *The rich are different-and not in a good way, studies suggest.* NBCNews.com. *http://www.nbcnews.com/id/44084236/ns/health-behavior/t/rich-are-different-not-good-way-studies-suggest/#.Vy_XKmyTXGE* August 10, 2011. Accessed May, 8, 2016

Allen, James. 2003. *As A Man Thinketh.* Borders Press/Grange Books. United Kingdom. 2003

Allen, Will. 2012. *Good Food Revolution, Growing Healthy Food, People, and Communities.* Gotham Books. New York, New York. 2012

Alleyne, Richard. 2016. *Insults are better taken lying down, claim scientists.* The Telegraph, 12 Aug 2009. http://www.telegraph.co.uk/news/science/science-news/6016087/Insults-are-better-taken-lying-down-claim-scientists.html . Accessed May 8, 2016

Angers, Trent. 1999. *The Forgotten Hero of My Lai: The Hugh Thompson Story.* Acadian House Publishing. Lafayette, La. 1999

Barrett, Deirdre. 2010. *Supernormal Stimuli: How Primal Urges Overran Their Evolutionary Purpose.* W. W. Norton & Company. February, 2010

Beckert, Sven. 2014. *Empire of Cotton: A Global History.* Alfred A. Knopf. 2014

Beckert, Sven. *How the West got rich and modern capitalism was born.* Making Sen$e. http://www.pbs.org/newshour/making-sense/west-got-rich-modern-capitalism-born/. 13-Feb-15

Bernal, Martin Gardiner. 1987. *Black Athena: The Afroasiatic Roots of Classical Civilization*. Rutgers University Press. 1987

Bible. New International Version (©1984). http://biblehub.com/

Bible. King James Version. http://biblehub.com/

Bible. New American Standard Bible. http://biblehub.com/

Bukhari. *Sahih Al-Bukhari*. http://www.sahih-bukhari.com/. Accessed May 8, 2016

Burne, Charlotte Sophia. 1914. *Handbook of Folklore-Traditional Beliefs, Practices, Customs, Stories and Sayings*. Senate. 1914

Carter, Jimmy. 2006. *Palestine: Peace Not Apartheid*. Simon & Shuster Paperbacks. 2006

Chapra, Muhammad Umar. 1979. *Objective of the Islamic Economic Order*. The Islamic Foundation. London. 1979

Clark, Josh. 1979. *Did the ancient Greeks get their ideas from the Africans?*. http://history.howstuffworks.com/history-vs-myth/greek-philosophers-african-tribes3.htm. May 4, 1979

Clymer, Dr. R. Swinburne Clymer. 1951. *The Mysteries of Osiris, Ancient Egyptian Initiation*. Philosophical Pub. Co. Quakertown, Pa. 1951

Cose, Ellis. 2011. *The End of Anger: A New Generation's Take on Race and Rage*. Ecco/HarperCollins. New York, New York. 2011

Covey, Stephen R. 1989. *The Seven Habits of Highly Successful People*. Free Press. 1989

Cowan. Milton J. 1976. *Hans Wehr Arabic dictionary*. Spoken Language Services, Inc. Ithaca, New York. 1976

Dawkins, Richard. 2006. *The God Delusion*. Mariner-Houghton Mifflin. New York, New York. 2006

Drake, St Clair. 1991. *Black Folk Here and There*. University of California Center for Afro. February, 1991

Ellison, Keith. *America's Best Days are Ahead*. Huffington Politics. http://www.huffingtonpost.com/rep-keith-ellison/americas-best-days-are-ah_b_982088.html. Accessed May 5, 2016

Emanuel, Ezekiel. 2013. *Brothers Emanuel: A Memoir of an American Family*. Random House. New York, New York. 2013

Emerson, Ralph Waldo. 1844. *Manners, Essays, Second Series*. 1844

Emerson, Ralph Waldo. 1841. *Compensation (from Essays)*. 1841

Essien-Udom, E. U. 1995. *Black Nationalism--The Search for an Identity*. The University of Chicago Press. 1995

Fanusie, Fatimah Abdul-Tawwab. 2008. *Fard Muhammad in Historical Context: An Islamic Thread in the American Religious and Cultural Quilt.* Howard University. 2008

Fillmore, Charles. 2005. *Revealing Word.* Charles Fillmore Reference Library Series. 2005

Fillmore, Charles. 1995. *Metaphysical Bible Dictionary.* Charles Fillmore Reference Library Series. 1995

Foner, Eric and John A. Garraty, Editors, *Manifest Destiny History.* www.history.com/topics/manifest-destiny. Accessed May 5, 2016

Gieringer, Ph.D, Dale. *Economics of Cannabis Legalization (1994) Detailed Analysis of the Benefits of Ending Cannabis Prohibition.* June 1994

Gladwell, Malcolm. 2009. *Outliers-the Story of Success.* Penguin Books Ltd. July, 2009

Gleick, James. 2011. *What Defines a Meme?* Smithsonian Magazine. http://www.smithsonianmag.com/arts-culture/what-defines-a-meme-1904778/?no-ist. May, 2011

Gleick, James. 2011. *The Information: A History, a Theory, a Flood.* Pantheon/Random House. 2011

Greenlee, Sam. 1969. *The Spook Who Sat by the Door.* Lushena Books, Inc. Chicago, Illinois. 1969

Haykal, Muhammad Husayn. 1993. *The Life of Muhammad.* American Trust Publications. 1993

Higginson, Thomas Wentworth. 1870. *Army Life in a Black Regiment.* Penguin Books, 2002.

Hill, Napoleon. 1937. *Think and Grow Rich.* Ralston Society. 1937

Holy Qur'an, Abdullah Yusuf Ali Translation

Holy Qur'an, Marmaduke Pickthall Translation

Howe, Stephen. 1998. *Afrocentrism: Mythical Pasts and Imagined Homes.* Verso. 1998

Hughes, Thomas Patrick. 1905. *A Dictionary of the Islam.* H. Allen & Company. London. March 9, 1905

Hurston, Zora Neale. 1939. *Moses, Man of the Mountain.* J. B. Lippincott, Inc. 1939

Ibn Ishaq, Sirat Rasul Allah. *The Life of Muhammad,* edited by Abu Muhammad 'Abd al-Malik bin Hisham

Ibn Majah, *Sunan Ibn Mājah.* Dar-us-Salam Publications. 2007

Jackson, Sherman A. 2005. *Islam And The Blackamerican: Looking Toward the Third Resurrection.* Oxford University Press New York, New York. 2005

Julia, *The People Who Walk In Darkness Have Seen A Great Light,* Imam W. Deen Mohammed's Address at "Savior Day" Feb. 26, 2002, in Charleston, SC. Muslim Journal. May 3, 2002

Key, Wilson Bryan. 1974. *Subliminal Seduction.* Signet. December, 1974

Klineberg, Eric. 2002. *Climactic Events in the Social Context: Heat Wave- a Social Autopsy of Disaster in Chicago.* The University of Chicago Press. 2002

Kornfield, Jack. 2002. *The Art of Forgiveness, Lovingkindness and Peace.* Bantam Dell. New York, New York. 2002

Larson, Charles. 1973. *Heroic Ethnocentrism: The Idea of Universality in Literature.* The American Scholar. Summer 1973

Lefkowitz, Mary. 1996. *Not Out of Africa: How "Afrocentrism" Became An Excuse To Teach Myth As History. Basic Books.* 1996

Lefkowitz, Mary and Guy MacLean Rogers. 1996. *Black Athena Revisited.* The University of North Carolina Press. 1996

Lunde, Paul. 1974. *Aesop of the Arabs.* Saudi Aramco World. March/ April 1974

Mandel, Jonah 2010. Jerusalem Post, Jewish News, *Rabbi Ovadia Yosef: Gentiles Exist Only to Serve Jews* http://crownheights.info/jewish-news/29404/rabbi-ovadia-yosef-gentiles-exist-only-to-serve-jews/ October 19, 2010. Accessed May 12, 2016

Maududi, Sayyid Abul Ala. 1972. *Tafhim al-Qur'an - The Meaning of the Qur'an.* http://www.englishtafsir.com/Quran/12/index.html. Accessed May 8, 2016

Mohammed, W. Deen. Many quotes included herein are taken directly from Imam W. Deen Mohammed's many public addresses between 1975 and 2008, delivered to his students, and throughout the world, from the beginning of his leadership in February, 1975 until his passing in September, 2008. The reader is encouraged to access this vast reservoir of wisdom through WDM Publications, at http://www.wdmpublications.com/ and through the ongoing propagation efforts of Imam Mohammed's son, W. Deen Mohammed II, President of The Mosque Cares, the not-for-profit charitable and educational organization formed by Imam Mohammed.

Motz, Lloyd and Jefferson Hanes Weaver. *The Story of Physics.* Plenum. US. 1989

Muhammad, Elijah. 1965. *Message to the Black Man in America.* Nation of Islam. Chicago, Illinois. 1965

Mumford, Lewis. 1961. *The City in History, Its Origins, Its Tranformations, and Its Prospects.* Harcourt Brace. New York. 1961

Muslim, ibn al-Hajjaj al-Naysaburi. Sahih Muslim. https://muflihun.com/muslim/39/6757. Accessed May 8, 2016

Myss, Dr. Caroline. 1996. *Anatomy of the Spirit: The Seven Stages of Power and Healing.* Crown Publishers. 1996

Nelson, Jill. 1993. *Volunteer Slavery: My Authentic Negro Experience.* Penguin Books. 1993

Nemeth, PH.D, Maria. 1997. *The Energy of Money.* Ballantine Publishing Group. 1997

Nurriddin, Dr. Abdel J. 2010. *Health is Predicated in Energy.* Muslim Journal. September 3, 2010

Omar, Abdul Mannan. 2003. *Dictionary of the Holy Qur'an.* NOOR Foundation International, Inc. Hockessin, DE. 2003

Parenti, Christian. 2000. *Lockdown America: Police and Prisons in the Age of Crisis.* Verso. 2000

Patterson, Orlando. 1982. *Slavery and Social Death: A Comparative Study.* Harvard University Press. 1982

Ponder, Dr. Catherine. 1978. *The Millionaire Joshua: His Prosperity Secrets for You!.* DeVorss & Company. January, 1978

Ponder, Dr. Catherine. 1985. *The Dynamic Laws of Prosperity.* DeVorss & Company. 1985

Prejean, Sister Helen. *Dead Man Walking.* 1994. Vintage Books/Random House, Inc. New York, New York. 1994

Saahir, Imam Mikal. 2011. *The Honorable Elijah Muhammad: The Man Behind the Men.* Words Make People Publishing, Inc. 2011

Sacks, Oliver. 1985. *The Man Who Mistook His Wife for a Hat, and Other Clinical Tales.* Summit Books. December, 1985

Shannon, Claude. 1948. *A Mathematical Theory of Communication.* The Bell System Technical Journal. http://worrydream.com/refs/Shannon%20-%20A%20Mathematical%20Theory%20of%20Communication.pdf. July and October 1948. Accessed May 8, 2016

Schoenman, Ralph, citing Brenner, Zionism. *The Hidden History of Zionism.* http://www.marxists.de/middleast/schoenman/ch06.htm. Accessed May 11, 2016

Tan, Amy. 2006. *The Joy Luck Club.* Penguin. 2006

Toffler, Alvin and Heidi Toffler. 2006. *Revolutionary Wealth: How it will be created and how it will change our lives.* Doubleday. 2006

Turner, Nat. 1905. *Confessions of Nat Turner - The Leader of the Late Insurrection in Southampton, Virginia*. http://docsouth.unc.edu/neh/turner/turner.html. Thomas E. Gray. January 4, 1905

ushistory.org. *Manifest Destiny*. U.S. History Online Textbook. http://www.ushistory.org/us/29.asp. Accessed May 5, 2016

Warren, Rick. 2002. *The Purpose Driven Life*. Zondervan. Grand Rapids, Mi. 2002

Wheeler, Brannon. 2002. *Prophets in the Quran: an Introduction to the Quran and Muslim Exegesis*. Continuum. London-New York. 2002

Williams, Dr. Chancellor. 1987. *The Destruction of Black Civilization*. Third World Press. Chicago. 1987

Zakaria, Fareed. 2015. *America's self-destructive whites*. The Washington Post. https://www.washingtonpost.com/opinions/americas-self-destructive-whites/2015/12/31/5017f958-afdc-11e5-9ab0-884d1cc4b33e_story.html. December 31, 2015. Accessed May 8, 2016

INDEX

A

B

C

D

E

F

G

H

I

J

K

L

M

N

O

P

Q

R

S

T

U

W

Y

Z

Printed in the United States
By Bookmasters